ALTERNATIVE DISPUTE RESOLUTION
IN NORTH CAROLINA

ALTERNATIVE DISPUTE RESOLUTION
IN NORTH CAROLINA

A New Civil Procedure

Second Edition

Editor
Elizabeth P. Manley

Assistant Editors
Frank C. Laney, Lynn P. Roundtree, and Catherine Brohaugh

Revised from the First Edition, edited by
Jacqueline R. Clare

Review Group of the ADR Book Committee
(Joint Committee of the North Carolina Bar Association
Dispute Resolution Section and the
North Carolina Dispute Resolution Commission)

Design & production by BW&A Books, Inc.
Manufactured in the United States of America.

Library of Congress Control Number: 2012945497
ISBN: 978-0-9858889-09

The first edition was originally published in 2003,
and reprinted in 2005.

The second edition was published in 2012
in both print and e-book formats.

This graphic of a multi-door courthouse, designed by Bobby Gill of the North Carolina Bar Association, first appeared in June 1985 on the cover of *Dispute Resolution, A Task Force Report* by the North Carolina Bar Foundation. The design represents the integration of alternative dispute resolution (ADR) procedures into the North Carolina justice system. Although the signs above each door depict litigation, arbitration, and mediation as the directions a dispute may take, the choices available to the parties have evolved since this graphic was introduced to provide for a wider array of alternatives for resolving disputes.

This book is dedicated to
former North Carolina Supreme Court

CHIEF JUSTICE JAMES G. EXUM, JR.,

without whose leadership many of the events
herein would not have occurred, and

CARMON J. STUART (1914–2004),

without whose efforts this book
would not have been written.

CONTENTS

Mediation Centers

ADR in Government Agencies

Arbitration

Other Uses of ADR

PART III

THE FUTURE DEVELOPMENT OF ADR IN NORTH CAROLINA

ADR BOOK COMMITTEE REVIEW GROUP AND EDITORS

Co-Chairs (First Edition): John C. Schafer and Carmon J. Stuart

Committee Members: Jacqueline R. Clare, Frank C. Laney,
J. Anderson Little, and Judge Ralph A. Walker

Chair (Second Edition): Frank C. Laney

Committee Members: M. Ann Anderson, Dawn S. Bryant,
Jacqueline R. Clare, J. Anderson Little,
and John C. Schafer

M. ANN ANDERSON is an attorney-mediator from Pilot Mountain, N.C. She practiced law with Womble Carlyle Sandridge & Rice (1981–1991) and Constangy Brooks & Smith (1993–1996). She received her undergraduate degree in psychology from the University of North Carolina at Chapel Hill in 1976 and her J.D. with honors from the University of North Carolina School of Law in 1981. Ms. Anderson served on the North Carolina Bar Association Board of Governors (2008–2011) and chaired the North Carolina Bar Association Dispute Resolution Section (2006–2007). Anderson, who writes a column for a Bar Association publication, *The Peacemaker,* currently serves as a member of the North Carolina Dispute Resolution Commission (2010–2013 term).

CATHERINE BROHAUGH, an assistant editor of the current edition of this book, is a graduate of Clemson University (B.A., 1987). Ms. Brohaugh has extensive publishing experience, having worked as a content editor, copy-editor, and indexer for F&W Publications and South-Western Publishing in Cincinnati, Ohio. As publications manager for the Cincinnati Art Museum, Ms. Brohaugh was responsible for the monthly members' magazine and a variety of museum catalogs and books. Most recently, Ms. Brohaugh was a Marketing Manager for IBM Corporation, leading marketing publications for advanced computer technologies.

DAWN S. BRYANT received her B.A. degree in international studies from the University of North Carolina at Chapel Hill in 1978 and her J.D. degree from the North Carolina Central University School of Law in 1981. She served as the police attorney for the City of Raleigh Police Department for twenty-eight years. Upon leaving the police department, she joined Carolina Dispute Settlement Services as Director of Education and Clinical Services. Ms. Bryant mediates and trains mediators. She is a current member of the North Carolina Dispute Resolution Commission.

JACQUELINE R. CLARE, formerly an associate with Womble Carlyle Sandridge & Rice, is a full-time mediator in Raleigh. Ms. Clare is a member of the North Carolina Dispute Resolution Commission and currently serves as chair of the Commission's Standards, Discipline, and Advisory Opinions Committee. She is a past chair of the Dispute Resolution Section of the North Carolina Bar Association (NCBA), a member of the Board of Governors of the NCBA, and a past recipient of the NCBA Dispute Resolution Section's Peace Award. Ms. Clare is also a member of the Alternative Dispute Resolution Subcommittee of the North Carolina State Judicial Council. She is past editor of *Dispute Resolution,* the newsletter of the NCBA Dispute Resolution Section, and *Disclosure Statement,* the newsletter of the NCBA Bankruptcy Section. She was the lead editor of the first edition of this book. Ms. Clare received her B.A. degree from East Carolina University in 1977 and her J.D. from the University of North Carolina School of Law in 1982.

FRANK C. LANEY is Circuit Mediator for the U.S. Court of Appeals for the Fourth Circuit, chair of the State Judicial Council Dispute Resolution Committee, and an ex officio member of the North Carolina Dispute Resolution Commission. A graduate of North Carolina State University (B.A., 1979) and the University of North Carolina School of Law (J.D., 1982), he served as Mediation Coordinator for the North Carolina Industrial Commission and is a former partner in Mediation, Inc. He has been a member of the North Carolina Bar Association (NCBA) Dispute Resolution Committee/Section since its inception and was a consultant with the NCBA's Court-Ordered Arbitration and Mediated Settlement Conference Pilot Programs. Mr. Laney is certified as a superior court and family financial mediator by the North Carolina Dispute Resolution Commission and as a practitioner member of the Academy of Family Mediators. He served as an assistant editor of the current edition of this book.

J. ANDERSON "ANDY" LITTLE is a graduate of Davidson College (B.A., 1966), Union Theological Seminary (M.Div., 1970), and the University of North Carolina School of Law (J.D., 1975). He practiced law in North Carolina for seventeen years with the firm of Northen, Blue, Little, Rooks, Thibaut, and Anderson in Chapel Hill. In 1992, Mr. Little formed Mediation, Inc., and since that time has worked as a full-time mediator and mediation trainer. He teaches forty-hour training courses for certification as a court mediator in North Carolina and is author of a book published by the North Carolina Bar Association (NCBA) entitled *Making Money Talk: How to Mediate Insured Claims and Other Money Disputes*. Mr. Little chaired the committees that drafted the mediation programs for North Carolina's superior and district courts and for the state's clerks of superior court. He also coordinated efforts to achieve the implementation of those programs. Mr. Little served as chair of the NCBA's Dispute Resolution Committee and as the first chair of the NCBA's Dispute Resolution Section. He currently serves as a member of the ADR Committee of the State Judicial Council and is a member (and past chair) of the North Carolina Dispute Resolution Commission.

ELIZABETH P. MANLEY served as an assistant editor for the first edition of this book and as the lead editor for the current edition. She was a labor and employment law attorney with the firm of Hunton & Williams from 1982 to 1986, and she worked in commercial litigation for Smith Helms Mulliss & Moore in Raleigh from 1986 through 1988. Ms. Manley worked as a legal editor for Lawyers Cooperative Publishing and as an independent editor for West Group Publishing for more than ten years. She is a certified mediator (inactive). Ms. Manley is a graduate of Mary Washington College (B.A., 1972), the University of Virginia (M.A., 1977), and the University of Richmond School of Law (J.D., 1982).

LYNN P. ROUNDTREE, an assistant editor of both editions of this book, is a graduate of Louisiana State University (B.A., 1980) and of the University of North Carolina at Chapel Hill (M.A., 1983, & M.S., 1985). A writer, historian, and antiquarian appraiser, he is the owner of Armadillo Books in Chapel Hill. Mr. Roundtree is the co-author of *Seeking Liberty and Justice: A History of the North Carolina Bar Association* and *The Changing Face of Justice: A Look at the First 100 Women Attorneys in North Carolina*. He is the author of *The Best Is Yet to Be: The First 125 Years of a Law Firm*, a history of Womble Carlyle Sandridge & Rice, LLP.

JOHN C. SCHAFER received his B.A. degree from the University of Notre Dame in 1981 and his J.D. degree from the Wake Forest University School of Law in 1984. Mr. Schafer served as a law clerk to the Hon. W. Earl Britt, Chief Judge of the U.S. District Court for the Eastern District of North Carolina, from 1984 through 1986. After a decade in private practice in the Research Triangle area, he joined the North Carolina Industrial Commission as its Dispute Resolution Coordinator in 1997. Since 1999, Mr. Schafer also has served as a Deputy Commissioner of the N.C. Industrial Commission. He served as chair of the North Carolina Bar Association's Dispute Resolution Section and is an ex officio member of the Dispute Resolution Commission and the ADR Committee of the State Judicial Council.

CARMON J. STUART (1914–2004) was a 1938 graduate of the Duke University School of Law. Mr. Stuart worked as an F.B.I. agent, as Solicitor for the Forsyth County Municipal Court, and as attorney for the City of Winston-Salem, N.C. From 1971 to 1983, Mr. Stuart served as Clerk of the U.S. District Court for the Middle District of North Carolina. Active in retirement as a member of the North Carolina and federal court bars, he was honored by the North Carolina Bar Association with the Judge John J. Parker Award in 1992. Carmon Stuart was a tireless advocate for the use of alternative dispute resolution, and he played a primary role in developing the original edition of this book.

JUDGE RALPH A. WALKER, a key member of the original ADR Book Committee, received his B.B.A. and J.D. degrees from Wake Forest University and its School of Law. A former practicing attorney, prosecutor, family court judge, and county attorney, Judge Walker served as a Superior Court Judge in Guilford County for eight years. He then served on the North Carolina Court of Appeals for nine years and as director of the Administrative Office of the Courts for five years. Judge Walker was the first chair of the North Carolina Dispute Resolution Commission. He now serves as a mediator, arbitrator, and emergency judge.

ACKNOWLEDGMENTS

(Reprinted from the first edition)

A work such as this would be difficult to research, write, and publish as a solo effort, so it was necessary to rely upon voluntary contributions from lawyers and others who were knowledgeable and willing to write chapters. An "ADR Book Committee," a joint committee of the North Carolina Bar Association (NCBA) Dispute Resolution Section and the North Carolina Dispute Resolution Commission, was formed, and a call went out asking for pro bono contributions. Accordingly, this book is a compilation of the work of many dedicated individuals who have shared their knowledge and experiences in the development of alternative dispute resolution in North Carolina.

The vision and tremendous dedication of the Review Group of the ADR Book Committee made this book a reality. Committee co-chairs Carmon J. Stuart and John C. Schafer provided inspiration and leadership, and never wavered in their commitment. Frank C. Laney, J. Anderson Little, and Judge Ralph A. Walker were steadfast members of the Review Group, giving generously of their time, memories, and editorial guidance. Ralph A. Peeples, Scott Bradley, and James E. Gates also served on the ADR Book Committee when the idea for the book was being formed.

Several individuals willingly contributed a significant number of chapters, even when asked to prepare some of them at a late date and on short notice: Leslie C. Ratliff, Ralph A. Peeples, J. Anderson Little, Carmon J. Stuart, Frank C. Laney, and John C. Schafer. Their extraordinary contributions of time and expertise were invaluable to the project. James E. Gates, Mark S. Thomas, and John C. Schafer consulted at length on copyright issues, and their work is greatly appreciated.

Much time was spent in gathering information about the history of ADR in North Carolina. At a meeting held on March 4, 2000, at the NCBA Bar Center in Cary, a number of individuals spent the day reminiscing about the development of dispute resolution in North Carolina. The recollections and memories shared on that day provided a good foundation for the historical sections of the book.

Special thanks go out to the following individuals who contributed the chapters which make up this book:

History Chapters

Scott Bradley	J. Anderson Little	John C. Schafer
Jane C. Clare	Ralph A. Peeples	Kathy L. Shuart
Barbara A. Davis	Leslie C. Ratliff	Carmon J. Stuart
James E. Gates	Andrew M. Sachs	J. Randolph Ward
Frank C. Laney	Miriam Saxon	

Procedural Chapters

M. Ann Anderson	Frank C. Laney	Diann Seigle
Robert A. Beason	Terry Leitner	Judge P. Trevor Sharp
Scott Bradley	J. Anderson Little	Kathy L. Shuart
Jacqueline R. Clare	Judge Julian Mann, III	Blythe Tennent
Jane C. Clare	Charles K. McCotter	Judge Ben F. Tennille
David W. Daniel	Mark W. Morris	Mark L. Van Der Puy
F. Joseph Diab	Ralph A. Peeples	Michel Vaughan
Jonathan R. Harkavy	Leslie C. Ratliff	George K. Walker
Susan E. Hauser	Andrew M. Sachs	Judge Ralph A. Walker
Judge Clarence E.	Miriam Saxon	Bobby D. White
Horton, Jr.	Allison B. Schafer	Jennifer Yarnell
Elizabeth M. Jordan	John C. Schafer	

Policy and Future Chapters

Roy J. Baroff	Former N.C. Supreme	James L. Lester
Dorothy C. Bernholz	Court Chief Justice	J. Anderson Little
	James G. Exum, Jr.	Carmon J. Stuart

The generous contribution made by each of these individuals has helped to memorialize the efforts of North Carolina's ADR pioneers. We hope that it will also provide guidance for those new to the ADR processes. Many thanks to all of these people for the countless hours spent in helping to make this book a reality. Special thanks also to the North Carolina Dispute Resolution Commission and the North Carolina Bar Association Dispute Resolution Section for their financial assistance. The funds provided by these organizations, along with a generous grant from the Smith Richardson Foundation, made sure that the contributed words of so many found their way into print.

INTRODUCTION TO THE
SECOND EDITION

This book was first published in 2003 and was reprinted without updates in 2005. As of 2011, approximately 5000 copies had been distributed throughout the world. The book remains in demand, primarily as a text for classes in law schools and dispute resolution graduate programs in North Carolina. There have been many changes to the programs and procedures described in the first edition of this book, and a number of new programs have been adopted and implemented since 2003. The purpose of publishing this edition is to update the book with regard to these changes in the ADR landscape in North Carolina so that the book will continue to be a useful resource, not only for ADR students and professionals, but also for attorneys, judges, court personnel, members of the legislature, state and local government administrators, and the general public.

The revisions to this edition were coordinated by a review group very similar to the review group that was involved with the first edition. This group was led by Frank C. Laney and Elizabeth P. Manley. Mr. Laney coordinated the participation of numerous contributors to the book revisions and oversaw the budgetary and other aspects of the publication process. He also served as a reviewer and an editor for all of the new material added to this book. Ms. Manley was the lead editor of this edition. They both spent countless hours working to ensure that the information in this edition not only is accurate, but also easy to understand and utilize. Mr. Laney and Ms. Manley were assisted by the other members of the review group for this edition, which included M. Ann Anderson, Dawn S. Bryant, Jacqueline R. Clare, J. Anderson Little, and John C. Schafer. Many of the same people listed in the acknowledgments to the original edition of this book also generously contributed many hours of their time to this updated edition. The work of all who contributed to this book is greatly appreciated.

Special thanks also to the North Carolina Dispute Resolution Commission and the North Carolina Bar Association Dispute Resolution Section for their financial assistance and to Beason & Ellis for their generous gift in honor of Carmon J. Stuart. The funds provided by these organizations allowed the publication of this updated revision to become a reality. North Carolina continues to be a national leader in the ADR field thanks to the contributions of all of these organizations and individuals.

AUTHORS AND CONTRIBUTORS TO THE SECOND EDITION

M. Ann Anderson
Catharine B. Arrowood
Zeb E. Barnhardt, Jr.
Robert A. Beason
Dorothy C. Bernholz
Nancy F. Black
Robert A. Brinson
LeAnn Nease Brown
Dawn S. Bryant
Judge David S. Cayer
Jacqueline R. Clare
F. Joseph Diab
Rene S. Ellis
Christie M. Foppiano

Billie Jo Garcia
Judge James E. Gates
Jonathan R. Harkavy
Sherrill W. Hayes
Sharon T. Howard
Frank C. Laney
Kathryn S. Lehman
J. Anderson Little
Judge Julian Mann, III
Jody K. Minor
Kate Neale
Ralph A. Peeples
Phyllis B. Pickett
Leslie C. Ratliff
Andrew M. Sachs

David Salvesen
Steven A. Savia
Jessica S. Scott
Allison B. Schafer
John C. Schafer
Judge P. Trevor Sharp
Ann M. Shy
DeShield Smith
Judge Sanford L. Steelman
Judge Ben F. Tennille
Michel Vaughn
George K. Walker

FOREWORD

*"The obligation of our profession is, or has long been thought
to be, to serve as healers of human conflicts.*

*To fulfill our traditional obligation means that we should
provide mechanisms that can produce an acceptable result
in the shortest possible time, with the least possible expense
and with a minimum of stress on the participants.
That is what justice is all about. . . .*

*Today, I address the administration of justice in civil matters,
which shares with criminal justice both delay and lack of finality.
Even when an acceptable result is finally achieved in a civil case,
the result is often drained of much of its value because of
the time-lapse, the expense and the emotional stress
inescapable in the litigation process."*

—United States Supreme Court Chief Justice Warren E. Burger,
Isn't There a Better Way?,
Annual Report on the State of the Judiciary,
Midyear Meeting of the American Bar Association,
Chicago, Illinois (January 24, 1982).

Alternative Dispute Resolution (ADR):
A Judicial Fact of Life

In the last decades of the twentieth century leaders in the legal community
set forth a new vision for conflict resolution within the American civil justice system. It was a framework that offered court-ordered alternatives to
traditional litigation. Their vision has become a revolution in the way disputes are processed in society through a movement known as "alternative
dispute resolution" or simply, "ADR."

Today ADR is an established part of the legal process in the United States.
ADR techniques such as mediation and arbitration have enabled judges,
lawyers, administrative tribunals, and private citizens to experience the

benefits of resolving disputes without resort to costly and time-consuming trials. The success of these methods has done much to restore what is "civil" in civil justice. ADR has radically altered many assumptions about the use of adversarial confrontations in general—and litigation in particular—as the primary way to settle disputes and to yield just results.

North Carolina has been a pioneer in exploring and adopting effective alternatives to litigation. Many of this state's ADR programs serve as models for other jurisdictions. This book tells the story of how North Carolina emerged as a national leader in the field of ADR.

A New Civil Procedure

The term "civil procedure" in the normal English lexicon refers to the somewhat complicated, significantly rigid, and sometimes frustrating rules by which lawsuits are managed within the court system. One of the early motivations of the ADR movement was to loosen these restrictive bands and to allow people more freedom in managing the resolution of their own disputes. Another motivation was concern that the procedural rules which structured the adversary process changed people from disputants to adversaries. Thus, one of the goals of ADR advocates was to reduce conflict by shifting the focus from a "win or lose" situation to a problem-solving situation. The result was not just a new set of processes, but processes that were more civil, being more genteel, more cooperative, and more moderate. This book is not just about new court procedures, but also about changing the tone of disputes. Thus, the subtitle of this book, "A New Civil Procedure," reflects these more civil processes—not only a change in court procedures, but also a change in the very tone of societal disputes.

Why This Book Was Written

With almost twenty years of successful experience with ADR, it was clear that North Carolina had a great story to tell of unselfish service to the judiciary and to society at large by the North Carolina Bar Association and many other citizen organizations. It also became clear to a number of those active in the movement that a record of these efforts ought to be made before memories fade and relevant documents disappear. With the many hundreds of lawyers and laymen becoming involved in ADR every year, it became obvious that this book should be more than a history—that it also should serve the newly created practice area of ADR as an instructional guidebook. We hope that this book, with its broad range of topics and perspectives, will serve as a handbook on dispute resolution for attorneys, judges, court personnel, members of the legislature, state and local government administrators, and the general public.

How to Use This Book

Alternative Dispute Resolution in North Carolina: A New Civil Procedure begins with an explanation of ADR and the most common ADR techniques. A section on the movement's history follows. After a brief discussion of the origins of ADR on the national level, several chapters chronicle the efforts to establish ADR in North Carolina, from the early days of experimentation with community-based mediation and court-ordered arbitration in the late 1970s and early 1980s to the establishment of the many legislatively sanctioned dispute resolution programs in existence today. The section concludes with two chapters that focus on ADR policies and practice in the state, including a discussion of professionalism and ethical considerations related to the use of ADR processes.

More than just a history, *Alternative Dispute Resolution in North Carolina* is also a guidebook on ADR practice in North Carolina. It provides information on the "nuts and bolts" of ADR procedures currently in use in the state, including court-ordered techniques, mechanisms used in administrative agencies, and procedures employed in community-based programs. For convenience and ease of use, each of these practical chapters has been designed to stand on its own, providing information on background, procedures, and resources for ADR in each practice area. As a result, many of those chapters have elements in common. It was more feasible to repeat them in each chapter than to refer the reader to other parts of the book. The editors recognize this as intentional redundancy, justified by convenience. This section of the book has been substantially reorganized for the current edition, with programs grouped together according to general themes or topics, such as mediation of civil claims, resolution of family matters, mediation centers, and ADR in government agencies.

The book's final section offers observations about the future of ADR in North Carolina. It discusses the continuing impact of technology on ADR processes and discusses current and future trends.

The contributing authors to this publication have exerted their best professional skills to assure the accuracy of its contents. All original sources of authority presented by the publication should be independently researched in dealing with specific legal matters.

ADR Book Committee
(Joint Committee of the North Carolina Bar Association Dispute Resolution Section and the North Carolina Dispute Resolution Commission)

Review Group (First Edition)
Co-Chairs: John C. Schafer and Carmon J. Stuart
Members: Jacqueline R. Clare, Frank C. Laney, J. Anderson Little, and Judge Ralph A. Walker

Review Group (Second Edition)
Chair: Frank C. Laney
Members: M. Ann Anderson, Dawn S. Bryant, Jacqueline R. Clare, J. Anderson Little, and John C. Schafer

PART I

The Development of
Alternative Dispute Resolution (ADR)
in North Carolina

THE HISTORY OF ADR
IN NORTH CAROLINA

CHAPTER ONE

An Overview of Alternatives
to Civil Litigation

"[W]e must move away from total reliance on the adversary contest for resolving all disputes. For some disputes, trials will be the only means, but for many, trials by the adversary contest must go by the way of the ancient trial by battle and blood. Our system is too costly, too painful, too destructive, too inefficient for a truly civilized people."
—United States Supreme Court Chief Justice Warren E. Burger, The State of Justice, Report to the American Bar Association, February 12, 1984, 70 A.B.A. J. 62, 66 (April 1984).

Why ADR? Policy Reasons for the Use of Alternatives

Alternative dispute resolution (ADR) appeals to different people for different reasons. As the ADR movement has developed over the past thirty years, it has served two distinct but not always consistent purposes. One is the desire of many ADR proponents to use alternatives to litigation as a way of making the civil justice system (especially the courts) more efficient. Other ADR adherents hold the conviction that the informed application of ADR techniques often leads to better outcomes for all parties in a dispute.

The first aim—improving the efficiency of the civil justice system—emphasizes the perspective of the courts. Alternative dispute resolution offers clear benefits for the court system because it allows certain types of disputes to be resolved without resort to litigation, or at least, without resort to trial. The resulting reduction of caseloads frees judges and other court personnel to handle only those matters that genuinely need to be tried. In either case, the administration of justice is expedited, saving both time and money.

The second purpose of ADR—the promotion of better outcomes—emphasizes the perspective of the parties in the dispute. Proponents of this approach point out that those involved ought to be able to select the technique that best suits their interests and the nature of their dispute. Studies have shown that self-determination, in conjunction with the collaborative approach employed in most ADR techniques, provides a high degree of satisfaction for participants and leads to more stable resolutions of disputes.

ADR has other practical advantages, particularly from the viewpoint of the parties involved. Unlike litigation, most ADR proceedings are private, and the results may be kept confidential. They are less formal than court proceedings and tend to be less expensive, less time-consuming, and less stressful. Cooperation between the parties—the hallmark of most ADR techniques—helps promote improved relationships in cases where the participants must continue to interact, e.g., divorcing couples who have children, employers and employees, neighbors, and businesses with ongoing relationships.

Through the years a diverse group of supporters in North Carolina has worked diligently to link these two general approaches to ADR. Court officials, members of the bar, legislators, representatives of state and local governments, and private citizens have worked in concert with mediators, arbitrators, and other ADR professionals to realize the vision of a more efficient and effective system of justice. While those involved continue to seek better ways to structure and regulate the practice of ADR in North Carolina, there is a consensus that dispute resolution methods often offer compelling alternatives to litigation.

The use of ADR has revamped the court system and the legal profession in many ways. Civil procedure in North Carolina in essence has been amended and improved by the implementation of mandatory settlement procedures, so that settlement efforts are part of the life of every civil case. Lawyers negotiating on behalf of their clients in the context of a settlement conference now understand the need for further education in the area of negotiations. Thus, the subject of negotiations is beginning to be recognized and taught in the law schools to an extent never conceived of prior to the implementation of mandatory ADR. The role of lawyers as "counselors at law" is being realized among attorneys throughout the state.

A Survey of ADR Techniques

A review of the *North Carolina General Statutes* and the rules associated with the statutes provides persuasive evidence of the extent to which ADR pervades the legal landscape in North Carolina. For example, a recent Westlaw search found 177 different times that mediation was mentioned, 232 instances of arbitration, and 103 references to dispute resolution.

All surveys of current ADR techniques suffer from the same problem: They rapidly become outdated. With that caveat in mind, a summary of common ADR processes is offered below. The overview begins with a discussion of the three most widely used forms of dispute resolution—negotiation, mediation, and arbitration—and goes on to describe more specialized techniques, which are often hybrids of the basic forms.

NEGOTIATION

Negotiation typically involves a series of communications between the parties, either directly or through their representatives, with the goal of reaching an agreement (deal making) or settling a dispute. Often used as a threshold technique for reaching accord, negotiation offers a simple, private, inexpensive, and highly flexible way to resolve differences. It also gives the parties the maximum freedom to fashion their own mutually acceptable outcomes. Effective negotiation is marked by an informed exploration of alternatives conducted in an atmosphere of good faith. It requires thorough preparation, careful listening, and an exquisite sense of timing on the part of the negotiator.

MEDIATION

Mediation is, at heart, a structured negotiation conducted with the assistance of a third-party neutral—the mediator. Unlike a judge, a mediator never has decision-making power, his or her role being to help the parties arrive at their own resolution of their differences. Mediation is typically consensual and confidential. It can be used to resolve past disputes or to come to agreement on the terms of a future relationship or interaction.

The mediation process usually consists of a combination of joint sessions and private caucuses. In joint sessions, the parties and their attorneys present and exchange information and proposals with the assistance of the mediator. In private caucuses, the mediator confers with each side individually to elicit information and proposals. In both processes, the mediator's objective is to help the parties move toward agreement.

Mediation can take a number of forms, depending on the nature of the underlying dispute. **Traditional** or **classic mediation** is entirely voluntary. It can take place anywhere at any time. Court involvement is not necessary. In traditional mediation, the mediator typically uses joint sessions more than private caucuses. He or she usually remains nondirective, asking questions but avoiding declarative statements. The parties themselves generate options and evaluate solutions. The mediator often emphasizes improvement of the relationship between the parties rather than the need for an immediate resolution of the dispute. Classic mediation agreements are usually forward-looking, anticipating the parties' continuing interaction.

Court-ordered mediation differs in that those involved in the dispute are not there of their own volition, but rather because they have been ordered to attend. Although the parties are not required to reach an agreement or even to bargain in good faith, court-ordered mediators usually place explicit emphasis on settling the case. Agreements reached are typically little more than settlement documents, with less importance placed on the future relationship (if any) of the parties. Court-ordered mediators are more likely to use private caucuses as a way of generating settlement offers and counteroffers.

Child custody mediation often includes features of both court-ordered and classic mediation. In child custody mediation the parents are usually present under court order, and the mediator is highly interested in helping the parents reach an agreement. The mediator emphasizes the future relationship of the divorcing couple, particularly their ability to communicate effectively. What makes child custody mediation unique is that, unlike in classic mediation or court-ordered mediation, the most important parties—the children—do not participate. The mediator plays a key role in keeping the parents focused on the best interests of their children.

Arbitration

Arbitration, like litigation, is a form of adjudication. The parties submit evidence and arguments to a third-party neutral, the arbitrator, who decides the dispute and makes an award. As in a trial, arbitration is usually a win-or-lose process, though the arbitrator's presence can have the incidental effect of facilitating a settlement.

Arbitration comes in a number of forms. In **private** or **contractual arbitration** the parties agree to submit their dispute to binding arbitration. A private arbitration agreement is voluntary, but once it is made, arbitration of any disputes covered by the agreement may be compelled in a court action. The agreement to arbitrate can be made at the outset of the parties' relationship, before a dispute arises, or after the dispute develops.

In contractual arbitration the parties choose an arbitrator who has expertise in the subject matter of the dispute. The parties usually agree to procedural and evidentiary rules, which may include limitations on discovery and the length of the hearing, as well as restrictions on the types of motions and papers that may be filed. As a result, contractual arbitration is usually quicker and less expensive than conventional litigation. The results are also confidential, unlike those in a civil trial. Private arbitration also provides a greater sense of finality to the parties, since arbitral awards are reviewable by the courts only on very narrow grounds.

Contractual arbitration is traditionally used to resolve a wide variety of conflicts: labor-management disputes under the terms of a collective bargaining agreement; construction industry disputes among parties such as developers, contractors, and architects; securities industry disputes between broker-dealers and customers; and international commercial disputes. In the last two decades the use of contractual arbitration has expanded to other areas as well, most dramatically in employment law. Many employers now require prospective employees to agree in advance to arbitrate any employment-related claims they may make, even charges of discrimination against their employer. Arbitration clauses can also be found in an increasing number of form contracts, ranging from hospital admissions documents to credit card agreements and any number of consumer-merchant transactions.

Court-ordered arbitration is the converse of contractual arbitration. It is designed to promote settlement rather than to provide for final adjudication of a dispute. In court-ordered arbitration, the parties are required to submit their dispute to the arbitration process, but the award is not binding and the opportunity for a trial de novo is preserved. The parties present streamlined versions of their cases to a neutral third party, who then makes a decision on the merits of the parties' claims. This objective assessment, combined with the opportunity to be heard by a judge-surrogate, is often enough to induce a voluntary resolution of the dispute.

Enabling statutes usually establish the criteria for ordering cases to arbitration, typically setting a specified dollar amount. In North Carolina, for example, most state district court civil cases are eligible for court-ordered arbitration. The court appoints an arbitrator, usually an experienced attorney trained in arbitration techniques. Court-ordered arbitration programs are used in about two-thirds of the states. Some federal district courts also use this form of arbitration.

Specialized ADR Techniques: Building on the Basic Forms

Since its beginnings as a discipline, the field of alternative dispute resolution has lent itself to innovation and experimentation. The basic forms of negotiation, mediation, and arbitration can be combined or adapted into an almost limitless number of specialized ADR techniques tailored to the needs of the parties involved. Some of the most common of these techniques are discussed below. It is important to keep in mind that the list below is not exhaustive. Because ADR is limited only by contract principles, numerous variations are possible.

EARLY NEUTRAL EVALUATION

In early neutral evaluation a "neutral" is selected by the parties or appointed by the court to review and assess the relative merits of the parties' positions. The neutral is usually an attorney or other professional with expertise in the subject matter of the dispute. He or she makes an assessment of the case based on the parties' presentations and prepares a written report for the parties. To encourage full and accurate disclosures, the report is generally not admissible at trial. As with most ADR techniques, the mechanics of early neutral evaluation may be altered to fit the needs of the parties or the requirements of the court. This approach, like court-ordered arbitration, is based on the belief that a timely, objective assessment of a dispute by a respected third party will facilitate settlement. As with mediation, early neutral evaluation can be used whether or not a civil action has been filed.

OMBUDSMEN

Ombudsmen typically work to resolve disputes in institutional settings, such as large corporations, hospitals, universities, and government agencies. They can be used to investigate consumer complaints, employee grievances, or other problems and to resolve them through informal, non-adversarial means. Ombudsmen rarely have any decision-making authority and must rely on persuasion as their primary tool. Ombudsmen are usually employed by the institutions for which they provide services and thus, arguably, are not true neutrals. In the public sector in North Carolina the use of ombudsmen is authorized by statute in several settings, including the North Carolina Industrial Commission and the Division of Aging and Adult Services of the Department of Health and Human Services.

SUMMARY JURY TRIAL

Summary jury trials are condensed mock trials with advisory juries. They are designed to facilitate settlement by giving the parties and their counsel a realistic idea of how a jury might view a case. Because they involve presentation of evidence, summary jury trials are used only after the completion of discovery and thus occur in the late stages of preparing a case for trial. Summary jury trials are generally used only in complex litigation where: (1) factual disputes predominate; (2) a long trial is likely; and (3) a significant amount of money is at stake.

In a summary jury trial, attorneys for the parties present accurate but abbreviated versions of their evidence to a jury selected from the regular jury pool. The proceeding is conducted in court before a judge or magistrate. To increase the likelihood of a careful, realistic decision, the jury is not told that its verdict will not be binding on the parties. The attorneys are often given the opportunity to question the jury about the verdict, and some courts schedule a mandatory negotiation session after the verdict is rendered. If the summary jury trial does not result in settlement, the advisory jury's verdict is not admissible at the subsequent trial of the case. A common variation on this procedure is for the summary jury trial to be binding pursuant to a "high-low" agreement between the parties. (For further explanation, see the discussion below of "high-low" arbitration.)

MINI-TRIALS

The mini-trial combines elements of negotiation, mediation, and arbitration. In this technique, attorneys for both parties present summary versions of their cases before a panel consisting of a third-party neutral and high-ranking representatives of the parties, usually executives with decision-making authority. Following the attorneys' presentations, the company representatives negotiate. If they are not able to reach a settlement, the neutral member of the panel will be asked to render an opinion on the merits of the case. The neutral's opinion is generally non-binding, and the parties usually stipulate that all of the proceedings are confidential, including the attorneys' presentations and the representatives' negotiations.

Like the summary jury trial, the mini-trial is best suited for high-stakes cases that would require a substantial amount of time and money to try. However, the mini-trial can be used whether or not a lawsuit has been filed.

Not surprisingly, the mini-trial has been used primarily in complex business disputes.

MEDIATION-ARBITRATION (MED-ARB)

In med-arb, the parties agree to attempt mediation before proceeding to binding arbitration. This technique offers the parties assurance that the dispute will be resolved. Nationally, the use of med-arb has been associated most often with public sector employment disputes, but med-arb has also been used in the information technology field, where the pace of technological change often argues for a rapid settlement of a dispute.

In the simplest form of med-arb the same neutral is appointed to function as both mediator and arbitrator. (Using the same neutral in both roles saves time and money.) If arbitration is necessary, the neutral will begin with at least a working knowledge of the facts in dispute. In some cases, the mediator and the arbitrator are appointed separately, out of concern for the integrity of each process. The mediation process can be undermined if the parties, knowing that the mediator may become a decision maker, become reluctant to disclose sensitive information. The process can also be compromised if the parties' attorneys attempt to influence the neutral before the arbitration session has started. The knowledge that his or her role may change from facilitator to judge at any moment can become a difficult burden for the neutral.

VARIATIONS OF CONTRACTUAL ARBITRATION

Contractual arbitration is usually effective because the parties understand and agree to the process. Because of its consensual nature, it lends itself to a wide range of variations on the basic theme of adjudication by a neutral. Two of the more common variations are "final offer" arbitration (or "baseball" arbitration) and "high-low" arbitration.

In *final offer arbitration*, the parties agree to submit their final offers to the arbitrator. The arbitrator must choose one of the proposals as the award. He or she cannot make a compromise. If the parties exchange their final offers with each other before the hearing, they may find that the difference between their positions is modest enough to warrant additional settlement negotiations. Final offer arbitration encourages reasonable settlement proposals because neither side wants to risk appearing more outlandish than the opposition.

In **high-low arbitration**, the parties negotiate both a "floor" (or minimum) and a "ceiling" (or maximum) on the amount of the arbitral award prior to the hearing. They often agree not to inform the arbitrator of the limits placed on the award. If the award is below the "floor," the claimant nonetheless will receive the minimum amount agreed to by the parties. If the award is above the "ceiling," the claimant will be entitled only to the maximum amount agreed to by the parties. In this way, the claimant will recover something and is insured against a "zero" verdict, while the defendant limits his or her exposure and is insured against an outrageous or runaway judgment.

Conclusion

As the foregoing discussion suggests, the demand for a more just and efficient civil justice system can be satisfied in great part by the increased use of ADR processes. ADR's emphasis on shared responsibility and innovative solutions provides businesses, institutions, and private citizens with superior mechanisms for resolving disputes. As ADR techniques enjoy continued acceptance and adoption, the trial of lawsuits may become the true "alternative"—the process used only when nothing else works.

CHAPTER TWO

Origins of the ADR Movement:
The "Legal Explosion" and Calls for Change

"There seems to be little doubt that we are increasingly making greater and greater demands on the courts to resolve disputes that used to be handled by other institutions of society. Much as the police have been looked to to 'solve' racial, school and neighborly disputes, so, too, the courts have been expected to fill the void created by the decline of church and family. Not only has there been a waning of traditional dispute resolution mechanisms, but with the complexity of modern society, many new potential sources of controversy have emerged as a result of the immense growth of government at all levels, and the rising expectations that have been created. Quite obviously, the courts cannot continue to respond effectively to these accelerating demands. It becomes essential therefore to examine other alternatives."

—Harvard Law School Professor Frank E. A. Sander, *Varieties of Dispute Processing*, Speech to the National Conference on the Causes of Popular Dissatisfaction with the Administration of Justice, Washington, D.C. (April 7–9, 1976).

The Impetus for Change

Alternative dispute resolution (ADR) emerged primarily in response to dramatic changes in American society during the late 1960s and early 1970s, particularly the social reform and civil rights movements of that era. The period also saw a proliferation of new laws and explosive growth in the number of lawsuits filed in state and federal courts. Seeking ways to alleviate the staggering burden of litigation while assuring access to justice, a group of legal reformers began to explore new methods of handling disputes in the civil justice system.

In 1965, a report issued by the Commission on Law Enforcement and the Administration of Justice (appointed by President Lyndon B. Johnson) focused national attention on the country's overburdened judiciary. It helped build a consensus for reforms in the court system and for new approaches to providing justice. Within a few years Congress would provide funding for pilot dispute settlement programs in Philadelphia, New York, Miami, and Columbus, Ohio. The goals of these early court-based programs were remarkably similar to those of today: to divert appropriate cases from overloaded dockets; to offer more appropriate dispute resolution processes for selected cases; to provide citizens with more efficient and accessible dispute resolution services; and to reduce case processing costs. These programs used arbitration, mediation, and other alternative methods of dispute processing and focused on minor criminal cases involving neighbors, friends, relatives, and other acquaintances.

At the same time, another alternative dispute resolution initiative was beginning to emerge: community mediation. Activists in a handful of cities founded community mediation programs as alternatives to court-based dispute resolution processes. Their emphasis was on early intervention in disputes and prevention of conflicts. At the heart of this grassroots movement were principles of civic democracy: citizen participation and the development of networks of community organizations. Proponents of community mediation hoped that the process would improve conditions in urban centers by fostering better intergroup and interpersonal contacts. Mediation was viewed as an "empowerment tool," offering participants a greater sense of control over their lives. It was also seen as a means of creating mutual respect and understanding, even in the midst of conflict.

These community-based programs shared some of the same goals as the court-based reform programs. But they also sought to democratize decision making within the community. They had several aims: developing indigenous community leadership; reducing community tensions by strengthening the capacity of neighborhood, church, civic, school, and social service organizations to address conflict effectively; and strengthening the ability of local citizens to actively participate in the democratic process.

By the mid-1970s, these two dispute resolution initiatives—sometimes in harmony, other times at cross-purposes—had laid the groundwork for a revolution in the civil justice system.

The "Pound Conference" of 1976 and the Expansion of the National ADR Movement

In April 1976, the Judicial Conference of the United States, the Conference of Chief Justices, and the American Bar Association (ABA) co-sponsored the National Conference on the Causes of Popular Dissatisfaction with the Administration of Justice. The meeting, which soon became known as the "Pound Conference," commemorated a memorable address on judicial reform given by the noted dean of the Harvard Law School, Roscoe Pound, at the ABA's annual meeting seventy years earlier. The conference—designed to stimulate discussion and long-range planning for changes in the civil justice system—was attended by more than 200 leaders in the legal field, including chief justices of the state courts, leaders of the federal courts, officials of the organized bar, and noted legal scholars from around the country. While many topics were discussed at the conference, dispute resolution without resort to litigation was a major theme.

In his keynote address, Supreme Court Chief Justice Warren E. Burger spoke eloquently of the need for change:

> What we seek is the most satisfactory, the speediest and the least expensive means of meeting the legitimate needs of the people in resolving disputes. We must therefore open our minds to consideration of means and forums that have not been tried before. Even if what we have now has been tolerable for the first three-quarters of this century, there are grave questions whether it will do for the final quarter, or for the next century.[1]

Harvard Law School Professor Frank E. A. Sander echoed the call for change in a speech titled *Varieties of Dispute Processing.* In his address, Sander noted the extraordinary increase in the judicial caseload over the previous decade and provided an analysis of alternative dispute resolution techniques (including arbitration and mediation) as a means of lessening the litigation burden.

The Pound Conference generated many calls for reform. The ABA appointed a task force, chaired by Judge Griffin B. Bell, to follow up on proposals made at the conference and to make specific recommendations to the Association. Among the task force suggestions were proposals for developing models for "Neighborhood Justice Centers" to process disputes, and the adoption by federal and state courts of specially designed programs for compulsory arbitration.

The studies and recommendations generated by the Pound Conference Task Force sparked broader interest in ADR techniques among judges, lawyers, and citizen activists around the country. Both federal and private funds began to flow to various dispute resolution pilot programs. Nevertheless, many members of the legal community remained skeptical. It would take another decade—and the proven successes of ADR pioneers in several jurisdictions—before alternative dispute resolution procedures gained widespread acceptance among members of the bar.

NOTE

1. Warren E. Burger, "Agenda for 2000 A.D.—A Need for Systematic Anticipation," Address Delivered at the National Conference on the Causes of Popular Dissatisfaction with the Administration of Justice, 70 F.R.D. 83, 93 (1976).

CHAPTER THREE

Community Mediation: Laying the Groundwork for ADR in North Carolina

"Community mediation offers constructive processes for resolving differences and conflicts between individuals, groups, and organizations. It is an alternative to avoidance, destructive confrontation, prolonged litigation or violence. It gives people in conflict an opportunity to take responsibility for the resolution of their dispute and control of the outcome. Community mediation is designed to preserve individual interests while strengthening relationships and building connections between people and groups, and to create processes that make communities work for all of us."

—"Preamble" to Mission Statement, National Association for Community Mediation.[1]

Just as national attention was beginning to focus on new methods of conflict resolution in America's civil justice system in the mid-1970s, North Carolina was beginning its own exploration into alternatives to litigation. In 1970—six years before the convening of the landmark Pound Conference—a group of community volunteers in Chapel Hill gathered to investigate ways of resolving conflicts outside the courtroom. Their efforts over a period of years resulted in the establishment of one of the earliest and most successful community mediation programs in the country. Founded in 1978, the Orange County Dispute Settlement Center soon became a model for similar programs in other communities and helped spark the community mediation movement across the state. It also helped lay the foundation for other ADR programs in North Carolina—such as court-ordered arbitration and mediation programs—by demonstrating that certain kinds of disputes could be resolved more efficiently and effectively without going to trial.

The Orange County Dispute Settlement Center

In the mid-to-late 1960s, the campus of the University of North Carolina at Chapel Hill, like many other college campuses in the United States, erupted in a wave of protests against the war in Vietnam and against continuing racial segregation in public accommodations. Both students and local residents were arrested for various acts of civil disobedience. In 1970, at the request of the Chapel Hill Interfaith Council, three women sympathetic to the students' causes began monitoring the local criminal courts on behalf of the Women's International League for Peace and Freedom (WILPF). Charlotte Adams, Beth Okun, and Ruth "Tan" Schwab regularly attended district court sessions for the next seven years, observing whether students in general—and African American students in particular—received equal justice from the court system.

The three Chapel Hill women soon became convinced that some matters on the court docket (minor assaults, trespasses, and similar misdemeanors) were in essence civil disputes between family members, co-workers, and neighbors. "So many squabbles can be worked out without going to court," observed Charlotte Adams. "You'd be amazed how many roommates get into scraps over telephone bills."[2]

While attending a WILPF meeting in Boston in the summer of 1973, Adams, Okun, and Schwab learned about a community mediation program in Roxbury, Massachusetts, a neighborhood in Boston. The program, which had been established with help from the American Arbitration Association (AAA), used trained volunteer mediators to help resolve minor disputes that otherwise might have gone to trial. The Roxbury model seemed to offer a better alternative for resolving personal disputes than the traditional remedies afforded by the court system.

Adams, Okun, and Schwab were excited about what they had learned in Roxbury, and upon returning home they contacted others involved in community mediation efforts. They also arranged for a speaker from the AAA's Washington, D.C. office to visit Chapel Hill and explain the concept of conflict resolution at a community meeting. The presentation by the AAA speaker was well received by those in attendance, but, at the time, there was neither sufficient interest nor adequate funding to implement a dispute resolution program in the area.

Over the next three years the three women held a number of meetings to educate their fellow Orange County residents about community mediation. Finally, their persistence paid off. In 1976, another AAA speaker was invited to speak at a second community meeting in Chapel Hill. There was a large turnout for this second gathering, and, this time, interest in the community mediation concept was strong. A group of volunteers formed a committee and developed a proposal for a local dispute settlement center. The proposal was endorsed by the Orange County Board of Commissioners in late 1976 and by both the Chapel Hill Town Council and the Carrboro Board of Aldermen in 1977. District Attorney Wade Barber, Jr., an enthusiastic supporter, was helpful in organizing support within the legal community. His willingness to refer cases to the Center after its founding had a major impact in establishing its credibility and building a framework for its future success.

During the next year and a half, a broad-based community planning committee contributed many hours and raised substantial funds to start the Center. Paul Wahrhaftig of the Conflict Resolution Center in Pittsburgh, Pennsylvania—a tireless promoter of community mediation on behalf of the American Friends Service Committee—spoke to a receptive group of interested citizens in Chapel Hill in the spring of 1977. In the fall of 1978, Marjorie Curet, an attorney with the Community Relations Service of the United States Department of Justice, provided free mediation training to a group of community members. These volunteer mediators became the first board of directors for the Orange County Dispute Settlement Center. Scott Bradley, who later became the Center's first full-time Executive Director, was also an early volunteer at the Center.

The Center mediated its first case in the fall of 1978 in a room provided by the Newman Catholic Student Center in Chapel Hill. By the end of 1979 Bebe Danzinger, a local businesswoman, had donated use of a three-room office; state representative Patricia Hunt had secured a state appropriation of $7,500; the local United Way had provided an additional $4,500; and a paid, part-time Executive Director, Evelyn Smith, had been hired.

At the time, the Orange County Dispute Settlement Center's program was unique in North Carolina. But the combination of factors that led to its development was fairly typical of the community mediation movement around the country. The success of nearly all of the early dispute settlement centers was built on the hard work and commitment of community volunteers. The centers began on shoestring budgets, often working in donated space. They were helped by court officials and politicians willing to take a risk on a new idea and typically drew their support from community agencies, churches and synagogues, local funding organizations, and philanthropic foundations.

Growth of Community Mediation in North Carolina

The Orange County Dispute Settlement Center became a model for new centers throughout North Carolina. Orange County Center board members and staff advocated for community mediation across the state and assisted emerging centers (chiefly in the Piedmont region) with training and program development. In 1982, the Chatham County Dispute Settlement

Program began, at first, under the nonprofit umbrella of the Orange County Center. A separate center was opened the same year in nearby Durham. They were followed in 1983 by the Charlotte/Mecklenburg Community Relations Committee's Dispute Settlement Program, Mediation Services of Guilford County, the Neighborhood Justice Center of Winston-Salem (now Mediation Services of Forsyth County), and Mediation Services of Wake County (now Carolina Dispute Settlement Services). Three additional centers were founded in 1984: the Alamance County Dispute Settlement Center; The Mediation Center in Asheville; and the Henderson County Dispute Settlement Center. By the end of 2010, there were twenty-three community mediation centers in North Carolina.

The Mediation Network of North Carolina

In the fall of 1984, the directors of four dispute settlement centers in North Carolina met to draft legislation addressing certain key issues of mutual concern to those involved in the nascent movement. Some of the matters discussed included: confidentiality of proceedings; legality of mediated agreements; mediator training requirements; funding for center operations through state appropriations; fees for services; and a range of concerns involving the relationship between the centers and the state's courts.

In January 1985, the North Carolina Association of Community Mediation Programs (NCACMP) was founded. Mike Wendt, Director of the Dispute Settlement Center of Durham, served as acting chairperson until Alice Phalan, Director of the Chatham County Dispute Settlement Program, was elected chair. Others active in the formation of NCACMP included Barbara A. Davis of Asheville; Joan Gantz and Lee Dix Harrison from Guilford County; Shirley Johnes from Henderson County; Lisa Menefee from Forsyth County; Claire Millar from Orange County; and Frank C. Laney of Wake County, then a staff member of the North Carolina Bar Association.

The new association established four objectives for its first year: (1) to pass legislation on dispute settlement centers before the General Assembly; (2) to establish policies and procedures for mediation in the context of domestic abuse; (3) to work with the Consumer Protection Division of the state Attorney General's Office to mediate consumer complaints; and (4) to develop the organizational structure of the NCACMP.

The Z. Smith Reynolds Foundation provided a grant of $25,000 to the NCACMP, which allowed the Association to hire Dee Reid, a freelance writer, editor, and part-time mediator at the Chatham County center in

Pittsboro. In 1985, the NCACMP became known as "MediatioNetwork." MediatioNetwork changed its name to "Mediation Network of North Carolina" in 1992, when Scott Bradley was named Executive Director. The establishment of this umbrella organization for North Carolina's community mediation centers spurred unified efforts in several areas: training standards; policies regarding domestic violence issues and mediation; mediator evaluation guidelines; qualifications and ethical standards for mediators; enforceability of mediated agreements; confidentiality and mediator privilege; and state appropriations for dispute settlement centers.

Current Organization and Governance
of Community Mediation Centers

Although most mediation centers in the state are members of the Mediation Network, from time to time, some centers have determined that independent status is more in line with their goals or structure. Together, the Mediation Network and independent nonprofit mediation centers in North Carolina represent the footprint of community mediation in the state. All are similarly structured in that each serves the legislative purposes outlined in North Carolina General Statutes Section 7A-38.5, and each is independently governed by volunteer boards of directors. Each center strives to promote and provide alternative dispute resolution (ADR) services that are most needed, but services can vary by district depending on factors such as the local economy, population, education levels, and access to state and municipal services. The strength and diversity of these programs has helped make North Carolina a recognized leader in the use of cost-effective and integrated approaches to ADR methods in courts, schools, and communities.

Support for Community Mediation from the North Carolina
Bar Association and the Z. Smith Reynolds Foundation

Community mediation centers in North Carolina derived crucial support from several organizations. Important early support came from the North Carolina Bar Association's Task Force on Dispute Resolution. Chaired by Pittsboro attorney Wade Barber, Jr., the Task Force was sponsored by the North Carolina Bar Foundation, with funds provided by the Z. Smith Reynolds Foundation and the National Institute for Dispute Resolution. The Task Force's Subcommittee on Community-Based Alternatives, chaired by Greensboro attorney Larry B. Sitton, was unequivocal in its support of the ten community-based mediation centers in existence at the time.

The Task Force's 1985 report recommended that the North Carolina Bar Association actively encourage the growth and development of dispute settlement centers. It encouraged attorneys to support the work of the centers, in part by referring appropriate cases. It also recommended that centers be assured of partial state support while maintaining local initiative, volunteer support, and community funding. The report called for the General Assembly to enact legislation addressing several key issues and suggested that centers become more active in resolving consumer-merchant disputes.

With a 1986 grant from the Z. Smith Reynolds Foundation supporting permanent, part-time staff, Mediation Network was able to: (1) assist in developing several new centers; (2) publish its first newsletter, *The N.C. Mediator*; and (3) sponsor its first training program, a Train-the-Trainer workshop conducted by the Community Board Program of San Francisco.

Additional help came in 1987 with an award from the North Carolina State Bar's Interest on Lawyers' Trust Accounts (IOLTA) program, the first of many IOLTA grants for community mediation efforts. IOLTA funds made it possible for the Mediation Network Board of Directors to set a formula for allocating funds to member centers. Subsequent grants from IOLTA were vital to the development of new initiatives at some centers and maintaining existing programs at others.

Funding from the Z. Smith Reynolds Foundation also had a major influence on the growth and development of new community mediation centers, as well as on program expansion at existing centers. Since its first grant of $25,000 to the Orange County Dispute Settlement Center in 1981, the Foundation has provided over $1.5 million in key grants to support innovative programs, including: peer mediation programs in schools; juvenile mediation programs; restorative justice programs; prejudice reduction programs; and life skills training programs.

The Z. Smith Reynolds Foundation has been a grant partner with North Carolina's community mediation centers for the past three decades. At a Mediation Network board meeting in August 1997, Z. Smith Reynolds Foundation Assistant Director Joseph Kilpatrick spoke of the state's mediation centers as "a private philanthropist's dream come true with their small dedicated staffs and their spirit, flexibility and innovation."

NOTES

1. The website of the National Association for Community Mediation, http://www.nafcm.org/about/purpose.

2. Phyllis Tyler, "Charlotte Adams," *Spectator Magazine*, December 17, 1981.

CHAPTER FOUR

Early Steps in Court-Ordered Arbitration in North Carolina: The Federal Court Arbitration Program (1983–1987)

"We recommend that the Judicial Administration Division consider the potential utility of programs of compulsory arbitration with a right of appeal de novo, tailored to local needs and circumstances, with a view to the development of a program for the federal courts."

—American Bar Association, *Report of the Pound Conference Follow-Up Task Force*, 74 F.R.D. 159, 169 (1976).

The year 1983 was a watershed period in the state's efforts to resolve disputes by methods other than traditional litigation. In that year both the North Carolina Bar Association and the United States District Court for the Middle District of North Carolina took the bold step of developing programs of court-mandated arbitration for pending civil actions. Consensual arbitration was already well established in North Carolina, but court-ordered arbitration for a pending case was considered a radical idea by many of the state's trial lawyers at the time. Nevertheless, some judges were willing to experiment in limited circumstances, as long as the arbitration advocates could ensure acceptance by members of the bar, expedite court business, and reduce costs to litigants without prejudice to the quality of justice. In the end, the pilot programs of court-mandated arbitration developed in North Carolina between 1983 and 1987 proved the wisdom of making measured changes in the state's legal procedures.

Court-Annexed Arbitration in the U.S. District Court for the Middle District of North Carolina

In August 1976, the Pound Conference Follow-Up Task Force, chaired by Judge Griffin B. Bell, recommended court-annexed arbitration as a means of reducing costs and delays in civil litigation. Judge Bell, who was appointed Attorney General by President Jimmy Carter the following year, soon became instrumental in obtaining congressional funds for this experiment in arbitration. A mandatory, court-annexed, non-binding arbitration program was launched in 1978 in three federal judicial districts: the Northern District of California (San Francisco), the Eastern District of Pennsylvania (Philadelphia), and the District of Connecticut. A 1982 evaluation of these three pilot programs showed that court-annexed arbitration had been successful in reducing case disposition time.

The Administrative Office of the United States Courts obtained a congressional appropriation to expand the pilot program to ten additional districts. The Middle District of North Carolina applied and was selected as one of the new districts. The groundwork for the pilot program was laid through a unique partnership between the court and the Duke University School of Law. In June 1983, Carmon J. Stuart, an advocate for court-annexed arbitration who had just retired as Clerk of the United States District Court for the Middle District of North Carolina, volunteered to help develop the pilot program. At the same time, the Duke University School of Law, led by Dean Paul D. Carrington, was investigating alternatives to litigation. The two groups decided to join forces, and with Stuart acting as liaison between the federal court and the law school, a plan was developed for a joint program of court-annexed arbitration in the Middle District. Senior Judge Eugene A. Gordon and Chief Judge Hiram H. Ward gave their full support to the initiative.

Officials at the Duke law school proposed a Private Adjudication Center (the Center) as a means by which the law school could continue its ADR studies and assist the court in implementing the pilot program. The Center was approved by Duke University President Terry Sanford and chartered as a nonprofit corporation in December 1983. The mission of the Center, as stated in its articles of incorporation, was:

> (a) to improve the administration of private law by exploring an alternative means of dispute resolution which will be efficient yet faithful to controlling law, (b) to provide instruction to students at the Duke University School of Law . . . , and (c) to pursue inquiry into the most effective procedures for resolving disputes regarding the application of private law. . . .

On March 2, 1984, the court appointed a Local Rules Advisory Committee composed of seven lawyers from throughout the Middle District. Thornton H. Brooks, a highly respected lawyer from Greensboro, was chosen as chairman. One of the committee's first tasks was to help Carmon Stuart assemble an information notebook on court-mandated arbitration. This background material—which included an evaluation of the arbitration programs in the three pilot federal district courts, information about the Center and its mission, and proposed rules for court-annexed arbitration—was sent to a group of leaders within the Middle District bar with a request for their "advice and comment." The favorable response to this survey allowed Chairman Brooks to report to Chief Judge Ward in September 1984 that "a majority of the [Advisory] Committee unqualifiedly agrees to this proposed Rule."

After a series of informational sessions hosted by members of the committee, drafts of the proposed local rules were submitted to the judges in the district, to the clerk of court, and to the magistrate judge. Magistrate Judge P. Trevor Sharp wrote the final draft of the arbitration rules, which were formally approved in an Order Adopting Rules for Court-Annexed Arbitration. The Order was signed by all active judges in the Middle District on October 24, 1984, and became effective on January 1, 1985. The decision of the judges to adopt an experimental court-annexed arbitration program made the United States District Court for the Middle District of North Carolina the first court in the state and the first federal court in the Southeast to adopt such a program. This action demonstrated that the judges were open to change, had faith in the bar, and had the courage to act.

The Arbitration Panel

From the outset, the Local Rules Advisory Committee and the Private Adjudication Center had four main concerns about the court-annexed arbitration program. First was the question of whether their innovative plan would actually work. Second, they wondered if judges and court personnel would give court-annexed arbitration a fair chance. A third concern was whether trial lawyers would accept arbitration in good faith or just use it as an opportunity for enhanced discovery. Finally, there was the issue of attracting able lawyers to serve on the arbitration panel for nominal compensation. (At the time an arbitrator's compensation was limited to $40 per hour with a maximum of $500 per case, which required some seven hours of work, on average.)

Despite these concerns, the program received overwhelming support from the bench and the bar. Forty-five lawyers from the Middle District responded to the court's initial invitation to serve on the arbitration panel, all of whom received a one-day training course in arbitration. Ultimately, the arbitration panel had some sixty-five lawyers.

Under the program rules, litigants had the option of choosing their arbitrators by agreement or by a "strike system" in which litigants would eliminate names from a short list of prospective arbitrators submitted to them by the Center. The parties chose by agreement in about eighty percent of the cases. Some arbitrators were chosen repeatedly. Ralph A. Walker (later a judge on the North Carolina Court of Appeals) was selected sixteen times in the course of the thirty-month experiment. On the list of arbitrators were seven former judges—a former federal district court judge, a former state Supreme Court justice, a retired state Court of Appeals judge, a retired chief bankruptcy judge, and three former state trial court judges—four deans (or former deans) of law schools, and thirty-four name partners in North Carolina law firms. It was the consensus of the federal judges and court staff that the program's success was due largely to the quality of service rendered by the arbitrators. A number of the arbitrators on the panel declined compensation, saying that they considered their service to be a contribution to the court and to the legal profession.

Local Rules Governing Arbitration

In many ways the local rules for the Middle District arbitration program were unique at the time of their adoption. Designed as an experiment, the rules featured a "sunset" provision terminating them at the end of thirty months, at which time the court would weigh the benefits of court-annexed arbitration. Another distinct feature of the local rules was the high limit set on the amount in controversy for cases referred to arbitration. Arbitration was mandatory for civil actions seeking monetary relief not exceeding $150,000, the highest "cap" of any known set of rules at that time. The rules exempted from arbitration specified types of cases and allowed for case exceptions at the discretion of the court. To avoid an arbitrary and absolute cap, there was a rebuttable presumption that the amount in issue did not exceed $150,000.

The Federal Rules of Evidence did not apply in arbitration proceedings in the Middle District, except for rules relating to privilege. A single arbitrator, rather than the customary three, was authorized to weigh all evidence presented and to assess its relevance, trustworthiness, and value. The arbitrator was required to file an award with the clerk of court, who would hold it for thirty days under seal. Written opinions were optional. After the thirty-day period, the clerk entered the award as the court's judgment, with the same effect as a consent judgment, unless one of the parties had demanded a trial de novo, as of right, or filed a stipulation of dismissal. This feature enabled parties to settle the case with the benefit of knowledge gained in the hearing—or from the arbitrator's award—without having a preclusive judgment appear on the public record. If, in a trial de novo, the demanding party did not gain a judgment more favorable than the arbitrator's award, the clerk taxed the cost of the arbitration to that party. The fact that there had been arbitration was not admissible in the trial de novo.

Role of the Private Adjudication Center

Perhaps the most noteworthy and unique aspect of the federal court-annexed arbitration program was the partnership between the court and the Duke University School of Law's Private Adjudication Center. The Center actively participated in the program from its inception in 1983 through completion of the pilot program in 1987.

During the experimental period, the Center assumed primary responsibility for managing cases referred to arbitration. It developed and maintained a list of qualified arbitrators. Court orders selecting cases for arbitration were received by the Center, which then advised the parties of their rights and explained the procedure for selecting an arbitrator from the Center's approved list. Once an arbitrator was chosen, the court referred the case to the Center for scheduling and the conduct of a hearing.

The Private Adjudication Center received a complete copy of the court's file in each case, both for its own use and for use by the arbitrator. It managed the pre-hearing procedure, which included the exchange of information regarding issues such as witnesses, exhibits, and the submission of pre-hearing briefs. Records of proceedings were filed with the Center rather than the court. Most of the hearings were monitored by Center Vice President Carmon Stuart, who also served the arbitrator as a de facto courtroom deputy. In short, once a case was selected and referred to the Private Adjudication Center, it was managed by the Center all the way through to the award phase (indeed, to the judgment phase) with no judicial involvement, unless there was a trial de novo.

The Center performed one additional and critically important management function. It arranged for a study and evaluation of the program by E. Allen Lind, a well-known and respected social science scholar and researcher for the Institute for Social Justice at the RAND Corporation. His 1990 report, "Arbitrating High-Stakes Cases: An Evaluation of Court-Annexed Arbitration in a United States District Court," was highly regarded for its methodology and widely cited in the professional literature.

On June 30, 1987, the end of the thirty-month experimental period, the Center's work with the court was complete. The court rules were changed, effective July 1, 1987, to make arbitration a feature of local practice in the Middle District and to bring the program under the supervision of the clerk, rather than the Center. This program remained in place until 1993, when mediation rules were adopted in response to legislative limits on court-annexed arbitration in the federal courts and to the success of the Mediated Settlement Conference Program in state court, making mediation the court-sponsored alternative dispute resolution program in the Middle District.

CHAPTER FIVE

Dispute Resolution and the North Carolina Bar Association: Lawyers as Peacemakers and the Beginning of Court-Ordered Arbitration

"The time has clearly come for lawyers to begin to emphasize their role as mediators, conciliators, and peacemakers—as counselors for what is right, not merely advocates for what is legally possible. Lawyers must begin to take advantage of alternatives to litigation for dispute resolution. . . . Lawyers need to remind themselves that the courtroom is often not a place conducive to peacemaking or conflict healing, yet peacemaking and conflict healing are first obligations of our profession."

—North Carolina Supreme Court Chief Justice James G. Exum, Jr., "The Lawyer as Peacemaker," 34 Bar Notes 8, 9 (1983).

In 1983, a small group of prominent North Carolina attorneys attended a conference at Wheaton College, in Wheaton, Illinois, sponsored by the Christian Legal Society. The conference focused on the role of lawyers in discouraging litigation and encouraging private resolution of disputes. North Carolina Supreme Court Chief Justice James G. Exum, Jr. delivered an inspiring address on the role of lawyers as peacemakers.

Justice Exum urged "a return by the legal profession to the fundamental principle that a lawyer's highest obligation to society and to clients is to be a peacemaker." He suggested that litigation often was "the product of the lawyer's failure" in this duty. Noting that the vast majority of cases brought to trial involve factual disputes, rather than important legal or constitutional issues, Justice Exum argued that such cases frequently could be resolved outside the courtroom. In these situations, he said, lawyers should "exhaust their skills as counselors" before "so readily assuming the role of advocates."[1]

Recalling the words of Judge J. Braxton Craven, Jr., Justice Exum identified a category of disputes that he characterized as involving primarily "people's problems," not "legal problems." In such cases, he said, litigation could be "especially harmful." Examples included cases involving "persons who, before the dispute arose, enjoyed some kind of meaningful, positive personal relationship" as with "petty criminal matters between relatives or friends, domestic disputes, disputes between business associates, boundary line disputes between neighbors, [and] squabbles between heirs over their ancestor's spoils. . . ." He concluded: "Where we are dealing primarily with people's problems, the courtroom does not have nearly the resolving power of other, less formal, less structured, dispute settling devices. Litigation in these cases is frequently a severe obstacle to reconciliation between the parties."[2]

Justice Exum repeated his Wheaton College address to several bar groups in North Carolina. Charles L. Fulton, then President of the North Carolina Bar Association (NCBA), heard one of these talks and was inspired to help explore this new concept of lawyers as peacemakers. When several of the lawyers who had attended the Wheaton conference suggested a task force to study what role North Carolina's lawyers should play, President Fulton took the lead.

The Dispute Resolution Task Force

In November 1983, Fulton appointed the Alternatives to Litigation Task Force, eventually known as the NCBA Dispute Resolution Task Force (Task Force). The group's goal was to study alternative dispute resolution (ADR) programs across the country and to make recommendations for the North Carolina bar. Wade Barber, Jr. was appointed to serve as the Task Force chair. As District Attorney for Orange County and Chatham County, he was well familiar with the work of the Orange County Dispute Settlement Center in taking minor criminal cases from the district courts and resolving them in a just and amicable manner. Other prominent lawyers, court officials, and active members of the bar were asked to join the Task Force. Justice Exum was appointed chair of the Task Force Subcommittee on Court-Based Alternatives. Larry B. Sitton, a Greensboro lawyer, was appointed chair of the Community-Based Alternatives Subcommittee. Professor Ralph A. Peeples, of the Wake Forest University School of Law, and Reagan H. Weaver, a Raleigh attorney, agreed to compile and edit the final Task Force report. The Z. Smith Reynolds Foundation of Winston-Salem provided a research grant to support the group's work, and the National Institute for Dispute Resolution in Washington, D.C. contributed additional funds.

The Task Force held its inaugural meeting in Greensboro on April 5,

1984, and resolved to hold monthly meetings on the relevance of ADR for the justice system in North Carolina. Leading ADR consultants and practitioners and a variety of experts were invited to speak to the group as a whole. After some deliberation, members recommended wider use of ADR. The focus then shifted to the kinds of programs or initiatives that would be proposed to the courts and the bar. Despite a very limited budget, both subcommittees sent representatives to visit existing ADR programs in Ohio, Michigan, California, Pennsylvania, Arizona, and Washington to interview participants and to learn first-hand how the programs operated. This effort was greatly aided by Task Force member H. C. "Jack" Roemer, then Senior Vice President and Secretary for R. J. Reynolds Industries, who secured use of his company's corporate jet for some of these visits.

In June 1985, the Task Force issued its report, with four key recommendations:

1. The North Carolina Bar Association should actively encourage the growth and development of dispute settlement centers;
2. North Carolina should establish a pilot project of court-ordered arbitration in three judicial districts to resolve civil disputes involving $15,000 or less;
3. Dispute resolution procedures such as child custody mediation, summary jury trials, and mini-trials should be investigated more thoroughly;
4. The North Carolina Bar Association should promote greater awareness on the part of the bar and the public about alternative methods of dispute resolution.

The report was the single most important product of the Task Force and became the working guide for the development of ADR programs in the state.

The Push for State Court Arbitration

The work of the Task Force ended with the issuance of its report. But when the North Carolina Bar Association adopted the recommendations at its annual meeting in June 1985, a group was needed to oversee their implementation. Larry Sitton was appointed chair of the new Dispute Resolution Committee (Committee) of the NCBA. Sitton's agreement to serve was contingent on the willingness of other prominent Task Force members to continue their involvement. The majority of the Task Force participants agreed. The Bar Association's beginning ADR efforts would be in good hands.

The new Committee was divided into four subcommittees, each charged with implementing one of the four Task Force recommendations. The recommendation that required the most time and effort was the design of court-ordered arbitration in cases involving $15,000 or less.

The Committee's work was greatly aided by the hiring of Frank C. Laney, a Raleigh attorney and member of the original Task Force, to work as the NCBA's Dispute Resolution Coordinator. Funds to establish Laney's position were obtained largely through the efforts of Roy J. Baroff, an NCBA intern during the summer of 1985. Baroff, a volunteer mediator with the Orange County Dispute Settlement Center and a law student at the University of North Carolina at Chapel Hill, secured a grant from the North Carolina State Bar's Interest on Lawyers' Trust Accounts (IOLTA) Program to help support the Committee's efforts. With Laney working full-time to pursue the Committee's objectives, the drive for a state court arbitration program began in earnest.

Enabling Legislation

With the approval of its Board of Governors, the NCBA formally sponsored legislation entitled "Pilot Program of Mandatory, Non-Binding Arbitration of Certain Claims." The bill was enacted as North Carolina General Statutes Section 7A-37 near the end of the 1985 session of the General Assembly. The statute authorized pilot arbitration programs to be established in three state judicial districts, to be selected by the Supreme Court of North Carolina, and to be operated according to rules adopted by the Court. Arbitration was to be permitted only in cases involving claims for damages of $15,000 or less. Unfortunately, no state funds were appropriated for the program. The General Assembly instead directed that funds should be sought "from such willing private sources as the Court may deem appropriate. . . ."[3]

State Arbitration Rules

A subcommittee of the Dispute Resolution Committee, composed of representatives of the bench, the bar, and the North Carolina Administrative Office of the Courts (AOC), worked diligently to produce a set of Rules for Court-Ordered Arbitration in North Carolina. Led by Carmon J. Stuart, chair of the Arbitration Subcommittee, and Professor George K. Walker of the Wake Forest University School of Law, the subcommittee loosely patterned the proposed rules upon the federal court-ordered arbitration rules. Drafts were circulated to Committee members and trial lawyers for comment. Members of the Committee made numerous appearances before bar groups to explain the proposed rules and to gather input. As suggestions were received from the various parties, the proposed rules went through five drafts before a final form was reached.

Consistent with the enabling legislation, the rules made all civil actions filed in the trial divisions of the General Court of Justice subject to court-ordered arbitration if they involved a claim for monetary relief not exceeding $15,000. Exceptions to the requirement were made for certain types of cases, such as class actions, claims for substantial equitable relief, family law matters, real estate claims, and decedents' estate matters. The drafters on the Subcommittee fixed the relief cap at $15,000, in keeping with the experience in other states of starting low and raising the cap as warranted. Moreover, the drafters thought that if mandatory arbitration was limited to the "small cases," the new program would be more acceptable to the trial bar. They hoped to increase the limit to $25,000 at the end of the two-year trial period set by the Supreme Court.

One unique feature of the rules was a provision that arbitration hearings were to be limited to one hour, unless the arbitrator determined at the hearing that more time was necessary to ensure fairness and justice to the parties. Another unusual provision was the rule authorizing sanctions for any party failing or refusing to participate "in a good faith and meaningful manner," a rule which in practice proved to be rather ambiguous.

Because the program involved a procedure that was entirely new to North Carolina, the drafters added extensive comments to many of the rules to explain their rationale and to serve as instructive guides in interpreting them. Although the comments were an important part of the rules, and therefore carried the imprimatur of the Court, the issue of whether they were to be deemed authoritative was never decided.

Finally, on August 28, 1986, the Supreme Court of North Carolina directed that a pilot program of mandatory, non-binding arbitration be operated for two years in the Third, Fourteenth, and Twenty-Ninth Judicial Districts pursuant to the Rules for Court-Ordered Arbitration, as proposed by the Subcommittee of the Dispute Resolution Committee. The Rules became effective on January 1, 1987.

Scores of conscientious lawyers and AOC personnel gave freely of their time, talents, and resources to assist in creating and establishing the pilot program. In tribute to all who worked on the rules and procedures, it should be noted that the Rules have stood the test of time without much change.

The Pilot Program Begins

The pilot program was launched on January 1, 1987, and ran for two years. Carmon Stuart prepared a *Benchbook for Arbitrators*, published by the NCBA and later revised and updated by the AOC, to assist novice court-approved arbitrators.

The three judicial districts that served as the testing ground for the pilot program had been carefully chosen to represent different geographic regions and various types of communities. Such diversity offered an optimal basis for evaluating the program's overall effectiveness.[4] The Third Judicial District was a semi-urban area in the eastern part of the state which included Carteret, Craven, Pamlico, and Pitt counties. The Fourteenth District, covering Durham County, was primarily an urban district located in the center of the state. The Twenty-Ninth District, a predominantly rural area in western North Carolina, consisted of Henderson, McDowell, Polk, Rutherford, and Transylvania counties.

The enabling legislation included a directive to evaluate the program for a reasonable period of time. Funding was secured to conduct an independent study during the pilot phase. The NCBA asked the Institute of Government at the University of North Carolina at Chapel Hill to design and supervise an evaluation of the pilot program. The study, led by Professor Stevens H. Clarke, examined the program's effect on eligible cases filed in the three districts from January through June 1987. Under the procedures designed for the study, half of the eligible cases in each district were referred to arbitration. The rest were handled according to standard court procedures. The disposition of cases in both groups was examined to determine if any improvements could be attributed to the arbitration process. The evaluators also conducted interviews with attorneys and litigants to determine rates of satisfaction with the different procedures and with the outcomes. The evaluation, published in 1989, concluded that the court-ordered arbitration program reduced the time required for disposition of cases in each of the three pilot districts and resulted in a high level of satisfaction among litigants and their counsel.[5]

Specifically, the study found that disposition time in contested cases was reduced by 33 to 45 percent. The study also found that trial rates were reduced by more than two-thirds in contested cases. Litigants who lost or settled were more satisfied with the arbitration program than with standard procedure.[6] During the pilot phase, a staff person was provided to each district. The importance of the use of attorneys as arbitrators was also noted: "Clearly, another key ingredient to the ultimate success or failure of the program is the quality of the arbitrators. Here significant efforts were made to insure arbitrator competence and impartiality."[7]

The evaluation of the program did not directly address whether court-annexed arbitration results in a cost savings per se. Anecdotal evidence reflected some significant savings. It is noteworthy, however, that in the Third District, the court-ordered arbitration program was credited with reducing the number of weeks of civil trial court scheduled. This permitted judges additional time to handle other disputes, particularly equitable distribution cases and criminal matters. The NCBA report on court-ordered arbitration concluded that "[u]ltimately, the benefit of the program lies not so much in reducing direct costs as in the improvement of the overall operations of the judicial system, including a consideration of the level of litigant satisfaction."[8] The benefits to the court system and the litigants are still being felt in those districts in which court-ordered arbitration is in place. To fund the pilot program and the evaluation, the NCBA raised $566,364 from numerous grantors, primarily in North Carolina, but also from across the nation.

Based on the success of the pilot program, the General Assembly enacted legislation during the 1989 Session authorizing court-ordered, non-binding arbitration statewide. Although authorized, the program has been implemented in only thirty-two judicial districts. Immediately following the pilot phase, eight districts were brought on board in 1990. From 1993 through 1999, twenty-one of the remaining districts were in place. Further expansion of the program was dependent upon funding from the General Assembly to provide for payment of the arbitration fees and to provide for any necessary staff. During the court-ordered arbitration pilot program, a staff person was provided to each judicial district participating. A study of North Carolina's program noted that "[i]n this respect, the North Carolina program clearly benefitted from careful attention to the importance of administration."[9] Once the program was expanded past the original districts, staff was not always provided. Staffing was based on case filings. To conserve state resources, staffing has been kept as lean as possible. The districts operate with part-time staff or utilize the personnel already serving as staff to the district court judges. Many districts started arbitration without adding additional staff. Although the court-ordered arbitration program was authorized statewide, extending the program into the remaining districts was slow, since expansion required the General Assembly to approve additional court personnel to administer the program.[10] (For further information about the program and its current operation, please see Chapter 32.)

The program was reviewed again in 1994. The North Carolina Supreme Court Dispute Resolution Committee, chaired by Justice Henry E. Frye, evaluated the program at the request of the General Assembly and the Director of the Administrative Office of the Courts, James C. Drennan. The results showed that the program continued to meet its goals.[11]

Other Work of the Dispute Resolution Committee

During the late 1980s, the NCBA's work began to receive national attention. As the NCBA Dispute Resolution Coordinator, Frank Laney fielded telephone calls and letters requesting information and manuals about the use of mediation, arbitration, and other ADR processes in the courts of North Carolina. These queries came from lawyers, judges, and court officials in a number of states. By the end of the decade North Carolina had become a national leader in developing and implementing ADR in a statewide, systematic fashion. The state's method of building support among members of the bench, the bar, the community, and court administration became a model for other programs. Much of the success was due to the quiet, behind-the-scenes support of Chief Justice Exum and other leading members of the North Carolina Bar Association.

While the arbitration program was enjoying wide success, the NCBA Dispute Resolution Committee continued to study and promote other aspects of ADR. The Subcommittee on Bar and Public Awareness, under the leadership of its chairman, D. Clark Smith, Jr. of Lexington, printed and distributed 10,000 copies of an informational pamphlet on alternatives to litigation describing sixteen different ADR programs operating in the state.

The Other Procedures Subcommittee, chaired by Leslie J. Winner of Charlotte, published a study of the Mandatory Child Custody Mediation Program in Mecklenburg County. This study was used by proponents in the General Assembly to begin the gradual expansion of the program statewide. The Child Custody Mediation Subcommittee, chaired by Charlotte attorney Sydnor Thompson, produced a series of *Divorce Mediation* newsletters for distribution to judges and lawyers around the state.

The Dispute Resolution Committee played a major role in developing explanatory materials for a pilot program authorized by the Supreme Court of North Carolina in June 1987. The program encouraged use of summary jury trials in three judicial districts in urban areas: Wake, Buncombe, and Mecklenburg counties. Catharine B. Arrowood, an attorney in the Raleigh office of Parker Poe Adams & Bernstein, and Lee A. Spinks, an attorney in Rocky Mount, produced the explanatory materials on initiating and conducting a summary jury trial (SJT). Although the number of cases submitted to the SJT process was small, the procedure resulted in settlement each time it was employed.

Further urging the use of ADR, the Committee published articles in NCBA newsletters and bar journals describing mini-trials and encouraging their use. Although convinced that mini-trials had been held around the state, the Dispute Resolution Committee could not determine the extent of their use, due to the private and usually confidential nature of the process. During the period mediation was being explored, and in cooperation with several dispute settlement centers, the first mediation training for North Carolina lawyers was conducted at the NCBA Bar Center on October 26–28, 1989.

Conclusion

During this early, experimental period of ADR in North Carolina, a time when many initiatives were being proposed and implemented, the bar was generally receptive to new ideas. Most of the active local bar associations invited members of the Dispute Resolution Committee to speak at their meetings. On such occasions, Committee members found welcoming audiences, by and large. The typical bar member may not have understood at that time what alternative dispute resolution was, but most were willing to listen and to keep an open mind.

At the beginning of the court-ordered arbitration program, a speaker from the NCBA recalls one particular address to a local bar in a pilot district. As the speaker stood in line at lunch, he heard a prominent local lawyer say, "This arbitration stuff is a waste of time, but they asked me to be an arbitrator and I'm willing to give it a try." The speaker remembered thinking, "That is all we ask: to give it a try."

Three years later, at the end of the pilot program, the same speaker returned to address the same group about the success of the arbitration experiment. The first person he met was the aforementioned local attorney, who said, "I don't know if you remember me," (the speaker certainly did) "but I have served as an arbitrator, and this program is great. I am active in politics and I know a lot of people locally and in Raleigh. When you go to the legislature, let me know and I will write letters, I'll make calls, I'll drive all the way to Raleigh. I'll tell everybody how great this program is and that we need to put it in every district in the state." The speaker said, "Thank you," and remembered thinking to himself, "All we asked was that you give it a try. This program *sells itself.*"

NOTES

1. James G. Exum, Jr., *The Lawyer as Peacemaker,* 34 Bar Notes 8, 8 (1983).

2. *Id.*

3. N.C. Gen. Stat. § 7A-37.

4. *See Court-Ordered Arbitration, Report to the Supreme Court of North Carolina By the North Carolina Bar Association* (March 1989).

5. *See* Stevens H. Clarke et al., *Court-Ordered Arbitration in North Carolina: An Evaluation of Its Effects* (Institute of Government, The University of North Carolina at Chapel Hill, 1989).

6. *Court-Ordered Arbitration, Report to the Supreme Court of North Carolina by the North Carolina Bar Association, supra* note 4, at 33.

7. *Id.* at 3.

8. *Id.* at 9.

9. *Id.* at 3.

10. *See* The North Carolina Court System, Court Ordered Arbitration in North Carolina, Expansion Programs, http://www.nccourts.org/Citizens/CPrograms/Arbitration/Default.asp?topic=8.

11. *Interim Report of the North Carolina Supreme Court Dispute Resolution Committee to the Supreme Court of North Carolina and the Administrative Office of the Courts* (April 8, 1994).

CHAPTER SIX

The Development of Mediated Settlement Conferences: From "Court-Ordered ADR" to "Settlement Procedures"

"Discourage litigation. Persuade your neighbors to compromise wherever you can. Point out to them how the nominal winner is often a real loser—in fees, expenses and waste of time. As a peacemaker, the lawyer has a superior opportunity of being a good man. There will still be business enough."

—Abraham Lincoln

The year 1989 was pivotal in the development of alternative dispute resolution (ADR) in North Carolina. During that year, bills were introduced in and enacted by the General Assembly that authorized the statewide expansion of two ADR programs whose pilot phases had just concluded: the Child Custody Mediation Program and the Court-Ordered Arbitration Program.

By 1989, the North Carolina Bar Association's Dispute Resolution Committee had reached several important conclusions. The Committee found: first, that litigants judged ADR programs to be effective and satisfactory alternatives to litigation; second, that these programs were remarkably successful in reducing the disposition time of civil cases; and third, that ADR had to be mandatory for it to have a major impact on the court system.

This decision marked a true milestone in the development of alternative dispute resolution in North Carolina. Although much of the country continued—and still continues—to debate whether or not ADR procedures should be court-ordered, the early successes of the experimental program of mandatory arbitration in the United States District Court for the Middle District of North Carolina and the State's court-ordered arbitration program led to this conclusion. The soundness of that conclusion has been validated as ADR has continued to evolve through the years.

Despite the success of these ADR initiatives, some observers in 1989 were cautious about ADR's future. One reason for skepticism was based on economics. The arbitration and child custody programs cost a great deal of money, and it was far from clear that funds would be available to create new programs. Already there were predictions of state budgetary shortfalls which, in 1991, would produce North Carolina's worst financial crisis since the Great Depression. With the prospect of cutbacks in all services, including those attached to the courts, some supporters of ADR believed that new programs simply would not pass fiscal muster in the future.

A second reason for concern was that there seemed to be no clear direction or advocacy for further development of ADR in the courts. Superior courts were the next logical venue for implementing ADR, but there was no consensus on the proper approach to take in those courts. Although court-ordered arbitration had proven successful in resolving certain kinds of disputes, its state-wide implementation in the courts was not favored by the Bar. Summary jury trials, which had been promoted and studied by the Duke University School of Law's Private Adjudication Center, had had too little impact to be seen as applicable on a statewide and everyday basis. And finally, the much studied concept of the "multi-door courthouse" (discussed later in this chapter) appeared too cumbersome to implement in North Carolina's many small, rural counties.

The Dispute Resolution Committee's New Agenda

Several events soon took place that turned uncertainty over ADR's future into optimism about its prospects. In August of 1989, the new Dispute Resolution Committee chair, Greensboro attorney Horace R. Kornegay, convened the Committee for a brainstorming session. It was a first step toward creating a new agenda for the Committee's ADR efforts. That meeting (and subsequent smaller meetings during the next several weeks) proved significant in several ways.

The first was the appearance of Robert A. Phillips, a Florida lawyer who had moved to North Carolina and opened a practice in the mountain town of Burnsville. Phillips told the Committee about Florida's court-based mediation program. He explained to the Committee that Florida lawyers had not liked non-binding arbitration as a settlement tool; that they rarely chose arbitration over mediation; and that mediation in Florida's circuit courts had been well received. Members of the Committee were intrigued. It was the first time most of them had heard of any court using mediation in civil cases (other than in family disputes).

Shortly after the August brainstorming session, Horace Kornegay conducted a series of subcommittee meetings to consider the ideas generated by the discussion. As a result, Kornegay made two decisions that organized and defined the Committee's efforts for that time and, as it turned out, for many years to come.

The first decision came from a suggestion by Chapel Hill attorney J. Anderson (Andy) Little to combine several mediation subcommittees into one. During the years from 1985 to 1989, when the main focus of the full Committee was the design and testing of an arbitration program, the number of mediation subcommittees had multiplied. There were subcommittees on child custody mediation, community center mediation, farm credit mediation, and school mediation. Although these groups gathered valuable information, none of them produced much that would be applicable to the courts. Combining them into one, so that the energies of all could be focused on one or two projects, seemed essential. Kornegay did that and later asked Little to chair the new consolidated Mediation Subcommittee.

Kornegay's second decision was to establish a "multi-door courthouse" committee, with Reagan H. Weaver as its chair. As noted earlier, Weaver was one of the original members of the North Carolina Bar Association Dispute Resolution Task Force and, along with Ralph A. Peeples, one of its reporters. The phrase "multi-door courthouse" was used in legal circles at the time to describe the infusion of ADR procedures into the legal system. Chief Justice James G. Exum, Jr. of the Supreme Court of North Carolina often used it in speeches during the 1980s, and an artistic rendering of a multi-door courthouse appeared on the cover of the Task Force's 1985 report (and in a number of other Committee publications in subsequent years). As a metaphor, the multi-door courthouse was a useful concept. However, by the end of the 1980s, it had come to be identified with a highly structured ADR case management system. Such programs had been created in Tulsa, Houston, and Washington, D.C., under sponsorship of the ADR Task Force of the American Bar Association (ABA).

Weaver's committee set out to explore the concept of the multi-door courthouse. Using grant money from the National Institute of Dispute Resolution obtained by Frank C. Laney (a Raleigh attorney and, at the time, Dispute Resolution Coordinator for the North Carolina Bar Association), the committee visited existing programs in Washington, D.C., Brunswick, New Jersey, and Philadelphia during the fall of 1990. Weaver's committee found that each program relied on a staff of administrators who assigned cases to specific ADR procedures. Such a method followed the conventional wisdom of the time that certain types of cases were best suited to specific

ADR procedures, and that administrators and judges were the appropriate people to make those determinations. That concept often was called "fitting the forum to the fuss."

At first, the Dispute Resolution Committee found the multi-door courthouse approach an appealing one. The Committee abandoned the concept later that fall, however, and it was never taken up again. In the end, the administrative costs of such a program proved to be too high. In each of North Carolina's one hundred counties, at least a part-time position would have been needed to provide the central screening function associated with the model. With forecasts of a dire fiscal year circulating around the state, proposing such an expensive program seemed untimely.

The Committee members also were beginning to doubt the current wisdom that one could identify cases by type for assignment to an "appropriate" ADR technique. Although other courts had spent considerable energy developing complex criteria by which staff could triage cases, the Committee members remained skeptical. Instead, they were beginning to believe that choosing an ADR process was a decision that could best be made by the parties and their attorneys.

But a far more compelling reason for abandoning the multi-door courthouse concept, with its bulky administrative components, emerged in November 1990. The Mediation Subcommittee had devised an entirely new proposal for the full Committee's consideration: a program of mediated settlement conferences, which needed no state funds and would require no new administrative structure.

The Focus on Mediation

The new Mediation Subcommittee began its work shortly after it was created in August of 1989. The Subcommittee's task was to develop objectives and a work plan to guide its efforts for several years into the future. It met at regular intervals throughout the fall and winter of 1989–1990, at times seeking and utilizing the resources of the ABA's ADR Task Force. At the April 1990 meeting of the full Dispute Resolution Committee, Andy Little reported the Mediation Subcommittee's objectives. They were to support the establishment and development of community settlement centers throughout the state, to monitor the child custody mediation program and make suggestions to its advisory committee, and to study whether and how other states were using mediation in civil cases. To further the last objective, the Mediation Subcommittee asked Frank Laney to obtain grant monies for travel in the fall of 1990 to four sites chosen for study. Those sites were picked with the aid of staff at the ABA, which served as a clearinghouse for information on ADR programs nationwide. (Ironically, Florida was not one of the proposed destinations.)

At the urging of the full Committee, Horace Kornegay made another important administrative decision at this time, one that would significantly bolster the Mediation Subcommittee's work and infuse it with new energy. In 1989 and 1990, as the Dispute Resolution Committee focused on district court and non-court related alternatives, participation of the bench in the efforts of the Committee diminished. Committee members believed that involvement of additional judges was crucial, especially if new programs worthy of implementation in the courts were going to be recommended. Kornegay asked Chief Justice Exum to appoint several judges to the Committee. Among the appointees were Judge James M. Long, senior resident superior court judge for Stokes and Surry counties, and Judge Robert (Bob) D. Rouse III, retired senior resident superior court judge and former Pitt County District Attorney. These men would play an important role in bringing mediation to the trial courts of North Carolina.

The Florida Model

During the month of August 1990, several events took place that changed the course of the Mediation Subcommittee's deliberations. Having learned more about Florida's court-based mediation program from Robert Phillips, Mediation Subcommittee Chair Andy Little decided to take a civil trial court mediation training seminar in Asheville taught by David Strawn, a former circuit court judge from Orlando, for vacationing Florida lawyers.

Little, who had already been trained in community center and family mediation, attended the seminar to find out more about mediation in the context of civil litigation, with lawyers participating in the process. He learned how the Florida program worked; how cases were selected; how mediators were assigned; how neutrals were compensated; how the program was funded; and how lawyers reacted to it. He discovered that while both mediation and arbitration were available in the Florida program, judges routinely ordered the parties only to mediation. In Florida, the parties and their attorneys rarely requested arbitration themselves. Little also learned that the Florida system required no additional administrative personnel at the local level, and, perhaps most important at the time, that the mediators were paid by the parties and not by the state. It became clear to Little during that week in Asheville that the key to new ADR initiatives in North Carolina was the coupling of mandatory mediation with the sharing of costs by the parties. He also surmised that a program based on these concepts would require some radical changes and might not be an easy sell to the bench and bar.

In late August 1990, Judge Rouse attended Judge Strawn's mediation seminar in Florida. He returned feeling just as excited as Little about the training, the Florida program, and the way that Florida lawyers seemed to like mediation. After many discussions over the course of several days, Little and Rouse concluded that the Mediation Subcommittee should plan for a sizeable group to make a trip to Florida to study its program in detail, rather than travel around the country to examine other model programs. The Subcommittee later agreed.

Little and Rouse thought it critical that the group making the trip include members of the legal community who were dedicated to the ADR effort, but who also would command the attention and respect of the bench, the bar, and the legislature. The individuals selected to make the trip included Senior Resident Superior Court Judge James M. Long, North Carolina Court of Appeals Judge Jack L. Cozort, North Carolina Supreme Court Justice Harry C. Martin, North Carolina Administrative Office of the Courts (AOC) staff member Kathy L. Shuart, Winston-Salem attorney Lisa V. Menefee, First Union Bank Corporate Legal Counsel Francis Charles (Chip) Clark, Robert Phillips, Retired Judge Bob Rouse, and Andy Little.

The trip took place over three days in October 1990. During that time Mediation Subcommittee members attended mediations, talked to judges and administrators, interviewed numerous lawyers, and talked among themselves about what portions of the Florida program might be useful in North Carolina. Robert Phillips arranged for attendance at mediations in both Orlando and Tampa. Chip Clark arranged conversations with a number of civil trial lawyers in Orlando. Judge Strawn spoke with the Subcommittee members and helped set up a number of meetings for them with court officials.

Because lawyers in Florida seemed to like the mediation component of the state's program, but not the non-binding arbitration part, the Subcommittee decided to limit its consideration to a court-ordered mediation program. Andy Little later recalled that those who made the trip to Florida seemed "on fire" about the idea and believed it could bring about needed improvements to the state courts. Their energy and enthusiasm would be put to good use, for designing and implementing the program in North Carolina would require countless hours of dedicated effort.

Building Support for the Mediated Settlement
Conference Pilot Program

Upon returning to North Carolina, the group began to draft a statute authorizing a pilot program of "mediated settlement conferences" in North Carolina's superior courts, along with a set of rules to implement it. The program's proponents used the name Mediated Settlement Conference rather than Superior Court Mediation to make this new format sound more appealing to judges and attorneys who were already familiar with judicial settlement conferences. The drafters worked at nights and on weekends upon their return to North Carolina and were ready with their recommendations at the meeting of the Dispute Resolution Committee in November 1990. The Committee enthusiastically endorsed the new program.

The next stop on the road to implementation was the office of Chief Justice Exum, who was a strong supporter of ADR and a member of the original Task Force. He had two important questions at the end of the Committee's presentation. First, he asked if the phrase "mandatory mediation" was a contradiction in terms. Committee members responded that it was not, because the parties would only be required to attend the conference and would not be required to make an offer or proposal during the conference. A tougher question followed. Justice Exum wondered whether the mediation costs would be too steep and run counter to the strong and long-standing North Carolina tradition of easy access to the courts.

The matter of placing the costs of the program on the shoulders of the parties to litigation was a critical feature of the program and the reason it could be implemented widely and quickly. Many people in the court system were understandably cautious about placing a greater financial burden on those who needed and used the courts for the redress of their grievances. They believed that the state should provide and pay for any programs or services that the courts order the parties to undertake.

The response to Justice Exum's concern was twofold. First, lawyers in Florida had stressed to the Subcommittee that paying for mediation services did not cost litigants more than proceeding to trial in the traditional way. Second, the pilot program's design included a professional evaluation, which would address the issue of costs, along with many other issues. Proponents hoped that the evaluation would reveal an overall reduction in costs to the parties. In fact, it ultimately concluded that the program did not result in a statistically significant reduction in costs,[1] but it also showed that the costs of litigation did not increase, even with litigants paying for the mediator.[2]

By the beginning of the 1991 legislative session, the Dispute Resolution Committee had successfully garnered support for the pilot program from both the North Carolina Bar Association (NCBA) and the Supreme Court of North Carolina. However, the Committee was not sure what kind of reception such an innovative program would receive in the General Assembly. The proposed legislation was introduced in the Senate by Alexander P. (Sandy) Sands III and shepherded through that body with the help of B. Davis Horne, the NCBA's lobbyist, and Lucius W. Pullen, a member of the bar and a lobbyist. Surprisingly, the bill sailed through the Senate without a single dissenting vote. Even more surprising, on June 4, 1991, the bill passed the House, also without opposition.

Many people contributed to the creation of the Mediated Settlement Conference (MSC) Pilot Program. Andy Little had the vision and drive to lead the effort. It was Little who first stimulated widespread interest in the Florida model and helped guide the process that resulted in the pilot program's adoption by the General Assembly and its implementation by the Supreme Court. Little has continued to contribute to the development of ADR through the years, including chairing the committees that designed and implemented mediation in family law cases in the district courts and in cases within the jurisdiction of the clerks of court. He has served several terms on the Dispute Resolution Commission and as its chair by appointment of Chief Justice I. Beverly Lake, Jr.

Three other individuals also stood out as major contributors to the design and support of the program. Judge Bob Rouse was one of them. He loved the courts of this state and made it his passion to work to improve them. His enthusiasm for the mediation program was infectious, and he worked tirelessly to make the program a reality. Sadly, he died of pancreatic cancer the day before the authorization bill passed the House in June 1991.

Judge James M. Long was another major contributor to the program's success. Judge Long made one of the first ADR presentations to the NCBA's original Task Force in 1983. Long spoke about what he called "judicial arbitration," which was his name for a bench trial with specified time limits for the presentation of evidence and summations. Judge Long's original vision of mediation in the civil trial courts included training judges as mediators who would attempt to settle the cases that came before them. He changed his mind, however, during the Florida trip and became convinced that lawyers needed a non-judicial mechanism to facilitate settlement negotiations. Judge Long came to believe that judges should hear motions and try lawsuits and be wary of engaging in judicial settlement efforts that might be perceived as being coercive by attorneys and litigants. Judge Long's commitment to court-ordered mediated settlement conferences became evident during the legislation drafting sessions, and his reputation and credibility throughout the state were great assets to the Committee's efforts. Later, during the pilot program, he served as chair of the Mediation Committee of the Supreme Court's Dispute Resolution Committee.

A special note of recognition should be made of Frank Laney. Laney served on the original ADR Task Force of the NCBA and continued his involvement through leadership in the creation of the mediation programs in superior court and many subsequent ADR programs. Laney's most notable contribution to the early development of ADR programs occurred in the realm of fundraising. He generated approximately one million dollars in grant money with which to fund the pilot program in non-binding arbitration from 1985 to 1989 and the MSC Program in superior court between 1991 and 1995, as well as studies of those and other ADR pilot programs. His contributions have gone far beyond that, however. For nearly three decades, Laney has been an ever-present contributor, educator, and ambassador for mediation and for ADR in general.

The Mediated Settlement Conference Pilot Program was authorized in June 1991. The rules were redrafted and submitted to the Supreme Court in August and promulgated in September of that year. Later that fall, eight pilot districts were selected to participate in the program, with Judge Long's district being the first to become operational. Two years later, four additional districts with large caseloads were added to the pilot program, thus signaling an early acceptance of the innovation known as "mediated settlement conferences" (MSCs). Finally, in 1995, a bill was introduced to authorize the implementation of MSCs in superior court throughout North Carolina. It passed unanimously in both houses. Within two years, MSCs became a reality throughout the court system. (See Chapter 12.)

Fine-Tuning the MSC Program

Few problems emerged during the pilot program, but the handful that did occur are worth mentioning. The first involved a rule that required mediators to send a report to the court at the conclusion of the settlement conference. The "Report of Mediator" provided bare-bones information about whether and when the conference was held, whether the case settled and who would prepare closing documents, how long the conference was, and what costs there were to the participants. In many counties the court uses this report to trigger a variety of administrative procedures within the judge's office, such as assigning the case to a trial calendar.

During the pilot program, trial court administrators and judicial assistants complained that mediators were not submitting their reports in a timely manner, causing disruptions in their case management timetables. Efforts to remedy this problem have been successful in districts where the senior judge has closely supervised the appointment lists. Presently, mediators who do not file with the court in a timely manner are subject to being removed from the list and are not allowed to practice mediation in those districts.

A second problem arose when some mediators complained that judges were using a "short list" of experienced mediators from which to make appointments. (Under the rules, the senior resident superior court judge appoints a mediator when the parties are unable to agree on one.) New mediators and mediators not well-known believed that they were effectively being removed from the appointment lists in some districts. Judges, on the other hand, were concerned that cases in which the parties could not agree on a mediator should have a fair chance of settlement. Accordingly, they tended to appoint mediators whom they knew and in whom they had a high degree of confidence.

Attempts to address this problem were made in two ways. First, a rule change made during the pilot program made it clear that the judges should select from a rotating list of mediators when making appointments. Second, judges were informed by memorandum and in personal conferences that use of such a rotating list increased the chances that the parties would select their own mediator, thus encouraging party selection and decreasing the number of court appointments.

Party selection of mediators was a component of the Florida program that the designers of the MSC Program felt was vitally important. They believed that MSCs would be more effective if the parties used a mediator in whom they had confidence. In addition, party selection of the mediator was the only real quality control mechanism in the MSC Program. Aside from a mandatory initial training period, mediators were not required to report to anyone about the quality of their work. And while gross violations of ethical standards subject mediators to discipline by the Dispute Resolution Commission, the real test of a mediator's effectiveness comes from the judgment of "the marketplace" of consumers—the parties themselves and their attorneys.

As judges began to rely on the parties' right to select their own mediator and let them take the luck of the draw if they did not, the number of mediators selected by the parties began to climb and the number of complaints began to diminish. In fact, complaints about the quality of mediation in the MSC Program have been few. Anecdotal evidence indicates that parties and their attorneys think mediators do a good job and are helpful in the negotiation process.

The 1995 Legislation

With pilot MSC programs up and running in twelve judicial districts, plans were made in 1995 to draft a bill authorizing a statewide MSC Program. The new legislation differed in several respects from the act that had established the pilot program. Drafters of the 1995 legislation recognized the need for a special body to oversee the statewide program. Thus, the North Carolina Dispute Resolution Commission (DRC) was created and charged with certifying mediators for the MSC Program, regulating their conduct, and approving mediator training courses. Until that time, the Administrative Office of the Courts had certified mediators, but no mechanism for regulating their conduct had been established.

Changes also were made to certain provisions of the program. A sentence was added to the legislation to make it abundantly clear that the parties did not have to make an offer or proposal of any kind at a settlement conference, if they believed it was contrary to their best interest to do so.[3] The change underscored the Dispute Resolution Committee's belief that the parties should be required only to attend and to pay for the services of a mediator. There was never a requirement that they negotiate in good faith. Such a duty was present in the Florida model, but was omitted intentionally from the MSC Program out of concern that it would only generate additional litigation, given the subjective nature of such a standard.

Another change concerned a provision on the inadmissibility at trial of matters related to settlement negotiations. The Florida program had created a privilege to protect communications that took place in circuit court mediation. Drafters of the North Carolina pilot program thought that such a provision was too strong a protection and, therefore, made it clear in the pilot legislation that the protections of Rule 408 of the North Carolina Rules of Evidence would apply to communications at mediated settlement conferences. Rule 408 provides that an offer to compromise a claim may not be received into evidence as an admission regarding the merits of a claim. The rule also prohibits admitting evidence of conduct or statements made in compromise negotiations.

Several problems with the rule developed during the pilot program, however, which sent the drafting committee back to the drawing board. A number of attorneys had been advising their clients not to say anything in settlement conferences, because they feared that Rule 408 did not provide the assumed protections. They believed that the rule and the case law developed under it, particularly in the federal courts, had left gaping holes in the protection that it was supposed to provide.

A related problem was that mediators were sometimes subpoenaed to testify about things said and done during settlement conferences, usually in proceedings to enforce an oral agreement allegedly reached at the conference or to interpret a written settlement agreement. The subject of whether or not the mediator could be compelled to testify had not been addressed in the pilot program legislation.

In response, a new "inadmissibility" section was drafted for the statewide MSC Program. It expressly prohibited a court from receiving evidence of statements made or conduct occurring in an MSC, except under specific circumstances set out in the statute.[4] An entirely new paragraph was also added to assure that mediators could not be compelled to testify.[5] That section was later amended to make agreements reached at a mediated settlement conference unenforceable unless they were reduced to writing.[6]

The final major change to the enabling legislation was the addition of a new provision authorizing the use of settlement procedures other than mediation.[7] Although the Florida model had included both mediation and non-binding arbitration, North Carolina's mediated settlement conference program at first offered no choice. A party either attended mediation or asked the judge to be excused from it. During the pilot program most judges routinely denied such requests. However, because a number of attorneys reported that mediation seemed inappropriate for some cases and some clients, the drafters of the legislation (principally, the Dispute Resolution Section of the NCBA) decided that alternative procedures were needed in such cases.

Emergence of the ADR "Menu" Approach

The 1995 statewide enabling legislation was originally drafted by Andy Little as "The Settlement Procedures Act of 1995" and was sent to a number of groups and committees for review. It provided for a menu of ADR processes, called "settlement procedures," from which the parties and their attorneys could choose to aid them in their settlement efforts. This approach was codified in the local rules of Mecklenburg County after the 1995 legislation went into effect, with MSCs designated as the default process. Under the Mecklenburg rules, lawyers met in a scheduling conference soon after a case was filed, chose the ADR process best suited to their case, and designated their neutral. The United States District Court for the Western District of North Carolina utilized the same approach when its ADR program was implemented.

The groups that reviewed the proposal for legislative drafting, including the Dispute Resolution Section of the NCBA and the North Carolina Supreme Court's ADR Committee, decided that it was too different from the program tested during the 1991–95 pilot program. They opted instead for a statewide authorization of MSCs in superior court actions, but included a provision that allowed the court to order a settlement procedure authorized by the Supreme Court (or by local superior court rules) in lieu of mediation if the parties requested and agreed to the procedure.[8] The provision embodied the notion that the parties themselves, rather than the court, are in the best position to determine what type of ADR procedure is most appropriate for their case. This approach also placed mediation in a default (or preferred) status among the various ADR procedures. Drafters of the legislation believed this to be the correct approach, because it focused the efforts of the parties on direct negotiations for their settlement efforts, rather than on trial or other adjudicatory process.

Once the MSC Program was expanded to permit other settlement procedures, rules to implement the provision were studied and proposed to a subcommittee of the newly created State Judicial Council. The proposed rules created a "menu" approach, allowing the parties to select an alternative settlement process from an array of court-approved ADR procedures in lieu of mediation. Thus, North Carolina created its own version of the multi-door courthouse where the parties (rather than court staff) select the best settlement option for their dispute. A final version of the rules was approved by the full ADR Committee and the State Judicial Council and adopted by the Supreme Court in December 2002.

It took seven years for "other settlement procedures" rules to be drafted, debated, and promulgated, largely because their creation and implementation drew criticism from staff of the AOC in charge of administering the arbitration and child custody mediation programs. Ironically, the rules have been used sparingly by the Bar and their litigant clients, which adds strength to the conclusion that mediation as it has been incorporated into the procedure of civil trial courts has been a welcome change and a great success.

The Family Financial Settlement Program

At the urging of the NCBA and the DRC, the General Assembly in 1998 authorized a pilot MSC program to be used in family financial cases in the state's district courts.[9] The Family Financial Settlement (FFS) Pilot Program was modeled after the superior court program, but it also incorporated a menu approach to selecting an ADR process. With the creation of the FFS program, all of the trial divisions in North Carolina's state civil courts required that parties participate in MSCs or some other form of ADR.

The enabling legislation for the FFS Pilot Program was enacted in the General Assembly's short session in 1998. The program began operating in seven judicial districts. Judges and lawyers were enthusiastic and expressed strong support for the program; and as its success became evident, new districts were added during the pilot program. The NCBA's Dispute Resolution Section and the DRC drafted a new statute authorizing statewide implementation of the FFS Program at the end of the pilot program. The legislation authorizing statewide implementation was adopted by the General Assembly effective October 1, 2001,[10] with the support of the Family Law Section of the NCBA and with the great assistance of J. Wade Harrison, a board-certified family law specialist from Alamance County. Shortly thereafter, the Supreme Court adopted rules to implement statewide expansion, effective October 16, 2001. (See Chapter 18.)

Evaluation of the MSC Program

Why did the MSC Program gain such popularity so quickly? An evaluation of the MSC Pilot Program, conducted by the University of North Carolina at Chapel Hill's Institute of Government and published in 1995, showed modest improvements in the time to disposition over cases not ordered to mediation.[11] While the study concluded that there was no statistically significant evidence to support the notion that more cases were being settled using the MSC format, anecdotal evidence indicated that sessions of civil court were being canceled because of reductions in caseloads.

Supporters of the program were, and still are, enthusiastic about the advantages of using mediation as a settlement tool. They cite reductions in case disposition time, a decrease in trial loads, and reduced costs of litigation as important benefits of the program. Because settlement is fully explored long before the litigants arrive at the courthouse steps, trial dockets are less subject to change and there is less time wasted in trial preparation.

Just as important, however, is the fact that MSCs have significantly improved the process used by lawyers to handle settlement negotiations. Before the MSC Program was established, settlement negotiations occurred most frequently in discussions between lawyers. Clients often played no active role in resolving their own disputes. Legal issues were settled, but other interests and needs of the client—often personal and sometimes unspoken—were left unresolved. Traditional settlement negotiations also tended to occur late in the life of a case, resulting in greater expenditure of time, money, and other resources. Sometimes this resulted from busy lawyers putting off negotiations until a trial was imminent. In other cases, one litigant or the other typically saw an advantage in avoiding compromise, assuming that his or her interests would be advanced only through trial. Moreover, most people who were forced to file suit to resolve disputes were extremely pessimistic about the prospect of reaching a compromise agreement. Requiring a settlement conference early in the process, under the guidance of a trained mediator, has greatly altered the pattern of prolonged adversarial "jockeying" and "eleventh-hour" settlements.

Another benefit of the MSC Program has been that it has revealed a lack of training in the art and science of negotiation in legal education, but also has provided a partial remedy for that problem. When the pilot program began, few attorneys in the state were adept at negotiating. Many lawyers had no appreciation of even the simplest elements of preparation, such as exchanging medical bills and records. Mediators, who often ask the parties questions designed to promote case evaluation, frequently had to teach attorneys what they needed to do to get ready for negotiations. With the advent of the statewide MSC Program, attorneys began attending mediator training programs simply to learn more about the negotiation process, even though they did not intend to become certified mediators. The advent of mediation has made a significant change in the curricula of law schools as well. Courses in ADR procedures, mediation clinics, and negotiation preparation and practice are springing up in many law schools in North Carolina, a development that eventually will make learning how to settle disputes as important as learning how to try cases.

The MSC Program has done much to achieve the original goals of the ADR movement. It has helped divert cases from the long and drawn-out process of litigation and has promoted both increased court efficiency and greater satisfaction of the parties. It also has resulted in better trained and better prepared lawyers, more able to fulfill their mission as counselors, as well as attorneys at law.

Notes

1. Stevens H. Clarke et al., *Court-Ordered Civil Case Mediation in North Carolina: An Evaluation of Its Effects* (Institute of Government, The University of North Carolina at Chapel Hill, 1995), at 45–46.

2. *Id.* at 58.

3. *See* N.C. Gen. Stat. § 7A-38.1(f).

4. *Id.* § 7A-38.1(*l*).

5. *Id.* § 7A-38.1(j).

6. *Id.*

7. *Id.* § 7A-38.1(i).

8. *Id.*

9. *Id.* § 7A-38.4.

10. *Id.* § 7A-38.4A.

11. Clarke et al., *supra* note 1, at 33–34.

CHAPTER SEVEN

The Governance of North Carolina's Court-Based ADR Programs

"In the midst of a task so great as this, there may come a time of discouraging reflection upon the immense needs of the administration of justice and the extreme difficulty of finding ways by which [we] can solve the problems. . . . [W]e cannot afford to take a defeatist attitude. . . .The most important lesson of the past is to strive and never be disheartened because of the immensity of the task. The ultimate goal may seem to recede as we advance, but we must press on."

— United States Supreme Court Chief Justice Warren E. Burger,
The State of Justice, Report to the American Bar Association,
February 12, 1984, 70 A.B.A. J. 62, 66 (April 1984)
(quoting former Chief Justice Charles Evans Hughes).

Early Guidance by the North Carolina Bar Association

During the period from 1983 to 1993, most of North Carolina's court-based alternative dispute resolution (ADR) initiatives were conceived, designed, and developed within the organizational structure of the North Carolina Bar Association (NCBA). The NCBA Dispute Resolution Task Force, established in 1983 to study and make recommendations on the use of ADR techniques in the state, became a standing committee of the NCBA, the Dispute Resolution Committee, in 1985. The Committee worked diligently to develop, monitor, and support a variety of ADR initiatives. It was comprised of representatives from the bench and bar, along with court administrators and interested citizens. The first major task of the Dispute Resolution Committee was to implement the recommendations of the Task Force to establish a pilot program of court-ordered, non-binding arbitration. When the legislature authorized the pilot program in 1985, it stipulated that no state funds should be expended for its implementation. The North Carolina Administrative Office of the Courts (AOC) thus could not provide significant staffing resources or oversight. Consequently, it fell to the Dispute Resolution Committee to establish and guide the pilot program. The AOC did provide valuable insight and assistance, however, through two of its officials, Daniel J. Becker and

Kathy L. Shuart, who served as members of the Committee. When the court-ordered arbitration program was adopted by the legislature, after completion of the pilot program in 1989, the AOC stepped forward and assumed complete responsibility for its continuing administration and growth.

With the development of the Mediated Settlement Conference (MSC) Pilot Program (Pilot Program) between 1991 and 1993, the implementation of the Program was overseen by the Dispute Resolution Committee and members of the AOC staff, particularly Kathy Shuart. Details relating to the certification of mediators and mediation training were hammered out jointly between the Committee and the AOC. Orientation meetings were held for lawyers in the pilot judicial districts and were chaired by the senior judges of the districts, AOC staff, and members of the Dispute Resolution Committee.

In 1993, the NCBA, at the urging of Raleigh attorney Frank C. Laney, created a new Dispute Resolution Section to replace its Dispute Resolution Committee. The Bar Association made the change in response to the success of the MSC Pilot Program and the rising number of attorneys seeking mediator certification. Chapel Hill attorney J. Anderson "Andy" Little was named as first Section chair by NCBA President J. Donald Cowan, Jr.

With the creation of the Dispute Resolution Section, whose membership at the time was focused primarily on mediation, the staff of the AOC believed that some organization other than the NCBA should have general oversight of the burgeoning, court-ordered ADR landscape. The AOC staff formally recommended to North Carolina Supreme Court Chief Justice James G. Exum, Jr. that a Supreme Court committee be established to coordinate the implementation, evaluation, and modification of existing court-ordered ADR programs.

The North Carolina Supreme Court
Dispute Resolution Committee (1993–1995)

An "Umbrella" for ADR Activities

Recognizing the growing impact of ADR on the court system, Chief Justice Exum established the North Carolina Supreme Court Dispute Resolution Committee in September 1993. In writing the Committee's purpose and charge, Exum noted that the Committee was to consolidate under one "umbrella" all ADR-related activities approved by the Supreme Court, and to advise the Supreme Court and the AOC on matters relating to the development, implementation, administration, and evaluation of dispute resolution programs serving North Carolina's courts.

Chief Justice Exum asked Justice Henry E. Frye to chair the new Committee. The remaining membership, drawn from across the state, included representation from the appellate, superior, and district courts; the NCBA; the Director of the AOC (or his designee); and others, such as law school professors and representatives from the University of North Carolina's Institute of Government (now the School of Government). The original members included judges: North Carolina Court of Appeals Judge Jack Cozort; Senior Resident Superior Court Judge J. Marlene Hyatt in Waynesville; Senior Resident Superior Court Judge James M. Long in Pilot Mountain; Senior Resident Superior Court Judge F. Gordon Battle in Hillsborough; Chief District Court Judge E. Burt Aycock, Jr. in Greenville; District Court Judge Resa L. Harris in Charlotte; and District Court Judge Clarence E. Horton, Jr. in Kannapolis. Also serving were attorneys Marshall A. Gallop, Jr. of Rocky Mount, James Harold Tharrington of Raleigh, and Frank A. Campbell of Greensboro; professors Ralph A. Peeples of the Wake Forest University School of Law, Fred J. Williams of the North Carolina Central University School of Law, Thomas B. Metzloff of the Duke University School of Law, A. Mark Weisburd of the University of North Carolina (UNC) School of Law, and Thomas H. Thornburg of UNC's Institute of Government; and AOC officials Daniel J. Becker and Kathy L. Shuart. At the inaugural meeting of the Committee, Justice Frye appointed J. Anderson "Andy" Little and Frank C. Laney as ad hoc members.

Two existing AOC committees, the Custody Mediation Advisory Committee and the Advisory Committee for the MSC Pilot Program, were subsumed under the new Supreme Court Dispute Resolution Committee. Chief Justice Exum's "umbrella" also covered the Court-Ordered, Non-Binding Arbitration Program, which operated primarily in state district courts. Subcommittees corresponding to each of the three programs were established to provide oversight for their activities and procedures, and mediators, arbitrators, and others with particular areas of expertise were recruited to serve.

Work of the Supreme Court Dispute Resolution Committee

The Supreme Court Dispute Resolution Committee held its first meeting in early 1994 and met regularly over the next two years. As an advisory and coordinating body, it did not administer or regulate specific ADR programs. But it did provide an important forum where rule changes could be discussed and examined, and, if appropriate, forwarded to the Supreme Court for adoption.

The Committee analyzed many important issues that had arisen as the number and type of ADR programs multiplied across the state. One such issue was access: whether dispute resolution services were available to all litigants and whether there was any danger that the programs would have the effect of denying litigants their "day in court." Case screening presented another issue. The Committee's inquiry focused on how cases that were not appropriate for ADR could be identified and sent directly to trial. For those cases in which ADR was appropriate, the Committee wanted to know how to determine which type of dispute resolution procedure would be best. The question of mandatory versus voluntary participation was also explored, along with the issue of whether the parties should pay the costs of the process. Finally, with the emergence of alternative dispute resolution as a profession, the Committee addressed such questions as certification and training requirements for neutrals, private versus public providers, the need for ethical codes for dispute resolution practitioners, and the regulation of dispute resolution providers.

Another task for the Committee was the evaluation of ADR programs. The Committee assisted the AOC in evaluating the Child Custody and Visitation Mediation Program and the Court-Ordered, Non-Binding Arbitration Program. The Committee's evaluations, submitted to AOC Director James C. Drennan in April 1994 for transmittal to the General Assembly, heartily endorsed both programs and recommended that their statewide expansion continue apace.

The Supreme Court Dispute Resolution Committee was also active in monitoring and evaluating the MSC Pilot Program, which had been authorized by the General Assembly in 1991. It facilitated the expansion of the program from eight to twelve pilot districts in 1993 and helped evaluate the feasibility of expanding the program statewide at the end of its trial period. As a part of its evaluation process, Committee members reviewed the independent study of the MSC Pilot Program conducted by UNC's Institute of Government, comparing their own experiences with the study's findings.[1] The Committee sent letters to a number of constituent groups, including the North Carolina Conference of Superior Court Judges, the North Carolina Association of Defense Attorneys, the North Carolina Association of Black Lawyers, the North Carolina Academy of Trial Lawyers, and the North Carolina Association of Women Lawyers, seeking their comments on the Pilot Program. The Committee also met with representatives of three insurance carriers—Nationwide, Allstate, and Medical Mutual—to solicit their views on mediated settlement conferences.

The results of the Committee's inquiry were clear: There was widespread support for expanding the MSC Program to all of the state's superior courts.

The Committee recommended this change and was active in supporting it, along with the NCBA. It also recommended important provisions in the enabling legislation and revisions to the Pilot Program rules, all of which were adopted by the Supreme Court. These changes allowed qualified non-attorneys to become eligible to be certified as mediators; built flexibility into conference attendance requirements; required lienholders to be notified of mediated settlement conferences and provided an opportunity for them to attend; provided that sanctions for failure to attend be limited to monetary penalties; authorized senior resident superior court judges, at the parties' request, to order some other settlement procedure in lieu of a mediated settlement conference; and modified requirements for mediator certification to exclude from eligibility any individuals disqualified from practicing law by attorney licensing authorities in any state. Many of these ideas were originated by the NCBA Dispute Resolution Section.

The Supreme Court Dispute Resolution Committee did not limit its work to the MSC Program. Members of the Committee also began the process of developing rules and forms for the Pre-Litigation Farm Nuisance Mediation Program (see Chapter 35), and helped produce award-winning arbitrator training films.

The Committee continued to meet until the North Carolina Dispute Resolution Commission was created by statute in 1995. Although the Supreme Court Dispute Resolution Committee did not meet again after the establishment of the Commission, the Custody and Visitation Mediation Subcommittee and the Court-Ordered, Non-Binding Arbitration Subcommittee continued to meet independently.

The North Carolina Dispute Resolution Commission

Regulation of the MSC Program

Established in 1995 by the General Assembly at the same time the state-wide MSC Program was authorized, the Dispute Resolution Commission (DRC or the Commission) was charged with certifying mediators for the MSC Program and with regulating mediator conduct. During the MSC Pilot Program, the AOC had been charged with certifying the program's mediators. However, the AOC is an administrative body, not a licensing entity. Neither the AOC nor the Supreme Court Dispute Resolution Committee thought it was appropriate for the AOC to continue performing certification and regulatory functions when the MSC Program was expanded statewide. Thus, the AOC proposed legislation establishing the DRC within the Judicial Department to allow the newly formed body to assume those duties. The proposal was adopted by the General Assembly in 1995 as North Carolina General Statutes Section 7A-38.2.

The DRC assumed the role previously played by the Supreme Court Dispute Resolution Committee in relation to the MSC Program. It continued to monitor the MSC Program as it was established throughout the state over the next two years, to propose rule changes to the Supreme Court for the MSC Program, and to develop new ADR programs.

The Dispute Resolution Commission originally consisted of nine members, including two judges, two mediators, two practicing attorneys not certified as mediators, and three citizens knowledgeable about mediation. Appointments to the DRC were made by all branches of state government: the Chief Justice of the Supreme Court (four appointments), the President of the North Carolina State Bar (two appointments), the Governor (one appointment), the President Pro Tempore of the Senate (one appointment), and the Speaker of the House of Representatives (one appointment). Judge Ralph A. Walker of the North Carolina Court of Appeals served as the DRC's first chairperson. The other original appointees were Judge Janet Marlene Hyatt, Vice Chair, of Waynesville; Robert A. "Bob" Beason of Durham; Scott Bradley of Chapel Hill; Carmon J. Stuart of Greensboro; Joseph "Joey" L. Ray of Tabor City; W. Lewis Sauls of Whiteville; Michael M. Jones of Goldsboro; and H. Edward Knox of Charlotte. Leslie C. Ratliff was named Executive Secretary.

DRC Operations

The Supreme Court's Rules for the Dispute Resolution Commission (Rules for the DRC or Rules) govern the DRC's operations. The Rules address appointment of officers, staff meetings, budgeting, powers and duties, and regulatory functions.

The DRC was designed to be self-supporting and to operate without expenditure of taxpayer dollars. It generates revenue through certification fees charged to mediators and mediator training programs. For most of its history, the DRC has been able to meet its expenses entirely through collection of such fees.

The DRC has established a number of standing committees, which meet as needed. Ad hoc committees have been established as necessary to address certain topics. The Commission meets quarterly in various locations around the state.

DRC meetings are attended by a number of liaison members who also actively serve as non-voting members of the Commission's committees.

Liaison members include the Dispute Resolution Coordinator for the North Carolina Industrial Commission, the Chair of the NCBA Dispute Resolution Section, and representatives of the Judicial Support Staff Conference, Mediation Network of North Carolina, the Administrative Office of the Courts, the mediation program of the North Carolina Court of Appeals, and federal court mediation programs.

The Commission's enabling legislation provided for it to have an office staffed by an Executive Secretary and support staff. The Commission's office is housed in the North Carolina Judicial Center.

Responsibilities of the DRC

CERTIFICATION OF MEDIATORS

Since its inception, the DRC has worked to assemble and maintain a large and well-qualified pool of mediators to serve the mediated settlement conference/mediation programs operating in North Carolina's courts. Requirements for certification are set by rules adopted by the Supreme Court of North Carolina. Each of the programs the Commission helps to support has separate certification requirements and application materials. Information about certification and application forms is posted on the Commission's website at www.ncdrc.org.[2] As of December 2011, there were 1,944 active and inactive mediator certifications outstanding for the four programs, which the Commission helps to support: the superior court's Mediated Settlement Conference Program, the district court's Family Financial Settlement and District Criminal Court Mediation Programs, and the Clerk Mediation Program. Of this number, the vast majority serve the MSC Program—1,252 active certifications and seventy inactive certifications. The majority of certified mediators, about 85 percent, are North Carolina attorneys, with the remainder made up of attorneys licensed in other states and non-attorneys. The list of certified superior court mediators developed by the DRC is used not only by the MSC Program, but also by the federal district courts, the North Carolina Industrial Commission, the North Carolina Office of Administrative Hearings, and a number of other state agencies and departments. Lists of certified mediators are available on the Commission's website. Each mediator's listing, or Mediator Profile, includes contact, availability (by district or county), and biographical information (if biographical information is provided by the mediator).

All applicants must meet threshold criteria relating to their education and work experience to be eligible for mediator certification. The threshold criteria vary from program to program. The Commission's office will issue preapprovals to applicants who want to verify that their education and work experience meet threshold requirements before registering for training. All applicants also must complete mediator training designed to prepare them to serve a particular mediation program, and they must complete several observations of mediations conducted by certified mediators. Non-attorney applicants also are required to complete basic training in North Carolina court structure, legal terminology, and civil procedure. All applicants must also demonstrate that they are of good moral character and must disclose any convictions or pending criminal charges, professional discipline or pending grievances, judicial sanctions, tax liens, civil judgments, and bankruptcies. In an effort to serve as a proactive regulator, the Commission's office carefully screens all applicants for certification and brings any significant concerns to the attention of the Commission's Standards, Discipline, and Advisory Opinions Committee. Upon occasion, applicants have been denied certification due to character concerns.

REGULATION OF MEDIATORS

As a regulatory body, the Dispute Resolution Commission has sought to focus on information sharing and skills development. In this spirit, the DRC uses e-mail to keep mediators abreast of policy, rules, and rule changes. The DRC also maintains a website where mediators and members of the public may download rules, receive program updates, and learn more about DRC activities. Ethical and continuing education materials posted on the website include links to other internet sites where mediators can research ethical or other questions; a list of suggested readings on dispute resolution; contact information for professional mediator organizations active in North Carolina; and a list of mediator blogs. The Commission also publishes a newsletter, *The Intermediary*, which provides information on training opportunities and highlights the work of the Commission and the activities of mediators, court officials, and others who are making important contributions in the dispute resolution arena.

As a means of encouraging skills development and awareness of ethical responsibilities, the Commission also asks every mediator to complete at least three hours of continuing mediator education (CME) every year and requires them to report on their efforts during its annual certification renewal period. Mediators may receive credit for attending programs, such as the NCBA Dispute Resolution Section's annual meeting, or for conducting their own independent research on a topic of interest to them. Those mediators who voluntarily comply and report at least three hours of CME annually are designated as having met the Commission's expectation on their Mediator Profile appearing on the Commission's website.

Through its Advisory Opinions Policy, the Commission and its staff provide direct assistance to mediators who are facing an ethical issue or dilemma. The Policy establishes two avenues by which mediators may request assistance from the Commission. The informal avenue provides for mediators to contact Commission staff when time is of the essence and they need immediate assistance; for example, the mediation is in progress or is scheduled to be held in the near future. Staff seeks to answer the questions or to help them think through the dilemma and how they may best respond. If staff is uncertain, a member or members of the Commission may be called in to provide assistance. While the advice given does not have the force of a written opinion issued by the full Commission, the inquiry is logged and the fact that the mediator sought assistance is taken into account if a complaint is subsequently filed. If time is not of the essence or a mediator is seeking to ascertain whether he or she responded correctly to a dilemma, a formal process allows the mediator to seek a written Advisory Opinion from the full Commission. Advisory Opinions are published in the Commission's newsletter and posted on the Commission's website. Opinions also are published in instances where a mediator has been disciplined privately by the Commission and the Commission wishes to alert other mediators to the situation and conduct that resulted in the discipline. (Such Opinions are intended for educational purposes only and the offending mediator is not identified.)

The Commission has worked hard to make information and assistance available to mediators and to encourage skills development, but it also has been mindful of its responsibility to protect the public. A committee chaired by DRC member Bob Beason drafted a set of professional and ethical rules governing mediator conduct, which were adopted by the Supreme Court of North Carolina in 1998. These Standards of Professional Conduct for Mediators (Standards) charge mediators with certain responsibilities, including competency, impartiality, and preservation of confidentiality. Over the years, the Standards have been revised periodically to reflect the growing experience of both the Commission and the larger dispute resolution community with mediation programs and processes. (See Chapter 11.) Rule VII of the Supreme Court's Rules for the DRC also addresses mediator conduct and provides that conduct reflecting a lack of moral character or fitness to practice as a mediator, or that discredits the Commission, the courts, or the mediation process, may also subject a mediator to discipline. The Standards and Commission Rule VII are enforced through the investigation and hearing procedures set forth in Commission Rule VIII. Since its inception, the Commission has addressed complaints regarding mediator conduct that have been filed by court staff, lawyers, and, most typically, by litigants. In some instances, the Commission has disciplined mediators.

CERTIFICATION AND REGULATION OF MEDIATION TRAINERS

The Commission's enabling legislation not only charges it with certifying and regulating mediators, but also with certifying mediator training programs and regulating the conduct of those who train and manage within those programs. The Commission has adopted detailed Guidelines for each program for which it certifies mediators. The Guidelines amplify the training program curriculum established in Supreme Court rules for each of the programs the Commission helps to support. Guidelines and lists of trainers are posted on the Commission's website.

OTHER RESPONSIBILITIES OF THE DRC

Although the DRC is principally charged with certifying and regulating mediators, it has performed a number of other important activities since its establishment in 1995. The DRC has assisted the Supreme Court and State Judicial Council in formulating policy on dispute resolution and has played a leading role in program development. It also has suggested program rules and rule revisions to the State Judicial Council and the Supreme Court, developed program forms, worked with state agencies and departments to aid them in establishing mediation processes and programs, and has served as a clearinghouse for dispute resolution information in North Carolina.

Establishment of the Family Financial Settlement Program

In 1997, the General Assembly charged the DRC with designing a new district court program for the mediation of equitable distribution actions. The DRC appointed an ad hoc committee, chaired by Andy Little, to assist with the project. The resulting proposal for Rules Implementing Settlement Procedures in Equitable Distribution and Other Family Financial Cases was adopted by the Supreme Court in December 1998 and initiated as the Family Financial Settlement (FFS) Pilot Program. Like the superior court MSC Program, the FFS Program now operates statewide and pursuant to rules that mandate referral of pending equitable distribution disputes to mediation. (See Chapter 18.)

With the establishment of the FFS Pilot Program, the General Assembly amended North Carolina General Statutes Section 7A-38.2 in 1998 to expand the number of members of the Dispute Resolution Commission to fourteen. The amendment provided for inclusion on the DRC of judges, mediators, and attorneys with district court and family law expertise. The 1998 revisions also provided that a number of groups may recommend names for appointment to the DRC. These groups include: the Family Law, Litigation, and Dispute Resolution Sections of the NCBA; the North Carolina Conference of Clerks of Superior Court; the Conference of Superior Court Judges; the Conference of Chief District Court Judges; and the Mediation Network of North Carolina.

Establishment of the Clerk Mediation Program

In 2005, the Commission was asked to help with the design of another mediation program. Andy Little and Frank Laney co-chaired an ad hoc committee charged with exploring the feasibility of establishing a mediation program for matters pending before clerks of superior court. The work of this committee led to the enactment of North Carolina General Statutes Section 7A-38.3B, establishing the new Clerk Mediation Program. (See Chapter 15.) Supreme Court rules implementing the new legislation were adopted effective March 1, 2006. The rules created a special certification for mediators wishing to mediate guardianship and estate cases, but permitted certified superior court mediators to mediate other matters referred by clerks. With the establishment of this new program, the Commission's enabling legislation, North Carolina General Statutes Section 7A-38.2, was amended, once again, to provide for a clerk of superior court to serve on the Commission, bringing the total number of members to fifteen.

Establishment of the District Criminal Court Mediation Program

In 2006, the DRC was approached by three community mediation center directors who asked for assistance in developing a system for the certification and regulation of district criminal court mediators. At the time, more than twenty community mediation centers around the state were providing district criminal court mediators, and some centers had been doing so since the 1970s. Proponents of the new regulatory system suggested that it should have statewide application; should be modeled, at least to some extent, on existing certification rules and requirements for other court-based mediators; and should be implemented pursuant to Supreme Court rules and under the DRC's umbrella. The proponents hoped that adoption of uniform, statewide standards set by the DRC would enhance the standing of their programs and mediators with the local courts.

Judge Sanford L. Steelman, Jr. established an ad hoc committee to consider the request and named Frank Laney as chair. As a result of the committee's efforts, North Carolina General Statutes Section 7A-38.3D was enacted in 2007, creating the District Criminal Court Mediation Program. (See Chapter 23.) Supreme Court rules implementing the legislation followed later that same year. The new legislation created an "opt-in" program. It allowed those courts and centers that believed mediator certification would be of benefit to adopt DRC certification requirements, but they were not required to do so. Centers that did not adopt the program were permitted to continue providing district criminal court mediators who were not certified. In the wake of this effort to formalize district criminal court mediation, North Carolina General Statutes Section 7A-38.2 was further amended to provide for a certified district criminal court mediator to join the DRC, bringing the total number of Commission members to sixteen.

Advancing the DRC's Mission in the Twenty-First Century

Evaluating, Monitoring, and Disciplining Mediators

Mediator Evaluations

Through the first decade of the twenty-first century, the DRC continued its mission of oversight and improvement of the dispute resolution process. One of the most difficult issues for the Commission was continuing education requirements for certified mediators (CME). While the majority of the Commission members believed that some CME should be required for the professional competence and development of mediators beyond their initial mediation training, the Commission never agreed on how that requirement would be implemented. A major stumbling block was the realization that the majority of certified mediators were attorneys who already had a heavy annual continuing legal education (CLE) requirement from the State Bar, especially those who were certified as specialists in particular areas of the law.

Two requirements that were viewed as conducive to professional development were adopted without disagreement. The first was a rule that required mediators to distribute an evaluation form to the parties and their attorneys at the end of mediation. It was intended to serve as a tool for mediator self-appraisal. The requirement was rescinded by the Supreme Court in 2011, however, at the recommendation of the DRC, because it was seen as a tool that had outlived its usefulness, particularly in cases where the mediator was selected by the parties.

The second rule change was a requirement that each mediator report his or her efforts to engage in professional improvement as part of the annual application for certification renewal. Activities that demonstrate such efforts can be as simple as reading a book on mediation process or skills or observing a mediated settlement conference conducted by another certified mediator. While it may seem unusual to require reporting of activities that are not mandatory, the rule has been effective in encouraging mediators to engage in professional improvement efforts.

Monitoring and Disciplining Mediators

The Commission spent considerable time refining its role in monitoring and disciplining mediators. As a result of some unsatisfactory experiences in screening applications, the DRC realized it needed to broaden the character information it was seeking in the application process. At the same time, the Commission found itself dealing with an increasing number of ethics queries and complaints. Fortunately, most of the complaints were not well founded, and none were determined to be serious. Several candidates were denied certification, but no mediators had certification revoked. Sanctions rarely went beyond the issuance of a letter of warning or caution.

ESTABLISHING CRITERIA FOR CERTIFICATION OF NON-LAWYER MEDIATORS

The Commission struggled to define the proper criteria as to what training, education, and experience should be required of certified mediators. While allowing individuals without legal training or other advanced degrees to be certified, the Commission required a certain number of years of high-level business or administrative experience. This rule necessitated a great deal of case-by-case analysis as to what constituted professional management or administrative experience. Under the same rule, business executives seeking mediator certification also were required to have a four-year college degree. That portion of the rule has been challenged frequently by applicants who had years of business experience, but who lacked a college diploma.

CLARIFYING AND PRESERVING CONFIDENTIALITY STANDARDS

The Commission also undertook a significant review and revision of the Standards of Professional Conduct for Mediators. In the midst of that effort, the North Carolina State Bar pointed out a potential conflict between its Rule of Professional Conduct 8.3, requiring attorneys to report certain unethical conduct of another lawyer, and a mediator's duty of confidentiality under Standard III. After years of discussion and negotiation, both codes were modified in 2010 to eliminate the conflict. Only certain delineated misconduct is subject to reporting under Rule 8.3, and the DRC Standards permit such reporting. (See Chapter 11 for a more thorough discussion.)

STRIVING FOR UNIFORM PROGRAM OPERATIONS

Programmatic issues remained high on the Commission's agenda. In 2005, the DRC proposed to the Supreme Court rule amendments that required all eligible cases throughout the state to be ordered to mediation through the MSC and FFS Programs. This recommendation arose in part from a concern that application of the programs varied widely and that program availability should not depend upon the county in which one's case was filed. It also stemmed from recognition that the mediation programs provided value, increased litigant satisfaction, and improved case management. In early 2006, the Supreme Court adopted the proposed changes, and referral to mediation requirements were made uniform statewide.

At the same time, the DRC was concerned that attorneys in some areas routinely selected untrained and uncertified mediators. As Commission member Sherman L. Criner observed: "If we think it is a good idea for mediators to be trained and certified, then we should require it." The DRC proposed mandatory certification in both the MSC and FFS Programs. Only the MSC rule was changed, however, leaving FFS Program participants free to select uncertified mediators.

RESOLVING MISCELLANEOUS PROGRAM ISSUES

Throughout the decade, the Commission was confronted with several recurring issues. One persistent problem involved courts using a "short list" of mediators from which they made appointments, rather than randomly appointing from a list of all interested mediators. By asking the Supreme Court to make the appointment rules more explicit, as well as engaging in efforts to educate judges across the state on the need to give all certified mediators an equal opportunity, the Commission made significant progress in resolving the issue.

Another persistent problem, and the chief complaint about mediators by judges and their administrators, was that mediators often did not submit their reports to the court in a timely fashion. The DRC addressed this concern in many ways at different times by recommending rule changes to the Supreme Court, by issuing Advisory Opinions, and by imposing sanctions when mediators failed to report as required. Those actions made it clear that mediators have administrative duties under the program rules that are important to the administration of the courts; that reports are required even when cases settle before mediation is scheduled or held; and that mediators can be decertified if they fail to perform this important function.

Another issue involved the ability of newly trained mediators to complete the observations required for certification. Unfortunately, observers occasionally engaged in inappropriate conduct during a mediation or their presence detracted from the process in some other way. The Commission at times had to balance the benefits of providing opportunities to attend mediations against the potential detriment that might result from such observations.

An additional recurring issue that confronted the DRC involved balancing the needs of parties and mediators when it became necessary to change a mediation date. The MSC Program rules eventually were modified to provide flexibility to mediation participants in the scheduling and holding of conferences, while protecting the mediators who blocked out a day of work to conduct a conference, only to have it cancelled at the last minute. The rules now generally require payment of a postponement fee to the mediator unless there is "good cause" for the postponement.

Achieving Administrative Excellence

Administratively, the DRC quite literally was exemplary. The staff advanced quickly into the age of desktop computers and the Internet. The Commission's website won national awards for design and ease of use. The DRC eliminated almost all of its mailing costs by communicating with mediators via e-mail. The Commission moved its mediator registration online and then, as soon as the technology was available, began allowing mediators to pay their annual registration fees online. The success of the mediation programs and the DRC led to so many mediators seeking certification and annual renewals that the Commission became self-supporting and did not rely on taxpayer funds for its operation.

The Alternative Dispute Resolution Committee of the State Judicial Council

Background: The Need for Ongoing Coordination and Policy Direction

Throughout the 1990s, dispute resolution programs and procedures developed in North Carolina at an incredible rate. In the course of this rapid expansion, the ADR governance structure became increasingly complex. As noted previously in this chapter, the Supreme Court's ADR Committee fell into disuse and no longer met after the General Assembly authorized state-wide expansion of the MSC Program in 1995. It was clear that the Supreme Court retained ultimate decision-making authority for ADR programs, but practical oversight and supervision of these programs fell to two other entities: the AOC, whose employees staffed the Child Custody Mediation and Non-Binding Arbitration Programs, and the DRC, which monitored and recommended rule changes for the MSC Program. The NCBA also re-mained active in ADR efforts, generating proposals for programmatic or rule changes and ideas for new programs.

Between 1995 and 1998, issues developed between the NCBA and the DRC on the one hand, and the AOC on the other, over the development of new ADR programs and rule changes for existing programs. The Dispute Resolution Section of the NCBA and the DRC put forward numerous initia-tives during this period, many of which the AOC opposed.

One such issue revolved around the development of rules to implement Section (i) of the 1995 MSC Program legislation, North Carolina General Statutes Section 7A-38.1. Section (i) permitted use of "other settlement procedures" (procedures other than mediation) in the MSC Program. The Dispute Resolution Section and the DRC proposed that an ADR "menu ap-proach" be adopted to give effect to Section (i). The AOC had opposed many features of the "other settlement procedures" provision in the 1995 legisla-tion, and, in the wake of efforts to implement the menu approach, the staff appeared ready to re-open the debate. An issue also arose over the proposal for a program of mediation and other settlement procedures for financial issues in divorce cases. With the leadership vacuum created by a dormant Supreme Court ADR Committee, the NCBA and the DRC had no forum to approve and carry forward such initiatives.

In August 1998, the NCBA Dispute Resolution Section formed a task force to consider whether a separate group should be established to study the ADR governance structure in North Carolina and to recommend neces-sary changes. The Section Task Force was headed by Section Chair James E. "Jim" Gates and included Section Vice-Chair John C. Schafer, Chapel Hill attorney J. Anderson "Andy" Little, and retired Clerk of the United States District Court for the Middle District of North Carolina Carmon J. Stuart. NCBA President Larry B. Sitton and AOC Director Judge Thomas W. Ross worked closely with the Section Task Force. On December 1, 1999, at the request of the Section Task Force, Chief Justice Henry E. Frye appointed an Ad Hoc Supreme Court Dispute Resolution Task Force to make recommendations to the Court about a new governance structure for all court-sponsored dispute resolution programs in the state.

Chaired by former Chief Justice James G. Exum, Jr., the Supreme Court Task Force included the following members: DRC Chair and Court of Appeals Judge Ralph A. Walker; DRC Vice-Chair and Superior Court Judge Catherine C. Eagles; District Court Judge E. Burt Aycock, Jr.; Professor James C. Drennan of UNC's Institute of Government; Dean Ralph A. Peeples of the Wake Forest University School of Law; Durham Trial Court Administrator Kathy L. Shuart; John C. Schafer, Chair of the NCBA Dispute Resolution Section; and James E. Gates, immediate past Chair of the NCBA Dispute Resolution Section. AOC Director Judge Thomas W. Ross attended the meetings as Chief Justice Frye's representative. Miriam Saxon of the AOC served as staff liaison to the Supreme Court Task Force. Andy Little participated in the Supreme Court Task Force discussions at all but the initial meeting, and Carmon J. Stuart also attended several of the meetings.

Independent of these debates about the governance of ADR, the state's dispute resolution governance structure was addressed in legislation creating the State Judicial Council in 1999. The Council was given a broad legislative mandate in the field of dispute resolution, including the authority to monitor ADR programs and to recommend guidelines on the use of ADR.[3] Precisely how the Council's responsibilities would fit into the rest of the dispute resolution governance structure was less than clear.

The members of the Supreme Court Task Force unanimously agreed there was a strong need for a single forum to provide ongoing coordination and policy direction for the court-sponsored dispute resolution programs in the state. They recommended the creation of a standing Dispute Resolution Committee of the State Judicial Council, to be composed "in such a way that as many dispute resolution perspectives and disciplines as possible be represented."[4] The Supreme Court Task Force recommended a twenty-three person Alternative Dispute Resolution Committee (ADR Committee) with a specified number of positions for various members of the dispute resolution community, including judges, attorneys, citizens, and others.[5]

The Supreme Court Task Force also recommended that the new ADR Committee "be structured: (1) to provide a forum for the resolution of interprogram issues, and (2) to provide policy guidance for all court-sponsored dispute resolution programs as the need arises."[6] The Task Force envisioned a body that could "provide a forum for the raising of larger issues about the future direction of the court-sponsored dispute resolution movement within the North Carolina court system" and suggested that the ADR Committee would also "serve as a clearing-house and incubator for rules that affect dispute resolution programs before they are reviewed by the Council and submitted to the Supreme Court for review and adoption."[7]

Finally, the Task Force recommended that "[t]he DRC should continue to exist and to fulfill its statutory mandate to certify mediators and training programs; to deal with ethical issues; and to provide advice and suggestions on the overall operation of the mediated settlement programs."[8]

As explained in the Supreme Court Task Force Report, the recommended governance structure was not the only alternative considered. In fact, the scope of the proposed ADR Committee's responsibilities was the subject of much debate. A proposal to create a single agency to carry out all ADR-related functions, including the current functions of the DRC, was seriously considered. Under that proposal, the single agency, whether as a Council subcommittee or as an independent entity, would: (1) coordinate all dispute resolution/settlement programs; and (2) handle mediator certification and make recommendations to the Supreme Court through the Judicial Council on rules, policy, and structure for all court-sponsored dispute resolution programs. This approach would have encompassed under one body the responsibility for rule generation and ethics determinations, along with oversight of program rules and policy. Some Task Force members believed that a single agency would minimize problems such as program duplication, questions of authority, and volunteer burnout. After much debate, however, the Task Force decided to recommend that the ADR Committee limit its focus to offering guidance on policy, leaving certification and other operational responsibility for specific programs to the entities already exercising such authority.

The Task Force recognized that future modifications might become necessary as the Council gained experience addressing system-wide policy questions and rule-reviewing needs. Its final recommendation was that the Judicial Council and the Chief Justice of the Supreme Court review the ADR Committee's charge and operation within two years after the group's creation to determine whether the ADR Committee met the needs of the public, the courts, and the dispute resolution community.[9] The Task Force recommended a wide-ranging review, to include an opportunity for input from the ADR Committee, the DRC, the AOC, court officials, and other interested parties.

The Supreme Court Task Force issued its report on May 22, 2000. Two days later, the Judicial Council voted unanimously to adopt the Task Force's recommendations. Pursuant to these recommendations, by order dated

July 13, 2000, the Supreme Court established a standing ADR Committee of the Council.

The governance structure recommended by the Task Force, approved by the Council, and adopted by the Supreme Court was an improvement over the earlier, fragmented system. The new framework was designed to allow dispute resolution programs and procedures to continue developing with a clearer understanding of the roles and responsibilities of the various agencies, persons, and groups involved in the process.

The original members of the ADR Committee of the State Judicial Council appointed by Chief Justice Frye were: Randy S. Gregory (Chair) and Clifton E. Johnson, Judicial Council members; Justice George L. Wainwright, Supreme Court appointee; Judge Ralph A. Walker, Court of Appeals appointee; Judges Catherine C. Eagles and Sanford L. Steelman, Jr., superior court judge appointees; Judges Alfred W. Kwasikpui and William M. Neely, district court judge appointees; Robert A. Beason, DRC member; J. Nicholas Ellis, James E. Gates, J. Wade Harrison, J. Anderson Little, Ralph W. Meekins, Jaye P. Meyer, and Carmon J. Stuart, attorney appointees; Elaine Cigler, child custody mediator appointee; Kathy L. Shuart, trial court administrator appointee; Scott Bradley of the Mediation Network of North Carolina, community settlement center appointee; Professor Thomas B. Metzloff of the Duke University School of Law and Dean Ralph A. Peeples of the Wake Forest University School of Law, law professor appointees; Miriam Saxon, AOC appointee; and Debi Miller Moore of the American Arbitration Association, citizen appointee. John C. Schafer, Dispute Resolution Coordinator for the North Carolina Industrial Commission, and Frank C. Laney, Circuit Mediator with the United States Court of Appeals for the Fourth Circuit, served as ex officio liaison members of the Committee. The ADR Committee held its first meeting on September 14, 2000, thereby beginning a new era in the governance of ADR in North Carolina.

Initial Work of the ADR Committee

The ADR Committee immediately began work on the backlog of proposals and ideas that had been accumulating over the previous five or six years. The main issues were a review and rewrite of the court-ordered, nonbinding arbitration program rules and implementation of a menu of alternatives in the MSC Program. On May 4, 2001, Chairman Randy S. Gregory appointed Jim Gates to chair the Ad Hoc Subcommittee on Arbitration and to review the existing rules for needed changes. Judge Ralph A. Walker was appointed to chair the Appellate Subcommittee, Judge Sanford L. Steelman,

Jr. the Superior Court Subcommittee, and Professor Thomas B. Metzloff the District Court Subcommittee. In September 2001, Judge Kenneth C. Titus was appointed chair of the ADR Committee. After leading the Committee through two years of hard work and heavy lifting, described below, Judge Titus stepped down and was replaced in September 2003 by Judge Ralph Walker.

THE AD HOC SUBCOMMITTEE ON ARBITRATION

The Ad Hoc Subcommittee tackled a number of issues:

- Should the court-ordered arbitration program be limited to district court cases only?
- What cases should be excluded from the arbitration process?
- Should insurance carriers be required to attend the arbitration hearings?
- May a corporation be represented at an arbitration hearing by a non-lawyer corporate officer?
- Could funding issues be resolved by changing the arbitration program to a party-pay model?

These issues were vigorously debated during numerous meetings over the next year and a half. One of the most controversial issues was the jurisdiction of the program. Originally, arbitration had been conceived of as a district court program. During the pilot phase, it was decided as an experiment to expand it into superior courts by setting the limit at cases with amounts in controversy up to $15,000, instead of the district court limit of $10,000. Although the pilot had little impact on superior court cases, when arbitration was permanently adopted, no reason was seen to limit it to district courts. Some members of the Ad Hoc Subcommittee wanted to scale arbitration back to district court, while others saw it as being a potentially useful tool in some superior court cases. At this same time, another subcommittee, dealing with adding a "menu" in the MSC program, was considering establishing arbitration as a superior court option through the MSC menu. Eventually, the Ad Hoc Subcommittee decided to continue allowing civil cases of up to $15,000 into arbitration.

On the issue of which cases should be excluded from arbitration, the Subcommittee spent much time seeking input from lawyers with experience in the vast array of cases that get filed in district court. After much consideration and debate, the list of cases subject to arbitration was largely unchanged.[10] The program's jurisdiction was expanded slightly to allow for cases that would otherwise be excluded to be arbitrated by consent of the parties and permission of the court. However, the new rules explicitly stated that consent must be expressed in writing by the parties and may not be presumed by the court. This requirement was to counter the possibility of a superior court in one county presuming consent and sending all of its cases to state-funded arbitration rather than utilizing the MSC party-pay program.

Initially, there was discussion of requiring representatives of insurance carriers to attend arbitrations, similar to the attendance requirement in the MSC Program. While arbitration decisions may lead to further dialogue and ultimate settlement, and the insurance carrier needs to be involved in those discussions, such communications are more likely to be conducted by telephone at a later date. It was concluded that having the carrier present would not be helpful in reaching a conclusion. Therefore, the attendance requirement was not changed.

A particularly murky issue was whether a corporation could "attend" an arbitration hearing through a corporate officer who was not an attorney. The common law rule is that a corporation, not being a person, cannot represent itself pro se and, therefore, may appear in court only through an attorney. The original arbitration rules restated this general proposition with the explicit requirement that corporations be represented by legal counsel. In many districts, however, especially in matters brought by small, local corporations ("mom and pop" companies), the corporation commonly was represented at hearings by an officer—often the "mom" or the "pop." Because the arbitration program rules promulgated by the Supreme Court explicitly prohibited such representation, the lawyer-arbitrators objected to allowing the hearings to go forward unless the corporation hired an attorney. This had the effect of arbitration clogging up the court process rather than making it run more smoothly. As the issue was examined more closely, the Ad Hoc Subcommittee discovered that the rule against corporations appearing without attorney representation was more nuanced and less clear than previously thought. After much discussion, it was decided that the arbitration rules were not the place to articulate the state policy on attorney representation of corporations. The rule therefore was changed to simply state that "[p]arties may appear pro se as permitted by law."

One of the most contentious issues addressed by the Ad Hoc Subcommittee was whether to convert the arbitration program to a party-pay model. After the tremendous success of the MSC Program, with its requirement that the parties pay their mediator, several Subcommittee members felt strongly that converting to a party-pay model would relieve the state of the burden of paying for each arbitrator and, thus, would allow for almost instant statewide expansion. After much vigorous debate, over many meetings, the decision was made to recommend that the state continue paying arbitrators. At the time arbitrators were being paid $75 to conduct a one-hour hearing. Studies showed that including preparation and travel, the attorneys typically devoted slightly in excess of three hours to each case. Thus, most attorneys saw serving as an arbitrator not as a profit-making venture but as a service to the courts. Many attorneys did not even submit the paperwork to get the $75 fee. Although, at present, arbitration continues to function under a state-pay model and the arbitrator's fee has increased to $100, the program was effectively converted to a party-pay model in 2003. That year the legislature added Section (c1) to North Carolina General Statutes Section 7A-37.1. The provision requires the $100 arbitrator fee to be assessed against the parties and divided equally among them. However, instead of paying the arbitrator directly, the parties pay the clerk of court, and the court pays the arbitrator. The rule revisions recommended by the Ad Hoc Subcommittee on Arbitration were finalized by the ADR Committee on May 3, 2002, and adopted by the North Carolina Supreme Court on December 19, 2002.

THE SUPERIOR COURT SUBCOMMITTEE AND THE MSC PROGRAM MENU APPROACH

The ADR Committee's Superior Court Subcommittee, under the leadership of Judge Steelman, began its work by developing a menu of options to be added to the MSC Program, as provided by Section (i) of North Carolina General Statutes Section 7A-38.1, the 1995 statute that expanded the MSC Program statewide. Section (i) authorized use of settlement procedures other than mediation, as permitted by state or local court rules.

Mediation was the only ADR technique used in the original MSC Program. From the mid-1980s to the early 1990s, the NCBA Dispute Resolution Committee (and Task Force) studied the many forms of ADR that had emerged around the country to identify methods that might be adopted by North Carolina's courts. The procedures examined included arbitration, mediation, summary jury trials, early neutral evaluation, mini-trials, med-arb, summary bench trials, and the so-called "multi-door courthouse." Some of the programs studied utilized several forms of ADR. In fact, the Florida program that became the primary model for North Carolina's MSC Program required the court to order either mediation or arbitration. However, arbitration was rarely requested in Florida, and judges there routinely ordered cases to mediation. For this reason, drafters of North Carolina's MSC Program created only a court-ordered mediation program. It met with great success in its pilot phase, which lasted from 1991 to 1994.

As efforts to establish a permanent, statewide MSC Program gathered momentum, several attorneys suggested that mediation was not the best settlement device for all of their clients or cases, particularly if mediators were forbidden to give opinions during mediation. Thus, the notion of adding a menu of "other settlement procedures" began to take hold as the 1995 legislation was being drafted.

By 1997, after enactment of Section (i) of the 1995 legislation, the NCBA Dispute Resolution Section, under the leadership of Andy Little, and the DRC had proposed a set of amendments to the Rules of the North Carolina Supreme Court Implementing Mediated Settlement Conferences in Superior Court Civil Actions (MSC Program Rules) to create a menu of options other than mediation that litigants could utilize by agreement. The menu proposal focused on three alternative procedures: arbitration, neutral evaluation, and summary jury trials. Arbitration was a familiar process for most North Carolina attorneys, and it had shown great promise in the pilot program. Summary jury trials also had gained acceptance through a more limited, but very successful, pilot program in the state. Although fewer than two dozen cases were submitted to a summary jury trial, all of those cases were resolved through the process. The option of early neutral evaluation (or neutral evaluation) was seen as a way to address the most common complaint about mediated settlement conferences—that sometimes the parties needed to hear what someone else thought about the merits of the case. Mediators generally do not offer such opinions, so the use of neutral evaluation was seen as a way to meet that need without pressuring mediators to assume a role with which they felt uncomfortable.

The menu proposal also carried forward certain policy decisions made earlier by the Supreme Court Dispute Resolution Committee. First, the proposal anticipated that the court would have minimal involvement in the process of choosing an ADR procedure other than mediation, selecting the neutral to conduct the procedure, and setting the costs of the procedure. It also provided that no new processes would be created to certify or discipline the neutrals who would conduct these "other settlement procedures."

Many features of the 1997 MSC menu proposal were opposed by the AOC staff and were never considered by the Supreme Court ADR Committee or by the Court itself. With the creation of the State Judicial Council's Dispute

Resolution Committee and its Superior Court Subcommittee in 2001, the proposal was revived and reconsidered. A number of issues were debated over the course of the next eighteen months. First was whether to have a menu at all. Those opposed to it were concerned about added layers of administration for the courts and confusion for lawyers and litigants. Although these concerns persisted, the Subcommittee moved forward with fleshing out the proposal and developing specific rules.

As the discussions proceeded, several foundational principles emerged, all of which are now embodied in MSC Program Rule 10:

- Mediation would be the default option.
- Other options could be utilized only upon the request and consent of all of the parties.
- The parties would select their neutral by agreement, with approval by the court.
- All details of the selected option would have to be stipulated to by the parties prior to filing the motion for use of a menu option.
- All of the options would remain funded by the parties themselves.

The effect of these decisions was to make clear that use of a menu option was a party choice. If the parties could not agree on a menu choice, then they would automatically proceed to mediation. The development and maintenance of the mediation process had proved to be challenging—regulating mediator training, certifying mediators, and prescribing the MSC process in detail, among other issues. To set up similar systems for each menu option seemed an unfruitful and unnecessary burden. To finesse this regulatory issue, the Subcommittee decided on a "free-market" model whereby the buyers and sellers would regulate the market. If parties wanted to arbitrate, they would determine who they wished to conduct the arbitration and hire that person, rather than the court providing an approved list. Similarly, the parties were required to agree to other details, such as neutral compensation, discovery limitations, timing and duration of the settlement procedure, whether the procedure would be binding or non-binding, and other details of the process not covered by the new rules. Also central to the menu approach was the concept that just as MSC Program mediations were entirely funded by the parties, so, too, would any menu option they might choose.

Chief among the initial menu issues was arbitration. Would having an arbitration option in the MSC Program menu damage or destroy the existing arbitration program? Eventually, this question was answered in the negative. Should the option be modeled after the non-binding, court-ordered arbitration program, or should it be reconfigured? The arbitration process that emerged was one that was modeled on the existing program, but modified in several respects. In the new menu arbitration, the parties would be participating voluntarily. This allowed for fewer rules related to setting up and attending the hearing. When and where the hearing was to be held, who was to be there, who the arbitrators would be and how they would be compensated, how evidence was to be submitted, and how long the hearing would last were all issues that the parties would agree upon prior to seeking permission to conduct an arbitration rather than a mediation. Initially, a detailed set of rules implementing arbitration was drafted, but they were discarded as the Subcommittee reached consensus that allowing the parties to shape their own process was better than requiring a set of predetermined, uniform rules. However, to reduce confusion, the final proposal was modeled as closely as possible on the existing court-ordered arbitration program. A major difference was that the parties could stipulate to making the arbitration binding, although the default was that the arbitrator's award would be advisory.

Summary jury trials also engendered considerable debate. On the heels of the successful Summary Jury Trial Pilot Program, the North Carolina Supreme Court in 1991 had adopted Rule 23 of the General Rules of Practice for the Superior and District Courts. Rule 23 provided for the use of summary jury trials in any superior court case upon motion of the parties. The rule also provided that state court judges and juries may be used in summary jury trials. Initially, the Subcommittee was inclined to follow Rule 23 by setting out a process using taxpayer-funded judges and juries for the MSC Program menu option. After much discussion, the Subcommittee decided to refer to Rule 23 for clarification purposes, but that the menu would require a party-pay model. It also would require that use of Rule 23 would not be a substitute for the settlement process mandated by the MSC Program Rules. Under the MSC Program menu, summary jury trials would use presiding officials and jurors procured and paid by the parties. The process could be binding or non-binding, as decided by the parties. A broad framework was outlined in the menu rules, but details remained for the parties to fill in by agreement.

The MSC Program menu also provides for summary bench trials. Although summary bench trials are not well known nationally, from the mid-1970s until his retirement in 1994, Judge James M. Long of Stokes and Surry Counties utilized a unique procedure he called "judicial arbitration." In that model, the parties would stipulate to a bench trial with a summary presentation of the evidence, lasting no longer than half a day, in exchange for a setting on a time and date certain. The rules of evidence did not apply. The menu included the option for summary bench trials based on this procedure.

Similar to arbitration, summary trials were envisioned as a settlement procedure, to aid the parties in reaching their own resolution. Also, similar to arbitration, the parties could stipulate to making the summary process binding. In fact, in the Summary Jury Trial Pilot Program, frequently, while the jury was deliberating, the parties would agree to make the jury's otherwise advisory verdict into a binding verdict.

Once the broad outlines discussed above were established, it was relatively easy to craft the program rules for neutral evaluation. Under those rules, the parties could retain any person whose opinion they believed was likely to aid them in settling their case. The parties could present the case in whatever manner they deemed appropriate. The neutral would conduct a conference to further discuss and explore the case and to give feedback and an oral evaluation to the parties. The rules laid out a pre-conference and conference process, but they could be amended by consent of the parties and the neutral.

The MSC Menu rules were finalized by the ADR Committee on May 3, 2002, and adopted by the Supreme Court on November 21, 2002.

The District Court Subcommittee

The Family Financial Settlement Program was originally implemented with a menu option; however, under Professor Tom Metzloff's leadership, the District Court Subcommittee continued to refine that program's rules to resolve problems as they arose in its day-to-day operation. A significant issue was newly trained FFS mediators getting the observations required for certification, particularly as the program went from its pilot districts to statewide implementation. While ideas were explored that helped alleviate the problem, no lasting solution was found. Ten years later, the Dispute Resolution Commission continues to discuss the problem of insufficient opportunities for observation of FFS Program mediations.

The Appellate Subcommittee

The Appellate Subcommittee worked with the North Carolina Court of Appeals to develop a voluntary mediated settlement conference program. A pilot program was begun in early 2002 using as mediators primarily sitting or retired judges who had completed the DRC's certification process. The program became permanent in late 2004.

Subsequent Work of the ADR Committee

After this initial period of intense effort, the ADR Committee found that the need for creating new programs ebbed. Under the leadership of Judge Ralph Walker, who was appointed as chair in September 2003, the Committee met frequently and served as a clearinghouse for ideas and information about ADR in the courts and in the state generally. Several new initiatives were introduced during this period.

Permanency mediation was proposed to address situations not involving divorce where children may be removed from the home due to abuse, neglect, or other circumstances. The program sought to avoid lengthy and contentious custody hearings by gathering all of the interested parties, including state or local agencies, to mediate placement and conditions. The program was formally established in 2006 under North Carolina General Statutes Section 7B-202. (See Chapter 20.)

Another area of discussion was statewide implementation of the Child Custody and Visitation Mediation Program. While it was agreed upon as state policy, such expansion depended on the allocation of additional funding. Eventually the Program was funded by the General Assembly for statewide operation. (See Chapter 19.)

A third topic of concern was mandatory certification of all mediators in the MSC and FFS Programs. The MSC and FFS Programs had always required court-appointed mediators to be certified, but both programs initially allowed the parties to select uncertified mediators, with approval by the court. The DRC became concerned that, in certain areas of the state, the use of untrained and uncertified mediators was becoming the rule rather than the exception. The DRC proposed a set of rule amendments that would require all mediators to be certified, whether court appointed or party selected. In the ADR Committee, members of the family law bar raised concerns as to whether requiring all FFS mediators to be certified would hinder the use of the Program. After consideration, the ADR Committee limited the rule amendment to requiring only MSC Program mediators to be certified.

Restructuring the ADR Committee

With the diminished workload of the ADR Committee, its membership seemed too large. In November 2004, Judge Walker asked Andy Little to chair a task force to investigate reducing and restructuring the committee. Before the task force could report, Judge Walker was appointed Director of the Administrative Office of the Courts and relinquished his leadership of the ADR Committee. Frank Laney was appointed Chair in October 2005.

The initial report of the Reorganization Task Force on October 14, 2005, was to reduce the twenty-four-member ADR Committee to five members. Some felt this was too extreme, so the Task Force decided to reconsider its recommendation. The Committee met several times over the next year, each time considering the issue of reorganization. The proposal that evolved was a Committee of fifteen members, appointed by the Chief Justice of the North Carolina Supreme Court, and other ex officio members appointed as needed by the Chair. Before the Committee could finalize this plan, perennial budget crises cut travel expenses and halted all meetings of the Committee. The Committee continued to function without physical meetings, handling rule amendments and other business by e-mail and telephone conference call. In December 2010, the restructuring plan was finally placed before the North Carolina Supreme Court and was adopted. Chief Justice Sarah Parker appointed new members. Frank C. Laney was re-appointed as Chair. Superior Court Judges Phyllis M. Gorham and A. Robinson Hassell, and District Court Judges Christopher B. McLendon and A. Elizabeth Keever were appointed. Kathy Shuart was appointed as Trial Court Administrator representative, and Michael Haswell was appointed as an interested citizen. Five attorneys recommended by the President of the NCBA also were appointed: J. Wade Harrison, Jaye P. Meyer, Lyn K. Broom, Jacqueline R. Clare, and J. Anderson Little. Other appointees were Judge Julius H. Corpening, Chair of the Child Custody Mediation Advisory Committee, and Judge W. David Lee, Chair of the Dispute Resolution Commission. The Director of the Administrative Office of the Courts selected Tammy J. Smith as his designee. DeShield Smith of the AOC Court Programs Division served as staff to the Committee. The newly appointed Committee set to work reviewing and commenting on rule revisions to the court-ordered arbitration rules, continuing its mission of meeting the needs of the public, the courts, and the ADR community.

Current Governance Structure and Processes

The governance of the court-related dispute resolution programs in North Carolina is not a linear model. Rather, as ADR programs were developed, their administration was assigned to various organizations and was handled in a variety of ways. The current governance structure reflects this gradual process of evolution.

Community mediation centers generally are local, nonprofit organizations (although a few are city or county agencies) governed by local boards. Historically, a substantial portion of the centers' funding came from the state and was paid through the AOC as compensation for the significant number of district court criminal cases that the centers mediated. Unfortunately, state funding for the community mediation centers was eliminated effective July 1, 2011. Now, centers that provide mediation in district criminal court matters receive only a portion of any fee paid by the defendant to the clerk of court after a successful mediation.

Child Custody Mediation Programs are jointly administered by the local district courts and the AOC, with a Child Custody Advisory Committee giving statewide oversight. The mediators are state employees and serve as court staff. Although the chair of the Advisory Committee sits on the State Judicial Council ADR Committee, the ADR Committee has no authority over the Child Custody Mediation Program operations.

The court-ordered arbitration program is run on a day-to-day basis by local court staff and is administered programmatically by the AOC. The AOC trains and certifies the arbitrators, who are appointed by local judges. Changes in the arbitration rules have typically originated either from the NCBA Dispute Resolution Section or the AOC. The DRC has no authority over the program. In establishing the ADR Committee of the State Judicial Council, the North Carolina Supreme Court required that the Committee review and recommend adoption or revisions to any arbitration rule amendments prior to their consideration by the Council and adoption by the Supreme Court. The ADR Committee provides periodic oversight for the arbitration program.

In the summer of 2011, the ADR Committee considered major revisions to the court-ordered arbitration program rules. This review culminated in a significant reorganization of the rules and some substantial changes in the Program. First, the Program was removed from superior court and was designated for use only in district court. Arbitration was used very rarely in superior court, and having it operate in both jurisdictions created drafting and operational headaches. Second, because very few parties selected their arbitrator, and allowing party-selection required several additional administrative steps, the new rules deleted the party-selection option, leaving it up to the court to appoint arbitrators. This change was intended to streamline Program operations and to speed up the arbitration process. Third, because of the adoption of "party-pay" in 2003, the rules were amended to better provide for those who could not pay to participate at reduced or no cost and to provide for improved collection from those who could pay. Lastly, the new rules allow parties to stipulate that the arbitration will be final and binding. Other changes were made to clarify existing rules but had no impact on the functioning of the arbitration program. The new rules were adopted by the Supreme Court in October 2011 and went into effect on January 1, 2012. An additional proposal to increase the arbitrator's fee to $150 will require legislative action, as will removing the $15,000 cap on cases submitted to arbitration.

The MSC and FFS Programs are primarily administered by the DRC. The DRC certifies mediators and mediation training programs, gives guidance to mediators, and sanctions mediators who violate the Standards of Professional Conduct. AOC staff usually is involved in issues related to workflow and integrating the MSC and FFS Programs into the other court processes on the local level. The DRC is the usual source for program changes and rule amendments. Proposed amendments are forwarded to the ADR Committee for review and comment. Once the ADR Committee endorses the changes, they are presented to the State Judicial Council for its consideration and, if approved, are then submitted to the Supreme Court for adoption. Working out the details of most rule changes occurs in the Commission. The ADR Committee often offers comment and, occasionally, either returns a proposal to the Commission for reconsideration or directly engages the Commission in discussion to arrive at a consensus proposal. Fortunately, after this process, proposals typically are sound enough that the State Judicial Council and the Supreme Court rarely find it necessary to make additional changes.

The Dispute Resolution Section of the North Carolina Bar Association has no direct role in governing any dispute resolution programs. But it is populated with interested and energetic advocates for ADR, so is frequently the seedbed for new ideas or proposals. It also is a wellspring of political support for existing programs. With access to the NCBA's fulltime lobbyist, the Section can and does advocate vigorously on behalf of implementation and continued funding for dispute resolution. In the economically challenging year of 2011, for example, the Section actively sought to educate legislators regarding the downside of balancing the budget by terminating programs that significantly reduce the courts' caseloads.

Conclusion

Court-based ADR programs in North Carolina are governed in various ways. Some programs, such as court-ordered arbitration and child custody mediation, are administered through the local courts and the AOC.

The Dispute Resolution Commission provides primary oversight for the MSC and FFS Programs, as well as the Clerk Mediation Program and certification of mediators in district criminal court. Rule and program amendments for those programs usually originate in the DRC and then are submitted to the ADR Committee of the State Judicial Council.

Rule changes for the state's arbitration program and the mediation programs are often proposed by the NCBA's Dispute Resolution Section. The Section also explores the potential for new applications of ADR in our courts and administrative agencies and works to improve the existing programs. It continues to serve as a think tank for dispute resolution.

The ADR Committee of the State Judicial Council serves an oversight and review role for all court-based dispute resolution programs. Specific proposals usually come to it from the DRC or the AOC for review, comment, and recommendation. The Committee collects the proposals and then forwards them to the State Judicial Council and the Supreme Court once a year. The Committee also gives oversight in working with the AOC regarding what statistics to gather and in giving feedback to the various programs.

NOTES

1. Stevens H. Clarke et al., *Court-Ordered Civil Case Mediation in North Carolina: An Evaluation of Its Effects* (Institute of Government, The University of North Carolina at Chapel Hill, 1995).

2. This URL is automatically redirected to the North Carolina Court System's website, http://www.nccourts.org/Courts/CRS/Councils/DRC/Default.asp.

3. N.C. Gen. Stat. § 7A-409.1(c), (d).

4. *Report of the Ad Hoc Dispute Resolution Task Force* (May 22, 2000), p. 3, available at http://www.ic.nc.gov/ncic/pages/taskforc.htm.

5. *Id.* at 8.

6. *Id.* at 3.

7. *Id.*

8. *Id.* at 4.

9. *Id.* at 7.

10. In 2002, on its own initiative, the legislature amended North Carolina General Statutes Section 7A-37.1(c) to exempt cases "in which the sole claim is action on an account."

CHAPTER EIGHT

The Continuing Role of the North Carolina Bar Association Dispute Resolution Section

"Coming together is a beginning.
Keeping together is progress.
Working together is success."
—American industrialist Henry Ford

The North Carolina Bar Association (NCBA) played a key role in initiating and advancing many of the state's most successful court-based dispute resolution programs. As those programs matured, their governance came to rest with other entities, such as the Dispute Resolution Commission (DRC or Commission). However, the NCBA—through its Dispute Resolution Section (the Section)—continued to serve as an educator, innovator, and advocate for the use of alternative dispute resolution (ADR). The Section continues to function as an important resource for the legal community, ADR professionals, and the public. It is active in the ongoing development and implementation of dispute resolution processes in North Carolina's courts and in the state's business community.

At times, it is hard to define the Section's role in the various dispute resolution initiatives. Almost all of the leaders in ADR in our state began their participation as members and leaders of the Section. So when individuals undertake to advocate for rule changes or initiate new programs, are they doing so as Section leaders, Commission members, or in any of the other myriad positions where Section members serve? It is safe to say that if all of the Section members were removed from the North Carolina dispute resolution landscape, it would be very different and somewhat barren. The Section has always been and remains the root from which a forest of ADR programs has sprung.

The Section as Dispute Resolution Educator

With the proliferation of dispute resolution programs throughout North Carolina in the 1990s, more and more people became aware of ADR and sought information about its uses and potential. The Section, through its role as convener and clearinghouse, helped to meet the expanding need for information in a variety of ways.

The Section became a major provider of continuing education on ADR. Its annual Continuing Legal Education (CLE) program featured a wide variety of local and national speakers on many cutting-edge topics. Attendance at these programs averaged between eighty to one hundred attorneys, mediators, and arbitrators. The programs became the primary place that mediators in the state would gather to share insights and experience. The Section also sponsored specialty programs, such as an annual, day-long seminar on international arbitration presented in coordination with the Duke University School of Law and led by Andrea Carska-Sheppard and Judge Sidney S. Eagles, Jr.

In 1997, the Section began publishing a newsletter (currently distributed to more than 500 subscribers) that provided information on ADR programs and initiatives around the state. The Section and the DRC co-published the original edition of this book in 2003 and then reprinted it in 2005. All of the leaders in that effort also served as Section leaders.

The Section also sponsored activities to call attention to dispute resolution and to garner support for it. In 1999, the NCBA marked its one-hundredth anniversary by organizing a series of events celebrating the accomplishments and vitality of the Bar Association and of North Carolina's lawyers. Among the most extensive and successful activities conducted that year were those organized by the Dispute Resolution Section as part of its Dispute Resolution Month Project.

The Dispute Resolution Month Project

The Section had much to celebrate during that centennial year. ADR had become a fixture in the state's court system, and North Carolina had risen to national prominence as a leader in the ADR field. From the early days of the NCBA Dispute Resolution Task Force in the 1980s through the development of mediated settlement conferences and other court-based programs in the 1990s, the NCBA and the Section had played a central role in encouraging alternatives to litigation throughout the state.

The Section began planning for its centennial project in September 1997, under the direction of Section Chair Dorothy C. Bernholz. In the spring of 1998, the Section formed a Centennial Project Committee to oversee the effort. The Project Committee was initially co-chaired by Court of Appeals Judge Ralph A. Walker and James E. Gates, Bernholz's successor as Section Chair. John C. Schafer joined as third co-chair of the Project Committee after he succeeded Gates as Section Chair in June 1999. Members of the Project Committee included: Allison B. Schafer, an attorney with the North Carolina School Boards Association; John R. Archambault, a Greensboro attorney; Leslie C. Ratliff, Executive Secretary of the state's Dispute Resolution Commission (DRC); Debi Miller Moore of the American Arbitration Association (AAA); Miriam Saxon, Arbitration Coordinator with the Administrative Office of the Courts; Kathy L. Shuart, Trial Court Administrator in Durham; and Charise Alexander, a member of the Legal Assistants Division of the NCBA.

FOCUS ON PUBLIC AWARENESS

In keeping with the objectives of the centennial celebration, the Dispute Resolution Section sought to highlight North Carolina's progress in enabling citizens to resolve disputes by using alternatives to trial, such as court-based ADR programs, educational initiatives, and community dispute resolution centers. The Project Committee reviewed ADR awareness programs in other states, but found that those states that undertook projects promoting ADR focused their efforts solely on attorneys. In North Carolina, members of the bar already had a good understanding of dispute resolution methods through the statewide superior court Mediated Settlement Conference Program, the Court-Ordered, Non-Binding Arbitration Program, and other ADR techniques. The Project Committee decided to focus instead on public education and awareness. With no similar programs to emulate, the committee developed its public awareness program largely from scratch.

THE GOVERNOR'S PROCLAMATION OF
DISPUTE RESOLUTION MONTH

A key part of the project, and one that significantly increased overall awareness of ADR throughout the state, was the official proclamation of October 1999 as "Dispute Resolution Month" in North Carolina. Governor James B. Hunt, Jr. issued the Proclamation on April 16, 1999. The Proclamation provided a concise and straightforward acknowledgment of the benefits and contributions of ADR. It began by noting that the mission of North Carolina's legal system is "to provide all citizens access to justice and a fair and prompt resolution of disputes." It went on to declare that "dispute resolution procedures that provide alternatives to litigation have significantly advanced these causes." It recognized North Carolina's role as "a national leader" in promoting ADR and lauded dispute resolution procedures for saving "substantial time and cost" to parties and the state. The Proclamation thus represented more than just the announcement of a special, bar-sponsored project during the month of October. It served as an official recognition of ADR's role in improving the state's civil justice system.

Celebrating the Success of ADR

Several other activities sponsored by the Section helped to focus state-wide attention on ADR before the official Dispute Resolution Month events began. Daniel Bowling, Executive Director of the Society of Professionals in Dispute Resolution, spoke at the Section's annual continuing legal education program in April at Wrightsville Beach. At the NCBA Centennial Convention in June 1999, the Section sponsored a speech by William K. Slate II, President of the American Arbitration Association. Slate's address, "ADR Knows No Boundaries," was well received by attendees. An NCBA-sponsored radio announcement, featuring North Carolina Supreme Court Chief Justice Henry E. Frye, ran statewide, informing thousands of listeners about Dispute Resolution Month. The NCBA also issued several press releases about the project to North Carolina news outlets.

During the month of October, Dispute Resolution Month activities took place across the state almost daily. Ultimately, more than 130 events—an average of more than four a day—were held. Some sixty volunteer speakers presented speeches on ADR at schools, local chambers of commerce, business clubs, libraries, and other venues.

Another important aspect of the project was the provision of mediation services on a pro bono basis. Volunteer mediators assisted in some sixty cases around the state, including matters pending before the district courts, the superior courts, and the North Carolina Industrial Commission. Public information booths were set up at shopping malls in Asheville, Wilmington, and other cities. Hundreds of citizens received materials on ADR in North Carolina through this effort.

The energy and enthusiasm that fueled the project were, in many respects, reminiscent of an earlier time, when an idealistic group of NCBA members banded together and first dedicated their efforts to serving as peacemakers and healers of conflict. The events of October 1999 and those held throughout the centennial year helped to fulfill the mission of those early ADR pioneers.

Dispute Resolution Month also greatly increased public awareness of ADR programs and allowed North Carolina citizens to experience the benefits firsthand. In achieving these results, the NCBA and the Dispute Resolution Month Project clearly helped to prepare the way for a new century of progress in meeting the goals of North Carolina's civil justice system.

The Section as Dispute Resolution Innovator

In the late 1980s and early 1990s, the NCBA was active in developing new ideas on the uses and application of dispute resolution in our state. Much of that focus passed to the DRC after its creation in 1995, as it developed and fine-tuned the MSC and FFS Programs. (See Chapters 12 and 18.) However, the primary leaders of these efforts through the DRC continued to be various members of the Section.

After the turn of the twenty-first century, the Dispute Resolution Section regained some of its early spirit of innovation. In 2004, the Section and the DRC jointly established a committee to investigate, and if prudent, to develop a mediation process for use in cases in which the clerks of court had original jurisdiction, such as estate matters, guardianships, and boundary disputes. The committee, jointly chaired by Frank C. Laney and J. Anderson "Andy" Little, met over a period of a year with various stakeholders and clerk representatives to hammer out implementing legislation and proposed rules for a mediation program in the clerk's office. (For more information, see Chapter 15.)

Throughout the middle of the decade, the Section also dedicated much time and effort to rejuvenating peer mediation in public schools. Various schools showed interest in the program. However, it was difficult for the Section, as an outsider to the education system, to cultivate and sustain that interest.

During the same period, the Section also sought to create a simple resolution system for the handling of disputes over real estate escrows. In most real estate sales transactions, a buyer typically deposits $1,000 or more with a real estate agent. If the sale is not consummated, a dispute may arise over whether the buyer or seller is entitled to the escrow funds. The agent holding the funds is caught in the middle. Although there are reasonably simple processes for adjudicating the issue through small claims court or filings with the clerk, real estate agents are often reluctant to use such court-based methods because they involve filing a lawsuit against the agent's own client. In an effort to develop a procedure that would avoid litigation, Section representatives met with staff from the North Carolina Real Estate Commission and the North Carolina Board of Realtors and began developing an arbitration-based alternative. As work on the program progressed, however, the North Carolina General Assembly passed a bill that allowed real estate agents to place escrow funds in the hands of the clerk of court and authorized the clerk to adjudicate the dispute. That solution has been met with mixed reactions, and the Section continues to seek a solution based on ADR processes.

The Pro Bono Mediation Project:
Conflict Resolution Day 2008

*"If we knew what it was we were doing,
it would not be called research, would it?"*
—Albert Einstein

The Section's most noteworthy efforts as an ADR innovator involved developing a pro bono resource from within its membership. The Pro Bono Mediation Project[1] was first conceived in the autumn of 2007 by members of the section in response to the first annual 4ALL Campaign, initiated by the NCBA. Lynn Gullick, then chair of the Section, and Dr. Joseph E. Johnson, Professor Emeritus of the Bryan School of Business and Economics at the University of North Carolina at Greensboro (UNCG) and a non-attorney member of the Dispute Resolution Section, began the initial collaboration. The 4ALL Campaign centered on lawyers providing free legal advice via telephone to citizens with simple problems. Because the Section's expertise was in assisting parties in resolving disputes rather than in providing legal advice, the Section felt compelled to develop its own pro bono project aimed at matching parties who could not afford a mediator with mediators who were willing to work with such parties without charge.

At the December 2007 Section Council meeting, after an inspirational presentation about the 4ALL Initiative by NCBA Immediate Past President Janet Ward Black, additional volunteers, including Lesley McCandeless, the Honorable Melzer "Pat" Morgan, and Dr. Sherrill Hayes, joined Gullick and Johnson to form a committee. This committee went to work immediately, identifying possible referral sources, finding locations to conduct mediations, and developing program forms and materials. Committee members met with representatives from local schools, courts, and the nonprofit community and monitored progress through the use of e-mail and weekly teleconferences.

A critical stage in the project was the development of several partnerships, which allowed the project to proceed. Key support was provided by

Legal Aid of Central North Carolina, Senior Resources of Guilford County, and the Family Life Council of Greensboro. Attorneys from Legal Aid of Central North Carolina helped secure referrals for mediations by providing a list and brief descriptions of ten potential cases from their files. They also helped the committee develop relationships with opposing counsel in these cases. The executive directors of both Senior Resources and the Family Life Council agreed to provide access to their spaces' facilities on the date of the proposed program (Saturday, April 5, 2008) in the Dorothy Bardolph Center in Greensboro. In addition, faculty and students from UNCG's Program in Conflict Resolution (now Conflict and Peace Studies) volunteered to conduct an evaluation of the project.

By the February 2008 Section Council meeting, much of the structure of the program had been developed, including a client referral source, program forms, materials for clients and attorneys, a location for holding the mediation sessions, and an evaluation strategy. All that remained was creating a list of volunteer mediators, a task accomplished at the meeting.

Also at the meeting, the Section's Pro Bono Committee formulated questions to submit to the DRC regarding the ethics of offering pro bono mediation. Because North Carolina's Mediated Settlement Conference Program was designed as a "party-pay" procedure, the Committee sought advice on whether mediators, consistent with MSC Program rules and the Standards of Professional Conduct for Mediators, could offer their services pro bono or at reduced rates to parties represented by legal aid organizations or in other cases in which one or more parties are, or appear to be, indigent. This inquiry resulted in the DRC's Advisory Opinion Number 08-14, which reasserted the Commission's commitment to serving indigent parties and established specific guidelines permitting mediators, when voluntarily selected, to assist clients of legal services organizations and other indigent clients without charge or at a reduced rate.[2]

Due to a combination of scheduling conflicts and pre-mediation settlements, none of the selected cases were in fact mediated on April 5th. The overall experience of this project is probably best summarized by an excerpt from an e-mail sent by Lynn Gullick to the committee members after the final decision to cancel the pilot project:

". . . I am so grateful for your hard work and effort to develop this innovative mediation program. I believe we have learned many valuable lessons in the design and implementation phase. More importantly we have discovered how to partner with other organizations in order to develop a blueprint for the future. The time constraint of a one-time, one-day voluntary program was our biggest liability. I believe this group has a design which can offer a real structure for future partnership between legal aid, private attorneys, pro bono mediators, university conflict resolution programs and other community organizations to open a dialogue and resolve conflicts. The written material produced by this group is outstanding."[3]

From that written material, the Section's Pro Bono Committee began developing a panel of mediators who could serve Legal Aid cases year-round, not just on a statewide day of public service.

In sum, the Pro Bono Mediation Project represented an example of the best type of collaboration between members of the Dispute Resolution Section and community organizations designed to improve the lives of North Carolina citizens through the use of alternative dispute resolution. Although the project did not reach the conclusion originally envisioned, it served as a starting point for a longer-term Section initiative and as a model that could be used by groups or other bar sections working on community-based projects.

Continuing Pro Bono Efforts

Under the continuing leadership of Judge Morgan and Durham mediator Rick Igou, the initial Pro Bono Day project evolved into a continuing collaboration between legal services attorneys and volunteer mediators. The Section's list of volunteers was expanded and continually updated. Over the next few years, legal services organizations called on these volunteer mediators to provide free mediation services in dozens of cases involving their clients of limited means. Section members' services thus were not limited to a single day each year, but were available when needed throughout the year.

The Section as Dispute Resolution Advocate

Throughout the first decade of the twenty-first century, the Section remained interested in and supportive of the state's myriad dispute resolution programs. The Section used the NCBA's legislative resources as well as the time and influence of it own members to advocate for continued and increased funding for court-based ADR programs. The Section kept a watchful eye on pending legislation. It pushed for bills that would expand the use of dispute resolution and opposed bills that would be harmful to the field. The Section sought to inform and influence discussions regarding the use of permanency mediation, consumer arbitration legislation, and the unauthorized practice of law by mediators.

The Section also provided education to judges and other court personnel through speakers and printed materials to encourage broader acceptance and use of ADR. Asheville attorney, William F. (Bill) Wolcott III, led a committee that worked closely with clerks of court in various counties to gain acceptance for and increased use of the newly developed clerk's mediation program. Pursuant to the statute establishing the DRC, the Section consistently made recommendations for well-qualified individuals to fill new and unexpired terms on the Commission.[4] In this way, the Section tried to make sure that the people responsible for much of the governance of court-based ADR were knowledgeable about and supportive of the programs.

Advocacy by Recognizing Outstanding Service:
The Peace Award

To recognize the tireless efforts of the many people who dedicated years to the development and fostering of dispute resolution in North Carolina, the Section began presenting its Peace Award in 2002. The award is given annually to an individual in North Carolina who has shown a special commitment to the peaceful resolution of disputes. The Section bylaws set out criteria for judging potential recipients. Particular emphasis is placed on an individual's overall contribution and commitment to the field of dispute resolution in the following areas:

- Development of new or innovative programs;
- Demonstrated improvements in service;
- Demonstrated improvements in efficiency;
- Research and writings in the area of dispute resolution;
- Development of continuing education programs;
- Leadership with local, state, and national boards and legislative bodies.

A list of Peace Award recipients appears in Appendix A.

Advocacy for Standards of Confidentiality:
The Rule 8.3 Controversy

The most significant advocacy campaign undertaken by the Section during the past decade was initiated in response to a question raised by the North Carolina State Bar that had serious implications for confidentiality standards in mediations. In March of 2006, a participant in the audience at the Section's Annual Meeting and CLE program asked a question concerning the apparent conflict between the Standards of Professional Conduct for Mediators (Standards) and the Revised Rules of Professional Conduct (RPC) for attorneys. Essentially, the question posed was: "What is an attorney-mediator to do if he or she becomes aware in the course of a mediation that an attorney representing a party at the mediation has committed a violation of the RPC?" Would the attorney-mediator be obligated to report the violation to the State Bar pursuant to Rule 8.3 of the RPC, or would he or she be required to keep the violation confidential, as required by Standard III of the Standards?[5]

Coming to grips with how to resolve this conflict led to intensive study, discussion, and careful thought by the Standards, Discipline, and Advisory Opinions Committee of the DRC, the Ethics and Professionalism Committee of the Section, under committee chair Zeb E. "Barney" Barnhardt, Jr. and the DRC itself. The result of that effort finally appeared as an amendment to RPC Rule 8.3, which was approved by the Ethics Committee of the NC State Bar, after publication for comment. It was then approved by the State Bar Council and finally approved by the North Carolina Supreme Court in October of 2010. The revised rule now permits attorney-mediators to keep confidential the statements and conduct of attorneys participating in a mediation, with limited exceptions, to encourage the candor that is critical to the successful resolution of legal disputes. (For a more complete discussion of the interaction of Standard III and the revised Rule 8.3, see Chapter 11.)

The Section's Role in Planning for the Future

At the end of the decade, the Section reaffirmed its commitment to educating, inspiring, and innovating by calling a meeting of representatives of every dispute resolution program it could identify in the state for an informal discussion of the past, present, and future of ADR in North Carolina. The meeting was an outgrowth of a suggestion from the Section's Long-Range Planning Committee to bring together the myriad providers of ADR in North Carolina to talk about coordination and coverage of services.

M. Ann Anderson, a mediator from Pilot Mountain and a member of the DRC, led the effort, providing the resources of her office to research and compile the list of invitees. The event was co-hosted by Dr. Sherrill W. Hayes, Assistant Professor of Conflict Resolution at UNCG, and by the

UNCG Program in Conflict and Peace Studies. It was held at the school's satellite campus at Browns Summit on February 24, 2011, the day before the Section's Annual Meeting and CLE. The event became known as "The Summit at the Summit."

More than thirty people attended the half-day session, including representatives from the United States District Court for the Middle District of North Carolina, the Administrative Office of the Courts, the North Carolina Office of State Personnel Mediation Program, the Dispute Resolution Commission, the North Carolina Industrial Commission, the Mediation Network of North Carolina, and many others.

Section Chair Barney Barnhardt welcomed the participants and asked each attendee to give a short personal introduction. After the introductions, the agenda began with presentation of a short history of ADR in North Carolina by Frank Laney. It was followed by networking through "speed sharing" of information by participants. Lynn Gullick concluded the meeting with discussions of possible future meetings and ways to publicize attendee program information. Participants indicated an interest in additional meetings, potentially in conjunction with CLE. They also provided contact information, including brief summaries of program-provider information, contact listings, and descriptions of qualifications of providers. At the time of publication, the Section plans to make the information available to its members, either on the Section's web page or through social networking media.

Through the individual efforts of its growing membership, the NCBA Dispute Resolution Section continues to be a convener, clearinghouse, innovator, and advocate of dispute resolution in North Carolina.

NOTES

1. For a more detailed discussion of this project, see Sherrill W. Hayes, PhD, "Examining the Dispute Resolution Section Pro Bono Mediation Project," *Dispute Resolution* 23(1) (2008): 5–7.

2. Advisory Opinion of the North Carolina Dispute Resolution Commission, Opinion Number 08-14, http://www.nccourts.org/Courts/CRS/Councils/DRC/Documents/14-08_011609.pdf.

3. Lynn Gullick, e-mail message to NCBA Dispute Resolution Section Pro Bono Committee, March 25, 2008.

4. N.C. Gen. Stat. § 7A-38.2(c).

5. Both the RPC and the Standards were approved or promulgated by the North Carolina Supreme Court. Rule 8.3 of the RPC required an attorney to report certain violations of the RPC to the North Carolina State Bar. Standard III of the Standards required mediators to keep confidential all information learned during the course of a mediated settlement conference and, with certain limited exceptions, not disclose anything that occurred. None of the exceptions in Standard III addressed the scenario in question. As a result, if the attorney-mediator disclosed a violation of the RPC to the State Bar, then he or she had breached Standard III; but, if the attorney-mediator maintained the information as confidential pursuant to the mandate of Standard III, then he or she had breached Rule 8.3 of the RPC. Mediators who were not attorneys had no duty to report conduct of participants to the State Bar.

CHAPTER NINE

Assessments of ADR Use and Acceptance in North Carolina

*"My joy was boundless. I had learnt the true practice of law. I had
learnt to find out the better side of human nature and to enter men's
hearts. I realized that the true function of a lawyer was to unite parties
driven asunder. The lesson was so indelibly burnt into me that a large
part of my time during the twenty years of my practice as a lawyer was
occupied in bringing about private compromises in hundreds of cases.
I lost nothing thereby—not even money, certainly not my soul."*
—Mohandas K. Gandhi, *An Autobiography; Or,
The Story of My Experiments with Truth.*

Summary of ADR Evaluations, Surveys, and Studies

The commitment to deliberate experimentation and careful evaluation of
experimental programs are two of the distinguishing features of the way
in which alternative dispute resolution (ADR) has developed in North
Carolina. Each of the major dispute resolution processes introduced in the
state has followed a predictable pattern of growth and development. A pilot
program is established and implemented in a specific geographic area for
a specified amount of time. A well-designed evaluation is then conducted,
followed by review, revision (as appropriate), and eventual expansion on
a statewide basis. Court-ordered arbitration, mediated settlement conferences in superior court, mediation of workers' compensation claims, and
child custody and visitation mediation are the most visible forms of ADR
in North Carolina, and each of them has benefitted from this tripartite process of experimentation, assessment, and revision. Other dispute resolution
techniques used in the state, including community-based mediation and
summary jury trials, also have been the subject of systematic study.

What follows are descriptions of the major formal evaluations of dispute
resolution programs in North Carolina. With only a few exceptions, these
evaluations were conducted by the Institute of Government (IOG) of the

University of North Carolina at Chapel Hill (now the School of Government). It should be noted that in addition to the published studies summarized in this section, committees of the Dispute Resolution Committee (later the Dispute Resolution Section) of the North Carolina Bar Association (NCBA) studied and reported on each of the ADR techniques as they were introduced in North Carolina. The majority of the studies summarized below were initiated and sponsored by the NCBA Dispute Resolution Committee or Section, which raised grant funds of almost $1,000,000 to pay for them. A list of published studies appears at the end of this chapter.

Court-Ordered Arbitration

The first major NCBA-sponsored ADR initiative in North Carolina was the use of mandatory, non-binding arbitration for civil cases with an amount in controversy of $15,000 or less. In 1987, a pilot program was established in three judicial districts: the Third (Pitt, Craven, Pamlico, and Carteret counties); the Fourteenth (Durham County); and the Twenty-Ninth (Rutherford, Polk, Henderson, Transylvania, and McDowell counties). Funded through grants raised by Frank Laney, staff to the NCBA Dispute Resolution Committee, an IOG study of the pilot program randomly assigned half of the eligible cases to arbitration. The remaining cases served as a control group to measure the effects of the arbitration program. (A second control group also was created. It consisted of cases filed in 1985 that would have been eligible for the program if it had existed at the time.)

In early 1989, the IOG issued a favorable evaluation of the arbitration program. The report was endorsed by the NCBA and was submitted to the Supreme Court of North Carolina, which recommended that the court-ordered arbitration program be established on a permanent, statewide basis. The North Carolina General Assembly subsequently enacted the authorizing legislation.

The IOG study found that the pilot program significantly reduced the median disposition time for cases ordered to arbitration in each of the three pilot judicial districts. In addition, the number of trials was reduced in cases assigned to the arbitration program. Surveys of litigants indicated a higher level of satisfaction with the arbitration program than with the normal civil litigation procedure. Finally, the program received high marks from attorneys practicing in the three districts. More than two-thirds of the attorneys responding to the Institute's survey stated that the program should be continued and expanded.

Court-Ordered Mediation in Superior Court

In 1991, the General Assembly authorized the establishment of a pilot program of court-ordered mediation for civil actions filed in superior court. The Administrative Office of the Courts (AOC) initially selected eight judicial districts, comprising thirteen counties (Halifax, Cumberland, Bladen, Brunswick, Columbus, Orange, Chatham, Guilford, Forsyth, Stokes, Surry, Haywood, and Jackson) to participate in the pilot program. Four additional judicial districts (covering Mecklenburg, Buncombe, Wake, and Wayne counties) were subsequently added. In 1995, an IOG evaluation of the program focused on three of the pilot counties: Guilford, Cumberland, and Surry. Like the arbitration program evaluation, the mediation program study was funded by grants raised by Frank Laney. In each of the counties studied, a control group was established, using random assignment of cases filed between March 1992 and January 1993. A "preprogram" group of cases filed in the last nine months of 1989 was also identified for comparison. Litigants and attorneys were surveyed about the program as well. (Data on trial rates and disposition times in the other original pilot counties were also collected and analyzed.)

The IOG's report found that the mediated settlement conference program reduced median case disposition time from fifty-eight weeks (406 days) to about fifty-one weeks (360 days), a reduction of about ten percent. Both attorneys and litigants rated the program highly. However, the researchers concluded that the program did not reduce court workloads. Neither the overall settlement rate for contested cases nor the overall trial rate changed significantly. While the data seemed to show a decrease in litigation costs to the parties, the differences were not statistically significant. The report concluded with suggestions for improving the design and operation of the program.

Workers' Compensation Mediation

In 1993, the General Assembly authorized a pilot program of mediation in workers' compensation cases. The IOG assisted the North Carolina Industrial Commission with an evaluation of its pilot program. Randomly assigning cases filed in 1994, a group of 349 mediation cases and a control group of 590 cases were selected for study. The progress of both sets of cases was tracked through June 1996, using the Industrial Commission's records. Attorneys and mediators involved in the pilot program were also surveyed as part of the evaluation.

The Institute of Government report was released in early 1997. The study findings were similar in several respects to the IOG's earlier study of court-ordered arbitration and mediation in superior court. For example, the median disposition time for cases in the mediation group was considerably shorter than that in the control group (312 days compared to 372 days, a difference of over eight weeks). As in the previous studies, the attorneys surveyed were quite supportive of the pilot mediation program, as were the mediators themselves. Litigants were not surveyed. A majority of the survey respondents, both attorneys and mediators, felt that mediation improved the quality of agreements between litigants.

IOG researchers also found that the hearing rate for cases in the mediation group was 23.2 percent less than the hearing rate for the control group cases (27.2 percent vs. 35.4 percent of filed cases). The study noted that the mediation program achieved a reduction in the number of hearings in spite of the fact that a mediation conference was actually held in fewer than half of the mediation group cases.

Child Custody and Visitation Mediation

In 1983, the General Assembly established a two-year pilot child custody mediation program in Mecklenburg County. The pilot program was extended in 1985 for two more years. During the second pilot phase, the NCBA Committee on Dispute Resolution and Chief District Court Judge James E. Lanning were concerned that with no data to evaluate, the General Assembly might decide not to reauthorize the mediation program. Therefore, in cooperation with the local bench and bar, the Committee undertook to evaluate the child custody mediation program by interviewing mediation participants, family law attorneys, and district court judges in Mecklenburg County. Data was gathered in the spring of 1986. The participant survey was developed and conducted by Phil Rutledge of the Urban Institute at the University of North Carolina at Charlotte. The attorney survey was developed and conducted by Leslie Winner, Chair of the NCBA Dispute Resolution Committee Subcommittee on Other Procedures.

Overall, the parents, judges, and attorneys were satisfied with the process, the mediators, and the resulting agreements. Mediation had the effect of moving the attorneys to a more peripheral role during the negotiations, allowing the parents to take a more central role in reaching decisions about their children. Mediation decreased the time to resolution by about two months. The court saved trial costs, which were calculated to cover all of the program's out-of-pocket costs to the state plus a return of about fifty percent. The program also saved parties' attorney's fees.

Later, with funds provided by the Governor's Crime Commission, the North Carolina Administrative Office of the Courts conducted a study of the Child Custody and Visitation Mediation Program from October 1997 through December 1999. The study made use of four data sets: (1) court records of cases in two mediation program samples and two non-mediation program samples, amounting to 880 cases in all; (2) an exit survey of parties immediately after their participation in mediation sessions; (3) a follow-up survey of parents involved in the sample cases; and (4) survey responses from attorneys practicing family law in judicial districts where mediation was used.

The AOC's report, issued in 2000, concluded that the Child Custody and Visitation Mediation Program had reduced the rate of litigation, and possibly the re-litigation rate as well. However, the mediation program had no effect on median disposition times. In other words, mediation had not shortened the process. Parenting agreements produced in mediation were generally found to be more detailed than non-mediated consent orders, or orders resulting from trial. Finally, both parties and their attorneys rated the mediation program highly. Party satisfaction with the process remained high, even when a mediation agreement had not been reached.

Community-Based Mediation

Community-based mediation, conducted by local nonprofit dispute settlement centers around the state, has long been an essential part of the North Carolina ADR landscape. A large proportion of the centers' cases come from referrals by local district criminal courts. Most of the cases involve misdemeanor charges, often stemming from interpersonal disputes.

In 1991, the State Justice Institute provided a grant to MediatioNetwork to fund a study of the dispute settlement centers' programs. MediatioNetwork commissioned the Institute of Government to design and conduct the actual study.

The IOG study, released in April 1992, focused on three of the state's nineteen dispute settlement centers—those located in Durham, Iredell, and Henderson counties. These three counties were matched with similar counties that did not have community-based mediation programs: New Hanover, Davidson, and Rutherford counties. A total of 1,421 cases filed in 1990 that met the study criteria for mediation were examined. Interviews were conducted with a strategic sub-sample of parties who had been involved in mediation through the dispute settlement centers.

The IOG's study found that the mediation programs had the potential to divert a substantial number of cases away from trial, and it characterized mediation as "a valuable resource for disputants and the courts." However, the report noted that realizing the programs' potential would require more efficient and more rigorous intake procedures to increase the number of cases handled through mediation. The study further found that mediated agreements were usually complied with by both complainants and defendants. Both parties reported a high level of satisfaction with mediation, and there were few reports of parties being pressured or coerced to participate.

Summary Jury Trials

In 1987, the Supreme Court of North Carolina approved a pilot summary jury trial program for the state's superior courts. By the mid-1980s the summary jury trial had been recognized as a promising settlement technique in the federal courts, and many observers felt that the state courts also could benefit from its wider use. Three predominantly urban counties (Wake, Mecklenburg, and Buncombe) were chosen for the pilot program. The Dispute Resolution Committee of the North Carolina Bar Association asked the Duke University Private Adjudication Center (the Center) to evaluate the pilot program and to make recommendations regarding the use of summary jury trials in state courts.

Because the summary jury trial is a specialized ADR technique, the nature of the study was necessarily quite different from studies of more common forms of ADR, such as arbitration and mediation. The Center identified all seventeen of the summary jury trials held between 1987 and early 1991, collected data from the court records for each of the cases, and interviewed the attorneys, judges, and court personnel who had participated in them.

The Center report, published in May 1991, included detailed descriptions of each of the summary jury trial cases, as well as a thorough discussion of the many variations that are possible using the summary jury trial model. The report found that the summary jury trial represented an innovative and potentially powerful settlement technique for complex civil cases, but noted that its use in the state court system faced a number of serious obstacles. For example, a summary jury trial requires the active involvement of the trial judge. At the very least, the trial judge must be in a position to identify cases that are good candidates for a summary jury trial. Due to the large number of cases handled by superior court judges, identifying likely cases, the report noted, "may be compared to looking for a needle in a haystack." The Center report concluded by recommending the adoption of a permanent rule of practice, authorizing the use of summary jury trials in appropriate cases, and calling for increased efforts to educate lawyers and judges about the potential benefits of the summary jury trial.

Court-Ordered Mediation in Medical Malpractice Cases

In 1995, the Robert Wood Johnson Foundation funded a study of the use of court-ordered mediation in medical malpractice cases in North Carolina. The researchers collected data on over 300 medical malpractice cases filed in the North Carolina courts between 1991 and 1995 in which a mediated settlement conference order was issued. The researchers also observed more than fifty actual mediated settlement conferences and surveyed physicians, attorneys, and mediators involved in these medical malpractice cases. The study found that mediated settlement conferences led to settlement less often in medical malpractice cases than in other cases, but that in cases where the parties had a genuine interest in resolving the case through settlement, the mediated settlement conference seemed helpful. Consistent with most of the other North Carolina program evaluations, attorneys for both the plaintiff and the defendant endorsed the use of mediated settlement conferences in medical malpractice cases.

Published Studies of ADR Techniques in North Carolina:
A Select Bibliography

Stevens H. Clarke et al., *Court-Ordered Arbitration in North Carolina: An Evaluation of Its Effects* (Institute of Government, The University of North Carolina at Chapel Hill, 1989).

Stevens H. Clarke, *Court-Ordered Civil Case Mediation in North Carolina: An Evaluation of Its Effects* (Institute of Government, The University of North Carolina at Chapel Hill, 1995).

Stevens H. Clarke and Kelly A. McCormick, *Mediation in Workers' Compensation Cases: An Evaluation of Its Effects* (Institute of Government, The University of North Carolina at Chapel Hill, 1997).

North Carolina Bar Association, *Mandatory Child Custody Mediation Program in Mecklenburg County, A Study and Evaluation* (January 1987).

Laura F. Donnelly and Rebecca G. Ebron, The Child Custody and Visitation Mediation Program in North Carolina: An Evaluation of Its Implementation and Effects (North Carolina Administrative Office of the Courts, January 2000).

Stevens H. Clarke et al., Mediation of Interpersonal Disputes in North Carolina: An Evaluation (Institute of Government, The University of North Carolina at Chapel Hill, 1992).

Thomas B. Metzloff et al., Summary Jury Trials in the North Carolina State Court System (Duke University Private Adjudication Center, 1991).

Thomas B. Metzloff et al., Empirical Perspectives on Mediation and Malpractice, 60 Law & Contemp. Probs. 107 (1997).

ADR POLICIES AND PRACTICE

CHAPTER TEN

Policy Issues in the Use
of ADR in the Courts

*"The courts of this country should not be the places where
resolution of disputes begins. They should be the places
where the disputes end after alternative methods of resolving
disputes have been considered and tried."*
— United States Supreme Court Associate Justice
Sandra Day O'Connor

Policy issues concerning the conception, design, and implementation of settlement procedures in the courts of North Carolina have arisen over the past three decades as alternative dispute resolution (ADR) processes have been integrated into the court system. Some of these issues were identified, discussed, and debated in the early stages of design and development, while others, not viewed as issues initially, arose as the programs were being introduced and implemented. Many of the issues tackled by the North Carolina Bar Association (NCBA) and judicial personnel over the years are summarized here, in the hope that other states might learn from our experiences as they consider whether and how to include ADR procedures in their systems as settlement procedures.

Mandatory Versus Voluntary

One of the first debates about the development of ADR in the North Carolina court system revolved around the question of whether ADR procedures should be mandatory or voluntary. The NCBA's investigation into ADR began in 1983 with the creation of its Task Force on Dispute Resolution. In its 1985 report, the Task Force recommended that the NCBA sponsor an experiment with non-binding arbitration in small civil cases. (A similar court-annexed arbitration program was being explored in the United States District Court for the Middle District of North Carolina.)

The question of whether or not arbitration would be mandatory was both a case management issue and a philosophical issue. It was a case management issue because of the court's need to monitor and administer the arbitration program; and, it was a philosophical question about the nature of ADR processes. At that time many people believed that there was something inherent in ADR processes that militated against their inclusion in the court system as mandatory procedures. Those people felt that ADR procedures should remain voluntary in all respects.

Others felt that inclusion of arbitration on a voluntary basis would have minimal impact and result only in a state-sponsored public education effort about the benefits of ADR. They also argued that mandatory participation in a non-binding procedure was not a significantly coercive process. Ultimately, it was decided that the non-binding arbitration program would be mandatory, and the design of the subsequent mediation programs followed suit.

One unexpected benefit of requiring participation in ADR processes as settlement procedures was that the voluntary use of ADR rose sharply. Most observers believed that the mandatory use of ADR increased attorneys' exposure to the benefits of those processes, and, consequently, attorneys began to recommend ADR to their clients earlier in the dispute process. Initiating settlement conversations became easier as attorneys could always say to their opponents that "we might as well go ahead and do it; the court will order it later anyway." This rise in the use of ADR was particularly true of mediation. Attorneys experienced and reaped the benefits of early, facilitated settlement discussions and began to seek the negotiation process, which is the hallmark of mediation, over the more adjudicative process of arbitration.

Binding Versus Non-Binding Arbitration

One of the earliest debates about the use of ADR in the courts involved the question of whether binding or non-binding arbitration would be used in the NCBA's inaugural ADR program. Implicit in this debate was the issue of whether ADR would be used primarily as a case management tool to clear backlogs in court dockets or whether it would serve more as a settlement tool for the parties. The debate was an important one, but was resolved rather quickly for reasons that had little to do with the nature of ADR processes. The constitutional right to a jury trial in matters at law made it impossible to consider the use of mandatory, binding arbitration.

One result of the debate, however, was the resolve on the part of the NCBA Task Force and the then NCBA Dispute Resolution Committee to create ADR processes that fostered settlement discussions rather than processes that served as substitutes for trial. This basic decision was responsible for the linguistic shift that occurred later in the ADR community in which the phrase "settlement procedures" started being used synonymously with the more generally accepted "ADR techniques." Ironically, it often has been asserted that the creation of mandatory settlement procedures has given the courts several case management tools that indeed have enabled them to eliminate backlogs and speed up the disposition of civil litigation.

"Fitting the Forum to the Fuss"

One important policy issue that was hotly debated at the turn of the twenty-first century initially surfaced in North Carolina with the 1995 legislation authorizing statewide implementation of mediated settlement conferences in the superior courts. Prior to that legislation, all existing ADR programs employed a single ADR procedure, such as mediation in superior court or non-binding arbitration in district court. No program required anyone to choose among various ADR procedures.

In 1995, the NCBA's Dispute Resolution Section recommended to the Supreme Court Dispute Resolution Committee the creation in superior courts of a menu of ADR processes from which the parties could choose. The notion of a "menu approach" to ADR was not entirely new. Professor Frank Sander of Harvard Law School introduced the concept at a conference in 1976 where he talked about a "multi-door courthouse." Florida's circuit court mediation program, which served as a model for North Carolina's program, included both arbitration and mediation as ADR processes. Members of the North Carolina delegation that visited Florida in 1990 were instrumental in drafting the 1991 legislation for mediated settlement conferences in superior court, and they wrote the statute so that mediation would be the only choice available to litigants in superior court. They made this choice based upon their belief that non-binding arbitration would not be chosen over mediation and upon Florida's overwhelming success with mediation.

However, during the pilot program for superior court mediated settlement conferences between 1991 and 1995, many came to believe that "other settlement procedures" should be added. Attorneys occasionally expressed the belief that mediation was not appropriate for their clients, and that there should be a procedure available in which a third-party neutral could render opinions about the value of the case and make recommendations about how the case should be settled. The drafters of the 1995 statewide expansion legislation therefore included a paragraph that allowed the use of "other settlement procedures" rather than mediated settlement conferences, if the parties agreed and if the senior resident superior court judge authorized it.

One of the fiercest debates concerning the development of ADR in the North Carolina court system began in January of 1995 and continued for seven years. The debate did not center on whether or not a "menu" of ADR processes should be included. In fact, there appeared to be unanimity that there should be a range of choices in most court-related ADR programs (with the exception of child custody cases). Rather, the debate centered on the question of who should decide which ADR processes would be used by the parties.

In the early days of considering court-ordered ADR processes, the choice of one particular ADR process over another for a particular case was often called "fitting the forum to the fuss." The model for making that choice in the 1980s and early 1990s was the "multi-door courthouse" model imbedded in programs in Tulsa, Houston, and Washington, D.C. Those programs implemented a system of case management wherein the court, through its "ADR experts," decided which ADR procedures were appropriate for particular cases or for classes of cases. In those programs, the court, through its administrative structure and personnel, made the choice of which ADR process would be used. The notion that "the court knows best" was supported by the then-current wisdom that particular types of ADR procedures were best suited to particular types of cases.

The majority view in the literature in the mid-1990s was that some cases are more suited to arbitration than mediation, such as declaratory judgment actions or cases involving substantial statutory or constitutional questions. By 1995, the "current wisdom" about this matter was being questioned by those most active in the development of the mediation program in superior court in North Carolina. The drafters of the 1995 legislative proposal for statewide expansion of superior court mediation believed that the parties and their attorneys were best able to determine which cases and which parties were best served by a particular ADR form. And, based on their experience with the superior court pilot program, the drafters developed a firm belief that it was impossible to predict which cases would settle in mediation and which cases would not. The belief was that those closest to the case—the parties and their attorneys—were those best able to make that judgment. Furthermore, it was not the type of case, but the parties' attitudes about the case, that usually drove or hindered settlement.

The debate on this subject uncovered differences of opinion between attorneys, administrators, and law professors. Lawyers took the position that the parties and their attorneys are in the best position to know which process is appropriate for their case. Law professors and administrators, on the other hand, took the approach that court procedures should be governed by the chief judicial official involved with case management. They were more inclined to believe that certain types of cases are appropriate to some ADR models and not to others. Judges were often split in their approach to this subject. The majority, however, decided on the approach advanced by the attorneys, based largely on their experiences during the mediated settlement conference pilot program that it was impossible to predict which cases would settle and which would not. Thus, since 1995, there has been a trend in the development of ADR in North Carolina toward creating a menu of settlement procedures from which the parties and their attorneys may choose the process they think is most appropriate for their case.

Which ADR Process Should Be the Default Procedure?

Closely related to the question of who should choose the ADR procedure used by the parties is the question of which ADR process should be designated as the default position within a menu of approaches. Driving the notion that a default proceeding is needed in the design of a menu approach to ADR was the belief that cases would languish in the court system if all decisions were left up to the parties. It was decided that the use of a default mechanism in a menu system is crucial to moving cases toward disposition and that it serves as an important case management tool.

If there has to be a default settlement procedure, which process should occupy that position? Heated debates have occurred on this topic. Once again, the debate falls along professional lines. Lawyers tend to suggest that mediation should be the default mechanism, while administrators tend to like arbitration.

Lawyers argue that mediated settlement conferences, or facilitated negotiations, are the least restrictive and least adjudicatory of ADR processes because they focus on direct negotiations between the parties. In other words, the focus should be not on preparing for a hearing, whether that hearing is abbreviated, as in arbitration, or not. Rather, the emphasis should be on direct negotiations and settlement. Administrators, on the other hand, tend to like the quicker time frames that the non-binding arbitration program operates on, believing that the goal of case disposition is better accomplished by arbitration than by mediation.

The resolution statistics for each program do not suggest a serious advantage of one program over the other. Studies have shown that 71 percent of cases resolve in district court arbitration,[1] while 68 percent of cases resolve in superior court mediation.[2] The overall disposition rate in the two programs is also comparable. Nearly 95 percent of cases in the court-ordered arbitration program[3] and 91 percent of cases in the mediated settlement conference program[4] resolved prior to trial.

Through the years, lawyers representing the NCBA in discussions regarding establishment of a default settlement procedure have argued that the two settlement processes are fundamentally different. Arbitration is an adjudicatory process; mediation is a negotiation-based process. Anecdotal evidence indicates that practicing attorneys tend to favor the latter over the former as a tool for themselves and their clients. Mediation thus has been promoted by the bar as the preferred default technique and has become the default ADR process for the programs that use a menu approach.

Exclusion by Case Type

Another important question in the design of court-ordered dispute resolution programs in North Carolina has been whether certain types of cases should be excluded from a particular ADR program. Sometimes the answer was based on practicalities, and sometimes the answer was based on philosophical grounds. This issue first emerged during the development of the district court's non-binding arbitration program between 1985 and 1989. Included in that program were cases involving civil litigation with amounts in controversy not greater than $15,000. Excluded from the program were cases considered to be "fast-tracked" in the existing court system and claims that could not be resolved easily with a monetary award, such as family law cases and cases involving injunctive relief. Complex cases resulting in significant findings and complex judgments also were excluded, making court-ordered arbitration an ADR program for the resolution of small money damages claims.

The question of inclusion or exclusion of cases based on case type became more complicated with the development of the superior court Mediated Settlement Conference (MSC) Program in 1992. The committee that drafted rules for the MSC Program discovered a fairly long list of exclusions by case type in the Florida program that served as its model. After considerable discussion and debate, and based partly on Florida's experience, in which many of the excluded cases were settled before trial, the committee decided to propose a minimal number of exclusions.

When the initial MSC rules were proposed, the only exclusions were claims for extraordinary relief, such as petitions for writs of habeas corpus and mandamus. In 1995, the rules were amended to exclude appeals from motor vehicle drivers' revocations as well. By that date, the general view was that claims involving injunctive relief and issues of law, as well as claims for monetary relief, could be negotiated to resolution based upon the parties' underlying interests. Exclusions by case type continue to be few in number.

Another example of the inclusion/exclusion by case type issue occurred in the district court settlement procedures program for equitable distribution cases. In such cases, judges are frequently called upon to order mediation in situations where there have been allegations of domestic violence. A substantial body of literature has developed on the issue of mediating cases in domestic violence situations. Many authors and organizations have come out against mediating in that context, arguing that the abused spouse occupies an inherently weakened negotiating position and cannot compete on a level playing field. On the national level, it has been accepted in some circles that a party who has made an allegation of domestic violence should not be ordered to attend mediation. North Carolina has taken a slightly different view on this subject.

Acknowledging that safety is a primary concern and that allegations of domestic violence should be taken seriously, while also recognizing that victims of domestic violence often reach negotiated settlements after having secured proper advice and legal representation, the rules for the district court program do not require judges to exclude family financial mediation where domestic violence is alleged. Instead, allegations of domestic violence are considered valid grounds upon which a party may seek to dispense with mediation. Rather than making a blanket rule, the court may decide on a case-by-case basis whether ordering mediation is appropriate in the face of an allegation of domestic violence. The decision for the court is whether the parties are empowered enough to participate on a level field, not simply whether there has been an allegation of abuse.

Who Should Administer ADR Programs?

An issue that had to be resolved in the design and development of ADR in the court system was the question of deciding who would administer the programs, issue orders, and enforce deadlines. For the most part, that question has been answered in North Carolina by designating the chief judicial official in each district to supervise the operation of ADR programs.

In the child custody and visitation mediation program and the court-ordered arbitration program, the chief district court judge is the responsible official. In superior court, the senior resident superior court judge is the chief official, and in the clerk's program, it is the clerk of court. In the family financial settlement procedures program in district court, however, a variation has been created. Inasmuch as case management authority for equitable distribution cases varies from district to district, and frequently is handled by a judge other than the chief district court judge (or by many different judges during the life of the case), all district court judges have the authority to enter orders for settlement procedures in such cases.

A related issue was the question of whether ADR processes should be mandated uniformly across the state, or whether each district through its chief judicial officer would be allowed to pick and choose the cases ordered to dispute resolution procedures. On this issue, attorneys and administrators were more closely aligned. Both groups felt that all eligible cases should be ordered to ADR processes, so that settlement procedures would become the norm for lawyers throughout the court system and case management systems would be strengthened. They argued that the provision in the court's rules allowing judges to exempt matters on a case-by-case basis afforded the judiciary sufficient authority and discretion to make exceptions.

However, in superior court in particular, some judges saw this idea as an erosion of their authority. They tended to prefer rules that gave them the sole discretion as to whether or not a case would be sent to mediation or other ADR procedure. This view resulted in a hodgepodge of administrative processes throughout the state for the first decade of the superior court MSC Program. In some counties, all cases were ordered to mediation. In other counties, the judge ordered settlement processes only where one party requested it. In still others, the court would not order an ADR process unless both parties requested such an order.

The view that all cases should be ordered to some ADR procedure ultimately carried the day. In 2006, the Supreme Court changed its rule to require that all cases be ordered to mediation or other settlement procedures in equitable distribution cases in district court and in all civil cases in superior court.

Qualification and Selection of Neutrals

North Carolina began its ADR experiments in civil courts with non-binding arbitration. It was always assumed that the neutrals (arbitrators in that system) would be attorneys. Thus, no great thought was given to opening up the qualification process to anyone other than lawyers. But with the advent of the mediated settlement conference program in superior court in 1992, the issue of the qualification and selection of neutrals emerged with full force.

The first set of rules dealing with the qualifications of mediators in the MSC Program clearly authorized only attorneys to be certified as mediators, although anyone could be selected by the parties if the court approved the selection. There was a strong feeling among the attorney and judge members of the drafting committee that such a strategy was necessary to win the approval of the bar and the bench for a brand new and potentially controversial program. Non-lawyer members of the drafting committee and lawyers who had been trained in the community mediation programs had misgivings about this decision, but at the time, the need to have this new program accepted by the constituents of the court system was the paramount consideration. While some believed that lawyers would be more easily supervised and disciplined by the courts because they were members of the North Carolina State Bar and deemed to be "officers of the court," others viewed this as a violation of fundamental fairness and sought legislation to allow non-attorneys to be certified as mediators. Ultimately, the rules of the Supreme Court were amended to make it possible for non-lawyers to qualify as mediators, and those rules were later changed to expand the ways in which non-attorneys may qualify for certification.

There continues to be much debate nationally about proper credentialing for mediators. Certain groups within the ADR profession have made clear policy statements against professional and educational prerequisites for certification. Non-lawyers have been well represented in the ranks of arbitrators for decades, particularly in the area of voluntary, binding arbitration. In the field of arbitration, non-lawyer arbitrators with subject matter expertise are often chosen to render substantive decisions in such areas. In mediation, it is not as clear that subject matter expertise is, or should be, related to mediator competence.

The selection of the neutral is another important issue in the design of any ADR program, whether the neutral be an arbitrator, mediator, or neutral evaluator. Initially, the rules for non-binding arbitration in North Carolina allowed the parties to choose their arbitrator from among those who had been approved for such service by the chief district court judge. The MSC Program in superior court provides that the court will appoint mediators only in the event that the parties do not choose within a certain time, or cannot agree upon the selection of the mediator. This "party selection" preference was written into the statute and rules authorizing MSCs by the drafting committee, which believed that part of the success of the model program in Florida was the fact that the parties could choose their own mediator.

Another issue that grew out of the pilot program experience for MSCs in superior court was the method by which the court chooses a mediator in the event that the parties are unable to or do not choose a mediator within the time allowed. During the pilot program some mediators complained that senior resident superior court judges were using a "short list" of mediators (who they deemed especially qualified) from which to select the neutral.

Most of the judges who used a "short list" justified it on the basis that they wanted to have confidence in the mediators they appointed. Mediators not on the list complained that they were not given an equal chance to prove their merit, even though they had been certified under standards set by the Supreme Court rules implementing the program. Those mediators also believed that the "short list" method of judicial appointment was discriminatory to those less well known in the bar, particularly women and minority attorneys. Although the court appointment rules were changed to prescribe a random judicial selection process, the phenomenon of "short listing" by judges has not completely disappeared.

Implicit in the question of mediator qualification is the issue of how a system, which depends upon a cadre of private providers of mediation services (as opposed to a system of state-hired and state-supervised mediators), ensures the quality of the mediators. The decision of the drafters of the MSC Program was to rely upon the experience of the mediators, their training in mediation, and, most importantly, the "market system" of selecting mediators. The theory supporting this "market approach" is that the parties will choose mediators who have a good track record and who have built a measure of respect among those who are doing the selecting. In addition to the training requirement for mediators, the most important quality-control device in the MSC Program is the ability of the parties to select their own mediator.

One of the concerns of the NCBA's Dispute Resolution Section regarding the tendency of judges to appoint mediators from a "short list" was that it undercut this method of insuring qualified mediators. If judges appoint only those they deem most qualified, the parties will be less inclined to exercise their right to select a mediator. This would also place more of a burden upon judges to exercise supervision, something that they have neither the time nor the training to do effectively. Thus, the Section has opposed selection of mediators from a judicial "short list" on the grounds of fairness and as an incentive to the parties to select their own mediators. As the appointing courts have moved away from using a short-list approach, the percentage of cases in which parties select their mediators has steadily risen, providing the kind of quality-control system that the drafters intended.

The establishment, in 1995, of the Dispute Resolution Commission (DRC) was an important step in improving the effectiveness of mediators. The DRC is charged with certifying and decertifying mediators and with regulating their conduct. Standards of Professional Conduct for certified mediators were recommended by the DRC in 1997 and later promulgated by the Supreme Court of North Carolina. The North Carolina Standards echo the model standards of conduct written by Robert A. Baruch Bush, a professor at the Hofstra University School of Law, for the National Institute of Dispute Resolution.

Complaints made to the DRC about mediators have come mostly from administrators and litigants. The major complaint of administrators is that some mediators do not convene settlement conferences within the time frame set by the court and do not file their Reports of Mediator in a timely fashion. Disciplinary action has been taken by the DRC for those reasons. The DRC remains concerned that mediators understand the importance of the administrative functions that are built into their role under the Supreme Court rules.

Litigants have made occasional complaints about mediator behavior that they considered to be coercive. Most of those complaints have been resolved in favor of the mediator based on factual grounds. However, one mediator was sanctioned for making judgmental remarks that demonstrated a complete loss of neutrality. Early disciplinary action by the DRC occurred in the family law context in which a mediator later served as legal counsel for an individual in a divorce against his spouse when she had mediated for the two of them. Complaints about mediators have been on the rise in recent years, but most of them have been resolved on a factual basis in favor of the mediator. It is now a policy of the DRC that most instances of discipline decided by the DRC will be written up in the form of an Advisory Opinion, so that all mediators can learn from the experiences of others.

Currently, no mandatory continuing mediator education (CME) requirements have been enacted by the DRC, although Standard I of the Standards of Professional Conduct for Mediators (Standards) requires that mediators be and remain competent in the skills of dispute resolution. The rules of the Supreme Court in all programs provide that any requirements for continuing education that are adopted by the DRC in the future must be followed by all mediators. It undoubtedly would be an incentive to the adoption of mandatory CME requirements if CME programs could be designed in such a way as to also qualify for continuing legal education (CLE) credits before the State Bar. Without incentives of this type or a significant increase in the number of serious complaints about mediator competence, CME is likely to remain a voluntary process into the near future.

Financing ADR Programs

When the NCBA began its experiment in non-binding arbitration, it did so with the legislature's prohibition against using state funds for program implementation. Over half a million dollars was raised by the NCBA to fund the operation and study of the pilot program. When the program proved successful, the 1989 General Assembly approved legislation to expand non-binding arbitration statewide, as funds became available. By 2007, the program was close to statewide implementation and cost approximately $1,000,000 each fiscal year. About 50 percent of the cost was allocated to administrative personnel to assist with the scheduling of hearings and handling of paperwork, and the other 50 percent was needed to pay the arbitrators a fee of $75 per case for conducting and deciding the arbitration.

Because of the ever-increasing cost of the arbitration program and the success of the superior court program of party-paid mediation, the General Assembly decided to require that the parties pay an equal share of the arbitrator's fee.

Before 1991, little thought was given to the idea that neutrals and court-ordered ADR programs could be funded by the parties themselves. ADR programs throughout the nation were publicly financed. The Florida model studied by the NCBA's drafting committee broke that mold, establishing a model of litigant financing in which the parties themselves (instead of the taxpayers) pay for the neutrals who assist them as mediators, arbitrators, or evaluators.

North Carolina's superior court mediated settlement conference pilot program ran from 1991 to 1995, and the legislation authorizing it specified that it would not be financed through the use of public funds. The NCBA once again raised about $500,000 to pay for the administration and study of the pilot, but the parties were required to pay the mediator's fee. There was great skepticism about the "party-pay" method of financing. However, because the pilot was only a test, it was decided that it could move forward. Some court officials today still adhere to the philosophy that any program ordered by the court should be paid for by the state, as a part of the financing of the General Courts of Justice. As of this writing, North Carolina, like most other states, faces a budget shortfall, and the projections for improvement for the short term are not optimistic. As a result, nationally the notion of party-pay financing for ADR programs is being examined anew. Those who use the court system may increasingly bear the cost by way of additional court fees.

The study conducted on the MSC Program during the pilot phase indicated that the program saved the litigants money, but that the savings were not statistically significant. However, the study also demonstrated that litigants did not spend more than in traditional litigation, even though they were bearing the costs of the mediated settlement conference.[5] The only logical explanation is that savings realized as a result of mediated settlements offset the cost of paying for a share of the mediator's fee. Whatever the explanation, complaints about payment of mediators by the parties have been few, and party-pay financing enabled the superior court program to spread to every judicial district within two years of statewide authorization in 1995.

The notion of party-pay financing for ADR programs has been very controversial in this state. Lawyers and administrators have had wide-ranging and often contentious discussions about the issue. However, even proponents of party-pay financing recognize that ethical dilemmas arise for mediators who operate within this system. Pressures that are not brought to bear on court officials (who are paid by the state) are often brought to bear upon mediators, and certainly may be felt by arbitrators as they are party paid. Neutrals are currently feeling pressure from attorneys not to conduct settlement conferences in cases that they believe will not settle. There are also pressures on mediators to excuse from attendance persons who are required to attend the settlement conference. There is an implied threat that refusal to excuse attendance will mean few selections to mediate cases in the future. These pressures raise ethical issues inherent in the party-pay method of financing that are real and should not be overlooked.

Another issue that has arisen as a result of the party-pay method of financing is the way in which indigent litigants are handled by the court system. One way of resolving this issue is to not require settlement procedures for those cases in which at least one party is indigent. Believing, however, that there was no good policy reason for excluding indigents from a useful settlement process, the drafters of the MSC Program devised ways in which indigent litigants could participate in those programs without having to bear the financial burden of the process. The North Carolina Industrial Commission handles this issue by requiring defendant employers or their insurers to pay the entire fee of the mediator, and then to deduct the plaintiff's portion from any settlement proceeds paid by the defendant to the plaintiff, or from any award that ultimately may be due. Otherwise, the defendant or its insurer bears the expense.

In the MSC Program, the problem was handled by requiring mediators to forgive that portion of the fee that was charged to the indigent litigants. In the district court settlement procedures program in equitable distribution cases, additional methods were devised, including a cost-shifting mechanism between the parties in the event that one party is able to pay and the other party is not. Mediators have been called upon to bear the burden of pro bono work built into the rules, but the number of cases in which indigent litigants have appeared has not been great, and the responsibility for uncompensated service has been shared by certified mediators throughout the state.

Attendance at ADR Processes

Related to the issue of whether court-ordered ADR processes are voluntary or involuntary in nature is the question of what the parties are required to do when they participate in those procedures. In North Carolina's court-ordered ADR programs, the parties are only required to attend. They must appear, but they are not required to present evidence, to negotiate, or to reach agreements unless they deem it in their best interest to do so. The drafters of the original pilot program rules for superior court mediation intentionally deleted the requirement in the Florida mediation program that the parties not only attend, but "negotiate in good faith." That change was made in recognition of two things: (1) that the "good faith negotiation" requirement in Florida had spawned additional litigation over who had or had not negotiated in good faith during mediation; and (2) that mediation should be a voluntary process, not a coercive one.

A different type of attendance question arose in the MSC Program in the superior courts and in workers' compensation cases, where insurance companies rather than parties have the ability to settle insured claims. To get the attendance of the real parties in interest (those who can make a decision about the settlement of litigation), it was decided that insurance representatives should be required to be present. How that could be accomplished in North Carolina was a source of some debate, the result being that the 1991 and 1995 legislation authorizing MSCs in superior court (and the 1994 legislation authorizing MSCs in workers' compensation cases) required attendance by insurance company representatives at the mediated settlement conference. Although this has greatly affected the practice of insurance companies, challenges to the legislation have not materialized. The reasons for that fact are subject to debate, but insurance companies appear to have found it in their interest to participate fully in the MSC Program.

Style of Mediation

It has often been said that mediation in a court-ordered context conducted with lawyers present is not true mediation. This view is bolstered by the perception that in superior court mediation the parties are frequently separated from each other and the mediator often conducts "shuttle" mediation. There has been great debate within the mediation community about whether this is good mediation and, if so, how a mediator can perform his or her services effectively and with due regard to the Standards.

It is generally accepted among superior court mediators that the style of mediation in that program is decidedly different from mediations conducted in other contexts. But most believe that this is not the result of being taught that the "shuttle diplomacy" style is a better way of mediating. Rather, the view is that "shuttle" mediation results from the nature of the claims that trial court mediators are called upon to mediate. As with mediation in the child custody and visitation context, the nature of the claim often dictates a different set of techniques and different styles. Civil litigation commonly involves insured claims in which money is the currency of settlement. In that context, the parties usually seek the sanctity and safety of private sessions, so that they can discuss their bottom and top lines, how to move toward settlement, and how to make proposals within their range of acceptable outcomes. Such a setting is very different from a family and divorce context, in which the parties are seeking to work out ways to raise their children together while separated or divorced.

Another criticism of the type of mediation that occurs in superior court

MSCs is that it is "evaluative" as opposed to "facilitative." Superior court mediators tend to agree that the mediation process is inherently evaluative, in the sense that a great deal of attention is paid to risk (or case) analysis. The fact that attorneys are present (whose job is at least in part to remind their clients of the "value" of their case), and that many of these claims arise between strangers and are settled only through the payment of money, means that the mediation-negotiating process is inherently evaluative.

On the other hand, the prevailing view among superior court mediators is that they should not be "directive" in their approach toward mediation. The Standards clearly prohibit this kind of approach. However, many of the attorneys who represent clients in MSCs want their mediators to tell their clients "what their case is worth." In recognition of this fact, the NCBA's Dispute Resolution Section has long advocated neutral evaluation as an optional procedure in the menu of settlement procedures available to litigants, and that mechanism has been included in the menu of ADR options available in superior court. Litigants who want a more directive approach as an aid to settling their case now have a choice of approaches.

Impartiality and the Courts

The literature of mediation often discusses the fact that it is difficult for a mediator to be impartial when he or she is reporting to, and is effectively an arm of, the court. The drafters of the mediation programs in North Carolina have been careful to address this criticism and have done so in part by making it a violation of the Standards to include any information in the mediator's report to the court that is not statistical in nature. Therefore, in North Carolina, it is unacceptable for a mediator to report to the court on the behavior of the parties other than the facts of whether or not they attended the conference, whether they settled the case, how long the negotiation took place, and how much the mediation cost the parties.[6]

Should ADR Be Required Before a Lawsuit May Be Filed?

The drafters of the settlement programs in North Carolina believed that once cases are in the court system, every effort should be made to ensure that parties have engaged in some bona fide settlement effort. That, of course, does not address the question of whether there should also be a pre-litigation ADR requirement. In other words, should one have to get his or her "ADR ticket punched" before being allowed to file a suit in court?

Some people have suggested that, in addition to creating ADR procedures within the court system, the goals of ADR would best be served by requiring some form of dispute resolution before a lawsuit can be filed. There are many responses to this issue, a number of which have been discussed from time to time by members of the North Carolina Bar Association.

As a philosophical matter, it is hard to understand why people who are seeking injunctive relief or other lawful process should have to wait for an ADR process to take place before they may file a civil lawsuit. As a practical matter, court-ordered settlement processes now in operation are generally handled within a well-prescribed and well-known structure administered by the judges of this state. If pre-litigation ADR processes were required, the certification that there has been pre-litigation mediation or other ADR process would fall squarely upon the shoulders of the clerks of court who have little experience with and little knowledge of ADR. For a pre-litigation ADR requirement to succeed, the clerks of court across the state will have to be educated about ADR processes and brought into the ADR administrative framework.

Another practical matter has arisen with regard to the wisdom of requiring pre-litigation ADR. Many mediators and litigators have experienced significant frustration with mediations conducted either pre-suit or early in the litigation process. The chief source of that frustration is the fact that the parties do not have the information necessary to make informed decisions. The information usually uncovered in the discovery phase of the litigation process is not present. Whether this is a reason to be cautious about requiring pre-litigation ADR remains to be seen, but it is a practical reality that needs resolving when the possibility of requiring pre-litigation ADR is discussed.

The North Carolina General Assembly enacted two pieces of legislation at the turn of the century that adopt the pre-litigation mediation requirement: the pre-litigation mediation of farm nuisance cases and the pre-litigation mediation of Year 2000 (Y2K) cases (described in Chapter 35). With regard to the farm nuisance mediation requirement, the NCBA Dispute Resolution Section took a position against the pre-litigation condition, believing that there would be greater safeguards if the case were first filed and then taken through the superior court MSC process. However, there is a public perception (or perhaps a legislative perception) that mediation and other ADR methods are a great way to keep cases out of court, and that the requirement of pre-litigation mediation is an effective way to achieve that result. Since that time, the legislature has created two other pre-litigation mediation programs for use in electrical supplier territorial disputes and early settlement of insured claims (also described in Chapter 35). The effect of pre-litigation mediation is largely unknown as none of these programs have been used enough to have a measurable impact.

The question remains whether the NCBA and other forces in the North Carolina court system should seek to reduce the number of conflicts that reach the court by requiring pre-litigation ADR, or whether similar goals should be accomplished by building ADR processes within the dispute resolution structures of clubs, businesses, professional organizations, and other societal associations. Whatever the method, the goal is the same: to make the courts of North Carolina a place of last, rather than first, resort.

Should an Attorney-Mediator Report Misconduct?

At the 2005 annual meeting of the NCBA's Dispute Resolution Section, a question was raised as to whether a lawyer-mediator should report to the State Bar improper conduct of a fellow attorney discovered in the course of mediation. A mediator bears a duty of confidentiality under the Standards promulgated by the North Carolina Supreme Court through the DRC. However, a lawyer has a duty pursuant to Rule 8.3 of the Rules of Professional Responsibility (also approved by the Supreme Court) to report conduct by an attorney who violates those Rules. A lawyer-mediator, therefore, was faced with the conflicting duties of confidentiality and responsibility to help preserve the legal profession's high standards of conduct.

After four years of debate, the DRC recommended to the State Bar that it create an exception to Rule 8.3 (in addition to the two exceptions that were already in existence) that would free attorney-mediators from the obligation to report improper conduct in a mediation. The State Bar debated the issue for a year. In the summer of 2010, the Bar voted to create the exception recommended by the DRC, but with one amendment. The rule for lawyer-mediators now is that they are under no duty to report Rules violations discovered in mediation unless such reporting is permitted by Standard III (Confidentiality) of the Standards. Standard III permits the reporting of bodily harm or threats of bodily harm that occur in mediation. This rule change is a testament to the success of North Carolina's court-ordered mediation programs and the value lawyers now see in mediation and to those who serve as mediators in our courts. (See Chapter 11.)

NOTES

1. *North Carolina Courts 2000–01 Statistical and Operational Summary of the Judicial Branch of Government*, N.C. Administrative Office of the Courts, pp. 51–53; *North Carolina Courts 1999–2000 Statistical and Operational Summary of the Judicial Branch of Government*, N.C. Administrative Office of the Courts, pp. 50–52.

2. Report of the N.C. Dispute Resolution Commission for Fiscal Year 2000–01; Report of the N.C. Dispute Resolution Commission for Fiscal Year 1999–2000.

3. *North Carolina Courts 2000–01 Statistical and Operational Summary of the Judicial Branch of Government, supra* note 1; *North Carolina Courts 1999–2000 Statistical and Operational Summary of the Judicial Branch of Government, supra* note 1.

4. Stevens H. Clarke et al., *Court-Ordered Civil Case Mediation in North Carolina: An Evaluation of Its Effects* (Institute of Government, The University of North Carolina at Chapel Hill, 1995).

5. *Id.* at 45–46.

6. *See* Willis v. Trenton Memorial Association, 166 F.3d 337 (4th Cir. 1998).

CHAPTER ELEVEN

Professionalism and Ethical Considerations in Dispute Resolution

"To me, the essence of professionalism is a commitment to develop one's skills to the fullest and to apply that responsibly to the problems at hand. Professionalism requires adherence to the highest ethical standards of conduct and a willingness to subordinate narrow self-interest in pursuit of the more fundamental goal of public service."
— United States Supreme Court Associate Justice
Sandra Day O'Connor

Mediation, arbitration, and other methods of alternative dispute resolution (ADR) have been accepted in North Carolina and throughout the United States as effective and often preferable methods of resolving conflicts. A primary reason that ADR has been so widely embraced, not only in community settings but also by attorneys, the courts, and governmental agencies, is the high degree of professionalism demonstrated by the mediators, arbitrators, and other neutrals who have guided these processes over the past thirty years.[1] Because ADR has evolved largely as part of the court system, the standards of conduct for ADR professionals in many ways reflect traditional ethical standards established for attorneys and judges. This chapter briefly examines the foundations of professionalism in North Carolina's ADR community and describes in more detail the ethical standards established for the state's mediators and arbitrators.

Defining Professionalism

Professionals in any field are individuals who have a high level of training, knowledge, and skill. They use their expertise and independent judgment to solve problems and attain goals. "Professionalism" can be defined as the specific style of behavior expected of a professional. It encompasses not just a foundation of knowledge and competence, but also the demonstration of reason, maturity, and good character in carrying out one's tasks. Some of the qualities associated with professionalism include honesty, reliability, respect, discretion, perseverance, and appropriate verbal and non-verbal communication. In its ideal form, professionalism involves a strong sense of personal responsibility and adherence to a core set of positive values that guide actions and decision making. For the vast majority of ADR practitioners in North Carolina, those core values are expressed in the Standards of Professional Conduct for Mediators and the Canons of Ethics for Arbitrators.

Professionalism in North Carolina's Legal Community and the Development of Standards for ADR Practitioners

The North Carolina legal community historically has placed a strong emphasis on professionalism, as reflected in adoption by the North Carolina State Bar and approval by the North Carolina Supreme Court of The Rules of Professional Conduct, which govern attorney behavior. Similarly, the state's judges have long been guided by The Code of Judicial Conduct.[2] As ADR programs became more common in court proceedings in the early 1990s, and especially with the success of the Mediated Settlement Conference Program, the North Carolina Bar Association and others in the legal community recognized a need to establish a separate set of ethical standards to govern the emerging mediation profession. Although many lawyers acted as mediators, the role was different from the role of legal counsel. It included such familiar and fundamental principles as competency, confidentiality, and avoidance of conflicts of interest, but it also required dedication to several distinctly different precepts, including impartiality, self-determination of the parties, and the separation of mediation from legal and other professional advice. A new and separate set of ethical guidelines for mediator conduct clearly was needed.

As the bar and the (then) newly created North Carolina Dispute Resolution Commission (Commission or DRC) struggled to delineate ethical requirements for the emerging profession of mediation, it also became clear that the state should establish a set of rules that would assure professionalism in the conduct of court-annexed arbitrations under North Carolina General Statutes Section 7A-37.1 (also known as court-ordered arbitration). The Code of Ethics for Arbitrators adopted jointly by the American Bar Association and the American Arbitration Association served as a roadmap in this process, along with the North Carolina Code of Judicial Conduct and the set of standards for mediator conduct implemented by the DRC.

The remaining sections of this chapter discuss the ethical standards by which mediator and arbitrator conduct is measured in North Carolina and describe the processes that led to their adoption.

Standards of Professional Conduct for Mediators

Introduction

The DRC first approved Standards of Professional Conduct for Mediators (Standards) on May 10, 1996. After soliciting comments from certified mediators around the state, the DRC recommended the Standards to the Supreme Court of North Carolina for adoption. They were approved on December 30, 1998. The Standards specifically address the following aspects of conduct and/or mediator responsibility: competency, impartiality, confidentiality, consent, self-determination, separation of the role of mediator from the giving of other professional advice, conflicts of interest, and the need to protect the integrity of the mediation process. Upon recommendation of the DRC, the Standards have been revised six times since their initial adoption by the Court: June 1999, August 2001, October 2004, January 2006, February 2010, and October 2011.

History

The development of North Carolina's Standards of Professional Conduct for Mediators proved to be a long-term project. Crafting the Standards was, by all accounts, a journey marked by false starts, multiple detours, and the pain of starting over midway through the process.

In 1993, the North Carolina Bar Association created a new Dispute Resolution Section as an outgrowth of its Dispute Resolution Committee. The new section was formed in response to the success of the MSC Program and the rising number of attorneys seeking mediator certification. J. Anderson "Andy" Little was named the Section's first chair, and as one of his first acts he established a Committee on Ethics and Professionalism. The Committee was created in recognition of the fact that the MSC Program was helping to create a new profession. The objective of this Committee placed it squarely on the path with other states (Florida and Texas) and organizations (the American Bar Association, the American Arbitration Association, and the Society of Professionals in Dispute Resolution) seeking to develop an ethics code for mediators. The Section appointed five of its members to spearhead North Carolina's consideration of mediator ethics: Robert "Bob" A. Beason (chair), J. Dickson Phillips III, Brenda D. Unti, Professor Walker J. Blakey, and Frank C. Laney. Little did this group know that their discussions, begun at their first meeting in November 1993, would last more than five years.

The Committee began its work by focusing on efforts already underway in Florida. Years earlier, members of the North Carolina Bar Association's

Dispute Resolution Committee (the precursor to the Dispute Resolution Section) had traveled to Florida to talk with court officials and mediators about the state's Circuit Civil Mediation Program and Family Mediation Program, which would later serve as models for North Carolina's Mediated Settlement Conference Program. At their November meeting, members of the Committee on Ethics and Professionalism were assigned responsibility for reviewing and reporting on various aspects of Florida's ethical requirements for mediators, comparing them with those of other states and assessing whether they would be effective in North Carolina. There was also discussion about whether North Carolina's Standards should be merely aspirational, in light of the DRC's statutory charge to regulate mediator conduct.

In the summer of 1994, additional members were added to the Committee. The group also began to look closely at Texas' standards for mediator conduct. Using the Florida and Texas materials as a springboard, the Committee was able to produce draft Standards by the spring of 1995. The draft was presented to Reagan H. Weaver (then Chair of the Dispute Resolution Section) and the Section's Council.

While the Council considered the draft, debate continued within the Committee and the larger dispute resolution community in North Carolina. There was much discussion about self-determinative aspects of the mediation process and about facilitative versus evaluative mediation, the latter discussion reflecting a debate occurring nationally. Many North Carolina mediators wanted to be able to offer an evaluation of a case when the parties requested or demanded it. After all, they argued, lawyers were accustomed to neutrals evaluating their cases, and they expected the mediator to do so when asked.

At a meeting of the Committee held sometime later, Andy Little suggested that the Committee consider the works of Robert A. Baruch Bush, a professor of alternative dispute resolution at the Hofstra University School of Law. Professor Bush, who had written extensively on the mediation process and mediator ethics, was a strong proponent of facilitative mediation. Bush argued that mediators should be about the work of supporting—not supplanting—the parties' discussions and decision making. He termed this "the practice of fostering empowerment in mediation." Professor Bush also argued forcefully for what he termed the "recognition effect" in mediation. By this he meant that when the parties are willing, a mediator should try to help them transform their current relationship and the confines of their dispute. Transformation, he suggested, would occur as the parties, with their mediator's help, learned to recognize and appreciate each other's diverse perspectives and to communicate more effectively.

After considering Professor Bush's views (and with some persuasion from Andy Little), the members of the Committee on Ethics and Professionalism made the difficult decision to withdraw the draft that they had delivered to the Council and upon which they had labored so long. Now the Committee would change course and start a new draft, one which would reflect Professor Bush's thinking. Little made the first attempt at trying to synthesize Bush's concepts with portions of the already existing draft. Eventually, a new set of proposed Standards emerged.

In the meantime, Judge Ralph A. Walker, Chair of the newly created North Carolina Dispute Resolution Commission, appointed Bob Beason to chair the Commission's Committee on Mediator Conduct and Ethical Standards. It was to this Committee that the new draft of proposed Standards was submitted.

Over the next several months, the Committee worked to further refine the Little draft. Finally, in May 1996, the Commission considered the Standards. As had often been the case in previous discussions of the Standards, the topic of facilitative versus evaluative mediation took center stage. Beason noted that, in his judgment, it was not good practice to evaluate a mediation case, even at the request of the parties. He believed that giving an opinion was damaging to the process in a number of ways: it potentially robbed the parties of the ability to determine the result of a negotiated process themselves; it inappropriately subordinated the parties' own intimate knowledge of the dispute to the mediator's newly discovered perspective; it potentially compromised the mediator's ability to continue to be perceived as neutral; and it could be a bad opinion on which the parties would ultimately rely as the foundation for decision making. Beason suggested that if the parties to a dispute desired an evaluative process, they should be encouraged to consider other ADR mechanisms such as early neutral evaluation. The facilitative perspective prevailed. Early versions of the Standards prohibited mediators from sharing their opinions about a case and how they thought a judge or jury would likely decide it.

This facilitative/evaluative debate continued long after the initial adoption of the Standards. Attorneys and other mediation consumers made it clear that in some instances the mediator's opinion could be crucial to the settlement of a case. The DRC eventually relented. In an effort to reach a compromise, the Standards were revised in 2004 to permit mediators to give opinions in certain narrow circumstances.

Since professional standards were first proposed in May of 1996, inquiries, concerns, and dilemmas of mediators at work have continued to cause the DRC to consider not only the interpretation of the Standards, but also revisions, as necessary. In August of 1998, in an effort to provide further assistance to mediators facing ethical dilemmas, the DRC produced and adopted its Advisory Opinion Policy. The policy allows the Executive Secretary to issue informal advice to mediator inquiries by phone, but requests that involve issues of greater consequence are addressed in formal advisory opinions published by the full Commission. Mediators may rely on these opinions as a guide to resolving their own ethical dilemmas.

There have been many small clarifying "tweaks" to the Standards over the years and some major modifications as well. Those modifications have included meaningful changes to Standard III, Confidentiality, and to Standard V, Self-Determination. As the number of complaints about mediators increased, the Commission found itself dealing more frequently with the disciplinary portion of its statutory charge. The members realized that the way in which the Standards were drafted originally made it difficult to perform those disciplinary functions. The conclusion of the Commission, first articulated by mediator and law professor Mark W. Morris, was that in places, the Standards were written in aspirational terms, rather than in "minimal standards" language that a regulatory body could apply consistently and fairly.

Thus, in 2008, then Commission Chair Judge Sanford L. Steelman, Jr. established an ad hoc committee to conduct the first systemic review of the Standards. Judge Steelman led the work of the committee himself. The committee's efforts were an attempt to update the Standards, consistent with what had been learned about mediation and mediator ethics over the previous decade. The committee's recommendations were well received by the DRC, and on February 17, 2010, the North Carolina Supreme Court approved the first set of comprehensive revisions to the Standards. Additional revisions were adopted in October 2011 and took effect on January 1, 2012.

The Standards

Following is a closer look at each element of the Standards of Professional Conduct for Mediators.

PREAMBLE

The original Standards adopted by the Court in 1998 applied only to mediators participating in mediated settlement conferences conducted pursuant to the superior court's Mediated Settlement Conference Program (MSC Program). Subsequent revisions to the Preamble took a piecemeal approach specifically extending their application to each new court-based mediation program as it was implemented. The 2010 revisions sought to move away from the piecemeal approach, providing that the Standards would apply, "to all mediators who are certified by the North Carolina Dispute Resolution Commission or who are not certified, but are conducting court-ordered mediations in the context of a program or process that is governed by statutes, as amended from time-to-time, which provide for the Commission to regulate the conduct of mediators participating in the program or process." The current Standards thus apply to all certified mediators even when they are working in programs operating outside the courts, such as the North Carolina Industrial Commission's mediation program (unless they are serving pursuant to a statutory provision that conflicts with the Standards), and to all mediators working in court-annexed programs regulated by the DRC.

The Preamble begins by explaining that the Standards are "intended to instill and promote public confidence in the mediation process and to provide minimum standards for mediator conduct." Though the Standards themselves address specific areas of conduct, the Preamble makes a broad statement about professional conduct, affirming that mediators are accountable not only to the parties but also to the public and the courts, and that they are to conduct themselves in a manner that merits confidence. (This language is echoed in Section VII of the Rules of the North Carolina Supreme Court for the Dispute Resolution Commission, discussed later in this chapter.) The Preamble goes on to explain the mediator's role in the mediation process.

STANDARD I. COMPETENCY

A mediator shall maintain professional competency in mediation skills and, where the mediator lacks the skills necessary for a particular case, shall decline to serve or withdraw from serving.

This Standard stresses that a mediator must be skilled in the mediation process and in his or her role as mediator, emphasizing that this is the most important qualification the mediator brings to the table. If a mediator knows that he or she does not have the skills necessary to conduct a mediated settlement conference in a particular case, the mediator should decline to serve at the outset or withdraw from the case.

Although mediators should have some level of awareness of the law and fact situation in dispute, this Standard does not require that a mediator be an "expert" relative to the law or the fact situation underlying the dispute.

Instead, Standard I envisions that the mediator will possess a basic substantive understanding of the area of the law involved in the dispute. If a mediator determines that his or her lack of technical or substantive knowledge will impair his or her effectiveness, then the Standard obligates the mediator to notify the parties and to withdraw if requested to do so.

Lastly, the Standard obligates a mediator to make conscious determinations about his or her ability to serve, whether it involves the ability to mediate or to understand the law and facts in issue. If the mediator realizes there is a problem, he or she cannot simply wait for the parties to raise the issue.

STANDARD II. IMPARTIALITY

A mediator shall, in word and action, maintain impartiality toward the parties and on the issues in dispute.

Impartiality means both the absence of prejudice or bias and the commitment to aid all parties, not just a single party, in exploring settlement options. Mediators must disclose all relationships or interests that affect or that might appear to affect their impartiality. If a mediator knows that he or she cannot be impartial, the mediator must withdraw. If a party objects to the mediator serving on the grounds of impartiality, and after discussion continues to object, the mediator must withdraw.

STANDARD III. CONFIDENTIALITY

A mediator shall, subject to exceptions set forth below, maintain the confidentiality of all information obtained within the mediation process.

Mediators are required to maintain strict confidentiality. As the DRC has noted in one of its Advisory Opinions, "[C]onfidentiality is essential to the success of mediation. Absent a statutory duty to disclose information, the Standards obligate mediators to protect and foster confidentiality."[3] In writing these words, the DRC recognized that parties will not speak freely in mediation if they believe that what they say will not be protected. Moreover, the fact that confidentiality is one of the hallmarks of mediation is exactly what makes the process attractive to many parties. (It is important to note, however, that Standard III governs the conduct of mediators only and not that of the parties or their lawyers. While statutes provide that evidence of what is said or done in mediation is not subject to discovery and shall be inadmissible in a court of law, subject to a few exceptions, a party is not otherwise prohibited from talking to others or the media about what occurs in mediation.)

Standard III also provides that a mediator shall not tell a party about any communication revealed in confidence to the mediator by another party to the mediation. For example, possible litigation tactics or negotiation bottom lines revealed in confidence to a mediator must not be shared with the other participants. In addition, a mediator must not reveal to a non-party, either directly or indirectly, any information communicated to the mediator during a mediation. Confidentiality protections attach to the entire mediation process and not just to private sessions.[4]

After stating a strong presumption in favor of confidentiality, the Standards spell out a few exceptions. It is indicative of the sanctity of confidentiality that the exceptions are limited to two areas: (1) situations where a statute requires or permits disclosure of the statement or conduct, and (2) situations where public safety is or may become an issue.

The four specific situations in which exceptions to confidentiality are allowed under Standard III follow:

- When a mediator has a statutory duty to report or is permitted to report the information communicated (e.g., statutes that require the reporting of child or elder abuse) or statutes that require a mediator to report on the outcome of a mediation (such as statutes requiring mediators in the Clerk Mediation Program to provide clerks of court with copies of agreements reached in estate or guardianship mediations for their review and endorsement).

- When a party communicates a threat to the mediator indicating that he or she intends to cause serious bodily harm or death to himself/herself or to another.

- When a party communicates a threat to the mediator indicating that he or she intends to cause significant damage to real or personal property.

- When a party's conduct during the mediation results in direct bodily injury or death to a person.

In drafting this Standard, the DRC recognized that during mediation, parties sometimes make idle threats to persons or property. For this reason, it was believed to be essential that mediators have some discretion in reporting. When a threat is made but a mediator does not believe that the party who issued the threat has the ability and intent to act, the mediator is not obligated to make a report. In allowing mediators to use discretion in identifying individuals who may pose a real danger to themselves or others, the Dispute Resolution Commission sought to strike a balance between protecting the public and safeguarding confidentiality.

Questions of confidentiality also arise in situations where a mediator has been asked to give a deposition or to testify in court about what was said at a mediation. In instances where none of the exceptions noted above apply, the DRC has consistently sought to protect confidentiality. In Advisory Opinion No. 01-03, the DRC advised a mediator who had been asked to give an affidavit that if he participated, he could be violating Standard III. The DRC took this position even though the mediator reported that the other party was not objecting to the affidavit. When a mediator receives a summons to testify, the DRC has consistently maintained that the mediator has no choice if compelled, but should strenuously resist and explain that although he or she will testify if ordered by the court, his or her testimony will violate both the Standards and statutes establishing mediated settlement conference programs in North Carolina courts, as well as the confidentiality protections afforded to discussions and offers made at settlement conferences.[5]

In 2006, the North Carolina State Bar requested comment from the DRC about the application of Rule 8.3 of the Revised Rules of Professional Conduct of the North Carolina State Bar in the context of mediation. Rule 8.3 requires an attorney to report conduct of another lawyer that the attorney knows to be in violation of the State Bar's Revised Rules of Professional Conduct when such conduct raises a substantial question as to the other lawyer's honesty, trustworthiness, or fitness to practice. However, Standard III requires a mediator to keep confidential things said and done in a mediation, including the statements and conduct of attorneys participating in the process. Thus, there appeared to be a conflict between the duties established by these two rules when the mediator was an attorney.

The apparent conflict between the two provisions engendered nearly four years of study and debate within the DRC, as well as among mediators and lawyers across the state. Ultimately, the State Bar recommended a new exception to the reporting requirements of Rule 8.3, which the North Carolina Supreme Court approved in the fall of 2010. Rule 8.3(e) and the supporting comment now permit attorney-mediators to maintain confidentiality with respect to statements and conduct of attorneys during mediation, with limited exceptions. The revised rule now provides as follows:

Rule 8.3 *Reporting Professional Misconduct*

(a) A lawyer who knows that another lawyer has committed a violation of the Rules of Professional Conduct that raises a substantial question as to that lawyer's honesty, trustworthiness, or fitness as a lawyer in other respects, shall inform the North Carolina State Bar or the court having jurisdiction over the matter.

. . .

(e) A lawyer who is serving as a mediator and who is subject to the North Carolina Supreme Court Standards of Professional Conduct for Mediators (the Standards) is not required to disclose information learned during a mediation if the Standards do not allow disclosure. If disclosure is allowed by the Standards, the lawyer is required to report professional misconduct consistent with the duty to report set forth in paragraph (a).

COMMENT

. . .

[7] The North Carolina Supreme Court has adopted Standards of Professional Conduct for Mediators (the Standards) to regulate the conduct of certified mediators and mediators in court-ordered mediations. Mediators governed by the Standards are required to keep confidential the statements and conduct of the parties and other participants in the mediation, with limited exceptions, to encourage the candor that is critical to the successful resolution of legal disputes. Paragraph (e) recognizes the concurrent regulatory function of the Standards and protects the confidentiality of the mediation process. Nevertheless, if the Standards allow disclosure, a lawyer serving as a mediator who learns of or observes conduct by a lawyer that is a violation of the Rules of Professional Conduct is required to report consistent with the duty set forth in paragraph (a) of this Rule. In the event a lawyer serving as a mediator is confronted with professional misconduct by a lawyer participating in a mediation that may not be disclosed pursuant to the Standards, the lawyer/mediator should consider withdrawing from the mediation or taking such other action as may be required by the Standards. See, e.g., N.C. Dispute Resolution Commission Advisory Opinion 10-16 (February 26, 2010).

Under the current version of Rule 8.3(e), a mediator is not required to report anything said or observed in the mediation process unless the Standards permit disclosure. Therefore, the mandatory reporting requirement of Rule 8.3 is triggered only if a lawyer participating in a mediated settlement conference conducts himself or herself in such a way that the conduct may be reported under Standard III.C.(2). Such conduct includes harming or threatening to commit harm to a person or property. Only under those limited circumstances must a lawyer-mediator report the matter to the State Bar. In all other circumstances, the lawyer-mediator is bound by the standard of confidentiality and may not voluntarily report what is said and done in a mediation.

STANDARD IV. CONSENT

A mediator shall make reasonable efforts to ensure that each party understands the mediation process, the role of the mediator, and the party's options within the process.

Standard IV places a duty on the mediator consistent with program rules to inform the parties about the mediation process and the role of the mediator. It is expected that every mediation conference will begin with such an explanation. The rules for the Mediated Settlement Conference Program, the Family Financial Settlement Program, the Clerk Mediation Program, the Pre-Litigation Farm Nuisance Mediation Program, and the District Criminal Court Mediation Program also discuss the duties of the mediator and list specific items to be discussed with the parties at the beginning of the conference.

Standard IV also provides that a mediator shall not exert undue pressure on the parties either to negotiate or to settle. This is not to say that mediators should not encourage parties to consider the options and alternatives available to them. Mediators should urge the parties to engage in the process and actively work to advance their negotiations. In fact, one of the most frequently heard complaints about mediators from attorneys is that "mediators give up too soon." However, a mediator must stop short of strong-arming parties into participating or accepting an offer or agreement.

Pursuant to Standard IV, if a party appears to have difficulty comprehending the process, the issues in dispute, or settlement options, the mediator must explore the circumstances and any accommodations or adjustments that could be made to facilitate the party's capacity to comprehend, participate, and exercise self-determination. If the mediator thereafter determines that a party cannot participate meaningfully, the mediator must either recess or discontinue the mediation. Before making a determination to discontinue, the mediator must consider all of the circumstances and ramifications involved, including the subject matter of the dispute, the availability of support persons for the party, and whether the party is represented by counsel.

Lastly, Standard IV provides that mediators shall, when appropriate, inform the parties of the importance of seeking legal, financial, tax, or other professional advice during or after mediation.

STANDARD V. SELF-DETERMINATION

A mediator shall respect and encourage self-determination by the parties in their decision whether, and on what terms, to resolve their dispute, and shall refrain from being directive and judgmental regarding the issues in dispute and options for settlement.

This Standard is the cornerstone of the North Carolina Standards of Professional Conduct for Mediators and the one that has probably generated the most controversy. It places a premium on the parties' determination of the outcome of a mediation and reinforces the notion that mediators are neither judges nor arbitrators and do not make decisions for the parties. When first adopted, Standard V prohibited mediators from giving their express opinion of the worth of a case, (i.e., stating what they believed the outcome of a case would be when tried before a judge or jury). It was the DRC's firm belief that such a practice only serves to drive parties further apart and could in fact alienate a party from a mediator and undermine the mediator's credibility, neutrality, and, most importantly, his or her ability to continue to assist all parties. In practice, however, attorneys often asked mediators to provide just this kind of assessment. In light of this reality, in 2004 the North Carolina Supreme Court, upon recommendation of the DRC, revised Standard V to permit a mediator to give an opinion about the merits of the case or any settlement proposal in the following circumstances: (1) a party or parties specifically request(s) the opinion; (2) the mediator has made an effort to help the parties evaluate the case or settlement proposal using their own resources; and (3) the mediator provides the opinion only as a last resort (i.e., he or she has exhausted all avenues available to move the process and parties forward and they are stuck). Only when all those elements are present should the mediator provide his/her own opinion.

While mediators may provide their opinions only under the circumstances described above, Subsection B of Standard V makes it clear that they may raise questions regarding the acceptability, sufficiency, and feasibility of proposed settlement terms—including their impact on third parties—and may make suggestions for the parties' consideration.

Subsection E of Standard V addresses another aspect of self-determination: situations where there is an underlying flaw that compromises the parties' discussions entirely. Examples of such circumstances include the inability or unwillingness of a party to participate meaningfully, inequality of bargaining power or ability, unfairness resulting from nondisclosure or fraud by a participant, or other circumstances likely to lead to a grossly unjust result. Whenever such circumstances exist, the Standard provides that a mediator must inform the parties of his or her concern. Consistent with the confidentiality requirements of Standard III, the mediator may discuss with the parties the source of concern. The mediator may discontinue the mediation if he or she believes that it is the correct course of action, but in doing so the mediator may not violate the obligation of confidentiality.

Standard VI. Separation of Mediation from Legal and Other Professional Advice

A mediator shall limit himself or herself solely to the role of mediator, and shall not give legal or other professional advice during the mediation.

Attorney-mediators are not permitted to give legal advice during mediation, even if a party requests it, and mediators should be mindful of this prohibition as they respond to questions or statements during mediation. Non-attorneys who give legal advice are engaging in the unauthorized practice of law.[6] Mediators who are licensed to practice other professions (accountants or therapists, for example) should also be mindful that they are not to practice their profession as they mediate.

The above notwithstanding, a mediator may provide information that he or she is qualified by training or experience to provide, if the mediator can do so consistent with the Standards. If a mediator believes there is some facet of the case that the parties have not considered sufficiently—for example, the tax ramifications of a proposed divorce settlement—the mediator could ask each party about such tax consequences. Attorney-mediators may respond to a party's request for an opinion on the merits of a case or the suitability of a settlement proposal, but only in accordance with Standard V, above.

Standard VII. Conflicts of Interest

A mediator shall not allow any personal interest to interfere with the primary obligation to impartially serve the parties to the dispute.

This Standard has a number of subsections that address various aspects of conflicts of interest. Essentially, a mediator is not to use the mediation process to further his or her own interests, but rather must keep the interests of the parties first and foremost in his or her words and actions. A mediator must *not*:

- place the interests of the court or agency that referred the case over the interests of the parties when such interests are in conflict;
- place his or her interest in maintaining cordial relations with a professional advocate or adviser of the parties over the interests of the parties when such interests are in conflict;
- advise or represent the parties in future matters concerning the subject of the dispute, an action closely related to the dispute, or an outgrowth of the dispute when the mediator or his/her staff has engaged in substantive conversations with any party to the dispute;[7]
- charge a contingent fee or any other fee based on the outcome of the mediation;
- use information obtained or relationships formed during a mediation for personal gain or advantage;
- knowingly contract for mediation services that cannot be delivered or completed in a timely manner as directed by a court;
- knowingly prolong a mediation for the purpose of charging a higher fee; or
- give to a party or representative of a party, or receive from a party or representative of a party, any commission, rebate, or other monetary or non-monetary form of consideration in return for referral or expectation of referral of clients for mediation services.

STANDARD VIII. PROTECTING THE INTEGRITY OF THE MEDIATION PROCESS

A mediator shall encourage mutual respect between the parties, and shall take reasonable steps, subject to the principle of self-determination, to limit abuses of the mediation process.

A mediator must not inject his or her vision of a "fair" agreement into the mediation process. Essentially, it is up to the parties to determine what they think is a fair settlement of their dispute. However, there are some circumstances under which fairness becomes an issue. If a mediator believes that one party is seeking to manipulate or intimidate another, then the mediator must take steps to try to ensure a balanced discussion and to eliminate further manipulation and intimidation. If the mediator believes that the actions of a participant jeopardize conducting mediation consistent with the Standards, the mediator shall consider appropriate steps including postponement, withdrawal, or termination.

Other Rules of Conduct

The Standards are not alone in circumscribing mediator conduct in North Carolina. The Rules of the North Carolina Supreme Court for the Dispute Resolution Commission, adopted in 1996, also address conduct and help to implement the Standards. Section VII of the Rules specifically addresses conduct:

> The conduct of all mediators, mediation trainers and managers of mediation training programs must conform to the Standards of Professional Conduct for Mediators adopted by the Supreme Court and enforceable by the Commission and the standards of any professional organization of which such person is a member that are not in conflict nor inconsistent with the Standards. A certified mediator shall inform the Commission of any criminal convictions, disbarments, or other revocations or suspensions of a professional license, complaints filed against the mediator or disciplinary action imposed upon the mediator by any professional organization, judicial sanctions, civil judgments, tax liens, or filings for bankruptcy. Failure to do so is a violation of these Rules. Violations of the Standards or other professional standards or any conduct otherwise discovered reflecting a lack of moral character or fitness to conduct mediations or which discredits the Commission, the courts or the mediation process may subject a mediator to disciplinary proceedings by the Commission.

The broader language in the Preamble excepted, the Standards address specific issues relating to conduct. The Supreme Court Rules cast a wider net, addressing any conduct that reflects a lack of moral character or fitness to mediate, or which discredits the DRC, the courts, or the mediation process.

When evaluating conduct reportable under Rule VII, the Commission is primarily concerned about serious breaches or indications of patterns. For example, if an applicant for mediator certification or certification renewal reported that he or she had filed a bankruptcy, that fact alone would not likely concern the Commission. However, a bankruptcy in conjunction with a number of tax liens and worthless check convictions or other evidence of fiscal irresponsibility might well raise concerns and even result in conditional certification or a denial of certification.

Enforcement of the Standards

The Standards are not simply aspirational in nature. North Carolina General Statutes Section 7A-38.2 charges the DRC with regulating mediator conduct as well as the conduct of trainers and managers operating Commission-approved mediator training programs.

The Rules of the North Carolina Supreme Court for the Dispute Resolution Commission address enforcement of the Standards, serving to "put teeth" in them. Section VIII of the Rules sets out complaint and hearing procedures for instances where a complaint is brought regarding a mediator's conduct. Complaints about mediator conduct are generally brought by members of the public, and most usually parties or attorneys, but complaints can be filed by court staff or even DRC staff or members. Complaints may address alleged violations of the Standards or program rules or behavior that runs afoul of Section VII of the Rules (i.e., conduct that evidences bad character, a lack of fitness to practice or that discredits the Commission, the courts, or the mediation process). Once a complaint is received, the DRC's Executive Secretary will review the complaint and conduct an investigation. Following completion of the investigation, the Executive Secretary may elect: (1) to refer the matter for conciliation; or (2) to refer the matter to the Chair of the Commission's Standards, Discipline, and Advisory Opinions (SDAO) Committee; or (3) to refer the matter to the full SDAO Committee.

CONCILIATION

The Executive Secretary may refer a matter for conciliation only if, after talking with the parties, he or she determines that: (1) the complaint appears to be largely the product of a misunderstanding or raises best practices concerns or technical violations only, and (2) that the parties are willing to participate in conciliation in good faith. If conciliation fails, the Executive Secretary will refer the matter to the SDAO Chair or the full SDAO Committee.

REFERRAL TO SDAO CHAIR

If after investigating the complaint, the Executive Secretary determines that no further action is warranted on the matter, he or she will prepare a summary containing a recommendation to dismiss and forward it to the Chair of the SDAO Committee along with a copy of the complaint, the mediator's response, and the responses of any witnesses or others contacted. The Chair reviews the materials provided and if he or she agrees with the recommendation will dismiss the complaint. If the Chair does not agree with the recommendation he or she may instruct the Executive Secretary either: (1) to refer the matter to conciliation (if conciliation has not already been undertaken) or (2) to refer the matter to the full SDAO Committee for consideration. If the Chair dismisses the matter, the complaining party may appeal the decision to the full SDAO Committee.

Referral to SDAO Committee

The Executive Secretary must refer complaints directly to the full SDAO Committee in situations where he or she believes that the complaint raises significant concerns about possible program rules or Standards violations or raises questions about a respondent's character, conduct, or fitness to practice.

SDAO Committee Review

When a complaint comes before the SDAO Committee—either because staff directly refers it, the SDAO Chair refers it, or a complaining party appeals a dismissal by the Chair—the Committee reviews the complaint, the mediator's response, the responses of any witnesses or others contacted, and the report and recommendations of staff. The Committee may request additional investigation or information as it deems appropriate. After concluding its review, the Committee may elect to dismiss the complaint, make a referral, or impose sanctions on the respondent mediator.

Dismissal

If the Committee finds no probable cause, it will dismiss the complaint and the complaining party has no further right of appeal.

Referral

If the Committee determines that there was a technical or minor violation of the Standards or program rules only or that the conduct at issue raises best practices concerns, it may elect to either provide the mediator-respondent with written guidance or to ask him or her to meet with a member of the Committee or a representative of the Chief Justice's Commission on Professionalism to discuss and address the concerns raised. If the Committee determines that the complaint raises significant concerns about the mediator-respondent's mental stability, mental health, lack of mental acuity, or possible dementia or raises concerns about alcohol or substance abuse, the Committee may elect to refer the mediator-respondent to the North Carolina State Bar Lawyer's Assistance Program (LAP) for counseling and treatment or, if the mediator is not a lawyer, to a licensed physician or a substance abuse counselor or organization.

IMPOSE SANCTIONS

If the Committee finds that probable cause exists to believe that the mediator's conduct violated the Standards (or any other ethical standards to which the mediator is subject) or program rules or that the conduct is inconsistent with good moral character, reflects a lack of fitness to practice, or discredits the DRC, the courts, or the mediation process, the Committee may impose sanctions, including: (1) private written admonishment; (2) public written admonishment; (3) additional training; (4) restriction on types of cases to be mediated in the future; (5) reimbursement of fees paid to the mediator; (6) suspension for a specific term; (7) probation for a specific term; (8) de-certification; or (9) any other sanction deemed appropriate. In appropriate situations, the Committee could also elect to couple one of the sanctions above with a referral to treatment or counseling. Though a complaining party may not appeal the Committee's determination to dismiss his or her complaint, a mediator may appeal a determination to impose sanctions to the full Dispute Resolution Commission for a de novo hearing. Members of the SDAO Committee who participated in issuing sanctions must recuse themselves from the hearing. The Commission's hearing procedures are set forth in Rule VIII. Jurisdiction for appeal of Commission decisions lies with the General Court of Justice, Wake County Superior Court Division. Copies of both the DRC's Rules and complaint forms can be obtained from the DRC's office or by visiting its website.[8]

All complaints are treated confidentially until such time as there has been finding of probable cause. Once there has been such a finding, the file is open to the public. Though the DRC may waive the requirement, the Commission Rules provide for publication of the names of those respondent mediators who have been publicly sanctioned.

Advisory Opinions

Since its inception, the Dispute Resolution Commission has endeavored to work proactively, seeking to educate and guide mediators rather than to punish them. Thus, the DRC adopted an Advisory Opinion Policy on August 28, 1998. The policy provides a means for mediators to seek both formal and informal advice from the DRC on matters of conduct. In essence, mediators may seek help in resolving any dilemma that arises in the course of their mediation practice, including situations that call for an interpretation of the Standards or program rules.

Mediators may contact the DRC's Executive Secretary or a member of the DRC and ask for informal advice. While informal advice does not carry the full weight of the Commission's authority, it is often the only way to provide guidance in situations where time is of the essence, e.g., when the issue comes up during a mediation and the mediator needs an answer quickly. If the DRC's Executive Secretary is contacted, he or she will seek to respond to the question and assist the mediator in interpreting the appropriate statutes, program rules, or the Standards. Often the question is one that the DRC has addressed before. If the Executive Secretary is unable to provide assistance and there is time, he or she will seek advice from the chair or another member of the Dispute Resolution Commission. The Executive Secretary logs in all such calls from mediators, noting the caller's name, the issue raised, and the advice given. If a complaint is later brought against the mediator, the log entry stands as evidence that the mediator sought help and was attempting to respond appropriately to the situation he or she faced. The log is maintained as a confidential document. Two versions are kept, one having the name of the caller and the other having such identifying information blacked out. The latter copy is reviewed periodically by the DRC's Standards, Discipline, and Advisory Opinions (SDAO) Committee to ensure that the advice being given is appropriate and consistent.

If a mediator has more time (e.g., the mediator made a decision and now questions whether the decision was appropriate or optimal for the situation), he or she may seek a formal, written advisory opinion from the DRC. Such advice can be helpful if the mediator believes that he or she may face the same or a similar situation in the future. To receive a formal opinion, the mediator must make his or her request in writing. The SDAO Committee will review the request and may decide to issue a written opinion. A written opinion will be issued only in instances where: (1) the request for advice is an outgrowth of actual events occurring or issues arising in a case the mediator was to conduct or did conduct; and (2) the opinion sought will have general application or will potentially benefit other mediators, the court, or the public.

The SDAO Committee submits any opinions it drafts to the full Dispute Resolution Commission for approval. As such, written opinions carry the full weight of the DRC and may be relied upon. Only mediators seeking advice pursuant to a mediated settlement conference may request an advisory opinion. Occasionally lawyers involved in a mediation have asked their mediator to seek an advisory opinion and, when the mediator has been willing, the DRC has responded. Normally, in instances where a party or an attorney has a concern about a mediator's conduct, it is the DRC's expectation that a complaint will be filed under the Rules of the North Carolina Supreme Court for the Dispute Resolution Commission, rather than by requesting an advisory opinion from the DRC. Copies of the Advisory Opinion Policy and advisory opinions issued to date may be viewed on the DRC's website.

A listing and synopsis of all advisory opinions adopted at the time of publication of this book is included at the end of this chapter. The opinions are also available on the DRC's website.

Applicant Screening Committee

The Dispute Resolution Commission has also sought to tighten its initial screening procedures to ensure that only applicants of good character are certified in the first place. The DRC's Applications for Certification ask applicants to respond to a number of questions involving character or conduct concerns, including disclosing any criminal convictions, pending grievances or disciplinary sanctions, judicial sanctions, civil judgments, tax liens, or bankruptcy filings. If a mediator served as a neutral in other states, he or she is asked to disclose such service and to provide contact information for the agencies governing the qualification of neutrals in the state(s) in which the mediator served. In the event an applicant reports an ethical concern and the staff considers it to be a serious matter, the application may be referred to the DRC's SDAO Committee. The Committee will review the matter or matters reported to determine whether the conduct involved was of such a serious nature as to bar the applicant's certification to conduct mediated settlement conferences. If so, the application will be denied. A disbarment, a suspension of a law or other professional license, or a series or pattern of less significant ethical violations indicating a lack of character are situations likely to result in denial.

The Commission also asks mediators renewing their certification during the annual renewal period to respond to questions about character and to report convictions, disciplinary matters, and other concerns that have occurred since their last certification. As with an original application, a disbarment, a suspension of a law or other professional license, or a series or pattern of less significant ethical violations indicating a lack of character are situations likely to result in the Committee's refusal to renew a certification.

Conclusion

North Carolina has done much to ensure that mediation services offered in its court-annexed mediated settlement conference programs will be provided by skilled, ethical practitioners. One of the DRC's first acts was to adopt Standards of Professional Conduct for Mediators, and the Standards have been updated and revised over time to assure that mediators have clear, concise guidance on matters of conduct. Without a doubt, the Standards and opportunities the DRC has provided for mediators to seek guidance on matters of conduct have strengthened North Carolina's mediation programs immeasurably.

Canons of Ethics for Arbitrators

Introduction

The North Carolina Canons of Ethics for Arbitrators were adopted by the Supreme Court of North Carolina to regulate arbitrator conduct in court-annexed arbitration proceedings under North Carolina General Statutes Section 7A-37.1, more commonly known as "court-ordered" arbitration. The Canons and their accompanying comments, issued as an order of the Supreme Court of North Carolina,[9] are binding rules for court-ordered arbitrations, referred to as "court-annexed arbitrations" in the Canons. The Canons do not apply to arbitrations by agreement unless the parties contract for them. The Canons, which became effective on October 1, 1999, are a "one-size-fits-all" set of principles, adaptable for use in cases involving nearly any subject matter.

The Canons follow the general format of the American Bar Association-American Arbitration Association Code of Ethics for Arbitrators in Commercial Disputes (ABA-AAA Code). They also draw on other state and national rules governing neutrals' conduct, particularly the North Carolina Dispute Resolution Commission's Standards of Professional Conduct for Mediators and the North Carolina Code of Judicial Conduct. Comments following each Canon include source references, which may be helpful if issues arise concerning construction of specific provisions.

There are eight Canons. Canons I through VII establish explicit standards for arbitrator conduct, while Canon VIII sets out governing choice of law and conflict of laws principles. Canons I–VII follow the ABA-AAA Code format but include revisions for style, additions applicable to court-annexed arbitration, and amendments suggested by other ethics rules for neutrals.

The Canons substitute the mandatory "shall" for "should," which appears in most of the provisions on which they were modeled. When the Canons refer to "court-annexed arbitration," it is a specific reference to cases governed by North Carolina General Statutes Section 7A-37.1, while the phrase "court-administered arbitration" is a generic term encompassing court-annexed cases and other situations where a court is involved in arbitration under the Federal Arbitration Act (FAA), the North Carolina Revised Uniform Arbitration Act (RUAA), or other arbitration statutes. The Canons do not refer to "court-ordered arbitration," because a court can issue orders in arbitrations under several different state and federal statutes.

General Analysis of the Canons

CANON I: UPHOLDING THE INTEGRITY AND FAIRNESS OF THE ARBITRATION PROCESS

Canon I sets out standards for upholding the integrity and fairness of arbitration. It covers an array of ethical obligations and concerns, all aimed at assuring an arbitrator's impartiality and adherence to "high standards of conduct." The Canon makes clear that arbitrators have a responsibility "to the public, the parties whose rights will be decided, the courts, and other participants in the proceeding."

One area of particular focus in Canon I is the limit on ways in which an arbitrator can market his or her services. The Canon declares that "it may be inconsistent with the integrity of the arbitration process for persons to solicit appointment for themselves" as arbitrators. Arbitrators nevertheless "may indicate a general willingness to serve" by listing themselves with courts that have court-annexed arbitration programs, or with institutions (such as the AAA) that sponsor arbitrations. Also, as in the case of advertising by attorneys generally, arbitrators may advertise, "consistent with the law."

Canon I also includes restrictions on "relationships" that might interfere with an arbitrator's impartiality. An arbitrator must avoid entering into relationships or interests that are likely to affect impartiality, or that might reasonably create an appearance of partiality or bias. This obligation also extends for one year after the decision in a case, unless all parties to the arbitration consent to the arbitrator's entering into a particular relationship or acquiring an interest before expiration of that time. The one-year rule, modeled on provisions of the FAA, is the same as the time limit for moving to set aside an award.

The reason for prohibiting the arbitrator from entering into certain types of relationships or acquiring certain interests is illustrated by the following example. A party to a court-annexed arbitration who wins an award may be impressed with the arbitrator's skill in conducting the proceedings. The party innocently asks the arbitrator, who must be a lawyer under the rules for court-ordered arbitration, to represent him or her in another matter. If the former arbitrator, now being approached as a lawyer, agrees to represent the former party, he or she might be faced with accusations of bias from the losing party in the arbitration. Canon I establishes a clear one-year exclusion rule to avoid this situation.

Other ethical requirements under Canon I are fairly straightforward. Arbitrators may not serve in a particular case if they do not have the necessary skills or expertise, and they may not accept an appointment if they are unable to conduct the arbitration promptly. They must be fair to all parties and cannot be swayed by public opinion. When an arbitrator's authority is based on an agreement by the parties, he or she must comply with procedures and rules set out in the agreement. The arbitrator must also make reasonable efforts to prevent abuse or disruption of the arbitration process.

The Canon states that these obligations begin when the arbitrator accepts an appointment and continues throughout all stages of the proceeding. In certain instances noted in the Canons, the obligation begins as soon as the arbitrator is asked to serve, and continues for a full year after the decision has been issued.

Finally, Canon I encourages arbitrators to "participate in development of new practitioners in the field," and to be involved in educating the public about "the value and use of arbitration procedures." It also states that arbitrators should provide pro bono services, as appropriate.

CANON II: DISCLOSURE STANDARDS

Canon II establishes standards for disclosure of interests that might compromise an arbitrator's fairness and impartiality. In general, disclosures must be made, before accepting an appointment, of: (1) any direct or indirect financial or personal interest in the outcome of the arbitration; (2) any existing or past relationships that are likely to affect impartiality, or that might reasonably create the appearance of bias; and (3) in the case of court-administered arbitrations, any information required by a court. Arbitrators must make reasonable efforts to determine if there are any such interests or relationships, and they have a continuing duty to reveal interests or relationships at any stage of the arbitration as they may arise, be recalled, or be discovered. Disclosure must be made to all parties, unless applicable rules or procedures provide otherwise. In cases where there is more than one arbitrator, the other arbitrators also must be advised of the interests and relationships that have been disclosed.

Canon II includes procedures to be followed in cases where the arbitrator is asked to withdraw as a result of partiality or bias. When the request is from all parties, the arbitrator must withdraw, except in the case of court-administered cases, where the arbitrator must advise the court of the request and then comply with any court orders that are issued.

If the request to withdraw because of alleged impartiality is not unanimous, the arbitrator must withdraw, except in three special situations. First, if the parties' agreement or the rules agreed to by the parties establish procedures for dealing with challenges to arbitrators, those rules or procedures must be followed. Second, the arbitrator is not obligated to withdraw if, after careful consideration, he or she determines that the reason for the challenge is not substantial; that he or she can act and decide the case impartially and fairly; and that withdrawal would cause unfair delay or expense to another party or would be contrary to the interest of justice. In court-administered cases, the arbitrator must comply with decisions of the court. Third, Canon II allows the parties to waive disqualification of an arbitrator after full disclosure. In court-administered arbitrations, any such waiver requires approval by the court.

Since the North Carolina International Commercial Arbitration and Conciliation Act (ICACA) has its own disclosure rules, Canon VIII (discussed below) requires that arbitrations under that legislation follow its standards. The same is true for arbitrations governed by the North Carolina RUAA and the revised Family Law Arbitration Act. This legislation, following the RUAA, has statutory disclosure standards. Canon II remains a catchall for those arbitrations that are not covered by the RUAA or the FLAA, e.g., those for which the repealed North Carolina UAA applies and for court-ordered arbitrations.

Canon III: Communications Between Arbitrators and Parties

The third Canon discusses standards for avoiding improprieties or appearances of impropriety in arbitrator communications with parties. It is based largely on the ABA-AAA Code and the state Code of Judicial Conduct.

Canon III states that an arbitrator must follow all rules and procedures concerning communications with parties that are contained or incorporated by reference in the parties' agreement, even if those rules and procedures are different from the standards set out in other provisions of Canon III. In the absence of any such agreement or applicable rules, arbitrators are forbidden from discussing a case with any party in the absence of other parties, except in two situations. First, an arbitrator can have ex parte discussions about such matters as setting the time or place of the hearing or making other arrangements for conducting proceedings. But he or she must inform other parties of the discussion promptly, and the arbitrator cannot make any final determination on the matters discussed before giving each absent party an opportunity to express its views. Secondly, ex parte discussions can take place if all parties request or consent to them.

When an arbitrator communicates in writing with a party, he or she must send a copy of the communication to other parties at the same time. Also, if the arbitrator receives a party's written communication that has not been sent to the other parties, the arbitrator must send the communication to the other parties.

Canon IV: Conducting Proceedings Fairly and Diligently

Canon IV requires arbitrators to conduct proceedings fairly and diligently. Like many of the other Canons, it follows similar provisions in the ABA-AAA Code and the state Code of Judicial Conduct. The Canon states that an arbitrator must be "patient, dignified, and courteous" to all with whom he or she has contact in the proceedings, and it obligates the arbitrator to encourage similar conduct by all participants. When necessary, the arbitrator may impose sanctions on the participants, if permitted by law or by the parties' agreement.

Canon IV includes a provision requiring the arbitrator to permit all parties the right to appear in person and to be heard after "due notice of the time and place of hearing." The arbitrator cannot deny any party the right to be represented by counsel. If a party who has been given due notice fails to appear and the arbitrator receives assurance that the notice was given, the arbitrator may proceed with the arbitration when authorized to do so either by law or by the parties. An arbitrator can ask questions, call witnesses, and request documents or other evidence if he or she determines that more information than has been presented by the parties is needed to decide the case.

Under the provisions of Canon IV, an arbitrator can suggest that the parties discuss settlement, but he or she may not pressure the parties to settle. The arbitrator cannot be present or participate in any settlement discussions unless asked to do so by all the parties. The Canon does not prevent an arbitrator from acting as a mediator, conciliator, or other neutral in the dispute if he or she is asked to do so by all of the parties or is authorized or required to do so by applicable law. If there is more than one arbitrator, the arbitrators must give each other the opportunity to participate in all aspects of the proceeding.

If one or more parties appear without counsel, Canon IV requires an arbitrator in a court-annexed proceeding to explain the arbitrator's role, the time for each party's case, the order of proceedings, and the right to trial de novo (if applicable) if a party not in default is dissatisfied with the award. Parties can waive this requirement. Waiver in pro se cases might occur where litigants appearing without counsel have been in court-annexed arbitration and feel that they already "know the ropes," but this requirement protects those unfamiliar with the state's civil justice system.

Canon V: Making Decisions in a Just, Independent, and Deliberate Manner

Canon V states that decisions must be made in a just, independent, and deliberate manner. The arbitrator must decide all issues submitted for determination, but only those issues. He or she may not be swayed by bias or by outside pressures and may not delegate the decision-making responsibility, unless the parties agree to the delegation.

If the parties agree to settle issues in dispute and ask the arbitrator to embody their settlement agreement in the award, the arbitrator may do so, but is not required to unless he or she is satisfied that the settlement terms are proper. If the arbitrator embodies a settlement agreement in the award, the award must state that it is based on the parties' agreement.

Canon VI: The Arbitrator's Relationship of Trust and Confidentiality

Canon VI requires an arbitrator to be faithful to the relationship of trust and confidentiality inherent in the office. The arbitrator cannot use confidential information acquired in the arbitration proceeding to gain personal advantage, advantage for others, or disadvantage for others. All matters relating to the arbitration proceedings and decision must be kept confidential unless the parties agree otherwise, or unless otherwise required by law or applicable rules.

The Canon forbids an arbitrator from disclosing the arbitration decision to anyone before it is given to the parties. In cases where there is more than one arbitrator, it is also improper to inform anyone about the arbitrators' deliberations. An arbitrator may not assist in post-arbitral proceedings, except as required by law or agreed by the parties.

Canon VI also addresses ethical concerns that may arise in situations where arbitrators receive payments for their services and expenses. When payments are to be made, arbitrators must avoid any actions "which would create an appearance of coercion or impropriety" with respect to such payments. The Canon contains "preferable" payment practices that must be followed if the parties' agreement does not specify payment procedures, or if there is no applicable provision contained in agreed-upon rules or applicable law. First, the basis for payment must be established before the arbitrator finally accepts appointment, and all parties must be informed of it in writing. Second, in cases being administered by an institution, the institution must make arrangements for payments so that the arbitrator will not have to communicate directly with the parties on the subject. Third, if an institution is not involved in administration of the case, discussions about payments to the arbitrator must take place in the presence of all parties. Fourth, if a case is court-administered, court orders, rules, and practices must be followed. This means that for court-annexed arbitrations, procedures established by the Rules for Court-Ordered Arbitration, the Administrative Office of the Courts, and the court administering the program will be followed.

CANON VII: ETHICAL CONSIDERATIONS RELATING TO ARBITRATORS APPOINTED BY ONE PARTY

Canon VII supplements Canons I–VI, setting standards in cases where parties appoint their own representatives as non-neutral arbitrators. In these situations, arbitral rules for a dispute generally provide that the party representatives must pick another arbitrator to serve as a final, neutral member of a multi-member panel. This procedure is used most often in construction or international arbitration. It usually does not apply in court-annexed arbitrations unless a court approves the procedure, which typically occurs only in high-dollar cases.

The non-neutral arbitrators are required to observe Canon I's obligations to uphold the integrity and fairness of the arbitration process, but Canon VII recognizes two exceptions to those obligations. It allows a non-neutral arbitrator to be predisposed to the party who appoints him or her, as long as the arbitrator acts in good faith and with integrity and fairness in all other respects. Accordingly, the non-neutral arbitrator cannot engage in delaying tactics or harassment and cannot knowingly make false or misleading statements. The other exception recognized by Canon VII is that the non-neutral arbitrator is not subject to the limits on relationships and interests imposed by Canon I.

CANON VIII: IMPACT OF OTHER RULES, PROFESSIONAL RESPONSIBILITY PRINCIPLES, AND CHOICE OF LAW REQUIREMENTS

Canon VIII states that if a Canon provision conflicts with state or federal constitutional, statutory, decisional, or administrative rules, those rules take priority if it is not possible to give effect both to the rules and to the Canons. For example, Canon II prescribes disclosure standards, as does the North Carolina International Commercial Arbitration and Conciliation Act (ICACA), the North Carolina RUAA, and the revised North Carolina Family Law Arbitration Act (FLAA). The ICACA, RUAA, and FLAA disclosure standards would take precedence in cases governed by those statutes.

If there are ethical standards that apply to an arbitrator in any other capacity, such as ethical rules governing attorney conduct, Canon VIII says these standards should be read *in pari materia*, if possible, giving effect to both the Canons and the other rules. If the arbitrator is subject to other arbitrator ethics rules, the Canons govern if there is a conflict, except that this rule of "primacy" does not apply to disclosure principles contained in Canon II or to payment principles contained in Canon VI. Canon VIII also declares that the Canons apply to arbitrations in North Carolina, to arbitrations administered by a court in North Carolina, to arbitrations where parties choose this state's law exclusive of conflict of laws principles in the contract, or if it is determined that North Carolina law (exclusive of conflicts principles) applies regardless of the location of the arbitration.

ENFORCEMENT OF THE CANONS

Although there is no express provision for enforcement of the Canons under North Carolina law, the senior resident superior court judge or the chief district court judge who is responsible for administering the court-annexed arbitration program in a particular district can exercise influence over an arbitrator's compliance with the Canons. The judge approves the arbitrator list and must approve party-requested arbitrators not on the list. Inherent in this authority is the discretion to remove arbitrators from the list, which a judge can do if an arbitrator runs afoul of the Canons. If a judge finds that an attorney acting as an arbitrator violates the Revised Rules of Professional Conduct in addition to the Canons, the judge can report that lawyer to the North Carolina State Bar, just as in any case where there is a Rules violation. A serious violation of the Canons could be a basis for setting aside an award.

Use of the Canons in Other Forums and in Arbitrations by Agreement

There are no local rules for court-annexed arbitration in the federal courts in North Carolina. Those courts generally use mediation rather than arbitration as an ADR procedure. If a federal district court order approves court-annexed arbitration instead of mediation, it can impose the Canons (or a variant of them) as standards for the arbitrator in the case. The Canons are not binding as law in a federal district court case, unless the court adopts them by order for a case or under a local rule of court. Parties considering court-annexed arbitration as the ADR technique in a federal case should consider submitting the Canons or a variant of them as part of a draft reference order.

Although mediation and neutral evaluation are the preferred North Carolina Industrial Commission ADR techniques, upon motion, the Industrial Commission may order a case to court-annexed arbitration. If the motion is granted, the Industrial Commission can order that the Canons apply to the proceedings. Arbitrations in other state administrative agency cases also may incorporate the Canons by reference.

The most common use of the Canons, apart from court-annexed arbitration, is in arbitration by the parties' agreement. A handbook for family law arbitrations pursuant to North Carolina's Family Law Arbitration Act (FLAA), *2006 Revised Handbook: Arbitrating Family Law Cases Under the North Carolina Family Law Arbitration Act as Amended in 2005*, is available from the North Carolina Bar Association and on its website and includes a form (in volume 1) to incorporate the Canons by reference, along with any desired amendments. The form can also be used to incorporate the Canons into other arbitrations by agreement. Incorporation by reference is the preferred method, but parties may write the Canons into a contract verbatim or with appropriate changes.

The question of whether violation of a Canon justifies setting aside an arbitral award may arise when the Canons apply as a result of the parties' agreement, or through adoption by a tribunal that has authority over the arbitration. In *ANR Coal Co. v. Cogentrix, Inc.*, the United States Court of Appeals for the Fourth Circuit held that provisions of the FAA, which governed the dispute, supplied the sole criteria for setting aside an award.[10]

Thus, reference to an ethics rule violation was not enough to justify setting aside the award. The decision in the *ANR* case follows Canon VIII's primacy rules, giving precedence to the governing statute. If a Canon coincides with legislated set-aside standards, the Canon might provide additional supporting authority. At the time of publication this issue had not arisen in the North Carolina courts.

Other Arbitrator Ethics Rules

As previously noted, the Canons do not bind parties considering arbitration by agreement unless parties contract for their standards. Subject to statutory limitations, parties may agree on different standards, although prospective arbitrators might refuse to serve under those terms.

The Canons are not the only arbitrator ethics rules. The ABA-AAA Code is available for commercial disputes, and there are other rules parties can use. Where common practice is to use other rules, particularly if there are no great differences, a party might be advised to agree to those rules. An example would be in commercial disputes where an agreement refers to the AAA commercial arbitration rules and the AAA as the administering institution. However, where there are no commonly used arbitration rules, as with FLAA-governed arbitrations, the Canons should be considered. There is nothing to stop parties from agreeing to arbitration under the FAA, North Carolina RUAA, or other legislation without arbitrator ethics standards, but such a course of action is not recommended.

Conclusion

The North Carolina Canons of Ethics for Arbitrators apply to court-annexed arbitrations in North Carolina. The North Carolina Bar Association Dispute Resolution Section developed the Canons to fit those cases and as a "one-size-fits-all" option for arbitrations in other settings. Parties considering these ADR options should examine the Canons for these purposes. Even if an award cannot be set aside because of arbitrator misconduct based on the Canons, the Canons are important and valuable in regulating arbitrator conduct.

Maintaining Professionalism

The Standards of Conduct for Mediators and the Canons of Ethics for Arbitrators are at the core of ADR practice and should be second nature to all ADR professionals throughout the state. Governing bodies like the North

Carolina Dispute Resolution Commission and the State Judicial Council, along with the North Carolina Bar Association's Dispute Resolution Section, continue to make professionalism a high priority by providing advice, assistance, and continuing education to assist practitioners in upholding these standards. The DRC has recognized the importance of professionalism for mediators, stating that "the Commission believes that all mediators must remain committed to improving their knowledge and skills through self-reflection, consumer assessment . . . and the completion of continuing mediator education hours."[11]

There may be situations, especially in the context of mediations, when the practitioner encounters circumstances where a course of action does not seem to be clearly spelled out by the rules or standards. Sometimes attorneys or parties are difficult to deal with. Sometimes a mediation that shows promise of reaching settlement drags on beyond what seems like a reasonable period of time. Occasionally, observers behave inappropriately. The ADR practitioner who has internalized the rules and the core values of his or her profession will instinctively meet such challenges with a cool head and common sense, often balancing the exercise of authority with old-fashioned good manners.[12] Moreover, by utilizing the many resources available through the DRC and the North Carolina Bar Association, ADR practitioners can better understand, achieve, and maintain the high standards that are expected of them. In the process, they will continue to solidify and expand opportunities for their profession.

NOTES

1. *See generally* "Continuing Education for Mediators," N.C. Dispute Resolution Commission, The North Carolina Court System, http://www.nccourts.org/Courts/CRS/Councils/DRC/Education.

2. This emphasis on professionalism became institutionalized on September 22, 1998, with the establishment by the North Carolina Supreme Court of the Chief Justice's Commission on Professionalism, whose primary obligation is to enhance professionalism among the state's lawyers. The Commission is required "to provide ongoing attention and assistance to ensure that the practice of law remains a high calling, dedicated to the service of clients and the public good." Melvin F. Wright was hired as the Commission's Executive Director in November 1999.

3. Advisory Opinion of the N.C. Dispute Resolution Commission, Opinion Number 01-03, http://www.nccourts.org/Courts/CRS/Councils/DRC/Documents/01-03_final.pdf.

4. *Id.*

5. *See* N.C. Gen. Stat. §§ 7A-38.1, -38.4, and -38.3.

6. Non-attorneys should consult *Guidelines for the Ethical Practice of Mediation and to Prevent the Unauthorized Practice of Law,* developed by the North Carolina Bar Association's Dispute Resolution Section Task Force on Mediation and the Unauthorized Practice of Law. The *Guidelines,* approved by the North Carolina Bar Association Board of Governors on June 17, 1999, may be downloaded from the DRC's website at http://www.nccourts.org/Courts/CRS/Councils/DRC/Documents/UnauthorizedPracticeofLaw.pdf. It also may be obtained from the Dispute Resolution Section by contacting the North Carolina Bar Association.

7. Substantive conversations are ones that go beyond discussion of the general issues in dispute, the identity of participants, and administrative issues and are those of which a party has some expectation of confidentiality. The prohibition regarding future advice and representation applies not just to the mediator, but also to the mediator's professional partners or co-shareholders.

8. The Commission's website can be accessed at http://www.ncdrc.org. This URL is automatically redirected to the website of the North Carolina Court System, http://www.nccourts.org/Courts/CRS/Councils/DRC/Default.asp.

9. 350 N.C. 877 (2000).

10. 173 F.3d 493, 497–501 (4th Cir. 1999).

11. "Continuing Education for Mediators," *supra* note 1.

12. The North Carolina Bar Association Dispute Resolution Section's newsletter, *The Peacemaker,* publishes the entertaining and enlightening feature "Ms. Mannerly Mediator," which shows how the MSC Rules and the Standards of Professional Conduct for Mediators provide guidance in dealing professionally with a number of challenging "real life" mediation dilemmas.

Summaries of the Dispute Resolution Commission's Ethics Opinions

ADVISORY OPINION NUMBER 99-01

Once a case has been ordered to mediation, a mediator has a duty to assemble the parties and hold the conference prior to the deadline for completion. A mediator may not simply report an impasse based on a representation by the parties that the case cannot be settled.

ADVISORY OPINION NUMBER 00-02

It is preferable for parties to physically attend a mediation conference rather than to participate by telephone. A mediator should not waive or modify the attendance requirement absent some compelling reason to do so.

ADVISORY OPINION NUMBER 01-03

Confidentiality is integral to the success of the mediation process. Mediators should be vigilant in their efforts to preserve confidentiality and should not give affidavits or testify in court as to statements and conduct occurring in connection with a mediation unless the communication is permitted by an exception set forth in a statute or Standard.

ADVISORY OPINION NUMBER 03-04

It is discretionary with individual mediators as to how long they retain mediation files, and mediators should consider confidentiality concerns in making decisions regarding file retention.

ADVISORY OPINION NUMBER 03-05

As long as he or she does not reveal any confidential information, a mediator may, following an impasse, continue to assist a party or parties who contact the mediator in an effort to revive discussions or to clarify something that was said at mediation. If the mediator believes that the party who contacted him or her has a motive other than settlement, the mediator is not obligated to respond or to involve himself or herself further in the matter.

ADVISORY OPINION NUMBER 04-06

A mediator who conducts a mediation for a couple that is separating may not thereafter represent either the husband or the wife in divorce proceedings.

ADVISORY OPINION NUMBER 04-07

Upon learning that a bankruptcy petition has been filed in a case, a mediator shall report to the court that the bankruptcy has been filed and shall request that the judge who referred the matter to mediation advise the mediator as to whether he or she should hold the conference.

ADVISORY OPINION NUMBER 05-08

It is the duty of the mediator, and not that of the parties, to schedule the mediation within the timeframe established by the court for completion.

ADVISORY OPINION NUMBER 06-09

The mediator has a duty to warn parties when confidentiality is breached and parties are at financial or other risk because of the breach. The situation which gave rise to this opinion involved financial information that was removed from a mediator's laptop during service and that could not be relocated and restored.

ADVISORY OPINION NUMBER 06-10

MSC Rule 4.A.(1) addresses who shall attend a conference. Pursuant to Rule 6.A.(1), the mediator has discretion to determine who else may be present. If there is a dispute between the parties regarding whether an individual may attend, it is best practice for the mediator to try and mediate the matter first. If the mediator cannot help the parties reach an agreement on the issue, then the mediator should make a determination as to whether the individual in question may attend.

ADVISORY OPINION NUMBER 07-11

Mediator failed to reduce the terms of an agreement reached in mediation to writing in accordance with MSC Rule 4.A.(2) and 4.C. Moreover, mediator should not have reported to the Senior Resident Superior Court Judge in his Report of Mediator that the case had been settled when there was no writing. Mediator should have accompanied the parties on their site visit to ensure that all the details were ironed out and then assisted them in reducing their agreement to writing.

ADVISORY OPINION NUMBER 07-12

A court-appointed mediator distributed a copy of an agreement to mediate and asked the parties to sign it prior to their mediated settlement conference. The agreement contained terms that modified and even ran counter to program rules and the Standards of Professional Conduct for Mediators. The Commission determined that a court appointed mediator may not, through the use of an agreement to mediate, modify program rules or the Standards.

ADVISORY OPINION NUMBER 07-13

A mediator should not compromise his/her neutrality by overtly accusing a party of being untruthful during mediation or by using language tantamount to such an accusation. A mediator should not confront a party in a hostile or abusive manner. Such actions compromise the mediator's neutrality. A mediator should not use profane language during mediation even if the parties or their lawyers are using such language.

ADVISORY OPINION NUMBER 08-14

This Advisory Opinion addresses a proposal to form a panel of volunteer mediators willing to serve pro bono in mediations involving clients of legal services organizations. The Opinion discusses fees, including disclosure of waiver and negotiation of the shifting of payment to another party, both in the context of service on the proposed panel and in the context of any other mediation where a mediator has agreed to serve pro bono or for a reduced fee relative to at least one party.

ADVISORY OPINION NUMBER 08-15

During a Clerk-referred mediation of a dispute over who should serve as an estate's administrator/fiduciary, the mediator agreed to allow the parties to appoint him as the administrator/fiduciary. The Commission believes that soliciting or even accepting such an appointment at the insistence of the parties can create the impression that the mediator manipulated the mediation process with the ultimate goal of furthering his or her own interests, e.g., receiving the administration fees. A mediator should remain focused exclusively on his or her role as mediator and should not solicit or accept such an appointment.

ADVISORY OPINION NUMBER 10-16

During a caucus session held during the mediation of a family financial dispute, the wife and her attorney told the mediator confidentially that they had intentionally failed to disclose the existence of a valuable marital asset on their inventory affidavit. The mediator asks whether the mediation can continue in the face of this nondisclosure. The Opinion provides that, in these circumstances, the best practice would be for the mediator to engage the offending party and encourage her and her attorney to disclose the asset. If they refuse, then the mediator must terminate the session and withdraw from the mediation without violating the requirements of confidentiality.

ADVISORY OPINION NUMBER 10-17

A mediator is not precluded from serving as an arbitrator in a case that he or she has previously mediated. This Opinion distinguishes the situation where a mediator transitions to the role of arbitrator from the situation where a mediator becomes a fiduciary. Opinion # 8-15 addresses the latter situation and advises that mediators should not solicit or accept an appointment as a fiduciary when that appointment flows from the mediation process. Opinion #10-17 provides guidance on making the transition from mediator to arbitrator.

ADVISORY OPINION NUMBER 11-18

Reports of Mediator serve an important case management function for the courts. If not filed timely, the efficiency that the MSC program provides to the courts is compromised. Therefore it is the duty of all mediators to promptly file a Report with the court at the conclusion of the mediation process. This opinion was initiated by the Commission issuing a reprimand to an experienced mediator for failing to file his Reports correctly over an extended period of time.

ADVISORY OPINION NUMBER 11-19

A party-selected, certified family financial mediator postponed a mediation due to one party being unable to pay his required advance deposit. A judge later dispensed with mediation after determining that the party could not pay her share of the mediator's fee. The Commission determined that while under FFS Rule 7 mediators and parties may agree on compensation, once retained FFS Rule 8 (which limits a mediator's fee arrangement if a party cannot pay) controls. Therefore a mediator should not refuse to conduct a mediation due to a party's inability to pay. Additionally, motions to dispense should not be allowed simply due to a party's inability to pay.

ADVISORY OPINION NUMBER 11-20

An attorney or non-attorney mediator who is also a notary public may notarize an agreement resulting from a mediation that he or she conducted.

ADVISORY OPINION NUMBER 12-21

When a mediator is asked by one party to a mediation to review documents in advance of the conference, a mediator may charge for the time spent in that review. However, to maintain neutrality, the mediator should obtain permission of all parties before undertaking the review, even if one party offers to pay the entire fee associated with the review. Mediators are urged not to charge for routine document review, such as short case summaries or briefs.

ADVISORY OPINION NUMBER 12-22

Standard III of the Standards of Conduct for Certified Mediators places a duty of confidentiality on mediators but not on anyone else involved in the mediation. The parties and their counsel are free to talk to the public or press about statements or conduct occurring in the mediation. Mediators should make it clear that it is the mediator, not the parties, who has a duty of confidentiality.

ADVISORY OPINION NUMBER 12-23

Program enabling legislation provides for mediator testimony at State Bar disciplinary hearings regarding an attorney's conduct in mediation. However, where no subpoena is involved, the Commission does not read the legislation broadly to permit mediators to answer a State Bar investigator's questions in preliminary stages of an investigation. A note following the Opinion addresses situations where an attorney-mediator is him or herself the subject of the investigation.

PART II
ADR Practice:
The Nuts & Bolts of ADR Procedures
in Use in North Carolina

MEDIATION OF CIVIL CLAIMS

CHAPTER TWELVE

The Mediated Settlement Conference Program in North Carolina's Superior Courts

"[T]o be a good mediator you need more than anything patience,
common sense, an appropriate manner, and goodwill. You must make
yourself liked by both parties, and gain credibility in their minds.
To do that, begin by explaining that you are unhappy about the bother,
the trouble and the expense that their litigation is causing them.
After that, listen patiently to all their complaints.
They will not be short, particularly the first time around."
—Prior of St. Pierre, *The Charitable Arbitrator* (1666)

Program Design

The North Carolina legislature established the Mediated Settlement Conference Program (MSC Program) in the state's superior courts to facilitate early settlement of civil cases and to make civil litigation more economical, efficient, and satisfactory to litigants. The Rules of the North Carolina Supreme Court Implementing Statewide Mediated Settlement Conferences in Superior Court Civil Actions (MSC Rules), promulgated under North Carolina General Statutes Section 7A-38.1, require senior resident superior court judges to order pretrial mediated settlement conferences in civil actions, except those actions in which a party is seeking the issuance of an extraordinary writ or is appealing the revocation of a motor vehicle operator's license. During a mediated settlement conference, a neutral third party, the mediator, meets with the parties to help them discuss and resolve the issues in dispute without the need for protracted litigation and trial. If the dispute cannot be resolved, then the case proceeds to trial.

Although mediated settlement conferences are mandated by statute and are the default procedure in superior court, the parties may request the use of an alternative settlement procedure if all agree to the alternative process and if the procedure is one that is authorized by the Supreme Court or by local court rules. Such a request is made by motion to the senior resident superior court judge in the judicial district in which the case is pending. The MSC Rules are not intended to limit or prevent the parties from voluntarily engaging in other types of settlement procedures at any time before or after those ordered by the court, including binding or non-binding arbitration.

Key Features of the MSC Program

Two key aspects of the Mediated Settlement Conference Program set it apart from other dispute resolution programs in use in North Carolina. First, the Program is designed as a "user pay" program; that is, the litigants—not taxpayers—compensate the mediator for his or her services. Second, in the MSC Program the parties have an opportunity to choose their mediator. Designation of a mediator by the parties was seen by the Program's designers as a "quality control" device in a system where mediation providers are independent contractors, not employees of the state. The court appoints a mediator only in instances where the parties fail to make a designation, cannot agree upon a mediator, or request that the court make a selection for them.

Characteristics of Mediated Settlement Conferences

The term "mediated settlement conferences," as used in North Carolina General Statutes Section 7A-38.1, refers specifically to mediated settlement conferences in the superior courts of North Carolina. The term was not intended to distinguish the general settlement process from what many consider a "pure" form of mediation, but rather to help gain acceptance in the legal community for a new concept: court-ordered mediation. What some might have seen as a potentially threatening innovation was recast as the familiar (if seldom used) settlement conference.

The mediated settlement conference is a mandatory event in the life of a civil case in the superior courts of North Carolina. The parties, their attorneys, and others with settlement authority (including insurance company representatives) are required to attend. However, the process itself is entirely voluntary. There is no requirement to negotiate in good faith or to negotiate at all. The mediated settlement conference process has proven successful because the decision makers and their advisors are required to attend and to work with the assistance of a trained mediator.

A typical conference begins with the parties working together in a "general session," at which the parties present their respective positions in the case and exchange any relevant information that was not provided during the discovery process. After the general session, the parties usually separate and meet with the mediator in "private sessions," sometimes referred to as "caucus sessions." During these sessions the mediator helps the parties analyze their positions, think through their needs, and develop options and proposals for settlement. Much of the time spent in mediated settlement conferences is in private sessions, with the mediator shuttling between the parties. Although the parties often return to general sessions, particularly in complex business cases, private sessions are seen as necessary components of a negotiating process. (The heavy reliance upon private sessions in mediated settlement conferences is probably due to the fact that most litigants view their case analysis as private information.) The typical conference is completed in one session usually lasting between two and four hours.

Program Operations

The North Carolina General Assembly charged the Supreme Court of North Carolina with adopting rules to implement the pilot MSC Program, and rules were first adopted in October 1991. The MSC Rules were revised after the Program was approved for statewide expansion in July 1995 and have been modified over the years as mediators and court personnel have gained a deeper appreciation of the mediation process and how it can be more effectively utilized in the courts. Copies of the MSC Rules are available on the website of the North Carolina Dispute Resolution Commission (DRC or Commission)[1] or through the DRC's office. Many superior court judicial districts have also adopted local rules, which supplement the MSC Rules. The framework for the MSC Program's operations as set forth in the MSC Rules is discussed below, along with some practical tips for mediators and attorneys.

Prior to Mediation

CONSULTATION WITH CLIENTS AND OPPOSING PARTY

The Rules place a duty on attorneys, upon being retained, to advise their client(s) regarding the settlement procedures available to them under MSC or local rules and to attempt to reach an agreement with opposing counsel as to which settlement procedure they will utilize in the case. Most attorneys and their clients choose the default procedure of mediated settlement rather than selecting an alternate procedure.

INITIATING THE CONFERENCE

The MSC Rules provide that the senior resident superior court judge of the judicial district in which a civil action is filed shall issue a written order requiring all parties, attorneys, and insurance company representatives to attend a pretrial mediated settlement conference. The only cases exempted from referral are those actions in which a party is seeking the issuance of an extraordinary writ or is appealing the revocation of a motor vehicle operator's license. The order must be issued as soon as practicable after the time for the filing of answers has expired. The deadline for completion of the conference is set by the judge at not less than 120 days or more than 180 days after issuance of the order. In districts that use scheduling conferences or orders pursuant to local rule, the MSC Rules require the senior resident superior court judge or his or her designee to set a completion date well in advance of trial. The deadline should be set at the scheduling conference or in the scheduling order or notice.

MOTION TO DISPENSE WITH MEDIATED SETTLEMENT CONFERENCE

For good cause, parties who have been referred to mediated settlement may move the senior resident superior court judge to dispense with the process. Good cause may include, but is not limited to, the fact that the parties have already participated in a settlement procedure or have elected to resolve their case through private arbitration. The fact that parties are indigent or live at considerable distance from the location of the conference should not be an impediment to mediation, and the MSC Rules address these situations. For example, Rule 4 provides for telephone participation, and Rule 7 provides that the mediator must waive fees for parties determined indigent by the court. As a practical matter, most judges have been reluctant to grant motions to dispense with mediation.

MEDIATOR SELECTION OR APPOINTMENT

One of the hallmarks of the MSC Program is that parties are given an opportunity to select or "designate" their mediator. Only in instances where the parties take no action to designate a mediator or cannot agree on their choice and ask the court for assistance does the court intervene and appoint a mediator. The MSC Rules provide that where the conference is initiated by court order, the parties have twenty-one days to designate a mediator and report their choice. Where the conference is initiated by local rule, the deadline for designation also is established by local rule. A Designation of Mediator form is used to notify the court of the parties' selection. The same form can also be used to request court appointment of a mediator if the parties cannot agree on one.

The Rules require that only certified mediators may serve the MSC Program (i.e., training and certification are required whether the mediator is serving pursuant to the parties' selection or a court appointment). The qualifications for mediator certification are set out in the MSC Rules. North Carolina licensed attorneys, attorneys licensed in other states, and non-attorneys are all eligible to be certified if they possess the requisite education and work experience; complete the training, observations, and other requirements set forth in MSC Rule 8; and demonstrate that they are of good moral character. A list of certified mediators is posted on the DRC's website. Each mediator's individual listing, or "Mediator Profile," includes contact information, availability by judicial district, and biographical information submitted by the mediator. The DRC has also published on its website a "Guide to Selecting a Mediator," which offers tips to attorneys and pro se parties on what to look for in a mediator and how to best utilize the Commission's website to locate mediators.

If the parties do not designate a mediator within the twenty-one-day period established by the MSC Rules or the deadline for mediator selection set by local rules, or if they report that they cannot agree on a mediator, the senior resident superior court judge will appoint a certified mediator to conduct their conference. In making appointments, judges are to rotate down the DRC's list of certified mediators available for appointment in the judicial district, departing from a strict rotation only when there is good cause to do so. Certified mediators who do not reside in the judicial district or a county contiguous to the judicial district may be included in the rotation only if, on an annual basis, they have informed the judge in writing that they agree to travel to the district to mediate cases.

Parties who do not submit the Designation of Mediator form within the appropriate time frame and then seek to substitute their selection for a mediator appointed by the senior resident superior court judge are required to pay a $150 substitution penalty to the mediator appointed by the court and to provide proof of that payment to the court before the substitution may occur. This penalty is intended to encourage parties to submit their form in a timely fashion, thus minimizing the frustration and inconvenience for court staff and court-appointed mediators alike. The DRC has adopted an approved form for requesting substitutions.

SCHEDULING THE MEDIATED SETTLEMENT CONFERENCE

The Mediator as Case Manager

Once selected, by agreement or appointment, the mediator becomes the case manager for purposes of scheduling the mediation conference and reporting its results to the court. The MSC Rules give the mediator responsibility for scheduling the conference, for reserving a location, and for giving timely notice of the date, time, and location to the persons and entities required to attend. The mediator must make a good faith effort to schedule the conference at a time convenient for the parties. The MSC Rules specify that the mediation must be held in a public place or a location agreed to by the parties. Most conferences are held in the offices of one of the lawyers involved in the case or the office of the mediator. If a mediator is advised that there may be safety concerns, he or she will likely hold the mediation in a courthouse or other secure facility. The mediator must schedule the conference for a date prior to the deadline for completion established by the court's order.

Requests for Extensions

The MSC Rules provide that a senior resident superior court judge may extend a deadline for completion of the conference upon the judge's own motion, upon stipulation of the parties, or upon suggestion of the mediator.

A party or parties may ask their mediator to reschedule a conference as long as the proposed new date is prior to the deadline for completion set by the court. (As noted above, only the court may extend a deadline past the completion date.) The mediator and the opposing attorney(s) must agree to the postponement. The DRC has warned mediators that there should be a compelling reason for such a request, even if the new date is before the deadline, since one of the main purposes of the MSC Program is to expedite settlement of cases. Postponements frequently work to the opposite effect, especially when no compelling reason exists for the delay. In requesting a postponement, parties should be aware that the MSC Rules provide for postponement fees to be assessed against a party who seeks to reschedule a conference without good cause. The penalty will be higher if the request is made on short notice and just prior to the scheduled date for the conference.

Preparing the Client for Mediated Settlement

An attorney should plan to spend time with his or her client prior to mediation, explaining what will happen at the conference and encouraging the client to come prepared to cooperate and to collaborate. A brochure about the MSC process, designed especially for litigants, is available from the DRC. Copies are provided at no charge to the parties and to law offices. The DRC's website also provides information about mediated settlement and the MSC Program. A visit to the website or a quick reading of the brochure can reinforce the information an attorney conveys about the MSC process during discussions with the client.

Prior to mediation, the attorney should also discuss a settlement range with the client and determine which issues are negotiable and which are not. Lastly, the attorney should advise the client that he or she will need to pay for the mediator's professional services at the conclusion of the conference, as provided in the MSC Rules, and advise him or her to bring a checkbook to the mediation.

Attorney Preparation for Mediated Settlement

Careful preparation by counsel can help to ensure that the mediation process will benefit the client. The following steps are essential prior to a mediated settlement conference:

- Complete sufficient discovery to form an educated opinion of what the case is worth and to document that opinion for opposing counsel.

- Arrange for settlement authority. If the client is a corporation or other form of business entity, the attorney should make sure that the representative sent to mediation has authority to decide whether, and on what terms, to settle the action. If an insurance carrier is involved, the defense attorney should seek to ensure that a claims manager or experienced adjuster is present and has authority either to make a decision on behalf of the carrier or to negotiate and to communicate during the conference with persons who have decision-making authority.

- Develop a strong presentation.

- Prepare a checklist of all items that, from the client's perspective, need to be discussed and resolved for agreement to occur.

At the Mediated Settlement Conference

ATTENDANCE

Who Must Attend

The MSC Rules provide that the following persons must attend the conference:

- All individual parties;
- A representative of any governmental or corporate entity that is a party, who is not the entity's outside counsel and has authority to decide whether and on what terms to settle the case, or can communicate with persons who do have authority;
- At least one counsel of record for each party; and
- A representative of each liability insurance carrier, uninsured motorist insurance carrier, and underinsured motorist insurance carrier that may be obligated to pay all or part of any claim presented in the action. The representative, who may not be the carrier's outside counsel, must have authority either to make decisions on behalf of the carrier or to negotiate on behalf of the carrier and to communicate with persons who do have decision-making authority.

Also, any party or attorney who has received notice of a lien or other claim upon proceeds recovered in the action must notify the lien holder or claimant of the date, time, and location of the mediated settlement conference and request his or her attendance at the conference.

Those who attend the conference should remember that mediated settlement, while an informal proceeding, is still a court-ordered event. Attendees should behave courteously and decorously. If litigants do not feel that the conference has given them the benefit of "their day in court," they may not be inclined to settle.

Waiver/Modification of the Attendance Requirement

Modification or waiver of the attendance requirement is allowed only: (1) by agreement of all parties, other persons required to attend, and the mediator, or (2) by order of the senior resident superior court judge upon motion of a party and notice to all parties and persons required to attend. Such requests may be made, for example, when one or more persons required to attend wish(es) to participate by telephone (as when a party or adjuster is located at a considerable distance from where the conference is scheduled to be held) or seek(s) to be excused from attending. However, the

DRC strongly favors physical attendance by the parties and representatives. Physical attendance gives parties an opportunity to come face-to-face with the other side, and to hear opposing views of the facts in dispute and the other side's assessment of the case. It also allows parties to be active participants in formulating offers and counteroffers and gives them a sense of ownership of any agreement reached during the conference. Thus, the DRC has issued an Advisory Opinion cautioning that the attendance requirement should not be casually waived or modified, even if all parties consent.[2]

Sanctions for Failure to Attend

The MSC Rules authorize a superior court judge to impose monetary or contempt sanctions on any person required to attend a conference, who, without good cause, fails to do so. MSC Rule 5 specifically provides that a superior court judge has the discretion to require such a party to pay the mediator's fees and related expenses.

AUTHORITY AND DUTIES OF THE MEDIATOR

The mediator alone has the authority to control the conference, not the parties or their attorneys. The MSC Rules permit the mediator to communicate privately with any participant or counsel prior to or during the session. If prior communications have occurred, the mediator must disclose that fact at the beginning of the conference.

The MSC Rules specify a list of topics the mediator must discuss at the beginning of the conference to explain the mediation process to the parties. The mediator also must advise the participants of any circumstance bearing on his or her possible bias, prejudice, or partiality. When appropriate, it is the mediator's responsibility to declare an impasse in the proceedings. In determining whether an impasse has been reached, the MSC Rules provide that the mediator is to consider the wishes of the parties.

FINALIZING THE AGREEMENT

If an agreement is reached at the MSC, the MSC Rules require that it be reduced to writing and signed by the parties. North Carolina General Statutes Section 7A-38.1 provides that an agreement reached at mediation is not enforceable unless it is reduced to writing.

COMPENSATION OF THE MEDIATOR

The mediator is to be compensated for his or her services at the conclusion of the conference. A party-selected mediator's fees are established by agreement of the parties and the mediator. The fees of court-appointed mediators, however, are capped. At the time of publication, court-appointed mediators receive $150 per hour for mediation services plus a one-time per case administrative fee of $150. The administrative fee, unlike the fee for professional services, is due upon the appointment of the mediator, although as a practical matter that fee generally is also paid at the conclusion of the conference.

If a case scheduled for mediation is rescheduled without good cause, the party seeking to reschedule must pay a postponement fee of $150 in addition to the one-time per case administrative fee. "Good cause" is defined as a situation over which the party seeking the postponement has no control, including, but not limited to, a party or attorney's illness, a death in a party or attorney's family, or a sudden and unexpected demand by a judge that a party or attorney for a party appear in court. If a case is rescheduled just before the mediation is to occur, the penalty is higher.

If the case settles prior to the scheduled date for mediation, the settlement constitutes good cause as long as the mediator was notified of the settlement immediately after it was reached and received notice of the settlement at least fourteen calendar days prior to the date scheduled for mediation.

Unless otherwise agreed to by the parties or ordered by the court, party-selected and court-appointed mediator fees are paid in equal shares by the parties, except that multiple parties represented by the same counsel are considered a single party under MSC Rules and pay a single share. MSC Rules provide that willful failure to pay a mediator's fee in a timely manner, following notice and a hearing, may result in a contempt ruling and monetary sanctions.

Under the MSC Rules, a party found by the court to be indigent is not required to pay mediator's fees. An attorney representing an indigent party may petition the senior resident superior court judge by filing a Petition and Order for Relief from Obligation to Pay Mediator's Fee. The determination of indigence will be made subsequent to the mediation. In ruling on the motion, the judge must not only apply the criteria enumerated in North Carolina General Statutes Section 1-110(a), but also must take into account the outcome of the action and whether a judgment was rendered in the movant's favor.

Following Mediation

REPORT OF MEDIATOR
The mediator is required to file a Report of Mediator (Report) with the senior resident superior court judge within ten days of the conclusion of the

conference. A Report must be filed whether or not a mediation was actually held. Recent revisions to MSC Rules also require the mediator to file a Report in cases that he or she mediates that are filed in superior court, but have not been ordered to mediation (i.e., cases filed that are voluntarily mediated). The Report advises the court who attended the conference and states the outcome: mediation not held, case settled pre-mediation, case settled at the conference, or parties reached an impasse. When a mediator reports a case settled either prior to, at, or during a recess of a conference, he or she must also indicate whether a voluntary dismissal or consent judgment will be filed in the case and provide the name, address, and telephone of the person who will file the closing document. In addition, the mediator must advise the parties that MSC Rule 4.C. requires that their consent judgment or voluntary dismissal be filed with the court within thirty days (or within ninety days if the state or a political subdivision of the state is a party to the action). Court staff use information contained in the Reports to help manage the court's docket. They also use the information to track program performance. Court staff members extract information from the Reports each month and forward it to the Administrative Office of the Courts (AOC). The AOC compiles the monthly caseload and outcome data submitted by individual districts for publication in an annual report. The DRC also distributes copies of the compiled caseload statistics along with its own annual report to senior resident superior court judges, members of the legislature, officials of the North Carolina Bar Association and the State Bar, the DRC's appointing authorities, and others.

The DRC takes mediator case management responsibilities, including reporting, very seriously. Mediators who do not file their Reports, or do not file them on time, risk discipline by the Commission and are subject to sanctions by the senior resident superior court judge to whom they failed to report.

When an Agreement Falls Apart

Occasionally a party will seek to renege on a settlement agreement. Under the MSC Rules, when a party reneges on an agreement reached at a settlement conference, an attorney cannot subpoena the mediator to testify about what occurred at the mediation, or to discuss or interpret the content of the agreement. In such cases, North Carolina General Statutes Section 7A-38.1(*l*) limits mediator testimony as follows:

> . . . No mediator shall be compelled to testify or produce evidence concerning statements made and conduct occurring in a mediated settle-

ment conference in any civil proceeding for any purpose, including proceedings to enforce a settlement of the action, except to attest to the signing of any such agreements, and except proceedings for sanctions under this section, disciplinary hearings before the State Bar or any agency established to enforce standards of conduct for mediators, and proceedings to enforce laws concerning juvenile or elder abuse.

If the attorney senses that there has been a true misunderstanding of the terms reached, he or she may want to invite the other side to meet with the mediator again in an effort to clarify the situation and to head off a motion to set aside or enforce the agreement.

When Impasse Results

An impasse is sometimes inevitable. When the conference ends in impasse but on a positive note, it often is possible to informally continue the dialogue begun at the mediation and ultimately settle the case without trial.

Oversight

Program Oversight

A senior resident superior court judge has broad administrative authority over the Mediated Settlement Conference Program operating in his or her district. Judges may also adopt local rules to supplement the Supreme Court's Rules for the MSC Program.

The Dispute Resolution Commission is charged with certifying mediators to conduct mediated settlement conferences in superior court and with regulating the conduct of mediators serving the MSC Program.[3] The DRC also serves as a "sounding board" for those involved in the MSC Program, working with court personnel, lawyers, mediators, insurance carriers, litigants, and others to improve the Program. In response to suggestions received from interested parties, the DRC often recommends additions or revisions to the MSC Rules.

On July 13, 2000, the Supreme Court authorized the State Judicial Council to establish an ADR Committee for Dispute Resolution as an "umbrella" agency for dispute resolution in North Carolina. The ADR Committee helps the Supreme Court set policies for dispute resolution in the state, including policies for the MSC Program. The DRC assists this Committee by recommending new rules and rule revisions for the MSC Program.

Mediator Oversight

THE CERTIFICATION PROCESS

The Dispute Resolution Commission has certified a large and talented pool of mediators. As of the date of this publication, there are nearly 2,000 mediator certifications. Of that number, more than 1,300 hold active or inactive superior court certifications. While both attorneys and non-attorneys may be certified to conduct conferences in superior court, the majority of certified mediators serving the Program—roughly 85 percent—are North Carolina-licensed attorneys.

An attorney applicant must be licensed to practice law in North Carolina or some other state and must possess at least five years' experience as a judge, practicing attorney, law professor, or mediator, or have equivalent experience. To complete the certification process an attorney applicant must attend a forty-hour mediator training course, observe two mediated settlement conferences, and pay a certification fee.

A non-attorney applicant must have significant mediation experience plus at least four years of relatively high-level management, professional, or administrative experience, or he or she must possess at least ten years of relatively high-level management, professional, or administrative experience. All non-attorney applicants must complete a forty-hour mediator training course; complete six hours of training on North Carolina court organization, legal terminology, civil court procedure, the attorney/client privilege, the unauthorized practice of law, and common legal issues arising in superior court; observe five mediated settlement conferences; provide three letters of reference; and pay a certification fee.

The DRC has developed an application process that seeks to ensure applicants not only meet these basic criteria, but also demonstrate that they are of the highest moral character. The DRC also certifies mediator training programs and has adopted Guidelines that flesh out the curriculum for the forty-hour superior court mediator training program set forth in the MSC Rules and mentioned above.

STANDARDS OF PROFESSIONAL CONDUCT

Upon recommendation of the DRC, the Supreme Court of North Carolina adopted "Standards of Professional Conduct for Mediators" on December 30, 1998. These Standards govern the conduct of mediators serving the MSC Program. Under the Standards the mediator must: (1) maintain competency in his or her professional skills; (2) remain impartial; (3) maintain confidentiality; (4) make reasonable efforts to ensure that each party understands the mediation process and the role of the mediator; (5) respect and encourage the parties' efforts to resolve their disputes on their own terms; (6) keep his or her role as mediator separate from other professional roles and not offer legal or other advice to the parties; (7) avoid conflicts of interest; and (8) protect the integrity of the mediation process.

The Rules of the North Carolina Supreme Court for the Dispute Resolution Commission (DRC Rules) provide for enforcement of the Standards by authorizing the DRC to investigate complaints brought against mediators, to conduct hearings, and when necessary, to discipline a mediator. Copies of the Standards, DRC Rules, and complaint forms may be obtained on the DRC's website or by contacting its office. The DRC Rules also discuss issues of moral turpitude and fitness to practice and provide that mediators must conduct themselves in such a way as not to discredit the DRC, the courts, or the mediation process.

In an effort to serve mediators in their practice and to establish a more uniform application of the MSC Rules, the DRC has adopted an Advisory Opinion Policy that states mediators may seek either an informal (oral) or formal (written) opinion on ethical issues or other dilemmas that arise in the course of the mediator's practice. The DRC publishes formal opinions in its newsletter and posts them on its website.

The Role of the Attorney

Prior to Mediation

THE IMPORTANCE OF ATTITUDE

Success in an endeavor often stems from a positive attitude. If an attorney is to be successful in mediation, it is important that he or she have confidence in the process and an appreciation of the benefits derived from mediation. It is also important for the attorney to be able to explain the advantages of mediation to the client and to make him or her comfortable with the process.

THE ADVANTAGES OF MEDIATION

Reduced Time, Stress, and Expense

Proponents of mediation cite first among its virtues the fact that the process can reduce time, stress, and expense. Mediated settlement conferences shorten the filing to disposition time in contested cases by about seven weeks.[4] Litigants are also spared the stress of protracted litigation and trial. This is a distinct advantage for most people. Many clients worry about going to court, fear testifying, and dread the consequences of an adverse ruling.

If successful, mediation may help contain the costs associated with litigation for litigants and for the legal system. Parties, particularly those with limited resources, are spared the expense of lengthy litigation and trial. Attorneys should also keep in mind that the traditional judicial system is expensive to operate. Each time new judges are added to handle mounting caseloads, judicial assistants, bailiffs, clerk staff, and courtrooms must also be added. Mediated settlement is designed to relieve some of the resulting strain on governmental resources. Mediation also aids the existing court structure. When cases are resolved in mediation, judges can devote more time to those civil cases that must be tried, or to criminal matters before the courts.

Relationships Preserved

Another advantage of mediated settlement conferences is the role they often play in preserving relationships (or rather, what is left of them) after a case is filed. This may be less critical in superior court cases than it is in district court family matters. However, an attorney should not overlook the fact that there may be relationship issues in some superior court cases as well. For example, mediation's emphasis on cooperation and collaboration may be just what is needed in a contract dispute between a wholesaler and retailer in which the parties need assistance to resolve a misunderstanding and do not want to alienate one another. Mediation may also be very effective in the case of a failing business owned by family members or by longstanding business partners. A party may need legal assistance in sorting out and securing a fair share of the assets of the business, but may not want to antagonize family members or lifelong friends in the process.

A cooperative and collaborative approach likewise may be effective where competing public interests have clashed. Undoubtedly, parties such as environmentalists, developers, agricultural interests, and governmental agencies, with differing views on the current and future state of North Carolina's environment, are destined to meet over and over again. A consensus-building approach to resolving their disputes—one that seeks to incorporate and, as much as possible, accommodate all points of view—may help minimize conflict and set the stage for better communication and increased cooperation in the future.

Privacy Preserved

In litigation, court files are generally open to the public and the press, and sensational trials may attract local and even national or international attention. Mediation, with its confidentiality protections, offers a much more private, low-key approach to conflict resolution.

A reticent client, even one whose situation is not likely to pique the interest of the public or press, may be fearful of appearing on the witness stand before a judge or jury and publicly reliving the intimate details that led to the filing of a medical malpractice, sexual harassment, or alienation of affection case. A corporate representative may not wish to have information about a company's business plans, accounting records, or research and development activity made public, and thus accessible to competing business interests. A successful mediation will render such testimony unnecessary and may eliminate the need to make such information public.

Except for some narrow exceptions, statements or conduct occurring in mediated settlement conferences are not subject to discovery and are inadmissible in any proceeding in the action or other civil actions on the same claim.[5] In addition, Standard III of the Standards of Professional Conduct for Mediators requires mediators to observe confidentiality in the broader sense, prohibiting mediators from talking with the public or press about what occurred at mediation. Standard III does not apply to parties or their lawyers, but MSC Rule 4 forbids parties or their attorneys from recording mediation proceedings, whether openly or surreptitiously.

Working with Pro Se Parties Made Easier

Although pro se parties are seen less frequently in superior court than they are in district court, an attorney may find that mediation can be helpful when pro se parties are involved. Many attorneys are uncomfortable handling a case in which the other party to the litigation is not represented by counsel. Even if the attorney's client wants to settle the case, the attorney may be uncomfortable in contacting the pro se party directly, or in having the party come to the lawyer's office to discuss settlement. Mediation can make such situations less awkward. During mediation, the mediator will secure a neutral place to conduct the mediation, and settlement discussions will occur under the direction of the neutral facilitator.

Increased Control and Finality

Mediation offers parties the opportunity to decide how to resolve their own dispute, rather than gambling that a judge or jury will rule in their favor. In mediation, the client is not likely to win on every point but is very likely to achieve satisfaction on some issues. Litigation offers no such assurances. Once a settlement agreement is signed the parties also have the security of knowing that the dispute is over. They do not have to wait anxiously through an appeals period or deal with the stress of initiating or resisting an appeal. Experience has also shown that parties are more likely to comply with agreements reached voluntarily, as opposed to decisions entered by the court.

Improved Public Image

In recent years the legal profession has suffered from image problems. Nearly everyone is familiar with "lawyer jokes," and attorneys continue to be a favorite target of comedians, talk show hosts, journalists, and many others. Attorneys who participate in mediation programs can do much to dispel the negative perception of attorneys as greedy, vicious, and unethical. Because the mediation process stresses cooperation and works to save time and money for all involved, mediation can, in a sense, serve as a good public relations tool for the legal profession.

SELECTING THE MEDIATOR

An attorney engaged in the process of selecting a mediator will find no shortage of talent from which to choose. A listing of certified superior court mediators is posted on the Commission's website. The Commission has published a "Guide to Selecting a Mediator," also available online, which provides information about searching its lists and gives tips on selecting a mediator. Because there is such a large group of mediators available, parties and their attorneys should consider the selection of a mediator carefully. Some factors an attorney may want to examine in selecting a mediator follow.

Criteria for Selection

Professional Background and Education. The mediator is an expert in the mediation process. Rarely does the mediator also need to be an authority on the type of dispute at issue or the case law in question. Nevertheless, if the case is an extremely complex one either factually or legally, an attorney may be more comfortable with a mediator who has some command of the technical vocabulary, who understands the context in which the dispute arose, and who appreciates the subtleties of the factual and legal issues raised by the parties. For example, parties who are involved in a complicated construction defect case may want to locate an attorney-mediator with an undergraduate background in engineering, or perhaps a non-attorney engineer mediator who has testified in court and who is familiar with the legal terminology and relevant case law.

Attorneys who are considering retaining such an "expert" as a mediator should be aware, however, of Section V of the Supreme Court's Standards of Professional Conduct for Mediators:

V. Self-Determination: A mediator shall respect and encourage self-determination by the parties in their decision whether, and on what terms, to resolve their dispute, and shall refrain from being directive and judgmental regarding the issues in dispute and options for settlement.

A. A mediator is obligated to leave to the parties full responsibility for deciding whether and on what terms to resolve their dispute. He/She may assist them in making informed and thoughtful decisions, but shall not impose his/her judgment for that of the parties concerning any aspect of the mediation.

. . .

C. A mediator shall not impose his/her opinion about the merits of a dispute or about the acceptability of any proposed option for settlement. A mediator should resist giving his/her opinions about the dispute and options for settlement when he/she is requested to do so by a party or attorney. Instead, a mediator should help that party utilize his/her own resources to evaluate the dispute and the options for settlement.

This section prohibits imposing one's opinions, advice and/or counsel upon a party or attorney. It does not prohibit the mediator's expression of an opinion as a last resort to a party or attorney who requests it and the mediator has already helped that party utilize his/her own resources to evaluate the dispute and options.

In short, Section V suggests that the parties should not select an "expert" mediator in the expectation that he or she will tell them the best way to settle their dispute, or proclaim how a judge or jury would decide the case.

Mediation Experience. Depending on the factors present in a case, an attorney may want to know about a mediator's professional experience: How many conferences has the mediator conducted? What types of cases has he or she mediated? What kinds of issues were involved in the cases? How complex were the issues? Were there multiple parties? Has the mediator had to deal with the press? Has the mediator ever worked with an interpreter? How successful has the mediator been?

One caveat: No mediator will ever be completely successful, and anyone making such a claim should be suspect as either an overzealous arm-twister, or a mediator more concerned with his or her "batting average" than with the durability of settlement agreements. However, a mediator should have a solid track record of having brought parties to agreement.

Mediator's Race, Ethnicity, Gender, or Sexual Orientation. In rare cases the race, ethnicity, gender, or sexual orientation of the mediator may make a difference. For example, if the case involves a claim of sexual harassment, a female plaintiff may feel more comfortable discussing her case with a female mediator.

Mediator Style. Mediation is an art, not a science. Each mediator has a unique approach to managing conflict and building consensus. An attorney should choose a mediator with whose style both the attorney and client will be comfortable. The attorney may also want to select a mediator whose style or approach to a case suits the client's temperament or mindset. For example, some mediators are more directive than others and tend to lean more on parties to settle. Some attorneys may not feel comfortable with this approach, and many parties will be intimidated or feel resentful. However, an attorney with a belligerent client who simply will not listen to reason may want a more "authoritarian" mediator, who presumably would intervene more forcefully.

Attorneys can learn about a mediator's style by talking with other attorneys who have used the mediator's services, or even by observing the mediator in action (with the permission of the mediator and others present, of course). An attorney should become familiar with the mediation process and the Standards of Professional Conduct for Mediators to differentiate acceptable practices and techniques from those considered questionable. Armed with such knowledge, an attorney can make an informed judgment about a mediator's capabilities and style.

PREPARING FOR THE MEDIATED SETTLEMENT CONFERENCE

Careful preparation by counsel is essential to ensure the success of a mediated settlement conference. Attorneys who do not begin preparing for mediation at least weeks in advance may compromise their chance for success.

Counsel must understand both the opponent's case and their client's case. At the pleading stage, broad allegations may be sufficient, but in preparing for settlement, the attorney must be able to articulate each element of harm. For example, in a construction case, the plaintiff must be able to list all alleged defects and support an assessment of damages for each defect. When preparation is neglected, an impasse is the likely outcome.

Completing Sufficient Discovery

The attorney's most important duty in preparing for mediation is to complete sufficient discovery to form an educated opinion of the worth of the case, and to document that opinion for the other side. The attorney should make sure that any physicians, accountants, actuaries, engineers, or other experts needed for the settlement conference have sufficient time to complete their work and make their findings available. If discovery is not completed or substantially completed beforehand, the mediation will likely fail. In a personal injury case, for example, if medical examinations are not completed before mediation and the full extent of the plaintiff's injuries is not yet known, it will be nearly impossible for the attorneys to make realistic settlement offers and counteroffers.

In cases involving a business or corporation in which many complicated financial records are at issue, an attorney may want to bring an accountant to the mediation session. During the mediation, the accountant may prove indispensable in interpreting the records and responding to the interpretations of opposing counsel. Again, the attorney must give sufficient notice to permit review of the documents prior to the mediation. Advance planning can mean the difference between success and failure. The mediation process itself, however, is not designed as a discovery tool. The conference should not be used as an excuse to depose a participating party or to gather evidence. Mediation is designed to explore *settlement* of the case. An attorney should be prepared in advance and not seek to turn the mediation into a discovery opportunity. An attorney who attempts to abuse the mediation process in this respect will likely alienate opposing counsel and hurt chances for settlement.

Arranging for Settlement Authority

If the client is a corporation or other form of business entity, the attorney should ensure that the representative sent to mediation on the client's behalf has authority to decide whether and on what terms to settle the action, as required by the MSC Rules. If the client is a governmental entity, the representative must have authority to decide on behalf of the entity whether and on what terms to settle the action, or have authority to negotiate on behalf of the entity and make recommendations to any board ultimately responsible for settling the matter. If an insurance carrier is involved, it is preferable to have a claims manager or an experienced adjuster present. The carrier's representative must have authority to make a decision on its behalf, or have authority to negotiate and to communicate during the conference with persons who have decision-making authority. If a representative of the carrier arrives at mediation with little or no authority to discuss settlement, the conference is not likely to get very far. Similar problems arise at conference for those insurance representatives who must "phone in" to get permission to sign off on a settlement agreement and the decision maker is unavailable.

Reviewing the Rules and Checking for Need of Case Summaries

Obviously, any attorney who is not familiar with the MSC Rules should review them prior to the conference. If an attorney has any questions about the Rules, he or she may contact the DRC for clarification.

Most mediators do not ask lawyers to prepare case summaries for them prior to a conference. However, if an attorney has not used a mediator previously, it might be good to check on this point. Also, if a case is exceptionally complicated factually or legally, the attorneys may want to approach the mediator and offer to provide summaries. Such summaries could cut down on the time spent at the conference providing background information to the mediator and bringing him or her up to speed.

Developing a Strong Presentation

Many attorneys who commit considerable time and energy to preparing for trial give mediation short shrift. But props (such as enlarged photographs, slides, or overheads) and audiovisuals can be very effective, and a polished case summary can have a very positive impact during a settlement conference. A strong presentation lets opposing counsel know the attorney and client are serious, and that if a settlement is not reached, the court fight will be a tough one.

Preparing the Client

Some attorneys do not take the time to prepare their clients for mediation. It may be their view that the mediator will explain the mediation process in his or her opening statement, so why should the attorney bother? It is important, however, that the attorney make the extra effort. An explanation and assurances are likely to mean more coming from the client's own counsel than from a stranger the client has just met, even though the mediator may have been handpicked by the lawyer. Also, discussing the mediation process with counsel well in advance can be very reassuring to a client and put him or her in a more positive frame of mind. A mediator's explanation and assurances at the mediation may come as cold comfort to a fretful party who endured a sleepless night prior to the conference and is already exhausted and out of sorts.

Explaining the Mediation Process. When preparing the client for mediation, the attorney should review a number of important matters. First, the attorney should explain the purpose and benefits of mediation: that it may save the client time and money and may involve less stress; that it is an opportunity for the client to have his or her say in resolving the dispute, rather than having a judge or jury decide the outcome; and that the client's privacy can be preserved during mediation. As mentioned earlier, the client's attitude is extremely important. A client who understands why he or she is participating in mediation will have more confidence in the process and will be in a better frame of mind than a client who is fearful, confused, and mistrustful.

Second, the attorney should discuss what will happen at mediation. The attorney might begin by explaining that mediation is an informal process where the parties will assemble to discuss their respective views of the case and then separate so that the mediator can discuss settlement with each of them in private. The client should be told that the mediator is not a judge and cannot force a party to agree to something the client deems unacceptable. The client should also understand that either party has a right to proceed to trial if the case cannot be settled satisfactorily at mediation. Nevertheless, the attorney should encourage the client to cooperate, emphasizing that the mediator is there to help, and that mediation offers an opportunity for parties to discuss their differences and resolve them on their own.

The attorney should also reassure the client that he or she will be present during the mediation and available to confer privately. The client should understand that he or she will not be called on to testify at mediation.

Discussing the Client's Role in Mediation. After explaining the mediation process, the attorney should discuss the client's role during the actual session. The client should understand that mediation is a process that contemplates active involvement of the parties in discussions. The mediator may encourage parties to explore issues, to suggest compromises, and to propose offers and counteroffers (with their attorneys' assistance, of course). Some parties, on the other hand, may prefer to have their attorney speak for them during the mediation. Some clients are not articulate. Some have hot tempers and short fuses. Others may be intimidated by the fact that they are involved in litigation at all. Such clients will probably rely heavily on their counsel during mediation.

Establishing a Settlement Range. The attorney should discuss the merits of the case with the client before mediation, presenting both its strengths and weaknesses. As part of this process the attorney must help the client separate "wants" from "needs." The attorney should ask not merely whether something is negotiable, but *why* it is or is not negotiable. The attorney may have to ask "why" many times to determine the client's real needs. Clients often have unrealistic expectations—for example, the personal injury plaintiff who wants to exit the case with a great financial victory despite a full or near full physical recovery. The attorney must help the client think realistically about what to expect. The attorney may also want to give the client a "best guess" as to the outcome of the case if it goes to trial and provide an estimate of what it will cost to try the case. Then, and only then, should the attorney and the client begin to decide on a settlement range.

The settlement range and demands must be realistic. Although proposals may be weighted in favor of the client, demands should not be outrageous. A party whose proposals are extreme or excessive risks alienating the other party and sabotaging the conference. Moreover, such demands are likely to provoke equally extreme proposals on the other side, resulting in an impasse and a waste of time and expense. In mediation, it is unwise to play too many games; it can offend the other side and exasperate the mediator. A straightforward approach is generally more effective.

Addressing Any Special Needs of the Client. If a party is deaf or hard of hearing or does not speak English well, counsel will need to arrange for an interpreter to attend the mediation. Although it is a good idea to let the mediator know that an interpreter will be attending, it is the attorney's responsibility—not the mediator's—to arrange for an interpreter. An attorney can locate a sign language interpreter by contacting the clerk of court's office in any judicial district and asking for names of certified interpreters. Information about foreign language interpreters is available in each judicial district from the office of the senior resident superior court judge or on the Administrative Office of the Court's website.

Although it may be difficult to locate a professional language interpreter, it will normally be in the client's interest to do so. Even a party who speaks English passably may benefit from having an interpreter present at mediation since he or she may feel nervous or unsure at the proceeding or may have difficulty comprehending legal or technical terminology that is not part of the vernacular. Try to discourage a client who wants to bring a relative or a friend to the conference to serve as his or her interpreter. The services may be offered for free, but the individual may know little about serving as an interpreter. For example, the amateur interpreter may fail to interpret words or thoughts he or she believes will be offensive or hurtful to a party, may misinterpret legal terms or concepts, may interject personal opinions into the process, or may argue with the other party or the mediator. The party is required to compensate a professional foreign language interpreter. The court is required to absorb the cost of obtaining a sign language interpreter.

If the client is in a wheelchair or has other limitations on mobility, the attorney should notify the mediator. The mediator can then make certain the location scheduled for the conference is accessible for those with disabilities. It also may be important to let the mediator know if a party is elderly and infirm, suffers from a physical or mental illness, or is taking medications that could affect his or her ability to focus or otherwise fully participate. Often, such a party may need a break because he or she is tired, confused, or feels overwhelmed, but is reluctant to ask for fear of "offending" or "inconveniencing" the mediator. If a mediator is alerted to potential concerns, he or she can be more alert to the situation and, if necessary, more solicitous of the party, even going so far as to insist on breaks or a recess if appropriate.

If the party is indigent, counsel should file a Petition and Order for Relief from Obligation to Pay Mediator's Fee and provide a copy to the mediator at the conclusion of the conference. The petition will be heard after completion of the conference or, if the parties do not settle their case, subsequent to the trial of the action. If the judge determines that the party is, in fact, indigent, the mediator, whether party selected or court appointed, must forego his or her fee. Legal services attorneys should be aware that the Pro Bono Committee of the North Carolina Bar Association's Dispute Resolution Section has recruited a panel of mediators who have expressed a willingness to provide their services at no charge to clients represented by legal services organizations.

Payment of the Mediator. The party should be advised that the MSC Rules require him or her to pay the mediator's fee at the conclusion of the conference. If the party is not indigent, but cannot afford to pay at the time of the conference, he or she should advise the mediator when payment will be forthcoming. A party-selected mediator may require a deposit toward his or her fee but cannot delay scheduling or holding a conference because the deposit has not been paid.

During Mediation

REPRESENTING THE CLIENT DURING MEDIATION

The lawyer has a number of important roles during the actual conference: helping to set the agenda for the conference, giving legal advice to the client, protecting the client's interests, planning and carrying out a settlement strategy, formulating offers and counteroffers, etc. In some situations, an attorney may also be faced with managing the client: e.g., calming an agitated or angry one, curbing a controlling one, supporting a distraught one, or reasoning with a self-righteous one.

The Importance of Attitude

If an attorney wishes to be successful in mediation, he or she must keep in mind the nature of mediation. While both mediation and litigation are avenues toward conflict resolution, they are fundamentally different means to the same end.

Litigation is an adversarial approach to resolving disputes; mediation is a conciliatory one. In mediation, parties are asked, with their attorneys' help, to cooperate with one another, search for compromises together, and construct their own solutions. Because mediation stresses conciliation, it is the more vulnerable of the two approaches. Intractable parties and rigid, posturing attorneys will not stymie a judge or jury, but they can spell disaster for a mediator, whose success is largely dependent on the goodwill and good-faith participation of the parties and their attorneys.

Although the mediation process is conciliatory, the process does not require an attorney to ignore the interests of the client. Clearly the attorney's primary obligation throughout mediation is to advance the client's interests. But mediation will fail if an attorney adopts a rigid, wholly adversarial approach, refusing to focus on anything but the other party's wrongdoing, dismissing any suggested compromise, or displaying an unwillingness to negotiate. If mediation is to succeed the attorney must: (1) be flexible; (2) listen thoughtfully when others speak; (3) recognize all parties' interests, not just those of the client; (4) propose compromises and trade-offs and encourage the client to consider them; and (5) be willing to give a little in one area to gain a little in another.

The Need for Decorum

Although the mediation process is less formal and less structured than a trial, the attorney should not appear too casual or informal while addressing the mediator. In many instances, mediation is the parties' first contact with the justice system. If counsel does not exhibit respect for the mediator and the process, and if the mediation is not conducted decorously, the parties may feel they are not receiving their "day in court." As a result, the parties' likelihood of settlement may be reduced. In addition, an attorney who shares a friendship with a mediator should be careful not to appear too chummy in the presence of the opposing party lest that party become convinced that the mediator cannot be neutral and that the process is "rigged" against him or her.

Setting the Agenda

At the outset of the mediation, after the mediator has explained the process and the mediator's role, the participants will need to set an agenda. The attorney will want to compile a checklist of all the items that, from the client's perspective, need to be discussed and resolved for agreement to occur. In a personal injury case, the checklist may be short, but in a business case or a dispute with many facets, the list may be much longer. It is important to be thorough in compiling the checklist, because one inadvertently omitted item can threaten an otherwise comprehensive agreement. Not only can an agreement be lost, but an enormous amount of resentment can be generated if one party later reneges on what the other thought was a "done deal." An attorney may want to share the checklist with the client prior to mediation to double-check its accuracy. Toward the end of the conference, the attorney should confer with the client again to determine whether any issue has been left out.

The attorney should also decide the order in which to discuss items on the checklist. If the client is willing to compromise on one issue in dispute, the attorney might suggest that issue as a starting place. It is more effective to generate early momentum and goodwill via successful resolution of some point in contention—even a minor one—than to begin with an issue on which the client will not relent, and over which deadlock seems certain.

Strategies for Moving Toward Settlement

In General. Attorneys help move a case toward settlement in mediation by: (1) making sure that they really understand their client's needs and expectations and bottom line; (2) formulating creative compromises and trade-offs; and (3) persuading the other party to listen to their perspective on the dispute.

Understanding the Client's Needs. A clear understanding of the client's wants, needs, and bottom line is essential if an attorney expects to formulate acceptable offers and compromises. Once the attorney has helped the client to distinguish "needs" from "wants," the client and the attorney are in a much better position to participate in mediation and to engage in the give-and-take necessary to settle a case. The task of educating the client to the realities (legal and otherwise) of the situation, and of helping him or her distinguish needs from unrealistic expectations, takes place throughout the mediation process.

Moving Toward Settlement. The following strategies can help an attorney encourage settlement:

- Respect the mediator's authority to control the conference (i.e., do not try to dominate the proceeding).
- Listen attentively to the other side.
- Avoid use of accusatory or inflammatory language.
- Don't overreact to the other side's use of accusatory or inflammatory language.
- Convincingly point out the strengths of the client's case.
- Gently point out the weaknesses of the opposing party's case.
- In appropriate cases (e.g., where liability has been admitted), acknowledge in a general and conciliatory way the other party's pain and suffering.
- Encourage the other party to look at the costs and risks involved in trying the case.
- Demonstrate goodwill by indicating some flexibility in the client's position.
- Make only realistic demands and avoid posturing.
- Think creatively in suggesting options for settlement. (Remember that the settlement does not have to approximate what a judge or jury might do with the case. For example, in a farm nuisance mediation involving noxious odors, the settlement provided for the absentee owner to live on the premises for a portion of the year.)
- Put your cards on the table early. If there is a big weakness in the case and the attorney knows the other side knows, the attorney

should mention it in the opening remarks rather than appearing to avoid or hide it.

- Reveal negative information about the opposing party's case at mediation rather than holding a "bombshell" for trial. (A mediator will be hindered in the negotiations if critical information is conveyed to the mediator and then he or she is told not to share it.)
- Advocate agreement on less important issues as a way of building momentum.

If opposing counsel takes a rigid and adversarial approach to mediation, an attorney may request a caucus in an effort to enlist the mediator's help in persuading the other attorney or party to be more cooperative. The attorney may also consider asking the other attorney to meet privately. The intransigent attorney may feel freer to speak when away from the client, and the posturing may cease.

When Settlement Is Reached. For an agreement reached in mediation to be enforceable, it must be reduced to writing and signed by the parties before leaving the mediation conference. Either one of the attorneys or the mediator does the drafting.

When Impasse Results. An impasse is sometimes inevitable. When an attorney senses that an impasse is going to be the likely result of a conference, he or she should try to end on a friendly note and stress what was accomplished. Sometimes the dialogue started at mediation can be continued afterward and may result in the case eventually settling.

Following Mediation

ATTORNEY RESPONSIBILITIES

As discussed earlier in this chapter, if an agreement is reached in mediation, it is important that attorneys promptly follow up by filing a consent judgment or voluntary dismissal with the court. If a party seeks to back out of a settlement agreement, an attorney cannot subpoena the mediator to testify about what occurred at the mediation.[6] However, the attorney may invite the other side to meet with the mediator again in an effort to clarify the situation and to prevent the filing of a motion to set aside the agreement. MSC Rules also provide that when a case is settled on all issues at mediation, all attorneys of record must notify the senior resident superior court judge within four business days of the settlement and advise him or her who will file the consent judgment or voluntary dismissal(s) and when.

PAYMENT OF THE MEDIATOR'S FEE

If a client does not pay the mediator at the conclusion of the conference, an attorney should encourage prompt payment and follow up to make sure that it is made. Attorneys who do not take seriously their clients' obligation to pay may risk losing the goodwill of mediators.

Conclusion

The Mediated Settlement Conference Program represents an important effort on the part of North Carolina's courts to expedite settlement of civil cases filed in superior court. The MSC Program has enjoyed great success over the last twenty years. Such success is due largely to the support the Program enjoys among North Carolina's attorneys—those who have become certified to mediate, those who have taken mediation training in an effort to better understand and utilize the mediation process, and those who have come to mediation prepared and with a positive attitude.

Mediation has much to offer. It provides an opportunity to deepen understanding of the nature of conflict and to search for ways of resolving it constructively and cooperatively. Many attorneys have said that mediation has enabled them to see their profession in a new light. Lawyers who once proudly proclaimed their skills as advocates now also speak in terms of their ability to negotiate successfully. They have come to value the ancient and honorable role of the attorney as counselor.

Mediation is not a panacea. Not every case can or should settle, but many disputes can be resolved without lengthy litigation. With a positive attitude, careful preparation, and thoughtful representation at the settlement conference, an attorney can help ensure that mediation will be successful and that everyone—the parties, the attorneys, the court, and the taxpayers—will emerge as winners.

NOTES

1. The Commission's website can be accessed at http://www.ncdrc.org. This URL is automatically redirected to the website of the North Carolina Court System, at http://www.nccourts.org/Courts/CRS/Councils/DRC/Default.asp.

2. *See* Advisory Opinion of the N.C. Dispute Resolution Commission, Opinion Number 00-02, http://www.nccourts.org/Courts/CRS/Councils/DRC/Documents/00-02_final.pdf.

3. N.C. Gen. Stat. § 7A-38.2.

4. Stevens H. Clarke et al., *Court-Ordered Civil Case Mediation in North Carolina: An Evaluation of Its Effects* (Institute of Government, The University of North Carolina at Chapel Hill, 1995), p. 31.

5. *See* N.C. Gen. Stat. § 7A-38.1(*l*).

6. *Id.*

CHAPTER THIRTEEN

The North Carolina Industrial Commission Mediation Program

*"The most significant development in the practice
of workers' compensation law in the last
three decades . . . is the advent of mediation."*
—Harry H. Clendenin III, Chair of the Workers' Compensation
Section of the North Carolina Bar Association, "The Chair's
Comments," *The Course and Scope,* Vol. 16, No. 1, Aug. 2002
(Newsletter of the Workers' Compensation Section
of the N.C. Bar Association), at 1.

Historical Development

The North Carolina Industrial Commission, a division of the Department of Commerce, was established by the General Assembly in 1929 to administer the state's Workers' Compensation Act. The Commission also has jurisdiction over tort claims against the state and certain claims by families of law enforcement officers, firefighters, and rescue squad workers. The Commission's primary mission, and by far the greatest percentage of its work, involves the administration and adjudication of workers' compensation claims in North Carolina. It receives and processes information related to claims under the Act and conducts hearings on contested claims.

In 1994, with an ever-growing backlog of cases waiting for hearing, the Commission implemented a pilot mediation program to determine whether mediating workers' compensation claims would help settle cases more efficiently. The pilot program's success led to the establishment of the highly effective mediated settlement program in place at the Commission today. This chapter describes the evolution of mediation as a primary mechanism for resolving disputes in cases under the Commission's jurisdiction and highlights procedures governing mediated settlement conferences.

Workers' Compensation: An Early Alternative to Litigation

Before the advent of workers' compensation, an employer could be held liable under tort law principles for workplace injuries or deaths. Litigation in these early cases frequently proved costly and burdensome for all parties. Employers often suffered heavy judgments, and injured employees had to struggle through protracted litigation to obtain needed financial relief. The Workmen's Compensation Act (Act), adopted in 1929, replaced the old system of tort liability with a requirement that employers provide insurance coverage to compensate employees for lost wages and medical expenses resulting from workplace injuries. Both employers and employees ceded significant rights under the new statutory scheme, but, as the Supreme Court of North Carolina noted in 1930, they received corresponding benefits:

> The [employer] in exchange for limited liability was willing to pay on some claims in the future where in the past there had been no liability at all. The [employee] was willing not only to give up trial by jury, but to accept far less than he had often won in court, provided he was sure to get the small sum without having to fight for it.[1]

Although the Act provided for adjudication of contested claims through an administrative hearing before the newly created North Carolina Industrial Commission (IC or the Commission), the workers' compensation process significantly reduced litigation during the first eleven years of its existence. Approximately 97 percent of claims settled in those early years, albeit in a far simpler legal context and with much less at stake than in the modern era.[2] In 1936, an original member of the IC and its first Executive Secretary, E. W. Price, suggested that "there should be little need for a lawyer" for a worker at an IC hearing, until the case is appealed to the courts.[3] As late as 1976, Justice J. Frank Huskins, a North Carolina Supreme Court justice and former IC Chairman, suggested that more than 95 percent of worker's compensation claims were being settled by agreement.[4]

A Mounting Backlog of Cases

By the late 1980s, however, adjudication of contested claims before the Commission had become a substantial burden, particularly in cases involving serious injury and potentially large liability. Hearing requests rose by 71 percent between 1984 and 1992, while employment in the state increased by only 22 percent during the same period. Despite the rise in the number of hearing requests, the IC backlog was not due to the volume of cases. The problem was the time required to try them. The legal issues involved in many workers' compensation claims had become dramatically more complex, and greater financial implications inspired more intense litigation.

Gone were the days when a party had "little need for a lawyer." In 1991, the Court of Appeals noted that "in contested workers' compensation cases today, access to competent legal counsel is a virtual necessity."[5] Although the settlement rate remained high (perhaps due to the lack of timely hearings), by 1992 it took an average of more than fourteen months to obtain a decision at the initial hearing level. The situation was deteriorating: 5,045 hearings were requested, but only 1,464 decisions were rendered.

Another reason for the backlog was that during the late 1980s, only nine IC deputy commissioners held initial hearings across the state. Only one half-time secretary assisted the Executive Secretary of the Commission. Thereafter, the Commission was very successful in obtaining additional resources, including a budget increase of nearly 25 percent in 1992, at the height of the state's worst budget crisis since the Great Depression.[6] A dramatic increase in the number of senior hearing officers followed two years later. But there was no realistic hope of increasing the staff of adjudicators enough to significantly reduce the backlog. The solution lay instead in reducing the demand for their services.

Averting Litigation

The Commission needed a series of "screens" to diffuse or facilitate resolution of disputes arising in typical contested cases. If procedures were available to expedite delivery of benefits in meritorious cases, hearing officers could be freed to decide only those matters that truly were not amenable to settlement.

The need for action at certain notorious "flash points" for disagreement was widely recognized among system participants. Workers' compensation benefits were a mystery to most employees and to many employers as well. Simple misunderstandings were transformed into bitter litigation with depressing frequency. IC employees, particularly the Executive Secretary and Commissioners, spent much time answering questions about law and procedure. Finally, in 1994, the Office of the Ombudsman was created to expedite requests for information and services. The Commission also revitalized the process for making interim decisions on termination of benefits and medical treatment disputes in cases of temporary disability, two areas where conflicts frequently arose. Yet in spite of these efforts the Commission continued to face an overwhelming caseload. Something else was needed.

Former Commissioner J. Randolph "Randy" Ward took the lead in investigating alternative dispute resolution procedures being developed in North Carolina and throughout the country. One of the first alternatives that he examined was the pilot program of court-ordered arbitration for civil cases in

North Carolina's district courts. Unfortunately, the arbitration process was not well suited to the circumstances confronting the IC, since it required the participants' acceptance of an experienced attorney's assessment of the case. In addition, the workers' compensation bar was sharply split between plaintiffs' and defense counsel, and neutrals who were both knowledgeable and acceptable to both sides were thought to be scarce.

"Settlement Day" programs, which had proven successful in other parts of the country, were studied. Such programs cloistered a group of attorneys and insurance adjusters in a comfortable setting, away from the distractions of the office, to facilitate unstructured negotiations in pending cases. Through Commissioner Ward's efforts one such program was held in Charlotte for workers' compensation cases in July 1990. While modestly successful, it was not clear that it could address the volume of cases necessary to alleviate the IC's backlog.

The Emergence of Mediation
as a Dispute Resolution Technique

North Carolina was not alone in facing backlogs and delays in resolution of workers' compensation claims during this period. By the early 1990s, most state-based compensation systems around the country had begun experimenting with programmatic, mandatory alternatives to formal hearings for case resolution. Many observers noted the irony of the situation. The administrative workers' compensation procedures used throughout the United States were intended as "alternatives" to conventional tort litigation. Exploring *alternatives to an alternative* was an unfortunate commentary on how bad things had become.

Many of the experimental procedures used in other states were labeled "mediation." They varied greatly in methodology, degree of government involvement, and settlement pressure on the parties, and they often differed markedly from the mediation procedures that eventually developed in North Carolina. But because of its relative success in promoting settlement, mediation quickly became the fastest growing alternative dispute resolution method used in the workers' compensation setting.

By early 1998, nearly forty states had incorporated some form of general purpose, informal dispute resolution into their compensation claims process.[7] In twenty-seven of those forums, the process was called mediation, and in eight of these twenty-seven jurisdictions the use of mediation was mandatory.[8]

Introducing Mediation at the Industrial Commission

The first major step toward mediation of IC cases was taken in September 1992, with the presentation of a continuing legal education program, *Mediation for Workers' Compensation Counsel/Workers' Compensation Law for Mediators*. The program, sponsored by the North Carolina Bar Foundation, drew more than ninety attendees, including workers' compensation attorneys, mediators interested in handling IC cases, and claims representatives from firms administering well over half of the insurance and self-insurance in force in the state. Participants were encouraged to use mediated settlement conferences on a voluntary basis in handling workers' compensation claims.

An encouraging trickle of workers' compensation cases were voluntarily mediated, but no forum has been successful in having most cases go to alternative dispute resolution without officially initiating referrals. In most contested cases, the attorneys have enough challenges without having to convince all parties to pursue alternative procedures.

In 1993, legislation enabling the North Carolina Industrial Commission to order parties into mediation was introduced in the Senate by Senator Roy A. Cooper III; and in the House by Representatives Philip A. Baddour, Jr., Martin L. Nesbitt, Jr., and Joe Hackney, and co-sponsored by Representatives James F. Bowman and Milton F. "Toby" Fitch. The legislation was offered at the behest of Attorney General Michael F. Easley, whose office represented the state's largest employer, the State of North Carolina. On the motion of Senator Cooper, similar language was added to Senate Bill 906, which a year later was the vehicle for the Workers' Compensation Reform Act of 1994. The House bill, H.B. 658, became law in 1993. Senate Bill 906 put the current mediation provision in North Carolina General Statutes Section 97-80(c).

The stated purpose of the Industrial Commission's pilot mediation program was twofold: (1) to determine whether mediation could help settle workers' compensation cases more efficiently for the parties; and (2) to save work for the Commission, thus freeing its resources to decide cases not amenable to settlement. The program had at least two features that were not common in other mediation processes. First, in other states that offered or required mediation in the workers' compensation setting, the mediator typically was an employee of the state agency responsible for administering the compensation program. In the North Carolina IC program, workers' compensation cases were ordered to outside mediation presided over by private mediators whose fees were paid by the parties. The IC's program was also distinct in that the defendant was responsible for advancing the plaintiff's share of the mediation fees until the conclusion of the case, an obligation not required of defendants in the state's superior court mediation program.

The Commission's 1994 appropriation from the General Assembly included the new position of Mediation Coordinator. Frank C. Laney, who had formerly provided staff support for the North Carolina Bar Association's Dispute Resolution Committee, ably filled this new position. Accepting the challenges involved in launching a fledgling program with limited resources, Laney moved quickly to build momentum for the new initiative. He was instrumental in developing criteria for selecting cases for mediation and in creating rules and policies for program administration. He advised participants when problems arose. He established procedures for compiling meaningful statistics to permit evaluation of program results and trends. Laney also obtained a grant from the Z. Smith Reynolds Foundation to make mediation services available for cases in which only small dollar amounts were at stake (where payment of a mediator's fee otherwise would have been a hardship).

In 1997, an evaluation conducted by the Institute of Government at the University of North Carolina at Chapel Hill concluded that the pilot program was very successful in meeting its goals. The study found that the average disposition time—the period from hearing request to case disposition—was considerably shorter in the mediation group than it was in the control group. The evaluation noted: "[T]he [mediation] program reduced the proportion of cases going to a single-commissioner hearing by one-fourth, lowering the hearing rate from 35.4% in the control group to 27.2% in the mediation group." The evaluation also concluded that "[a]ttorneys and certified mediators responding to a survey generally expressed favorable views toward the mediation program."[9]

Laney left the Industrial Commission in March 1997. He was succeeded by John C. Schafer, who has administered the ongoing development and growth of the Commission's mediation program since then. The title "Mediation Coordinator" was changed to "Dispute Resolution Coordinator" when a neutral evaluation procedure was made available in IC proceedings, pursuant to the Commission's 1998 rule revisions. The position was later given the classification of Deputy Commissioner in recognition of the importance of dispute resolution procedures to the Commission's work.

Automatic Referral of Contested Claims to Mediation

The initial use of mediation as a litigation "screen" helped alleviate the backlog of workers' compensation cases, but the state's rapid economic growth in the 1990s and the continuing need for hearings within a reasonable time kept the Industrial Commission struggling with its workload. Reorganization and special expenditures were used to improve efficiency. By the spring of 1996, widespread support among system participants and the ready availability of qualified mediators permitted IC Chairman J. Howard Bunn, Jr. to make a watershed policy decision: from that point onward *all* cases would be referred to mediation whenever a request for hearing was filed.

At the time many observers feared that settlement rates and the overall effectiveness of the mediated settlement conference program would be adversely affected if all cases were referred to mediation, instead of only claims that appeared most suitable for negotiated resolution. Such fears proved groundless. As the volume of cases referred to mediation grew dramatically, from fewer than 900 cases during the 1994–1995 fiscal year to more than 8,700 cases during the 1999–2000 fiscal year, the mediation settlement rates actually *increased*, from 60 percent to 73 percent. If cases resolved prior to scheduled mediation conferences also are included, the IC mediation settlement rate increased to almost 80 percent during the period. (These figures do not include the large number of cases that are resolved *after* mediation conferences, but prior to hearing.)

Despite a 50 percent *increase* in the number of hearing requests from 1994–1995 to 1999–2000, there was a 50 percent *reduction* in the number of hearings actually conducted, the huge hearing backlog that existed in the early 1990s was eliminated, and the disposition time for contested cases was substantially reduced. Clearly, mediation was the primary reason for these dramatic improvements. Soon after Buck Lattimore was appointed Chairman of the Industrial Commission on July 22, 2000, he hailed the success of the mediation program, describing it as the Commission's "saving grace."[10] More than 8,500 cases have been referred to mediation each year in the most recent ten-year period for which data were available at the time of this book's publication (i.e., the 2001–2002 fiscal year through the 2010–2011 fiscal year).

Summary of ICMSC Rules and Procedures

The North Carolina Industrial Commission adopted Rules for Mediated Settlement Conferences (ICMSC Rules) on July 29, 1994. Amendments and additions to these Rules were adopted and became effective as of June 1, 2000, and January 1, 2011. Many of the revisions simply updated the Rules to reflect changes in statutory and case law as well as changes that had been made in the superior court mediation program. In addition, the January 1, 2011 revisions were designed to expedite the mediation process and the resolution of pending disputes. The ICMSC Rules and related forms are available on the Industrial Commission's website. Also available on the website are the mediator databases of the IC and the Dispute Resolution Commission. Copies of these documents are available upon request from the Commission's Dispute Resolution Coordinator. The information that follows is a summary of the ICMSC Rules and procedures and the MSC forms currently in use.

Initiating the Mediation Process

Under the ICMSC Rules, the mediation process in a worker's compensation or state tort claims case may be initiated through any one of four basic methods:

- by Order for Mediated Settlement Conference issued by the Commission;
- by automatic referral upon the filing of a Request for Hearing by a party;
- upon a request for an Order for Mediated Settlement Conference by a party; or
- by consent of all parties.

MEDIATION BY ORDER OF THE COMMISSION

Authority of the Commission to Order Mediation
The Commission may require the parties and their representatives to attend a mediated settlement conference concerning any dispute within the tort and workers' compensation jurisdiction of the Commission by issuing an Order for Mediated Settlement Conference, pursuant to the ICMSC Rules.

Content of the Order for Mediated Settlement Conference
The Order for Mediated Settlement Conference must include the following provisions:

- a requirement that a mediated settlement conference be held in the case;
- a deadline for completion of the conference;

- a deadline, prior to the conference, for exchange of pertinent documents and completion of any specified discovery;
- a time period for selection of a mediator by mutual agreement of the parties;
- the rate of compensation of the Commission-appointed mediator, if the parties do not agree to one; and
- a statement that the parties are required to pay the mediator's fee at the conclusion of the settlement conference, unless otherwise ordered by the Commission.

The order may also specify a date for an Industrial Commission hearing if the parties fail to reach a settlement.

AUTOMATIC REFERRAL TO MEDIATION UPON FILING OF REQUEST FOR HEARING

Under the automatic referral procedures commenced during the 1996–1997 fiscal year, whenever a party files a request for hearing on a workers' compensation claim, an Order for Mediated Settlement Conference is sent to all parties along with the IC's acknowledgment letter. The only cases that are not automatically referred to mediation are claims against the state brought by prison inmates, which are excluded by law, and appeals of administrative orders. However, many administrative appeals are mediated voluntarily or pursuant to a Commission order.

REQUEST FOR MEDIATION BY A PARTY

Petition or Letter Requesting Order to Mediated Settlement
A party who does not file a Request for Hearing may request a mediated settlement conference by submitting either: (1) the IC's "Petition for Order Referring Case to Mediated Settlement" form; or (2) a letter to the Dispute Resolution Coordinator containing the IC case number, the names of the parties, the attorneys representing the various parties, a request for entry of a mediation order, and the reason that mediation is being requested.

The stated reason for the request may be used to evaluate the appropriateness of mediation in a particular case and generally is needed only if the opposing party objects to mediation. Failure to state a reason for the mediation request is not a fatal flaw, however, and an objection to mediation based upon such failure will generally not be granted. A copy of the petition or letter requesting mediation should be sent to all parties. Objections are ruled on after receipt of a response to the objections or after expiration of the ten-day response period. In all cases ordered to mediation by the Commission, the mediation conference must be scheduled to convene within 120 days of the mediation order.

MEDIATION BY CONSENT OF ALL PARTIES

If all parties agree to mediate, they may proceed to mediation in either of two ways. They can schedule and proceed to mediation on their own, without permission from the Industrial Commission, or they can jointly request an Order for Mediated Settlement Conference.

When the parties agree to mediate the dispute without an Order, they choose a mediator, set up the settlement conference, and proceed to mediation on their own. However, the mediator must report the results of the settlement conference to the Commission. This allows the IC to track mediation cases and prevents the appointment of another mediator in a case that has already been mediated.

The parties may also choose to jointly request an Order for Mediated Settlement Conference, which will set a deadline for the selection of a mediator. If an Order for Mediated Settlement Conference is entered in a case, the parties must, of course, comply with the deadlines set forth in the Order. The parties may select a mediator, rather than have the Commission appoint one, by submitting a form request or by providing other appropriate notice of the request. If the parties are unable to agree on the selection of a mediator, they may submit suggestions for consideration and appointment by the Commission.

Dispensing with Mediation

Mediation may be dispensed with or excused by the Commission. For example, while claimants who are not represented by an attorney are allowed to opt into the mediation process, such cases typically are excused from mediation if the claimants do not notify the Commission that they want to mediate their claim. Likewise, cases involving non-insured defendants are generally excused from mediation.

Mediation may not be dispensed with or excused by the parties or the mediator unless the parties have agreed (subject to Commission approval) on a full and complete resolution of all disputed issues set forth in the request for hearing filed in the case and have given notice of the settlement to the Dispute Resolution Coordinator.

Neutral Evaluation

Use of Neutral Evaluation in Lieu of Mediated Settlement Conference

The parties may ask the Commission to authorize the use of a neutral evaluation procedure in lieu of a mediated settlement conference. If the parties can agree on the selection of a neutral and the persons or entities excused from attending the proceeding, then the Commission may order use of the proceeding in lieu of a mediated settlement conference. If the parties are unable to agree on the above matters, the Commission will deny the motion for neutral evaluation, and the parties must attend the mediated settlement conference as originally ordered by the Commission. In addition, the Commission will not order the use of a neutral evaluation proceeding in any case in which the plaintiff is not represented by counsel.

Description of the Neutral Evaluation Process

Neutral evaluation is an informal, abbreviated presentation of facts and issues in a case by the parties to an evaluator at an early stage of the case. The neutral evaluator is responsible for evaluating the strengths and weaknesses of the case; providing the parties with a candid assessment of liability, settlement value, and a dollar value or range of potential awards if the case proceeds to a hearing; identifying areas of agreement and disagreement; and suggesting necessary and appropriate discovery.

Modification of Rules

Subject to the approval of the evaluator, the parties may agree to modify the procedures required by the Commission's rules for neutral evaluation, or such procedures may be modified by order of the Commission. The modified procedures may include the presentation of submissions in writing or by telephone in lieu of the physical appearance at a neutral evaluation conference and may also include revisions to the time periods and page limitations of the parties' submissions.

Report of Evaluator

The neutral evaluator must file a Report of Evaluator with the Commission in all cases, even if no conference is held. The only exception is when the neutral evaluator receives an order from the Commission dispensing with the neutral evaluation. If the Report of Evaluator indicates that there has been an impasse in a case with a pending hearing request, the case will then be set for hearing on the next available calendar.

Selection of the Mediator

SELECTION BY THE PARTIES

The parties have the right to select a mediator on their own and may do so within the time periods set out in the ICMSC Rules. In cases that have been ordered to mediation, the mediator must be certified by the DRC to mediate superior court cases, and when the mediator is selected the parties must confirm that the mediation conference is scheduled to convene within 120 days of the mediation order. In cases that have not been ordered to mediation, the mediator can be anyone with the skill or experience that would enable him or her to assist the parties in resolving the disputed issues. Any mediator, attorney, or other person with experience in the workers' compensation field normally qualifies. If the parties do not have a specific mediator in mind, they can select one from a list of mediators, available on the Commission's website or from the Dispute Resolution Coordinator's office.

If the parties want to select a mediator, but need more time, an extension of the selection deadline may be requested. Extensions of time to select a mediator are liberally granted and may be requested orally, if followed by a written confirmation.

Designation of Mediator

Once the parties agree on the selection of a mediator, they must submit a Designation of Mediator form or a letter containing comparable information to the Dispute Resolution Coordinator. The form or letter must be received within the time designated by the ICMSC Rules. Upon the receipt of a timely Designation of Mediator form or letter, an order will be entered approving the parties' selection of the mediator. Any party may submit the form, as long as all parties have agreed on the selected mediator. The failure of an opposing party to respond to inquiries concerning the selection of a mediator does not automatically entitle a party to have its chosen mediator selected by default.

SUGGESTIONS BY THE PARTIES

If a party sends a letter to the opposing party and to the Commission suggesting one or more mediators for consideration, and the Commission receives no response to the suggestion(s) from the opposing party, then the Commission usually appoints a mediator suggested by a party. However, if the opposing party objects to a suggested mediator, that mediator generally will not be appointed. To be eligible for appointment when not selected by the parties, the suggested mediator must be on the Commission's list of mediators available for appointment, and must have agreed to travel to the county where the case is pending. Some mediators are not on the Commission's approved list because they do not accept the appointed rate of pay (see ICMSC Rules for current rate), or otherwise set compensation terms that are different from the Commission's terms. Nevertheless, such mediators may be selected by the parties, since a selected mediator may charge any amount that is agreed upon by the parties.

APPOINTMENT BY THE COMMISSION

Procedure for Assignment

If the parties do not select a mediator within the required time period or request an extension of the deadline for designation, the Commission appoints a mediator from its list of approved mediators. Mediators generally will be selected at random for specific cases, or chosen by a system that attempts to assign each mediator to an equal number of cases over a period of time. However, the Commission has discretionary power to appoint a particular mediator in a particular case, given the special circumstances of that case.

Qualifications of Mediators Appointed by the Commission

To be appointed by the Industrial Commission, a mediator must be certified by the Dispute Resolution Commission to mediate cases in North Carolina's Superior Court Mediated Settlement Conference Program. The mediator must also have a Declaration of Interest and Qualifications form on file with the IC. The declaration must state, if the mediator is an attorney, that: (1) he or she is a member in good standing of the North Carolina State Bar; (2) he or she agrees to accept and perform mediations of disputes before the Commission with reasonable frequency when called upon, for the fees and at the rates of payment specified by the Commission; and (3) if the applicant desires to be appointed by the Commission to mediate workers' compensation cases, he or she has completed at least six hours of continuing legal education approved by the North Carolina State Bar in workers' compensation law during the previous two years.

REQUEST FOR SUBSTITUTION OF MEDIATOR

If the parties request the approval of a selected mediator after the appointment of another mediator by the Commission, and the substitution of mediators is allowed, the Commission will generally require the parties not only to pay a substitution of mediator fee to the Commission, but also to pay the administrative fee owed to the mediator initially appointed by the IC.

The Conference

SETTING UP THE CONFERENCE

The parties and the mediator arrange the time and place of the conference. The mediator is responsible for coordinating the scheduling of the conference, with the assistance of the parties. If a party does not respond or cooperate adequately, the mediator has the authority to set the conference without the parties' consent. If a party does not appear, the opposing party may file a motion for sanctions.

The parties and mediator may agree on the location of the conference. If the parties do not agree, the conference will be convened in the county in which the case was filed. As noted above, the Commission appoints only mediators who have previously agreed to travel to the county in which the case was filed.

COMPLETION DEADLINE

The deadline for completion of the mediated settlement conference is generally 120 days after the entry of the mediation order in the case. Limited extensions of time may be granted in appropriate circumstances. Anyone may request an extension, including the parties or the mediator. If the parties select a date for the conference that is after the completion deadline, they should immediately notify the Commission of the scheduled date and the need for an extension. An extension through that date, or through the end of that month to allow for any necessary follow-up, may be granted. An Order allowing an extension of time to complete mediation does not necessarily mean that the mediation conference will convene prior to the date of the hearing in the case, especially when the request for hearing has been pending for an extended period of time.

POSTPONEMENTS OF SCHEDULED CONFERENCES

After a conference is scheduled to convene on a specific date, it may not be postponed unless the requesting party first notifies all other parties of the grounds for the requested postponement and the mediator or the Dispute Resolution Coordinator approves. The ICMSC Rules address the fees that may be owed to a mediator when a scheduled conference is postponed.

Conflicts with Scheduled Hearings

If the original or extended deadline for mediation conflicts with a Deputy Commissioner's hearing calendar, the parties have two options. First, the case may be mediated before the hearing date. If the case settles, the hearing is unnecessary. If it does not settle, the parties may proceed to the hearing. Alternatively, the parties may request a continuance of the hearing, or request the removal of the case from the hearing docket, by filing a motion and proposed order with the appropriate Deputy Commissioner. Granting the motion is within the Deputy Commissioner's discretion.

Duties of Parties, Representatives, and Attorneys

Attendance

All parties and attorneys of record are required to attend the mediated settlement conference. The ICMSC Rules contain special provisions that apply to employers, insurance companies, and governmental entities, which are described below.

Attendance by Representative of Employer in Workers' Compensation Cases

In a workers' compensation case, a representative of the employer at the time of injury is required to attend only if:

1. the employer, instead of or in addition to the insurance company or administrator, has decision-making authority with respect to settlement; or

2. the employer is offering the claimant employment and the suitability of that employment is at issue; or

3. the employer and the claimant have agreed to simultaneously mediate non-compensation issues arising from the injury; or

4. the Commission orders the employer representative to attend the mediation conference.

Attendance by Representative of Insurer

Each insurance carrier or self-insured that may be obligated to pay all or part of any claim presented in the action must be represented at the conference by an officer, employee, or agent who is not such party's outside counsel, and who has the authority to make a decision on settlement of the claim, or who has been authorized to negotiate on behalf of such carrier or self-insured and can promptly communicate during the conference with persons who have such decision-making authority.

Attendance by Representative of a Governmental Entity

Any party that is a governmental entity must be represented at the conference by an employee or agent who is not such party's outside counsel or by the Attorney General's Office counsel responsible for the case. The representative must have authority to decide on behalf of such party whether and on what terms to settle the action. If proposed settlement terms can be approved only by a board (e.g., a board of county commissioners), the representative must have authority to negotiate on behalf of the party and to make a recommendation to that board.

APPEARANCE BY TELEPHONE

In appropriate cases, the Dispute Resolution Coordinator or the mediator, with the consent of all parties and persons required to attend the conference, may allow an insurance carrier representative or other person who is required to attend a mediated settlement conference to attend via telephone, conference call, or speaker telephone. The person(s) so attending must bear all telecommunications costs. The mediator may communicate directly with the insurance representative with regard to the matters discussed in mediation and may set a subsequent conference at which all persons will be required to physically attend.

FOREIGN LANGUAGE INTERPRETERS

When a person who does not speak or understand the English language is required to attend a mediation conference, the person must be assisted by a qualified foreign language interpreter unless the right to an interpreter is waived by both parties. The procedures for retaining an interpreter at a mediation conference are very similar to the procedures for retaining an interpreter for a hearing.

FINALIZING THE AGREEMENT

If an agreement is reached in the mediation conference, the parties must reduce it to writing, specifying all of the terms bearing on the resolution of the dispute before the Industrial Commission. The agreement must be signed by the parties and their counsel. By stipulation of the parties and at their expense, the agreement may be electronically or stenographically recorded. All agreements for payment of compensation must be submitted in proper form for approval by the Commission and must be filed with the IC within twenty days after the mediation conference is concluded.

ATTENDANCE IN RELATED CASES

The ICMSC Rules set out a procedure for obtaining the attendance of an attorney, party, or insurance carrier representative in a case pending before the Commission at a mediated settlement conference conducted in a related case, regardless of the forum in which the related case is pending. The Supreme Court of North Carolina has adopted a similar rule for the superior court mediation program.

Sanctions

The Commission may impose sanctions against any person or party who violates the ICMSC Rules without good cause. Any sanctions that may be assessed against a party under these Rules may also be assessed against the party's principal or attorney, depending on whose conduct necessitated the assessment of sanctions.

Authority and Duties of Mediator

AUTHORITY

Under the ICMSC Rules, control of the settlement conference and the procedures followed rests with the mediator at all times. This is a fact that often bears repeating with the parties or their representatives. The mediator's control, of course, is constrained by the standards of conduct established for mediators by the North Carolina Dispute Resolution Commission. It is also bound by applicable restrictions of the ICMSC Rules, such as provisions limiting the recording of negotiations and discussions at the settlement conference.

The mediator must make a good faith effort to schedule the settlement conference at a time that is convenient for the parties, attorneys, and mediator. If the parties cannot agree on the scheduling, the mediator may select the date.

The mediator is authorized to meet privately with any of the parties or their counsel either before or during the settlement conference. If private communications occur before the conference, the mediator must disclose that fact to all participants at the beginning of the conference.

DUTIES

Providing Information to the Parties

The mediator has a duty to define and describe the following aspects of the mediation process at the beginning of the conference:

- the overall process of mediation;
- the differences between mediation and other forms of conflict resolution;
- the costs of the mediated settlement conference;
- the facts that the mediated settlement conference is not a trial or hearing, that the mediator is not acting in the capacity of a commissioner or deputy commissioner, that the mediator will not act in the capacity of a commissioner or deputy commissioner in the case at any time in the future, and that the parties retain their right to a hearing if they do not reach a settlement;
- the circumstances under which the mediator may meet alone with either of the parties or with any other person;
- whether and under what conditions communications with the mediator will be held in confidence during the conference;
- the inadmissibility of conduct and statements made at the conference, in accordance with applicable rules of court and the ICMSC Rules;
- the duties and responsibilities of the mediator and the parties; and
- the fact that any agreement reached will be reached by mutual consent of the parties.

Disclosure
The mediator has a duty to be impartial and to advise all parties of any circumstances that might bear on possible bias, prejudice, or partiality.

Declaring Impasse
The mediator has a duty to determine in a timely way when mediation is not viable, that an impasse exists, or that mediation should end.

Reporting the Results
The mediator must file a Report of Mediator in all cases, even if no conference is held. The only exception is when the mediator receives an order from the Commission dispensing with mediation. The mediator should *not* attach a copy of the parties' memorandum of agreement to the report.

Scheduling and Holding the Conference
As discussed above, the mediator has the authority to select the date for the settlement conference, in consultation with the parties and their counsel

or other representatives. The mediator also has a duty to conduct the conference within any time limits established by the Commission. Deadlines for completion of the conference must be strictly observed unless they are changed by the Commission.

Standards of Professional Conduct

All mediators conducting mediation conferences pursuant to the ICMSC Rules must adhere to the Standards of Professional Conduct for Mediators adopted by the North Carolina Dispute Resolution Commission.

Compensation of the Mediator

MEDIATION AND ADMINISTRATIVE FEES

When the mediator is selected by the parties, compensation is paid at a rate and in a manner agreed upon between the parties and the mediator. When the mediator is appointed by the Commission, he or she is compensated by the parties at an hourly rate set by the ICMSC Rules. The parties also pay the mediator a one-time per case administrative fee, established by the Rules, unless written notice is given to the mediator and the Dispute Resolution Coordinator (within the time specified by the Rules) that the issues for which the request for hearing were filed have been fully resolved, or that the hearing request has been withdrawn. If a mediated settlement conference is postponed without good cause, the mediator is entitled to a postponement fee, the amount of which is set by the ICMSC Rules. The postponement fee varies depending on how close to the date of the scheduled conference the postponement is requested. The settlement of a case prior to the scheduled date for mediation constitutes good cause for a postponement provided that the mediator is notified of the settlement immediately after it was reached and the mediator receives notice of the settlement at least fourteen calendar days prior to the date scheduled for mediation. Upon application of the party or parties charged with the fee, the Commission may waive the postponement fee.

Parties obligated to pay a share of the costs are responsible for equal shares. However, in workers' compensation claims the defendant pays the plaintiff's share, as well as its own. The defendant is reimbursed for the plaintiff's share, when the case is concluded, from benefits that may be determined to be due to the plaintiff, and the defendant may withhold funds from any award for this purpose. In the event the plaintiff is not entitled to benefits, the plaintiff is generally not responsible for any share of the mediator's fee. Unless the Dispute Resolution Coordinator enters an Order allocating such fees to a particular party, the fees may be taxed as other costs by the Commission. Payment is generally due upon completion of the conference, except that the State of North Carolina is billed at the conference and may pay within thirty days of receipt of the billing. Insurance companies or carriers whose written procedures do not provide for payment of the mediator at the conference may pay within fifteen days of the conference. Sanctions may be imposed if mediation fees are not paid in a timely manner.

Miscellaneous Procedures

MOTIONS AND RESPONSES

Unless otherwise indicated, motions pursuant to the ICMSC Rules must be addressed to the Industrial Commission's Dispute Resolution Coordinator. Motions must be served on all parties to the claim and the settlement process and are decided without oral argument. Responses may be filed with the Commission within ten days after the date of receipt of the motion. Notwithstanding the above, for good cause the Commission may act upon oral motions, or act upon motions prior to the expiration of the ten-day response period. Any appeals from orders issued pursuant to a motion under these rules shall be addressed to the attention of the Commission chair or the chair's designee for appropriate action.

WAIVER OF RULES

In the interest of justice, or to comply with the law from time to time as it may be amended or declared, the Commission may waive any requirement of the ICMSC Rules.

NOTES

1. Conrad v. Cook-Lewis Foundry Co., 198 N.C. 723, 725–26 (1930).
2. J. M. Keech, *Workmen's Compensation in North Carolina 1929–1940* (Duke University Press, 1942), at 63–64.
3. *Id.* at 53.
4. Pruitt v. Publishing Co., 289 N.C. 254, 258 (1976) (citing Smith v. Red Cross, 245 N.C. 116 (1956).
5. Church v. Baxter Travenol Laboratories, 104 N.C. App. 411, 416 (1991).
6. *See* Joe Dew, "Budget Wars to Heat Up in General Assembly," *The News & Observer* (Raleigh, N.C.), March 11, 1991 (quoting Senator Marc Basnight, Chairman of the Senate Appropriations Committee).

7. Duncan S. Ballantyne, *Dispute Prevention and Resolution in Workers' Compensation: A National Inventory, 1997–1998*, Table B (Workers' Compensation Research Institute, 1998).

8. *Id.* at Table 4.1.

9. Stevens H. Clarke and Kelly A. McCormick, *Mediation in Workers' Compensation Cases: An Evaluation of Its Effects* (Institute of Government, The University of North Carolina at Chapel Hill, 1997), pp. 1–2.

10. "New Chairman Calls for Tighter Deadlines, Fewer Continuances," *North Carolina Lawyers Weekly*, Sept. 25, 2000.

CHAPTER FOURTEEN

ADR in the North Carolina Office of Administrative Hearings

"The central quality of mediation . . . is its capacity to reorient the parties toward each other, not by imposing rules on them, but by helping them to achieve a new and shared perception of their relationship, a perception that will redirect their attitudes and dispositions toward one another."

—Lon Fuller, *Mediation—Its Forms and Functions*, 44 So. Cal. L. Rev. 305, 325 (1971).

Creation of the Mediation Program

With the creation of the Office of Administrative Hearings (OAH) in 1985, the North Carolina General Assembly established as public policy that administrative law disputes should be settled. North Carolina General Statutes Section 150B-22 provides as follows: "It is the policy of this State that any dispute between an agency and another person that involves the person's rights, duties, or privileges, including licensing or the levy of a monetary penalty, should be settled through informal procedures."

By statute, in 1993, private mediation was introduced into the OAH administrative law process, and in February 1994, the OAH began referring contested cases to private mediation.[1] This mediation legislation also included a "sunset" provision, effective on June 30, 1995. But due to the positive response from both the public and private sectors, the General Assembly removed the sunset provision from the legislation at its 1995 session and confirmed that the program of mediated settlement conferences would continue in the OAH.

The initial difficulty during the start-up period was identifying which cases should be selected for mediation. Many of the early cases referred to mediation had substantial economic value and sought complex statutory remedies. Such cases do not readily fit the pattern of civil actions in which monetary remedies alone are sought. Also, due to the penal nature of many contested cases, administrative litigation may take on both criminal and civil law characteristics. For example, a substantial environmental penalty is analogous to a criminal fine or forfeiture in superior court. Cases involving penal sanctions arguably are more difficult to mediate than are cases where the relief sought is purely compensatory. All of these characteristics are carefully considered when identifying cases for mediation.

Operation of the OAH Mediation Program

Referral to Mediation

Mediated settlement conferences in the OAH setting are conducted substantially in compliance with the Rules of the North Carolina Supreme Court Implementing Statewide Mediated Settlement Conferences in Superior Court Civil Actions (MSC Rules). The OAH procedures are virtually identical to the procedures set forth in the MSC Rules. (See Chapter 12, "The Mediated Settlement Conference Program in North Carolina's Superior Courts," for a full description of the MSC Rules.)

Not all contested cases before the Office of Administrative Hearings are referred to mediation. The chief administrative law judge selects certain cases for referral, according to guidelines set forth in the North Carolina Administrative Code. Before being referred to mediation, a contested case must meet these established guidelines. However, any contested cases not selected for a mediated settlement conference, upon request of any party by motion, may be referred to mediation, and the presiding administrative law judge (ALJ) may issue such an order. Conversely, if a case is assigned to mediation and a party wishes to dispense with mediation, the party may request by motion that the presiding ALJ dispense with the conference. The presiding ALJ may grant the motion to dispense, with good cause.

Mediator Selection

While the parties involved in mediation typically choose a certified mediator, a non-certified mediator who is qualified by training or experience to mediate all or some of the issues in the action may also be selected. The OAH website, www.ncoah.com, contains a link to the North Carolina Dispute Resolution Commission's Mediator List. The OAH does not provide print copies of the mediator list. The parties may select a mediator by agreement within twenty-one days after either the chief or presiding ALJ orders the contested case to mediation. If the parties are unable to agree upon a mediator, the petitioner's attorney may request that the presiding ALJ appoint one.

The Mediated Settlement Conference

Once selected, the mediator is responsible for setting the time and place for the mediated settlement conference and for giving timely notice to the attorneys and the parties. Unless all parties and the mediator agree otherwise, the mediation is held in the local courthouse or another public building in the county where the case is pending. Although the initial order must clearly state a date for completion of the conference, a party or the mediator may request an extension of the deadline. Mediation can occur as early as the discovery phase or as late as the ALJ's recommended decision but before the final agency decision has issued.

All parties, attorneys, and representatives having authority to settle a claim must attend the settlement conference, unless excused by the presiding ALJ. If a person fails to attend without good cause, the presiding ALJ may impose a monetary sanction. If an agreement is reached in the conference, the parties must reduce its terms to writing and sign the agreement, along with their attorneys.

After the Mediated Settlement Conference

Following the conference, the mediator must file a written report with the parties and the presiding ALJ, stating whether the parties reached an agreement. If the parties reach a full agreement, the mediator's report must state specifically how the action is to be concluded. If the parties do not reach a full agreement, the report will set out the terms of any partial agreement.

Compensation of the Mediator

When the parties select the mediator, the mediator's compensation is established by agreement of the parties. When the OAH appoints the mediator, the mediator's compensation is established at the uniform hourly rate set by rule, plus a one-time administrative fee of $150. Currently, the rate of compensation for a certified mediator is $150 per hour. Fees for postponement may also be applicable. If a party is found to be indigent, the indigent party will not be required to pay any part of the mediator's fee.

The Judicial Settlement Conference

Mediation is not the only alternative dispute resolution technique available to the parties in OAH contested cases. In certain situations a settlement conference is held in lieu of mediation. The major difference between the two methods is that a settlement judge presides at the settlement conference, rather than a mediator. The types of cases typically referred for judicial settlement conferences include all public employee discharge cases and routine contested cases, particularly where the citizen petitioner is not represented by an attorney.

Most of the administrative law judges in the OAH have substantial training in mediation, and several have been certified as mediators. These judges bring not only extensive skills but also years of experience in presiding over similar cases. However, the settlement judge is never the judge who will preside at the hearing. As a result, statements made at the settlement conference will not prejudice a party's position at the contested case hearing.

Mediation in Contested Medicaid Cases

Upon receipt of an appeal, Medicaid cases are referred to the Mediation Network of North Carolina. Within five days of the referral, the mediator will contact the parties to set a time for the mediation. The parties may elect or decline to participate in mediation. If the parties choose to participate, the mediation must occur within twenty-five days of submission of the appeal. The mediator will coordinate with the parties' schedules to meet the deadline and to work diligently to reach a settlement. Most mediations will be conducted by telephone conference. Within twenty-four hours of the mediation, the mediator will file a report with both the OAH and the Department of Health and Human Services about what was determined in the mediation. If a settlement was not reached or the mediation failed for lack of appearance, the contested case will move to a contested case hearing.

Mediation of Medicaid contested cases has been mandatory since 2008. Over half of all of these contested cases have been successfully mediated. The success rate has consistently increased each year. (For a more complete discussion of the North Carolina Medicaid Mediation Program, please see Chapter 24.)

Conclusion

The judicial settlement conference offers a slightly different alternative dispute resolution dynamic than mediation, but both approaches encourage, complement, and enhance settlement opportunities at the Office of Administrative Hearings. Given the success of the program, the chief administrative law judge continues to refer an increasing number of contested cases to mediation or to a judicial settlement conference. The success of the Medicaid contested case mediations demonstrates the effectiveness of alternative dispute resolution and, in the future, may be used as a model for all contested case hearings.

NOTE

1. N.C. Admin. Code tit. 26, r. 03.0201–0208 (Oct. 2009).

CHAPTER FIFTEEN

Court-Ordered Mediation for Cases within the Jurisdiction of the Clerk of Superior Court

"Common sense often makes good law."
—United States Supreme Court Justice William O. Douglas

The Clerk as an Adjudicator

The court official known as the clerk of superior court often is regarded as an administrative person who runs the day-to-day functions of the county courthouse. The clerk and the clerk's employees maintain the files generated for each case in all the trial courts within the county. They time and date stamp, file, and safeguard all pleadings in all cases, whether they are civil or criminal in nature. The clerk also is present in the courtroom when court is in session, keeping minutes and preparing orders for the presiding judge to sign.

In North Carolina, the clerk also is an adjudicator in cases specified by statute. The list of cases for which the clerk is "the decider" is a long one. On that list is a category of cases called "Special Proceedings," which include a number of real estate issues. The clerk also performs the function of what in other states is called a judge of probate. In that regard, the clerk is both an administrative official who keeps records, sends notices, and receives and reviews accountings, and an adjudicator who hears evidence and arguments of counsel and makes judicial rulings in disputes arising out of decedents' estates. Some of those issues involve appointing or removing estate administrators, issuing orders for the recovery of property, and deciding issues that arise in the interpretation of wills. The clerk is also the judicial official who handles foreclosures in both their administrative and adjudicatory aspects.

Another category of cases handled by the clerk is adult guardianships. In that role, the clerk not only performs administrative functions, but also decides the two crucial substantive issues: (1) whether or not an adult is competent to manage his or her affairs; and (2) in the event of a finding of incompetency, who should be appointed as guardian of the person and/or estate of the ward. It is in the realm of adult incompetency that the story of North Carolina's Clerk Mediation Program begins.

Program Background and Development

In 2003, Lynne Berry, an employee of the Department of Aging for the North Carolina Department of Health and Human Services, approached a number of people in Wake County who were interested in mediation and/or elder care issues about the possibility of starting a program of guardianship mediation. The proposal was based on a successful elder care mediation effort in Ann Arbor, Michigan, and had only a tenuous connection with the courts. In the Michigan program, the clerk's office served as a source of information about the availability and benefit of family mediation in guardianship situations, and it actively steered potential petitioners to the nonprofit mediation program.

Ms. Berry organized a meeting of North Carolina clerks and mediators to discuss the idea of promoting eldercare mediation by clerks of court across the state. At that meeting, J. Anderson "Andy" Little, a mediator from Chapel Hill, urged that the proposal offered an opportunity to design a program of mediation for all types of cases within the clerk's jurisdiction. Little subsequently presented the idea to a much larger group of clerks, who expressed interest in the possible benefits of such a program. After obtaining input from that group, Little proposed creation of a clerk mediation program to the North Carolina Dispute Resolution Commission (DRC or Commission). The Commission enthusiastically endorsed the proposal.

Little and Frank C. Laney served as co-chairs of the committee formed to design the program and to draft enabling legislation. Also participating was a cross section of clerks from around the state and their legal advisor from the Administrative Office of the Courts (AOC), Pamela Best. The group included Ken Babb, an attorney from Forsyth County; Leslie Ratliff, Executive Secretary of the DRC; Mary Ann Dalton, an attorney from Wake County; James Stanford, Clerk of Superior Court (CSC) for Orange County; Martha Curran, CSC for Mecklenburg County; Jan Pueschel, CSC for Wake County; Catherine Graham, CSC for Moore County; Selina Brooks, Assistant CSC for Mecklenburg County; Whit Gibson, CSC for Scotland County; June Ray, CSC for Haywood County; Shirley Randleman, CSC for Wilkes County; Tommy Thompson, CSC for Henderson County; Jerry Brewer, CSC for Polk

County; Jerry Roten, CSC for Ashe County; and Eleanor Farr, CSC for Pitt County. The committee quickly realized that the design of a program for the entire range of cases within the jurisdiction of the clerk's office would present many challenges that did not exist in the design of other court-ordered mediation programs.

First, although many of the clerks on the committee believed that their counties were experiencing the beginning of a tidal wave of adult guardianship cases brought about by the demographics of an aging baby boom population, no clerk on the drafting committee believed that the mediation program would serve a significant case management function in his or her office. This skepticism was surprising to the non-clerks on the committee, partly because they believed that the other court-ordered mediation programs in the state had proven to be effective case management tools.

Complicating the issue was the reality that clerks typically have a more personal, or "hands-on," approach to case management than the judges in superior court. This is so partly because clerks perform both administrative and adjudicatory roles in their cases. Moreover, clerks often feel an intensely personal responsibility to the litigants who appear before them. Clerks are elected in local county elections and often know the litigants or their families personally. Their approach may also be explained by the nature of many of the cases within their jurisdiction, such as those dealing with personal, family, and sensitive matters where there may be issues of personal integrity (e.g., the malfeasance or misfeasance of guardians and estate administrators). For these and other reasons, there was a strong reluctance among the clerks to hand over their cases to someone (a mediator) they were not sure would approach the issues and the parties with the same sense of responsibility that they possessed.

Another complicating factor was that cases within the jurisdiction of the clerk come in many different forms. Some are handled like superior court actions, and others are handled through rules and processes not covered in the North Carolina Rules of Civil Procedure. The procedures also vary from case type to case type. Foreclosure cases, estate matters, and guardianship cases all have procedures that are different from each other. The design of a mediation program to fit all of these different types of proceedings was a more daunting task than that undertaken in other court-based mediation programs.

Two specific questions illustrate this drafting challenge. First was the issue of how to define the parties who would be ordered to mediate. The "parties" in matters before the clerk often are not known at the time the case is initiated, and in some cases, such as estate matters, they can change from issue to issue. Second was the question of how to deal with the fact that some matters in the clerk's jurisdiction, such as partition proceedings, may conclude with an agreement of the parties, while other matters may be concluded only with an order of the clerk, as in guardianship and estate cases. Rules for finalizing agreements reached in mediation thus would have to vary for different types of cases. The remainder of this chapter outlines those and other design challenges and discusses their ultimate resolution.

The 2005 Enabling Legislation: North Carolina General Statutes Section 7A-38.3B

The drafting committee began work on proposed legislation in 2004. The committee envisioned a party-pay system, as with other statewide, court-based mediation programs. Since only the legislature could authorize that type of cost to the parties, it was clear that statutory authorization would be required. On May 23, 2005, the General Assembly enacted North Carolina General Statutes Section 7A-38.3B, establishing a mediation program for matters referred to mediation by clerks of superior court.

Matters That May Be Referred to Mediation

Section (b) of the statute allows the clerk of court to order mediation in matters (the drafting committee rejected the word "action" as being too legalistic) within the clerk's original jurisdiction, except for foreclosures under Chapter 45 and adoptions under Chapter 48 of the General Statutes. Matters that may be referred to mediation include:

- Adult guardianships/incompetency;
- Estates administration; and
- Special proceedings—
  - Legitimations,
  - Name changes,
  - Motor vehicle liens,
  - Private condemnations,
  - Partition proceedings,
  - Boundary proceedings,
  - Torrens Act proceedings, and
  - Cartway proceedings.

In light of the foreclosure crisis that began in 2008, it may be hard to understand why the drafting committee exempted foreclosures from the list of available cases. However, in 2004–2005, foreclosures were a speedy and efficient process in which borrowers' rights appeared safely guarded. At that time, the clerks did not want to create a new process that solved no apparent problem and that might lead to significant delay. The committee also surmised that a move to require mediation in foreclosure proceedings would engender opposition from the banking community to the entire legislative proposal. For these reasons, the committee decided not to include foreclosure proceedings in the list of those matters in which mediation could be ordered. In light of the many mediation programs for foreclosures that have grown up across the nation since 2008, many have wondered whether this legislation should be amended. Thus far, however, the mixed success of those programs has not stimulated a strong movement in North Carolina for a program of foreclosure mediation.

As noted above, the drafting committee also decided not to include adoption proceedings in the program. There did not appear to be any problems in adoption cases that would be solved through the mediation process.

Attendance

Section (c) of the statute specifies the persons who are required to attend mediations ordered by the clerk. This was the most difficult part of the statute to draft because of the many different people who might be ordered to participate, depending on the issue in question. (As noted above, the persons relevant to the mediation may change from issue to issue.) The statute authorizes the clerk to order the following persons to attend:

- Named parties. This includes those persons whose names appear on the pleadings.

- Interested persons, meaning those persons who have a right, interest, or claim in the matter. This could include creditors, heirs, devisees, next of kin, or other persons or entities the clerk deems necessary for the adjudication of the matter.

- Non-party participants. The clerk may designate persons or entities who possess information that would be relevant and beneficial to the mediation (such as health care providers in an adult guardianship mediation).

- Fiduciaries, meaning persons or entities holding assets of another, as defined in Chapter 36A of the General Statutes.

This seemingly amorphous list of people who need to be notified and scheduled for mediation presented new challenges for mediators, who were used to determining who should receive notice simply by looking at a pleading. As a practical matter, some collaboration between the mediator and the clerk is involved in getting the mediation conference scheduled, noticed, and held.

Selection of the Mediator

Section (d) of the statute adopts the same methods for selection of the mediator as used in the superior court's Mediated Settlement Conference Program (MSC Program) and the Family Financial Settlement Program (FFS Program). (See Chapter 12, "The Mediated Settlement Conference Program in North Carolina's Superior Courts," and Chapter 18, "The Family Financial Settlement Program in North Carolina's Courts" for a full discussion of mediator selection procedures in those programs.) The parties may choose a certified mediator, but if they can't agree, the clerk will designate one.

Immunity

Under the provisions of Section (e) of the statute, mediators who are appointed or selected for matters ordered to mediation by the clerk have judicial immunity in the same manner and to the same extent as judges of the General Court of Justice.

Costs of Mediation

Named parties, fiduciaries, and interested parties each pay a share of the mediator's fee, pursuant to Section (f) of the statute. Non-party participants are not taxed with any portion of these costs. Costs can be assessed against the estate of a decedent, an adjudicated incompetent, a trust corpus, or a fiduciary only if there is a written order of the clerk. (This is consistent with estate law.)

Inadmissibility of Negotiations

Section (g) of the program legislation deals with the inadmissibility of things said and done in mediations ordered by the clerk. It tracks the comparable statutory provisions of both the MSC Program and the FFS Program. Under this provision, statements and conduct that occur in mediation generally are not subject to discovery and are inadmissible in hearings before the clerk, except in incompetency, guardianship, or estate proceedings (along with certain matters, listed in the statute, which are excluded from discovery in other court-ordered mediation programs).

The clerks who served on the drafting committee felt strongly that they could perform their functions fairly and prevent collusion, fraud, and undue influence in estate and family cases only if they had all the evidence, even those things said and done during mediation. Thus, the persons who attend a clerk-ordered estate or adult guardianship mediation may testify about things said and done in that mediation. Mediators, however, may not be compelled to testify, except in very limited circumstances, pursuant to the language in Section (h) of the statute.

Agreements

The process of finalizing agreements in the Clerk Mediation Program is strikingly different from the procedures in other court-based mediation programs, a fact that arises from the different duties of the clerk in certain types of cases. Under Section (i) of the statute, if an agreement is reached at the mediation that can be binding as a matter of a law (as in partition proceedings), then the parties must reduce the agreement to writing and sign it, along with their attorneys. They have a binding agreement enforceable without any action on the part of the clerk.

In all other matters (estate and guardianships), if an agreement is reached on some or all of the matters ordered to mediation, the parties must reduce its terms to writing and sign it, along with counsel. Such agreements are not binding upon the clerk, but may be offered into evidence at a hearing before the clerk.

Sanctions

The failure of a person to attend mediation was the only grounds for sanctioning someone in the original legislation under Section (j). Some years later, this and the other court-ordered mediation program statutes were amended to also allow sanctions for failing to pay the mediator's fee. With that amendment, the clerk now has contempt powers, as well as the power to impose monetary sanctions authorized in the original legislation.

Authority to Supplement Procedural Details

Section (k) of the statute states: "The clerk of superior court shall make all those orders just and necessary to safeguard the interests of all persons and may supplement all necessary procedural details not inconsistent with rules adopted by the Supreme Court implementing this section." This provision was based on the language of another statute granting similar authority to the clerks of court. It derives from the belief of the drafting committee that procedures in the Clerk Mediation Program will be more fluid and adaptive than in any other court-ordered mediation program.

Program Rules

Rules Implementing Mediation in Matters Before the Clerk of Superior Court (Rules) were adopted by the North Carolina Supreme Court effective March 1, 2006. They were revised in 2010 and were modified to conform with other mediation program rules in 2011. The Rules provide a framework for initiating and conducting mediations in matters referred by clerks of superior court and establish standards for mediator training, certification, and conduct. They are published on the DRC's website.[1]

Beginning the Mediation Process

RULE 1—INITIATING MEDIATION IN MATTERS BEFORE THE CLERK

The mediation process commences with an order of the clerk, which names those persons required to attend. Unlike the mediation programs in superior and district courts, entering the order is entirely at the discretion of the clerk. It is up to the clerk to decide which of the cases within his or her jurisdiction are appropriate for mediation. However, if a matter or an issue in a matter is not ordered to mediation, a party may request such an order.

Importantly, and to prevent fraud and undue influence, a petitioner may not voluntarily dismiss a petition for guardianship after mediation is ordered. The issue must come back to the clerk for review before a dismissal may be taken.

RULE 2—DESIGNATION OF THE MEDIATOR

This rule essentially tracks the provisions of the enabling statute, allowing the parties to designate a DRC-certified mediator by agreement and authorizing the clerk to appoint a certified mediator if the parties do not make a designation.

Conducting the Mediation and Sanctions for Failure to Attend or to Pay the Mediator

RULE 3—THE MEDIATION

Rule 3 sets out guidelines for where and when the mediation may be held and requires the mediator to make arrangements for the time and place. It specifies that the clerk's order to mediation must state a deadline for completion, but allows for extensions of time upon request. The rule also provides that mediation is not to cause delay of other proceedings in the matter.

RULE 4—DUTIES OF PARTIES, ATTORNEYS, AND OTHER PARTICIPANTS

Rule 4 describes the duties of the persons ordered to mediation by the clerk. It also gives wide discretion to the mediator to include in mediation discussions persons who were not ordered to attend, if their presence would be helpful to resolving any issue.

The duty to finalize agreements reached in mediation is set out in Rule 4, and the rest of the language tracks Section (i) of the legislation. If an agreement is reached at the mediation that can be binding as a matter of a law (as in partition proceedings), then the parties must reduce the agreement to writing and sign it, along with their attorneys. In all other matters (estate and guardianships), if an agreement is reached on some or all of the matters ordered to mediation, the parties must reduce its terms to writing and sign it, along with counsel. Such agreements are not binding upon the clerk, but may be offered into evidence at a hearing before the clerk.

RULE 5—SANCTIONS FOR FAILURE TO ATTEND MEDIATION OR TO PAY THE MEDIATOR'S FEE

Rule 5 tracks the language of the statute regarding sanctions that may be imposed on a person who, without good cause, fails to attend mediation or fails to pay the mediator's fee. Such persons may be found to be in contempt of court and subjected to monetary sanctions.

The Mediator

RULE 6—DUTIES OF THE MEDIATOR

The language of Rule 6 is similar to the comparable section of the rules implementing the MSC Program. It establishes the mediator as the person "in control" of the mediation. It permits the mediator to have private communications with the parties and their attorneys and requires disclosure that such communications have taken place. The rule sets out a list of procedural items that the mediator must discuss with the parties at the outset of the mediation. It places an affirmative duty on the mediator to consult with the parties to ensure the voluntariness of the mediation process. The mediator also has the responsibility of determining when an impasse has been reached and of declaring an end to the mediation. The mediator's "administrative" duties are also set out in the rule. They include scheduling and holding the mediation prior to the completion date established by the clerk's order and reporting the results of the mediation to the court on an AOC form within five days of completing the mediation.

RULE 7—COMPENSATION OF THE MEDIATOR

This rule tracks Rule 7 of both the FFS Program and the MSC Program as to setting the mediator's fees and determining whether a participant is an indigent person who does not have to pay a share of those fees. However, there are important variations with regard to fees in guardianship and estate matters. In those matters, the mediator's fees are paid in shares, which are determined by the clerk. Mediators who are accustomed to issuing invoices to the parties at the end of the mediation must adjust to this significant change of procedure in how they get paid. In the Clerk Mediation Program, mediators submit an invoice directly to the clerk, who then decides which parties, participants, and entities are responsible for paying a share of the fee and whether a participant does not have to pay due to indigence. (A person ordered to attend the mediation may submit a motion for a finding of indigence and to be relieved of the duty to pay the mediator. The motion is heard and decided by the clerk after the mediation is concluded.)

RULE 8—CERTIFICATION

If certified mediators want to mediate adult guardianship and estate matters, they must take a ten-hour training course, as prescribed by Rule 9. That course is comprised of substantive subject matter, such as the basics of estate administration, the physiology and psychology of the aging process, and adult guardianship procedures. There are no additional mediation skills or observation requirements. Any mediator certified in the superior court or family financial programs may be selected by the parties or appointed by the clerk to mediate the other matters within the clerk's jurisdiction.

Miscellaneous Provisions

The rules include several miscellaneous provisions. Rule 10 tracks Section (k) of the enabling statute, stating that: "The Clerk of Superior Court shall make all those orders just and necessary to safeguard the interests of all persons and may supplement all necessary procedural details not inconsistent with these Rules." Rule 11 includes definitions, and Rule 12 clarifies how certain time limits are determined.

Use of the Clerk Mediation Program

There are one hundred county clerks of court in North Carolina. Only a few of them have utilized their authority to order mediation, although most clerks will do so if the parties request it. They do not refer matters to mediation in any systematic way, however, and the program is largely underutilized, particularly when compared to the other court-ordered mediation programs.

Some of the likely reasons for this situation have been touched on in this chapter. The clerks are used to having a hands-on approach to their cases. They are protective of the people and processes that are in place to resolve family disputes in estate and guardianship cases without fraud or coercion. They worry that mediation will add an extra layer of time and expense to the disposition of cases within their jurisdiction. They also are worried that mediators who do not regularly handle cases within their jurisdiction will make mistakes of law and procedure, to the detriment of the litigants.

As important as any of these concerns is a fact noted several times in this chapter: the many different types of cases within the clerk's jurisdiction, each with its own procedures and rhythm. Clerks of court will have to determine how the mediation process fits within the parameters of different types of proceedings, what forms will be needed, and what new procedures will be added to their already voluminous procedures manual.

Realizing that these challenges exist, the leadership of the North Carolina Bar Association's Dispute Resolution Section has undertaken an effort to involve clerks in the creation of a mediation manual that will help them recognize markers to identify cases (and issues within cases) that are appropriate for mediation, to create procedures and forms for each of the case types represented in their caseload, to plan and implement a pilot program in several counties with willing clerks, and then to train other clerks in the use of mediation with the materials and experience developed in the pilot counties. It is an ambitious undertaking that, as of this writing, is being spearheaded by Zeb E. "Barney" Barnhardt, Kenneth P. Carlson, Jr., William F. Wolcott III, and L. G. "Nick" Gordon (a former Clerk of Forsyth County).

Conclusion

Many of the matters within the jurisdiction of the clerk of superior court are well suited to resolution by mediation rather than by adjudication, especially matters involving family members or others in ongoing relationships. As more clerks become familiar with the Clerk Mediation Program and its potential to assist them with case management, it seems likely that utilization of the program will increase and that citizens will benefit from the process of working more amicably to resolve their conflicts.

NOTE

1. *See* http://www.ncdrc.org. This URL is automatically redirected to the website of the North Carolina Court System, where information about the Clerk Mediation Program is available at http://www.nccourts.org/Courts/CRS/Councils/DRC/Clerks/Default.asp.

CHAPTER SIXTEEN

ADR in the North Carolina Business Court

*"Litigation is the basic legal right which guarantees
every corporation its decade in court."*
—David Porter

In 1995, the Supreme Court of North Carolina created the position of Special Superior Court Judge for Complex Business Cases to expedite business cases filed in superior court. Judge Ben F. Tennille of Greensboro was appointed as the first judge for the newly created "Business Court" in January 1996. In 2005, the Court was expanded to three members, with courtrooms in Raleigh, Charlotte, and Greensboro.

At the time of his appointment as the first business court judge, Judge Tennille was already a certified mediator. He had extensive experience with arbitration in the textile industry, where the arbitration of commercial disputes is commonplace. Because he had managed litigation for a large corporation, he was familiar with internal corporate decision-making processes. He believed that mediation and other forms of alternative dispute resolution (ADR) would help resolve complex business cases, and the experience of the Business Court judges in the intervening years has confirmed that belief.

ADR Procedures

The North Carolina Business Court is a specialized forum of the trial division of the North Carolina state courts. Cases involving complex and significant issues of corporate and commercial law are assigned by the Chief Justice of the Supreme Court of North Carolina to the Business Court's special superior court judges, who oversee resolution of all matters in their cases through trial.

At the outset of every new case assigned to the Business Court, judges hold a case management conference. Attendance by a corporate executive from each party is required. During the conference the judge not only encourages the parties to consider using mediation or other forms of ADR early in the litigation process, but also stresses the importance of maintaining direct communications to resolve business disputes. In business cases, as in all litigation, close to 95 percent of cases settle before trial. The only real question is how much time and money will be invested before settlement is reached. Business Court judges do not mandate a time for mediation; rather, they encourage the parties and their attorneys to tell the Court when they have enough information to use mediation effectively.

Most cases assigned to the Business Court are ordered to mediation or some other ADR procedure before trial. The majority of mediated cases settle either during mediation or as a result of having been through the process. The judges prefer mediation to court involvement in settlement negotiations. It is their belief that the parties and their counsel are more open during the mediation process than they are in settlement negotiations conducted by the judge who will try their case.

Why Mediation Is Successful in Business Court Cases

Mediation of corporate disputes is successful for several reasons. First, mediation and other forms of ADR give business executives an opportunity to assess the risks, rewards, costs, and time involved in litigation. Having assessed the risks, they are often willing to explore alternative solutions to resolving the dispute.

Second, mediation helps narrow the issues. Mediation usually results in the parties focusing on the basic issues from a *business* perspective, rather than a legal one. Multiple mediation sessions are common in business disputes, because the parties typically use mediation as a way of working toward a business resolution.

Third, mediation enables business people to use their negotiation skills to find practical solutions. Unlike most people involved in litigation, business people are comfortable with negotiating. Litigation leaves negotiation to the lawyers, whose adversarial culture often makes negotiated settlement more difficult to reach. While business people are often uncomfortable in the witness box or in litigants' roles in the courtroom, mediation encourages them to assume their accustomed role of negotiating to solve problems. Most importantly, it reinforces the notion that they have a business problem, not a legal one, and ultimately business issues—rather than legal ones—must shape the settlement. Mediation makes the client reassume responsibility for the problem, responsibility that otherwise is transferred to the lawyer.

Once clients take responsibility for resolving their problem, they often discover solutions that are practical and creative. The opportunities for resolution in a business context are broader and more flexible than in the legal realm, because legal remedies are generally limited and circumscribed. Mediation encourages companies to control their own destinies and to craft business results that neither judge nor jury can fashion.

Many of the disputes before the Business Court involve types of family disputes that often arise after a parent who founded the business dies without a clear succession or estate plan. Others involve small businesses that have been run like partnerships. In both instances, emotions can cloud business judgment. Mediation often helps to overcome emotional barriers to settlement and encourages the parties to use their business judgment.

Fourth, one of the other significant benefits of mediation is the opportunity for the executives to meet on neutral ground and communicate with one another. This opportunity to speak directly often eliminates misunderstandings or helps to clear the air, so that substantive progress can be made toward settlement. Mediation helps an executive understand not just his or her own position, but also the needs and desires of the opposition. A genuine understanding of the adversary's position is often crucial in reaching a creative business solution. (One complex case in the Business Court settled within ten minutes after the responsible managers on each side talked directly to each other.)

Mediation provides a safe setting for this important communication, because statements made in the mediation process are confidential and cannot be communicated to the court or admitted into evidence. The parties thus are free to speak openly and honestly, and to explore different business solutions without fear that their statements or suggestions will be used against them in court.

One advantage of mediation is that it can be used at any point in the dispute process, from before the suit is filed to after trial. Mediation is usually most effective when some discovery has taken place and all parties have a firm grasp on what the evidence will show.

Mediation can be used for many purposes. It is not limited to resolution of the entire case. For example, mediation can be used to resolve costly discovery disputes or to settle some (but not all) of the issues in a case. It may also provide a means for the parties to agree upon ADR mechanisms (e.g., arbitration or submission of technical issues to a panel of industry experts), a strategy that typically produces better results and fewer errors.

Finally, effective use of mediation offers a means of reducing the increasing costs of business disputes. The increasing expense of producing electronically stored information by businesses is making mediation and other forms of ADR more attractive. Litigation rarely adds to revenues but always adds to expenses. Controlling costs is an important aspect of business litigation.

Increasing the Effectiveness of ADR in the Business Court

Although the use of mediation in the North Carolina Business Court is increasing, several areas of possible improvement remain. First, more business executives should serve as mediators in business disputes. Although lawyer-mediators serve well in most cases, they sometimes lack the business perspective that senior executives can bring to the dispute resolution process. Recruiting new mediators with extensive backgrounds in business would help remedy the situation as only about 10 percent of the MSC certified mediators are non-attorneys.

Also, too few business executives use mediation and other ADR techniques to avoid litigation. Executives should be encouraged to use mediation earlier and more often. Business organizations such as the Chamber of Commerce could help promote the use of alternatives to litigation and educate their members on the benefits of ADR procedures. Organizations like the Wake Forest University Family Business Center could help educate family members on alternatives as well.

Conclusion

Mediation and other forms of ADR are ideally suited for use in business litigation. They reduce costs and produce better, more business-focused results. Mediation, in particular, permits business managers to use their negotiation skills to arrive at a business rather than a legal solution to the problems at issue. Usually the business resolutions are more productive for all parties. The North Carolina Business Court will continue to make extensive use of all forms of ADR to help resolve business conflicts and expedite justice.

CHAPTER SEVENTEEN

The North Carolina Court of Appeals Settlement Conference Program

*"The world is wide, and I will not waste
my life in friction when it
could be turned into momentum."*

—Educator and social reformer
Frances Willard (1839–1898)

Early Program (1981–1993)

Background

The North Carolina Court of Appeals was established in 1967. Throughout its early years, the Court's caseload increased dramatically, and by 1980 the Court was hearing appeals in virtually all matters from all the trial tribunals. Appeals from the district courts, superior courts, Industrial Commission, Commissioner of Insurance, Property Tax Commission, Utilities Commission, and all other state agencies came directly to the Court of Appeals. Within a decade of the Court's establishment, some of its members came to believe that many cases containing meritorious questions could be settled if the proper procedures were used before oral argument. They concluded that the use of the procedure known as the "settlement conference" would result in a savings in time, money, personnel, and equipment for all parties.

Other states were already using the settlement conference in their courts, with positive results. It was estimated that the program could produce settlement of as many as fifty cases in the first year. Also, as the program became more widely used, it was expected that the attorneys would become more accustomed to it and that the savings in the expense of further appellate costs would be greater each year.

The basic premise of a settlement conference at the appellate level was the same as that for a settlement conference at the trial level. If the topic of settlement was introduced by an experienced and impartial person not involved in the litigation, and if the discussion was to take place in a neutral forum, the Court felt that parties and counsel would be more likely to arrive at a fair and satisfactory settlement. Counsel and parties often appeared reluctant to introduce the topic of settlement for fear that it might be taken as a lack of confidence in their case or as a sign of weakness. Such reluctance often resulted in a case proceeding through the entire appellate process, despite the fact that a settlement was both possible and practical.

The original Court of Appeals Settlement Conference Committee consisted of Judge Harry C. Martin and Judge Willis P. Whichard. The Committee determined that several steps were necessary to initiate the settlement conference program.

The first step was to select the appropriate person to conduct the settlement conference. It was proposed that a retired judge should be selected, one who enjoyed the respect of lawyers throughout the state. A retired judge conducting the settlement conference would have two very important advantages. First, he or she would not feel under any compulsion to produce a successful record of settlements, as a non-judge might. Second, the fact that a judge was holding the conference would give instant legitimacy to the idea of settling cases after the trial had been concluded and one party to the litigation had lost. The Settlement Conference Committee noted that states using settlement conferences at the appeals court level had employed both retired trial judges and retired appellate court judges as neutrals with apparently equal success.

The second step was to design an information form to be filed with the Court of Appeals at the same time that the notice of appeal was given in the trial court. This form would give the settlement judge the information needed to conduct the conference before the time for filing the record had expired and, preferably, before the preparation of the trial transcript.

On May 14, 1981, Supreme Court Chief Justice Joseph Branch and Court of Appeals Chief Judge Naomi E. Morris announced the receipt of a grant from the Z. Smith Reynolds Foundation to implement the experimental settlement conference program at the appellate level. The program took effect a month later in three pilot districts covering the counties of Buncombe, Durham, Cumberland, and Hoke. The first settlement judges for the respective districts were Judge Francis "Frank" I. Parker, Judge Hamilton H. Hobgood, and Judge Henry A. McKinnon, Jr. By 1983, the settlement program had been expanded to thirteen additional counties overseen by five additional settlement judges.

Procedure

When notice of appeal was given in the districts participating in the program, the appellant's attorney completed and mailed to the clerk of the Court of Appeals a civil appeal statement. This form consisted of a single page providing basic information about the case, including a statement of the grounds for the appeal. Originally, this form went to a special panel of the Court of Appeals, which determined whether the case should be referred to a settlement judge. Shortly after Judge Earl W. Vaughn became Chief Judge, he directed that the forms be referred to Judge Whichard for determination.

If the case was assigned to a settlement judge, the Court issued an order to all counsel and to the settlement judge. The order had the effect of tolling (or stopping) the running of time for docketing the appeal. The settlement judge then attempted to settle the case by conference with counsel and, if necessary, the parties. The settlement judge had the responsibility for arranging the details of the conference and had wide discretion in the management of the settlement process. The Court of Appeals paid settlement judges $100 per day for their services, plus $0.25 per mile for travel expenses.

If the case was settled, the settlement judge advised the Court to that effect. A judge of the superior or district court then signed the necessary documents to implement the settlement.

If the case was not settled, the Court was also notified. The settlement judge did not in any way indicate an opinion on the merits of the appeal. If the case was not settled, the Court then issued an order withdrawing the case from the settlement judge and setting the time frame for perfecting the appeal.

The settlement conference program did not provide for any sanctions for attorneys who failed to file the civil appeal statement, even though those attorneys who failed to file were in violation of a local rule of practice promulgated in each of the judicial districts covered by the program. Because of the lack of such sanctions, some counties had a poor record for the number of civil appeal statements filed.

Results of Early Mediation Program

As of February 7, 1985, data collected for the first three and one-half years of the program showed that approximately one-third of the cases submitted to the settlement judge had been settled. Because of a lack of sanctions available to enforce the filing of the civil appeal statement, and with judges leaving the Court who had been instrumental in its operation, the settlement program was terminated in early 1993. During the twelve-year existence of the program, 663 civil appeal statements were filed. Of that number, 284 cases were referred to a settlement judge. This resulted in a settlement in ninety cases, or 32 percent of the cases referred to the settlement conference program.

Current Mediation Program (2002–Present)

Commencing August 1, 2002, an eighteen-month pilot program of Court of Appeals mediation was ordered into effect by North Carolina Supreme Court Chief Justice I. Beverly Lake, Jr. In February 2004, it became a permanent program. The program originally was supervised by Judge Robin Hudson. When she was elected to the North Carolina Supreme Court, Judge Sanford L. Steelman, Jr. assumed the supervision of the mediation program.

Civil cases (which include workers' compensation and domestic cases) are eligible for mediation, when both parties consent. There are three classifications of mediators for these cases: current Court of Appeals Judges, retired Court of Appeals Judges (Recalled Judges), and private mediators. The current Court of Appeals Judges do not charge a fee for their services. Recalled Judges and private mediators are paid by the parties for their services.

If a current Court of Appeals Judge conducts the mediation, he or she is prohibited from any future involvement in the case. This can be done because there are fourteen other judges available to hear the case who were not involved in the mediation.

The parties are requested to state whether they wish to mediate early in the appellate process. The objective is to schedule the mediation session as quickly as possible so that the parties can minimize their appellate costs if the case is settled.

Upon request of the mediator, the parties each provide a brief "Mediation Statement" (no more than four pages) that includes: a brief history of the litigation; the history of any efforts to settle the case, including any offers or demands; a summary of the parties' legal positions; the present posture of the case, including any related litigation in the trial court; and any current proposals for settlement. The Mediation Statement must *not* be filed with the clerk of the Court of Appeals.

The parties and their counsel must be present for the mediation unless excused by the mediator. Mediations usually are held in the Court of Appeals facilities, unless agreed otherwise by the parties and the mediator. Mediations also may be conducted by telephone if all parties and the mediator agree.

All information shared during the course of the mediation, including the Mediation Statement, is kept confidential. It does not become part of the record on appeal and is not disclosed to others, including the judges on the panel if the appeal moves forward. Neither the parties, the attorneys, nor the mediator may disclose any statements, discussions, or actions taken in the course of mediation except to the extent necessary to complete the Report of Mediator Form that must be filed within five days after completion of the mediation conference or to inform the Court whether mediation was successful or not. If the mediation is successful, the appellant is responsible for moving to dismiss both the appeal and the case in the trial court, if necessary.

One of the interesting dynamics of appellate mediation is that there already has been a decision on the merits of the case by the trial tribunal. The uncertainty of a trial result thus is not present in appellate mediation. There is only the uncertainty of the result of the appeal. Since the rate of reversal of trial court decisions in the Court of Appeals is readily calculable, it would seem that there would not be a compelling motivation for parties to mediate in many cases.

So what motivates parties to mediate and settle cases at the appellate level? Certainly, one factor is the desire for finality. Many parties have been litigating for several years and simply want the case to be over. Another factor is the sharply rising cost of appellate litigation. Resolving a case through mediation can end the matter at an early point in the appeals process, and costs can be greatly reduced. Finally, there are certain cases where a decision of the appellate court may not finally resolve the litigation. Workers' compensation cases, domestic relations cases, and interlocutory appeals may fall into this category. Appellate mediation offers the opportunity for a final, global settlement of all issues, a result that may not be achieved with an appellate ruling.

What has been the rate of settlement of cases in the Court of Appeals mediation program? Anecdotal evidence indicates that approximately one-half of the cases have settled at mediation. Also, in a number of cases, the parties made substantial progress toward settlement through mediation but were just not quite able to close the gap.

A study of the program was conducted, covering the time period January 2010 through March 2011. The study looked not at whether the case was settled at the mediation hearing, but instead at whether the Court of Appeals had to write an opinion in the case. The results of this study were as follows:

Cases submitted to mediation:	61
Cases withdrawn after mediation:	27
Opinions filed by the Court of Appeals:	15
No opinion filed/still pending:	19

Of the cases where the result was known (appeal withdrawn or opinion filed), 64.28 percent were withdrawn without an opinion being filed.

Conclusion

The Court of Appeals mediation program has afforded parties an opportunity to participate in the resolution of their case before it is finally decided by the Court. (For most civil cases in North Carolina, the Court of Appeals is the final court.) The program also allows the Court of Appeals to dispose of a number of cases every year without a written opinion, saving valuable Court resources for other cases.

RESOLUTION OF FAMILY MATTERS

CHAPTER EIGHTEEN

The Family Financial Settlement Program in North Carolina's Courts

"Emphasis on collaboration and problem solving can help soothe strained relationships, improve communication, and enhance prospects for positive future interaction."
—North Carolina Court of Appeals Judge Ralph A. Walker
(Chair of the North Carolina Dispute Resolution Commission),
"Family Financial Settlement Program to Assist Divorcing Couples,"
Press Release from The North Carolina Court System (April 7, 1999).

Program Design

Purpose and Scope

The Family Financial Settlement Program (FFS Program) is designed to facilitate settlement of district court cases involving disputes over equitable distribution, alimony, or support. "Equitable distribution" describes the process a court uses, upon application of a party to a divorce proceeding, to "equitably" divide marital property between the parties. The FFS Program encourages parties to focus their attention in these cases on settlement rather than on litigation and provides a structured opportunity for settlement negotiations to take place. At the scheduling conference, which is mandatory under state law, the court may order the parties in an equitable distribution action to attend a mediated settlement conference (mediation) or other settlement procedure agreed upon by the parties. Once the court enters the order, participation by the parties is required. Note that although the enabling legislation for the FFS Program and the program rules use the terminology "mediated settlement conference," that designation usually is associated with the superior court's Mediated Settlement Conference (MSC) Program. To avoid confusion, this chapter frequently uses the more generic term "mediation" to refer to the mediated settlement process used in the district court's FFS Program.

The parties are not limited to discussion of equitable distribution at the mediation. Other issues, including child support and alimony, may also be included in the negotiations. Custody and visitation issues may be discussed and negotiated upon agreement of the parties.

The Rules of the North Carolina Supreme Court Implementing Settlement Procedures in Equitable Distribution and Other Family Financial Cases (FFS Rules) allow the parties to select a settlement procedure from a dispute resolution menu. Among options available to the parties are mediations, neutral evaluations, judicial settlement conferences (if available in the district), or any other settlement procedures permitted by a district's local rules. Mediation is the default procedure (i.e., a court must order that a mediation be held if the parties do not select one of the other procedures). Parties generally opt for mediation, with the other alternatives selected only rarely.

During a mediation, a neutral facilitator or "mediator" meets with the parties and their attorneys to help them discuss and try to settle the issues in dispute. If the parties are successful in settling their case, the dispute is resolved without the need for protracted litigation and trial. If the dispute cannot be settled, the case proceeds to trial.

Features of the Program

The Family Financial Settlement Program was modeled to a large extent on the MSC Program, which has operated in North Carolina's superior courts since 1991. The programs share many important characteristics, including two in particular that differentiate them from some of the other court-based dispute resolution programs operating in North Carolina. First, the MSC and FFS Programs are designed as user-pay programs (i.e., litigants, rather than taxpayers, compensate the mediator for his or her services). Second, in each of these programs the parties have an opportunity to select their mediator, rather than having one appointed by the court. The court appoints a mediator only in instances where the parties fail to make a designation, cannot agree, or request that the court make the selection for them. Another important feature shared by both the MSC and the FFS programs is the menu approach, noted above, which offers a wide range of ADR alternatives.

Program Background and Development

The FFS Program's original enabling legislation, North Carolina General Statutes Section 7A-38.4, authorized the North Carolina Dispute Resolution Commission (DRC or Commission) to design a pilot program. J. Anderson "Andy" Little, a mediator from Chapel Hill, was appointed to chair an Ad Hoc Committee to develop pilot rules for the program's implementation. Members of the Committee included chief district court judges in pilot program sites, members of the DRC, family litigators, family mediators, and court administrators. Proposed rules developed by the Committee were approved by the DRC which, in turn, recommended them to the Supreme Court of North Carolina. The Court adopted the FFS Rules on December 30, 1998, with an effective date of March 1, 1999.

During the 2001 legislative session, FFS proponents encouraged the North Carolina General Assembly to continue the pilot program and to expand it statewide. These efforts were successful, and on July 28, 2001, Governor Michael F. Easley signed legislation continuing the FFS Program and expanding it throughout the state.[1] While this effort was underway in the General Assembly, Andy Little and other members of the DRC's Ad Hoc Committee worked to refine the pilot FFS Rules, taking into account lessons learned during the pilot period. On October 16, 2001, upon recommendation of both the DRC and the Alternate Dispute Resolution Committee of the State Judicial Council, the Supreme Court adopted the Ad Hoc Committee's proposed rule revisions.

The program's enabling legislation, FFS Rules, and program forms are available on the DRC's website[2] or through its office. Mediators and attorneys should also check with individual districts to determine whether local rules supplementing the FFS Rules have been adopted.

The framework for the FFS Program's operations (as set forth in the FFS Rules) is described below. Some practical tips for mediators and attorneys working in the family law area are also included.

ADR Options in the FFS Program

Mediation

MEDIATED SETTLEMENT CONFERENCE DEFINED

As noted above, the mediated settlement conference (or mediation) is the mandatory settlement procedure selected most often by parties in equitable distribution and other family financial cases in district court. It typically occurs early in the life of such actions. Attendance by the parties and their attorneys is required, but participation in the process is entirely voluntary. There is no requirement that the attorneys or parties negotiate in good faith, or that they negotiate at all. The mediation process generally is successful, however, because in most cases the decision makers and their advisors choose to work toward settlement with the help of their mediator.

A typical conference begins with the parties working together in a general session. The mediator first explains the mediation process and his or her role as mediator. Then, the parties present their respective positions in the case and may exchange information that was not delivered during the discovery process. After the general session, the parties usually separate and meet with the mediator in a private session often referred to as a "caucus." During the caucus, the mediator helps the parties put aside their anger and frustration. He or she assists the parties in analyzing their situation realistically and in thinking through their needs and those of their children. The mediator also helps the parties generate options and proposals for settlement. As the parties develop offers and counteroffers for settling issues in dispute, the mediator carries the offers and counteroffers back and forth between the parties and their attorneys. Although the parties may return to a general session from time to time, private caucuses are more common since the focus of family financial mediation is primarily property and money, not custody or visitation, issues which require more interaction between the parties. (Custody and visitation issues are the subject of the Custody and Visitation Mediation Program, discussed in Chapter 19.) The heavy reliance upon private sessions is probably due to the fact that most litigants view their case analysis and "best positions" as private information. The typical family financial mediation usually involves no more than two sessions, and most conferences are concluded in a single session lasting from half a day to a full day.

Prior to Mediation

Duty of Counsel to Consult with Clients and Opposing Counsel
Concerning Settlement Procedures

The FFS Rules require counsel to advise his or her client of the settlement procedures available in actions involving equitable distribution, child support, alimony, post-separation support, separation agreements, premarital agreements, or contracts between the parties regarding distribution of marital property or quitclaims of certain rights. In addition, the FFS Rules compel attorneys to confer with opposing counsel at or prior to the scheduling conference to determine which settlement procedure they and the parties wish to elect.

Order for Settlement Procedure

At the scheduling conference in an equitable distribution action, or at such earlier time specified by local rule, the court may enter an order requiring the parties to engage in a settlement procedure. The order must require that a settlement procedure be held, establish a deadline for its completion, and state that the parties are required to pay the neutral's fee, except in the case of a judicial settlement conference. The court's order for a settlement procedure may be contained in the scheduling order or, if one is not entered, must be included on the form titled "Order for Mediated Settlement Conference in Family Financial Case." (The form is available on the DRC's website.)

Selection of a Procedure Other Than Mediation. The FFS Rules acknowledge that the parties themselves, rather than the court, are in the best position to know which settlement procedure will be most effective in their case. The Rules therefore permit the parties to elect—and the court to authorize —an alternate settlement procedure, such as neutral evaluation, judicial settlement conference (if available in the district), or any other procedure provided for in local rules. The parties must agree upon the procedure to be used, the neutral to be employed, and the neutral's rate of compensation. If the parties cannot reach agreement on these points, the judge must order the parties to attend a mediation, the default procedure under the FFS Rules. If the parties desire to use an alternate settlement procedure, they must file either: (1) a Motion for an Order to Use a Settlement Procedure Other Than Mediated Settlement Conference or Judicial Settlement Conference in Family Financial Case; or (2) a Motion to Order Judicial Settlement Conference in Family Financial Case and to Appoint a Judge to Conduct Conference. (The motions are available in fillable form on the DRC's website.)

Motion to Dispense with Settlement Procedure. A party may move that the court dispense with its order to attend a settlement procedure. The motion must be in writing and must state why the relief is sought. For good cause, the court may dispense with the process. Good cause may include a history of domestic violence, the fact that the parties have already participated in a settlement process, or that they have elected to resolve their case through private arbitration under the Family Law Arbitration Act. The fact that parties are indigent or live at considerable distance from the location of the settlement conference should not be an impediment, and the FFS Rules address these situations. For example, Rule 4 provides for telephone or other electronic participation, and Rule 7 provides that a mediator must waive fees for parties determined by the court to be unable to pay their full share (or some portion of it). As a practical matter, most judges have been reluctant to grant motions to dispense with mediation (or other settlement procedures available under the program menu).

Designation of a Mediator

By Agreement of the Parties. As noted, the FFS Program is a user-pay program where the parties themselves, not the state, compensate the mediator. Since the parties bear the cost, it is important that they also have an opportunity to choose their mediator. This element of choice not only engenders a greater sense of confidence in the process, but it also helps to assure a measure of quality control, since attorneys and parties are not likely to recommend a mediator who proves ineffective. Only in those instances where the parties take no action to select a mediator or cannot agree on their choice does the court intervene and appoint a mediator to conduct the conference. The FFS Rules allow the parties to either designate a trained and certified family financial mediator or nominate a non-certified mediator to conduct their conference. The parties must designate their mediator at the scheduling conference, or at such earlier time specified in local rule, by filing with the court a Designation of Mediator in Family Financial Case form (available on the DRC's website).

Once the parties choose a mediator, they must submit the Designation of Mediator in Family Financial Case form to identify their mediator for the court, confirm that the mediator has agreed to serve, and state the rate of compensation to which they and the mediator have agreed. Parties nominating a non-certified mediator must also explain to the court why the individual they selected is qualified to serve. This is done by demonstrating the non-certified mediator's training, experience, or other qualifications. The court has the option of either approving or disapproving a nominated mediator. (As a practical matter, most courts routinely approve the nominations submitted to them.)

The DRC is charged with certifying family financial mediators. If the parties designate a certified mediator, they can be assured that their mediator has completed the required training and fulfilled the other requirements established by the North Carolina Supreme Court and the DRC for certification. Moreover, they may be assured that the mediator's conduct is governed by the Supreme Court's Standards of Professional Conduct for Mediators, and that the DRC is available to take complaints if a participant in the process believes his or her mediator is of bad moral character, has violated the Standards, or has otherwise acted unethically.

Once certified, a mediator's name and contact information are added to the master list of certified family financial mediators, which is maintained by the DRC and regularly updated on its website. The judicial districts that a mediator is willing to serve for purposes of court appointments and party designation are also indicated, and biographical information for the individual mediator appears on the website. If parties are interested in using a particular mediator but do not know much about him or her, they may visit the Commission's website and enter the name on the mediator search screen to access biographical material for the individual (provided that the mediator has supplied such information to the Commission). The material typically will include information on the mediator's education, work experience, and special skills or interests. In instances where attorneys or parties are working with a complex or specialized fact situation or with difficult legal issues, a keyword search function permits users to search biographical information for all mediators, or for mediators serving a particular district or districts for the purpose of identifying those who possess special skills or experience.

Most mediators selected by agreement are usually known by the parties' attorneys, either personally or by professional reputation. If parties are considering hiring a particular mediator, they may want to ask about his or her professional experience with family matters—how many family cases he or she has mediated, what issues were involved, how complex the cases were, and how successful he or she was in resolving them. (No mediator is successful all of the time, and anyone making such a claim probably should be viewed with suspicion. Nevertheless, a mediator should have a record of overall success in bringing parties to agreement.)

When appropriate, the attorney may also want to ask whether the mediator has ever worked with an interpreter or has had experience dealing with the press. The attorney may also want to inquire about the mediator's style to find out whether the mediator is more relaxed or will push the parties along vigorously. Attorneys can learn about a mediator's style by talking with other attorneys or even by observing the mediator in action, with the permission of the mediator and others present. An attorney should also take responsibility for becoming familiar with the mediation process and the Standards of Professional Conduct for Mediators (available from the DRC on its website). It is important that an attorney be familiar with accepted mediation practices and techniques and have an awareness of what is considered questionable, so that informed judgments can be made about a mediator's abilities, style, and ethics. (See "Selecting the Mediator," Chapter 12.)

By Appointment of the Court. If the parties cannot agree on a mediator or they take no action to designate one, the court will make an appointment. To request court appointment of a mediator, the parties file a Designation of Mediator in Family Financial Case form at the scheduling conference, or at such earlier time as specified by local rule. The form includes a Motion for Court Appointment of a Mediator and an Order of Appointment. The FFS Rules require that the court appoint a certified mediator to conduct the mediation. The DRC provides the court with a list of certified family financial mediators who are willing to accept court appointments in that district. The Rules also provide for judges to make their appointments by rotating down the list of certified mediators provided by the DRC.

Scheduling the Mediation

The Mediator as Case Manager. It is the responsibility of the appointed mediator to set the date, time, and place for the settlement conference and to give timely notice to the parties. The mediator must make an effort to consult with the parties prior to scheduling the mediation and attempt to hold it at a time and location convenient for them. The mediation must be scheduled for a date prior to the deadline for completion designated in the court's order. The FFS Rules provide that the court's deadline must not be more than 150 days after issuance of the court's Order for Mediated Settlement Conference in Family Financial Case, unless extended by the court. As a guiding principle, the scheduled date should give the parties time to complete discovery, but be set well in advance of the trial date. The mediator is specifically authorized by the FFS Rules to assist the parties in establishing a discovery schedule that allows discovery to be completed prior to the mediation conference.

The FFS Rules allow the mediation to be held in any location agreeable to the parties and the mediator. Most conferences are held in the office of one of the lawyers involved or in the mediator's office. They can also be held in the local courthouse. Attorneys should be sure to let the mediator know if anyone scheduled to attend has limitations on his or her mobility. If a client requires an interpreter due to hearing difficulties or a lack of familiarity with the English language, the attorney or party will need to engage an interpreter to attend the conference. If an interpreter will be attending, it is advisable to inform the mediator beforehand. Unfortunately, violence or extreme hostility can sometimes be issues in domestic mediations. In such cases, the parties may want to ask the court to dispense with mediation or to ask the mediator to conduct the mediation in a secure location such as the local courthouse. Mediators may have no ex parte communications with counsel or the parties before or outside the conference, except with regard to scheduling matters.

Extensions of Time. A district court judge may extend the deadline for completion of the mediation upon the judge's own motion, upon stipulation of the parties, or at the suggestion of the mediator.

A party or parties may ask the mediator to reschedule a mediation, as long as the new date selected for the conference falls within the deadline for completion set by the court. Only a judge can extend the deadline for completion set out in the court's order referring the case to mediation. However, the DRC has cautioned mediators to ensure that there is a compelling reason for the request, even when it falls within the deadline. Mediators should bear in mind that one of the purposes of the FFS Program is to expedite settlement of cases. Postponements often have the opposite effect, especially when no compelling reason for the delay exists. When a mediator postpones a conference without a finding of good cause, the rules provide for the party or parties requesting the extension to pay a postponement fee, both as penalty and to compensate the mediator for the unanticipated opening in his or her schedule. When a mediator encounters a situation where attorneys or pro se parties are uncooperative—they will not return calls or e-mails, will not agree upon a date, or request an unreasonable number of extensions, for example—the mediator will likely need to be assertive and simply pick a date for the mediation and notify the parties. As noted above, it is ultimately the mediator's responsibility to ensure that the deadline set by the court for completion of the mediated settlement conference is met.

Preparing the Client for Mediated Settlement

An attorney should meet with his or her client prior to mediation to explain the process and make sure that the client knows what to expect. A brochure designed especially for litigants, which explains the mediation process and the FFS Program, is available from the DRC. Law offices may order copies at no charge or may download them from the DRC's website. The DRC's website also contains additional information about mediated settlement and the FFS Program. While both the brochure and website are useful supplementary sources of information about mediated settlement, they are not substitutes for the time an attorney should spend with his or her client explaining the mediation process and planning for the negotiations that will occur.

Explaining the Benefits of Mediated Settlement. An attorney may begin discussions with the client by telling him or her that mediation offers an opportunity for the parties and their attorneys to meet face-to-face with a neutral facilitator to discuss and try to resolve their disputes. The attorney also should briefly explain how the process works and then tell the client how he or she may benefit from participating.

- Mediated settlement offers the parties an opportunity to work things out themselves and to design an agreement that truly meets their needs and those of their children. In effect, *they* are making the decisions, rather than a judge or an arbitrator who knows much less about their situation and their children.
- Mediated settlement eliminates the risks involved in a trial.
- Mediated settlement gives parties an opportunity to set a precedent for amicably resolving their disputes. If there are children involved, this can be critical to preserving whatever goodwill may be left between the parents. A successful mediation can instill faith in parents that they will be able to work through the inevitable issues that will arise over the years as they continue to parent, such as disputes over visitation and money. On the other hand, a bitterly fought trial will only exacerbate tensions between parents and likely lead to further litigation.
- Mediated settlement reduces time and stress and may reduce expense.
- Because mediated settlement is a confidential process, it offers parties an opportunity to resolve their disputes privately, without exposing their marital difficulties, personal problems, and individual failings to public scrutiny.[3]

It also may be important to explain to the client what mediation is *not*:

- The mediator is not a judge, and the mediation is not a trial.
- The client will not have to testify at the mediation.
- The mediator is not a therapist or marriage counselor. The mediation process is about dividing assets and debts, not about saving the marriage or deconstructing it and assigning blame.

Encouraging Constructive Behavior. During discussions, the attorney should counsel the client to try to put emotions aside for purposes of the mediation. Because the mediator is not a decision maker (unlike a judge or arbitrator), a party has nothing to gain by vilifying his or her spouse during the mediation. Also, the client should be advised that, although mediation is not a trial, it is a legal proceeding, and the client should dress appropriately and act civilly and with restraint. Emotions may be raw, and some venting is to be expected; but yelling, cursing, and name calling are not appropriate and will not be helpful in furthering a process wholly dependent upon the goodwill and cooperation of both parties.

The attorney also may want to explain that he or she will make an effort to be cooperative during mediation, and that mediation is intended to be a collaborative approach to dispute resolution, not an adversarial one. While posturing and objections may be effective at trial, they are not likely to produce positive results in mediation.

Reassuring the Client. It is important for an attorney to reassure the client about mediation. The client should understand that the attorney will be present during the conference to lend support and give advice. The client may be very uncomfortable if he or she thinks family financial mediation will require him or her to meet alone with the spouse to divide marital assets and set a child support or alimony amount, particularly if there has been a power imbalance within the relationship. While cases involving severe physical or psychological abuse are probably not appropriate for mediation, an attorney and client should be aware that participating in a successful mediation can be an empowering experience for a client who has not been allowed to assert himself or herself during the marriage. A successful mediation can also send a signal to a former spouse that communications will have to be handled differently in the future, if the parties are to remain out of court.

If a party has health concerns or other issues that may affect his or her ability to participate, counsel should let the mediator know before the mediation or when the private session begins. Counsel should reassure the client that if he or she needs frequent breaks or needs more time to think about the settlement proposal, the mediator is likely to be receptive to such requests and to allow breaks or a recess. A marathon mediation session that, in effect, deprives a client of breaks, food, or opportunities to take needed medication may result in a situation where the client is not able to make quality decisions. An agreement reached under such circumstances may not be durable. If, on reflection, a party realizes errors in judgment due to these types of pressures, he or she not only may refuse to comply with the agreement, failing to turn over property or make payments in accordance with its terms, but also may have recourse against the lawyer and mediator by filing complaints with regulatory authorities.

The attorney should stress to the client that not every case will be resolved in mediation and that the client is not required to settle the case at the conference. If the case does not settle, the dispute will simply proceed to trial. In other words, mediation will not compromise the client's right to a trial, nor will it delay the trial date. The client also should be aware that mediation is a confidential process. North Carolina General Statutes Section 7A-38.4A(j) and the FFS Rules prohibit the introduction at trial of any statements made or any conduct occurring at the conference.[4]

Finally, the attorney should explain to the client that the mediation process is specifically intended to give parties a chance to participate in the resolution of their case. If a party wishes to play an active role in the general discussions, that is appropriate. However, if a party is uncomfortable and wishes to let his or her attorney do all the talking, that also is acceptable.

Planning for the Conference. The attorney should help the client understand that mediation is designed as a win-win process, not a zero-sum game. Accordingly, the client needs to differentiate between his or her wants and needs. The goal is to draft an agreement that will meet the needs of both parties and their children, if any. While no party is likely to emerge from a mediation with a complete and total victory, many needs may be met and, in the process, the risks inherent in trying a lawsuit are eliminated. During discussions with the client, the attorney should attempt to learn where there is room for compromise on the issues. The attorney and client should develop a checklist for the mediation to ensure that all issues necessary to arrive at a full settlement are discussed. The attorney also should decide the sequence in which he or she plans to cover the issues. For example, the attorney would not want to open discussions with a "hot button" issue. Instead, it usually is better to start with a matter that can be resolved easily, in the hope of building some goodwill and momentum toward overall settlement.

Attorney Preparation for Mediation

Prior to a mediation, an attorney should do each of the following things:

- Convey a positive, constructive attitude about mediated settlement to the client. The client's attitude and actions will very often mirror those of counsel. If the client senses that the attorney views mediation as a waste of time, he or she probably will not come to mediation prepared to settle.

- Complete sufficient discovery to have a solid understanding of the couple's assets, including valuations of any business or professional practice that may be involved, and document the assessment of assets for opposing counsel. Also, the attorney should be able to document any special needs of a spouse or child, or any claims that certain property is separate from the marital estate.

- Review the case and develop a strong presentation. Many attorneys who commit considerable time and energy to preparing for trial may not give mediated settlement the same attention. It is important that the attorney have a thoughtful, polished case summary and be prepared to negotiate. Such preparation and presentation sends a powerful message to the other side that the trial will be an uphill battle and makes settlement look more attractive.

- Prepare a checklist of all items that, from the client's perspective, need to be discussed and resolved for agreement to occur. Counsel should meet with the client to ensure that the checklist is complete and to discern which matters on the checklist the client views as negotiable, and which issues are ones where there is little (if any) room for concessions. Reinforce with the client that even though it may be unpalatable, she or he may have to consider compromising. Talk with the client about how the court is likely to decide the issues in dispute, especially in instances where the client seems to be taking an unreasonable or unrealistic position.

- Advise the client that the mediator's fee is due and payable at the end of the conference. Make sure the client brings his or her checkbook to the mediation or comes prepared to make arrangements with the mediator for payment at a specified future date.

- Advise the mediator if the client has any mobility limitations so that the mediation is held in an accessible place and arrange for any interpreters that will be needed.

AT THE MEDIATION

Attendance

Who Must Attend. The FFS Rules require that the parties and their attorneys attend the mediation conference until an agreement is reached or the mediator declares an impasse. Under Rule 4, which permits telephone or other electronic participation, the attendance requirement can be modified by agreement of the parties and the mediator, but the DRC strongly favors the physical presence of the parties. Attending the mediation in person affords parties the opportunity to express their views and demands, to hear the views and demands of each spouse, to actively participate in the discussions and negotiations, and to take ownership of the agreement, including signing it at the end of the conference. By attending in person, the parties also are more likely to feel that they have had their day in court, and they may be more inclined to settle their case.

It may be helpful to have other parties attend the mediation, if their presence can help facilitate settlement. For example, if there are complicated tax, pension, or business valuation issues involved in the divorce, the parties may want to have their accountants or appraisers attend the mediation session.

Sanctions for Failure to Attend. The FFS Rules provide that a party who, without good cause, fails to attend a settlement conference is subject to the contempt powers of the court and monetary sanctions. These sanctions may include, but are not limited to, the payment of fines, attorney's fees, mediator fees, expenses, and earnings lost by persons attending the conference.

Authority and Duties of the Mediator

The mediation conference is controlled by the mediator, not by the parties or their attorneys. The FFS Rules list several topics that the mediator must explain at the beginning of the conference: the mediation process, the differences between mediation and other forms of conflict resolution, the costs of mediated settlement, that mediation is not a trial, that the process is confidential, and other topics. The mediator also must advise the participants of any circumstances bearing on his or her possible bias, prejudice, or partiality. The mediator has authority to declare an impasse when appropriate and should do so in a timely manner.

The Attorney's Role in Moving the Mediation Conference Forward

An attorney can encourage settlement in the following ways:

- Respect the mediator's authority to control the conference. Do not seek to dominate the proceeding.
- Listen attentively and respectfully to opposing counsel and his or her client.
- Avoid the use of accusatory or inflammatory language.

- Remind the client to be civil and respectful and to avoid blaming or shaming the spouse.
- Acknowledge in a general and conciliatory way the pain that both parties and their children, if any, are suffering as a result of the divorce.
- Ask the other party to look at the costs and risks involved in trying the case, including deterioration of the parties' relationship and potential emotional damage to any children.
- Demonstrate goodwill by indicating some willingness to compromise.
- Make only realistic demands and avoid posturing.
- Advocate agreement on less important issues as a way of building momentum.
- Invite parties to put their hurt feelings and anger aside for the sake of their children, if any, and their own emotional well-being.
- Even if a case cannot be settled, try to end the discussion on a positive note. When the conference ends positively, it is often possible to informally continue the dialogue begun at the mediation, which may result in eventual settlement of the case.

Finalizing the Agreement

To be enforceable, an agreement reached at a mediation conference must be reduced to writing, signed, and acknowledged by the parties in accordance with North Carolina General Statutes Section 50-20(d). A mediator who is also a notary public may notarize the parties' signatures on the agreement. If the parties are able to reach an agreement at the conference, but are unable to have it written, signed, and acknowledged, they are required to summarize the terms of their understanding in writing and use it as a memorandum and guide to drafting the agreement and any orders necessary to give legal effect to their terms. The parties must execute their final agreement and any other dispositive documents and file judgments or voluntary dismissals with the court within thirty days after reaching agreement at the mediation.

Compensation of the Mediator

The FFS Rules provide that the mediator is to be compensated for his or her professional services at the conclusion of the conference. A party-selected mediator is compensated in an amount and according to terms agreed to by the parties and the mediator. The fees of court-appointed mediators are capped at $150 per hour for mediation services, plus a one-time per case administrative fee of $150. The administrative fee, unlike the fee for professional services, is due upon the appointment of the mediator, though as a practical matter it is generally paid with the other fees. Court-appointed mediators are not permitted to seek reimbursement for travel time, mileage, lodging, or any other out-of-pocket expenses associated with their travel to and from a mediation. For that reason, most mediators limit the judicial districts that they serve for purposes of court appointments to those within a relatively short driving distance of their homes or offices. A party-selected mediator may require a deposit as an advance on his or her fee, but once the case has been accepted, the mediator cannot delay scheduling or holding a conference because the deposit has not been paid.

The fees of both party-selected and court-appointed mediators are to be paid in equal shares by the parties. Rule 7 provides that a mediator must waive fees for parties determined by the court to be unable to pay their full share or some portion of it. Such parties may petition the court for relief by filing a Petition and Order for Relief from Obligation to Pay All or Part of Mediator's Fee in Family Financial Case. In ruling on such motions, the judge may consider the income and assets of the movant, and the outcome of the action. In its order, the court may require that fees of the party be paid out of the marital estate. In certain circumstances, mediators may also assess a postponement or cancellation fee. Parties who willfully fail to pay a mediator's fee may be found in contempt of court.

FOLLOWING MEDIATION

Report of Mediator

The mediator is required to file a Report of Mediator (Report) with the court within ten days of the conclusion of the conference or of being notified of a settlement. A Report must be filed whether or not a mediation was actually held. Recent revisions to the FFS Rules also require the mediator to file a Report in family financial cases that he or she mediates that are filed in district court, but that have not been ordered to mediation (i.e., cases filed but voluntarily mediated). The Report advises the court who attended the conference, if one was held, and states the outcome: mediation not held, case settled pre-mediation, case settled at the conference, or that the parties reached an impasse. Court staff use the information supplied on the Reports for scheduling purposes. They also use the reports to prepare monthly caseload statistics, which they provide to the Administrative Office of the Courts on behalf of the FFS Program.

The DRC takes mediator case management responsibilities, including reporting, very seriously. Mediators who do not file their Reports (or who do not file them in a timely manner) risk discipline by the Commission and are also subject to sanctions by the court.

When a Case Settles

When a mediator reports a case settled either prior to, at, or during a recess of a conference, he or she also must indicate whether a voluntary dismissal or consent judgment will be filed in the case and provide the name, address, and telephone number of the person who will file the closing document. In addition, the mediator is required to advise the parties that FFS Rule 4.B.(2) requires that their consent judgment or voluntary dismissal be filed with the court within thirty days or before the expiration of the mediation deadline, whichever is longer.

When an Agreement Falls Apart

Parties and their attorneys may not leave a mediation until an impasse has been declared or a summary memorandum of their agreement has been reduced to writing or the parties have reached a full agreement, reduced it to writing, and signed and acknowledged it. The summary memorandum is used as a guide in drafting the final agreement and any orders necessary to effect it. If the parties fail to agree on the wording or terms of the final agreement or court order, the mediator is authorized to schedule another session if he or she believes it will assist the parties in moving forward.

If a party seeks to renege on a final agreement, the mediator cannot be subpoenaed to testify about what occurred at the mediation or to talk about or interpret the content of the agreement. North Carolina General Statutes Section 7A-38.4A(j) limits mediator testimony as follows:

> No mediator, or other neutral conducting a settlement procedure under this section, shall be compelled to testify or produce evidence concerning statements made and conduct occurring in a mediated settlement conference or other settlement procedure in any civil proceeding for any purpose, including proceedings to enforce a settlement of the action, except to attest to the signing of any of these agreements, and except proceedings for sanctions under this section, disciplinary hearings before the State Bar or any agency established to enforce standards of conduct for mediators, and proceedings to enforce laws concerning juvenile or elder abuse.

If the attorney senses that somehow there has been a true misunderstanding of the terms reached, he or she may want to invite the other side to meet with the mediator again in an effort to clarify the situation and to head off a motion to set aside the agreement.

When Impasse Results

An impasse is at times inevitable. No participant should think of an impasse as a failure. Even if no settlement was reached, it is likely that useful information was exchanged and that issues and positions were clarified. When the conference ends on a positive note, it frequently is possible to continue the dialogue begun at the mediation and to settle the case later, avoiding a trial.

Other Settlement Procedures within the FFS Program

THE OPTIONS

If the parties elect a settlement procedure other than a mediation or a judicial settlement conference, they must advise the court by filing a Motion for an Order to Use Settlement Procedure Other Than Mediated Settlement Conference or Judicial Settlement Conference in Family Financial Case. If they elect to participate in a judicial settlement conference, they must advise the court by filing a Motion to Order Judicial Settlement Conference in Family Financial Case and to Appoint Judge to Conduct Conference.

PROCEDURES APPLICABLE TO BOTH NEUTRAL EVALUATION AND JUDICIAL SETTLEMENT CONFERENCES

Scheduling

The FFS Rules authorize neutrals to schedule the settlement procedure. Specifically, a neutral must schedule the conference and conduct it within the deadline established by the court, or within 150 days of the court's order for the procedure. A party or the neutral may request an extension of the deadline for completion by filing a written request stating the reasons the extension is sought.

Confidentiality

The settlement procedure is confidential. Evidence of statements made and conduct occurring during the process is not subject to discovery and is not admissible at trial. The neutral cannot be compelled to testify or to produce other evidence of what occurred at mediation, and the parties are prohibited from making any record of the proceedings. In addition, Standard III of the Standards of Professional Conduct for Mediators more broadly prohibits mediators from speaking with the public or press. (Note that the Standards do not apply to parties or their lawyers.)

Duties of the Parties

The parties and their attorneys are required to attend the settlement proceeding. Just as with mediation, if the parties reach an agreement, it must be reduced to a written summary memorandum before the procedure is concluded. Within thirty days of the proceeding, a final agreement and any other dispositive documents must be executed and notarized, and any judgments or voluntary dismissals must be filed with the court. The parties are also responsible for paying the neutral. Time spent by the neutral reviewing materials, conducting the proceeding, and making and reporting the award is compensable. However, under court rules, a judge who conducts a judicial settlement conference receives no compensation.

Selection of the Neutral

The parties may select any person who they believe can assist them to serve as their neutral, except in the case of a judicial settlement conference. They must notify the court of their selection at the scheduling conference by filing a Motion for an Order to Use Settlement Procedure Other Than Mediated Settlement Conference or Judicial Settlement Conference in Family Financial Case.

Authority and Duties of the Neutral

The FFS Rules require the neutral to assume the following responsibilities:

- Control the proceeding.
- Schedule the conference at a time convenient for the parties.
- Explain the procedure at the beginning of the conference.
- Be impartial and disclose any circumstances bearing on his or her neutrality.
- Submit the results of the conference to the court within ten days of the proceeding on a Report of Mediator or Other Neutral in Family Financial Case form.
- Enforce the court's deadline for completion of the procedure.

RULES SPECIFIC TO NEUTRAL EVALUATION

Neutral Evaluation Defined

A neutral evaluation is defined in the FFS Rules as an informal, abbreviated presentation of facts and issues to an evaluator by the parties. The neutral evaluates the case by pointing out strengths and weaknesses, by assessing the merits, and by assigning a settlement value and a dollar value (or range) of potential awards if the case goes to trial.

Pre-Conference Submissions

Each party must furnish the evaluator and all other parties with written information about the case twenty days before the date set for the neutral evaluation conference, including a summary of significant facts and issues and copies of any supporting documents. No later than ten days before the neutral evaluation conference, any party may (but is not required to) send additional written information to the evaluator in response to the earlier submissions. The evaluator may also request additional written information prior to the conference. All documents must be furnished to all other parties. The evaluator may address questions to the parties at the conference and provide the parties with an opportunity to present brief oral statements.

Evaluator's Duties

The FFS Rules require the evaluator to:

- Explain at the beginning of the conference that neutral evaluation is not a trial, that the evaluator's opinions are not binding, that the parties retain their right to trial, and that any settlement reached will be by mutual consent of the parties.

- Issue an oral report to the parties at the conclusion of the evaluation, advising them of his or her candid assessment of the merits of the case, estimated settlement value, and the strength and weakness of each party's claims if the case proceeds to trial. The oral report must also contain a suggested settlement or disposition and the reasoning behind it.

- File a Report of Neutral Conducting Settlement Procedure Other that Mediated Settlement in Family Financial Case with the court within ten days after the evaluation is completed.

Evaluator's Authority

The parties may agree to modify the procedures required by the FFS Rules for neutral evaluation, subject to approval of the evaluator. If all parties at the neutral evaluation conference request and agree, the evaluator may also assist the parties with settlement discussions, functioning like a mediator at that point.

RULES FOR JUDICIAL SETTLEMENT CONFERENCES

Under the FFS Rules, the parties may request that the chief district court judge appoint another district court judge as the settlement judge to conduct a judicial settlement conference. The role of the settlement judge is to assist the parties in reaching a resolution of all claims, not to impose his or her judgment on them. The settlement judge, however, does determine the form and the manner in which the conference is conducted. As with other settlement procedures, judicial settlement conferences are confidential, and no records of the proceedings may be made. Within ten days after completing the conference, the settlement judge must file with the court a Report of Neutral Conducting Settlement Procedure Other than Mediated Settlement in Family Financial Case.

Oversight

FFS Program Oversight

A chief district court judge is ultimately responsible for the FFS Program operating in his or her district and has broad authority for its administration, including adoption of local rules not inconsistent with the FFS Rules. On the state level, the DRC certifies mediators to conduct mediations in district court and regulates mediator conduct. It helps support court staff administering the program and responds to questions and requests for information from attorneys and the public. The DRC also recommends program rules and rule revisions to the Alternative Dispute Resolution Committee of the State Judicial Council, which in turn makes recommendations to the North Carolina Supreme Court.

FFS Mediator Certification

The FFS Rules specify the qualifications for mediator certification. Both attorney and non-attorney applicants who hold membership in the Association for Conflict Resolution (ACR) as Advanced Family and Divorce Mediator Practitioners are eligible for certification. The FFS Rules also specify a number of professions whose members are eligible for certification, including judges and attorneys who have been licensed to practice law for at least five years in North Carolina or another state; psychiatrists, psychologists, marriage and family therapists, clinical social workers, and professional counselors who have been licensed to practice in North Carolina for at least five years; and certified public accountants who have held their certification to practice in North Carolina for at least five years. In addition to meeting these threshold requirements, applicants must also complete family mediation training and demonstrate familiarity with North Carolina family law. Non-attorney applicants must also complete a six-hour course on legal terminology, court structure, and civil procedure. All applicants for certification must complete observations of mediations (two for attorney applicants and five for non-attorney applicants) and demonstrate that they are of good character. As a condition of certification, all applicants must also agree to waive their mediator fees in instances in which the court has determined that a party is unable to pay some or all of the amount owed. Applicants must also complete an approved application form and pay a certification fee. A mediator's certification must be renewed every year. During the renewal period, the mediator must report on his or her efforts to complete continuing mediator education hours (mediators are asked to complete at least three hours annually) and to disclose any criminal or disciplinary matters in which he or she was involved since the date of his or her original certification or last renewal. All materials needed for certification and certification renewal are posted on the Commission's website.

The DRC also approves and certifies the trainers who provide the forty-hour family financial mediator training course. (Note that certified superior court mediators need complete only a sixteen-hour family financial mediator training course to become certified since they have already had basic mediation training.) The curriculum for the forty-hour training program is set forth in the FFS Rules.

Standards of Professional Conduct

On December 30, 1998, the Supreme Court of North Carolina adopted Standards of Professional Conduct for Mediators. These standards apply to all mediators conducting mediations under the FFS Program, whether they are certified or not (although the DRC has little power to control or discipline a non-certified mediator). The Standards of Professional Conduct require that each mediator:

- Maintain professional competency relative to his or her mediator skills.
- Remain impartial.

- Keep information obtained in the course of mediation confidential.
- Make reasonable efforts to ensure that each party understands the mediation process and the role of the mediator.
- Respect and encourage the parties' efforts to resolve their dispute on their own terms.
- Keep his or her role as mediator separate from other professional roles and not offer legal or other advice to the parties.
- Avoid conflicts of interest.
- Protect the integrity of the mediation process.

The North Carolina Supreme Court Rules for the DRC set forth complaint and hearing procedures for use when a mediator's conduct is called into question. The DRC is directed and authorized to investigate complaints brought against mediators, to conduct hearings, and, when necessary, to discipline a mediator. The North Carolina Supreme Court Rules for the DRC discuss issues of moral turpitude and provide that mediators are to conduct themselves in such a way that they do not discredit the DRC, the courts, or the mediation process. The DRC has adopted a complaint form, which is available on its website.

In an effort to better serve the ADR community, the DRC has adopted an Advisory Opinion Policy. Mediators may seek either an informal (oral) or formal (written) opinion on ethical or other dilemmas that arise in the course of their practices. Informal advice is given by DRC staff or individual DRC members. Formal written Advisory Opinions are issued by the full Commission and are posted on the DRC's website. (See also Chapter 11, "Professionalism and Ethical Considerations in Dispute Resolution.")

Conclusion

Divorce is always difficult. It is a painful process not only for the estranged spouses, but also for any children. The FFS Program is designed to help parties make the best of a difficult situation. If parties can settle their disputes with mediation or with one of the alternate procedures available, they benefit significantly. They avoid the time and stress involved in protracted litigation and trial. They may save money. Perhaps most important, they will have the satisfaction of knowing they worked things out themselves— a judge did not have to tell them how to divide their possessions and property, pay their debts, or support their children. By settling their disputes themselves, the parties establish an important precedent for their future interactions. The hope is that as other issues arise over time—arguments over visitation or child support, for example—the parties will be able to sit down together and work things out.

It is not only the parties who benefit from the FFS Program. Court staff save time when cases settle expeditiously. Judges are able to better manage their dockets, turning their attention to other, more intractable family disputes that could not be settled, or to criminal or other matters. Taxpayers benefit as well. Courts are expensive to operate and programs that help make courts more efficient conserve tax dollars. Ultimately, society benefits. We all have an interest in encouraging parties to take ownership of their conflicts and to resolve them responsibly. When those disputes involve families, and especially families with children, that interest becomes even more compelling.

NOTES

1. *See* N.C. Gen. Stat. § 7A-38.4A.

2. The DRC website can be accessed at http://www.ncdrc.org. This URL is automatically redirected to the website of the North Carolina Court System, http://www.nccourts.org/Courts/CRS/Councils/DRC/Default.asp, where extensive information and resources are available.

3. Except for some narrow exceptions specified by statute, statements made and conduct that occurs during mediation are not subject to discovery and are inadmissible in any proceeding in the action or in other civil actions on the same claim. (*See* N.C. Gen. Stat. § 7A-38.1(*l*).) In addition, Standard III of the Standards of Professional Conduct for Mediators requires mediators to observe confidentiality in the broader sense, prohibiting them from talking with the public or press about what occurred at mediation. Standard III does not apply to parties or their lawyers, but FFS Rule 4.D. strictly forbids parties or their lawyers from recording mediation proceedings, whether openly or surreptitiously.

4. *See* N.C. Gen. Stat. § 7A-38.1(*l*). *See also* Standard III of the Revised Standards of Conduct for Mediators, available at http://www.nccourts.org/Courts/CRS/Councils/DRC/Documents/StandardsConduct.pdf.

CHAPTER NINETEEN

The Child Custody and Visitation Mediation Program in North Carolina's Courts

"We now have in place, and operating well, a number of new programs designed to help ... families, and most important, our children. Most of these programs might be described broadly under the term 'therapeutic justice.' This simply means that litigants and those close to them normally spend more time receiving counseling and related services and less time in the courtroom. These innovations include such programs as ... custody mediation."
—North Carolina Supreme Court Chief Justice I. Beverly Lake, Jr.,
State of the Judiciary Address to the
N.C. General Assembly (March 26, 2001).

Introduction

When parents decide to separate, tremendous changes occur within the family. Matters such as custody, visitation, child support, alimony, and division of property become sudden, pressing issues that must be resolved. Separating or divorcing parents often turn to the legal system to work out their disputes, but when the court must resolve conflicts, it is generally through difficult negotiations or a bitter and protracted trial. Parents often feel like outsiders in the legal process as attorneys and a judge determine issues that go to the very core of their personal lives. The negotiation process and courtroom battles frequently intensify the stress within the family and frequently leave the parents further estranged than they were before. The emotional trauma and the long-term effects of this type of legal battle often take the greatest toll on the children involved.

Disputes of separating, divorcing, or never married parents are especially appropriate for mediation, in part due to the importance of establishing time-sharing routines for children quickly, and because of the continuing nature of the co-parenting relationship. While litigation in custody cases typically creates an environment of stress, distrust, and animosity between the parents, the North Carolina Child Custody and Visitation Mediation

Program provides a forum where parents can step back from their personal conflicts, focus on the best interests of their children, and structure their own parenting agreements.

History of the North Carolina Child Custody and Visitation Mediation Program

North Carolina courts began to order mediation in cases involving child custody in 1983, when a pilot program was initiated in the 26th Judicial District (Mecklenburg County). The 1983 General Assembly authorized the pilot program and granted funding until 1985. Mediation services were provided on a contract basis by United Family Services, a United Way agency. The Mecklenburg program was considered a success by both judges and attorneys and was extended by the 1985 legislature for another two years. In 1986, the program was also extended into neighboring Gaston County. The 1987 General Assembly gave the North Carolina Administrative Office of the Courts (AOC) a mandate to determine whether custody mediation should be recommended for statewide expansion or be allowed to expire.

Over the period of a year, an eight-member advisory committee of judges researched and analyzed various court-based mediation systems and provided a written recommendation for statewide expansion. (Also see Chapter 9.) In 1989, enabling legislation governing the North Carolina Child Custody and Visitation Mediation Program was enacted. As recommended by the committee, custody mediation was authorized as a mandatory practice, with oversight and administration to be developed by the AOC and substantial operational decision making left to the judicial district's discretion.

Gradually, the Child Custody and Visitation Mediation Program was implemented statewide, with the first programs established in metropolitan areas such as Buncombe County (Asheville), Wake County (Raleigh), and Cumberland County (Fayetteville). Many of these programs initially functioned as contract-based partnerships with local community mediation programs, but it was determined that staff mediators reporting directly to the judge functioned more efficiently and effectively to provide ongoing quality service. Over time, the districts have become more uniform in mediation culture, replicating local rules and developing standard policies and procedures. In 2010, the AOC developed a Best Practices Guide for Child Custody Mediation in North Carolina. It also revised and updated training standards and Uniform Rules and Standards of Practice for Mediators to guide and support the local district programs.

In 1997, the AOC obtained a grant from the North Carolina Governor's Crime Commission to evaluate the Child Custody and Visitation Mediation Program. The study assessed customer satisfaction with the mediation services provided through the program, identified differences in implementation across the state, and noted the impacts of custody mediation on the court system. The study concluded that the Child Custody and Visitation Mediation Program was effective, with parents and attorneys reporting high levels of satisfaction with the mediation process, even when no agreement was reached. The study also found that custody mediation was associated with a reduction in the trial rates and a decrease in relitigation compared to trial judgments.[1]

Child Custody and Visitation Mediation is now funded for the entire state of North Carolina, with forty-one of forty-two judicial districts offering a court-based custody mediator to provide mandatory mediation services without charge to parents and custodians involved in custody litigation. The program continues a model of local management, with chief district court judges determining the best procedures and operations for their own courts and directly supervising the mediators. The program also has the support of two contract mediators who provide emergency coverage and assist in understaffed districts as directed by the AOC. The AOC provides oversight through operational consultation, recruiting, hiring, and general administration assistance and ongoing mediator training, mentoring, and assessment.

Program Methods and Values

The mediation process allows parents to discuss child-related issues with the assistance and guidance of a neutral, professional mediator in a structured and confidential setting. The goal of the process is to facilitate discussion and negotiation of custody and living arrangements, ideally to assist the parents in creating a parenting agreement that is workable and satisfactory to them both. Above all, it is hoped that mediation will minimize the stress and anxiety for parents and their children as they resolve their differences without the acrimony that may be involved in extended litigation.

Mediation offers parents (or those identified as guardians for the child or children) a structure that encourages them to work cooperatively and to discuss issues of custody and visitation thoroughly in an attempt to resolve their disputes and improve their co-parenting skills. The mediator maintains an impartial position and focuses on recognizing needs and concerns of both parents. The mediator does not dictate the terms of the custodial and visitation arrangements, but helps the parties create their own parenting agreement, after discussing the issues affecting the children's health, education, and welfare. Self-determination and direct involvement in the decision-making process are effective in promoting positive and lasting results for parents and children.

Mediators do not generally meet with children, nor do they provide information to third parties, including the Department of Social Services (DSS), parenting coordinators, judges, or attorneys. Mediators cannot facilitate the resolution of non-custody issues such as child support, alimony, or distribution of property. (See Chapter 18, "The Family Financial Settlement Program in North Carolina's Courts," for a discussion of the alternative dispute resolution district court program dealing with cases involving equitable distribution, alimony, or support.)

Program Procedures

According to the legislative mandate set out in North Carolina General Statutes Sections 50-13.1 and 7A-494, all cases involving contested custody and visitation issues must be sent to mediation before those issues are tried in court. The only exceptions are cases waived for good cause, generally those cases involving serious allegations of domestic violence, child abuse, or substance abuse. Although courts may also waive cases in which a party resides more than fifty miles from the court, this has become less common. There is no cost to the parents for the mediation service and although attendance at the sessions is mandatory, the court does not require the parents to reach an agreement.

The first step in the mediation process is for parents with child custody and visitation issues to attend an orientation session. This group presentation delivered by the mediator is designed to provide participants with more information about the mediation program, the logistics of scheduling and attending a mediation session, the creation of the parenting agreement, and general advice concerning parenting from two homes. Parents watch an award-winning video, "Putting Children First," and are usually given the opportunity to speak personally with the mediator and ask questions. During or immediately after the orientation, parents are scheduled for a mediation session.

The parents meet in an informal setting with the mediator. Meetings are usually scheduled within thirty days of the date of referral by the court. A typical mediation case will last no more than one to three sessions, with each session typically lasting about two hours. The sessions are confidential, and the only documentation that leaves the mediation program is a parenting agreement, once it has been signed by the parties and the judge. Mediators do not provide information about the session, recommendations, or reports to the court, the parents, or their attorneys.

In the mediation session, the mediator helps the parents identify, clarify, and articulate their concerns related to custody or visitation with their children. The parents may discuss points of disagreement, brainstorm options, and plan time-sharing schedules that function for everyone involved. The mediator remains balanced and non-judgmental, facilitating the dialogue and exploring possibilities with the parents. The mediator helps them remain focused on the best interest of the child or children. Because North Carolina law requires custody mediators to have an advanced degree in a human relations discipline, many come from counseling or therapy backgrounds. Nevertheless, they clearly distinguish their roles as mediators and facilitators from those of the helping professions.

If parents are able to reach agreement on the issues in mediation, the mediator prepares a draft parenting agreement, sends it to the parents and their attorneys, and allows them at least ten days to review it. The mediator encourages parents to review the parenting agreement carefully with their lawyers before signing. Once the parents sign the agreement, it is reviewed and signed by the judge and becomes an enforceable order of the court. Parents do not return to court, although they may continue with litigation or private mediation on other matters. More than 60 percent of the cases sent to custody mediation result in a drafted parenting agreement.

If there is no agreement in mediation, the parents are referred to the court system. Judges and attorneys often note a change in perspective after mediation, with parents more willing to settle matters quietly rather than through extended litigation. Parents with complaints against the mediator or about the mediation process itself are encouraged to submit their concerns in writing to the chief district court judge in the district where the mediation was held.

Conclusion

Custody and visitation cases are often complex and involve contradictory claims by the parents, hurt feelings and resentment, concerns about loss of an important relationship, and fears about being distanced from a child or children. While parents suffer from the stress and anxiety associated with separation and divorce, their children are affected even more deeply. The intimate nature of these disputes and the intense emotions lend themselves well to resolution through mediation.

Mediation provides parents with an opportunity to create a positive model for working as partners in a new co-parenting relationship. The process allows parents to affirm their affection and concern for their children at a time when everyone involved is feeling a sense of loss and insecurity. Research shows that parents who invest time and energy putting together a plan for their children are more likely to adhere to their plan. In addition, many attorneys have found that mediation of custody and visitation disputes improves the ability of couples to successfully negotiate a settlement of the financial and property issues accompanying separation and divorce.

Parents and attorneys report high levels of satisfaction with the mediation process, suggesting that it improves communication between the parents. Parents have been pleased to be able to decide the custody and visitation arrangements for their children, rather than have strangers decide the matter. In sum, the custody and visitation program appears to be very beneficial to those who experience it and is held in high regard by attorneys as well as parents.[2]

NOTES

1. Laura F. Donnelly and Rebecca G. Ebron, *The Child Custody and Visitation Mediation Program in North Carolina—An Evaluation of Its Implementation and Effects,* North Carolina Administrative Office of the Courts (Jan. 2000).

2. *Id.* at 65–67.

CHAPTER TWENTY

Permanency Mediation in North Carolina: Resolving Issues of Child Placement in Cases Involving Abuse, Neglect, and Dependency

"In the middle of difficulty lies opportunity."
—American physicist John Archibald Wheeler (1979).

The Permanency Concept

A basic principle of child welfare theory is that "children grow up best in nurturing, stable families."[1] Public policy places an emphasis on preserving biological families but recognizes that there are circumstances where a child's safety requires removal from the home and placement in an alternative setting. This is particularly true in cases involving abuse or neglect of a dependent child. In the mid-twentieth century, alternative placements for children often involved long-term foster care and a series of different care providers. By the 1970s, however, researchers had concluded that children need "permanency" in their lives.[2] The goal became either reunification with the biological family or adoption. The findings of at least one demonstration project in the early 1970s showed "that intensive services and aggressive planning" could help achieve this goal, even with children "who had been adrift in long-term foster care."[3]

The federal Adoption Assistance and Child Welfare Act, passed in 1980, redefined foster care as a temporary service. It required court review for cases where there were allegations of abuse, neglect and/or dependency (A/N/D) and tied foster care funding for states to "reasonable efforts" to keep children in the home or return them as soon as possible. Later, the Adoption and Safe Families Act (ASFA) of 1997 further clarified "reasonable efforts" and set timelines to accelerate reunification or adoption. ASFA established the standard of achieving permanency no later than one year from the child's removal from the home, a norm that encouraged courts to consider innovative alternatives—including mediation—to resolve A/N/D cases more quickly.

Overview of Permanency Mediation

North Carolina's Permanency Planning Mediation Program began as an innovative way to remedy obstacles to permanency after a child was removed from the home in A/N/D cases. These cases tend to entangle families in protracted legal proceedings with an array of professionals, including Department of Social Services (DSS) social workers, DSS attorneys, parents' attorneys, guardians ad litem, and others. Children involved in the process often undergo significant stress due to the uncertainty of placement, the loss of contact with loved ones and friends, and new living arrangements with foster parents, distant family members, or other guardians.

Mediation, a process using a neutral third-party to assist in the clarification and negotiation of a dispute, can be effective in helping the multiple players involved in A/N/D cases to reach a facilitated agreement. In other areas of the country, the process goes by many names: child protection mediation, adoption mediation, and dependency mediation. In North Carolina, it is referred to as permanency mediation. Mediation can help at any stage of the A/N/D process—from establishing services for the parents that are needed for reunification to discussing termination of parental rights. Permanency mediation facilitates the information sharing required for a more rapid and thorough resolution of the case.

The overarching goal—to help determine a permanent placement for a child in a safe and stable home—is achieved through mediation in two important ways. First, the mediator's facilitation allows for a confidential discussion about the allegations, possible and realistic solutions, and the obstacles that impede them. A benefit of mediation in A/N/D cases is that it is conducted in a less adversarial environment, so the negotiations can be expanded to include explanations and conversations that can be especially helpful to bewildered parents and stalemated professionals. Second, mediation helps the parties to develop detailed and truly individualized case plans. The detailed case plans that result from mediation could rarely emerge from the litigation process. Professionals and parents can incorporate innovative and practical details that improve parents' ability to understand and comply with requirements to regain custody.

In situations where parents are facing termination of their parental rights, mediation facilitates a conversation about the choices still facing parents. The majority of children who are removed from the home are placed with relatives and will have some type of contact with the biological parents after adoption. North Carolina is not an "open adoption" state, however, and arrangements discussed in mediation for the time after parental rights are relinquished or terminated are not binding. Nevertheless, mediated conversations at this stage often are the linchpin for the entire family to make the adjustments needed for children to truly settle in permanently with the adoptive parents.

Mediation is also beneficial in assisting the courts in managing and hearing A/N/D cases. Conflicts that arise during the implementation of the case plan that would normally occupy a judge's time are resolved privately outside the courtroom. This allows judges to devote more time to monitoring hearings and other important matters. In addition, because agencies participate more actively, a collaborative spirit develops, leading to the formation of more detailed and nuanced plans than typically result from a litigated hearing. This creative partnership to help families benefits the entire juvenile court.

The Mecklenburg County Pilot Project

The first permanency mediation program in North Carolina to address the needs present in A/N/D cases began in Mecklenburg County as a grant-funded program called the Child Abuse, Neglect, and Dependency Mediation Pilot Project. It was initiated by the Charlotte Model Juvenile Court. The goal of the project was to create a mediation-based means to achieve the 1997 ASFA timeline that permanency be achieved within one year. This new standard required that courts accelerate the process of handling children caught up in the welfare system by moving them to a permanent living situation within one year. If courts could not meet the standard, they might lose the funding extended through the Adoption Assistance and Child Welfare Act of 1980.

The Mecklenburg County Child Abuse, Neglect, and Dependency Mediation Pilot Project began scheduling and holding mediation sessions in January 2001 using experienced local mediators on a contract basis. Adjudication and disposition hearings continued to be held, and mediation took place at the pre-adjudication stage, addressing issues raised in petitions and helping formulate individualized case plans. Although difficult to initiate, permanency mediation gradually gained support, in large part because of its advantage in creating detailed case plans for families to work toward reunification. The apparent success of the Mecklenburg project led the General Assembly to approve a second pilot program in neighboring Gaston County, which benefitted from using the same trained mediators. Cases going through the mediation programs were tracked, assessed, and compared to non-mediated cases over the three-year period from 2001 to 2003.

The Charlotte pilot project was evaluated by independent researchers from the University of South Carolina. The study found that more than 90 percent of the mediated sessions resulted in an agreement. It also found that the case plans were significantly better, participants were more satisfied, and court hearings were reduced. An unexpected benefit of the program was an improvement in communication, not just between DSS and the parents, but also among the involved family members and among participating professionals. These overall positive benefits and the consistency of the results confirmed that the Mecklenburg pilot was a success.[4]

The Statewide Initiative

Assured by the success of the pilot programs in Mecklenburg and Gaston Counties, the North Carolina General Assembly in 2006 made a determination that permanency mediation should be available statewide. North Carolina General Statutes Section 7B-202 required the Administrative Office of the Courts (AOC) "to establish a Permanency Mediation Program to provide statewide and uniform services to resolve issues in cases . . . in which a juvenile is alleged or has been adjudicated to be abused, neglected, or dependent, or in which a petition or motion to terminate a parent's rights has been filed." The statute further stipulated that the AOC "promulgate policies and regulations necessary and appropriate for the administration of the program." Protections were written into the statute, with confidentiality extended for both written and verbal communications made during or in furtherance of mediation sessions. Such communications were deemed absolutely privileged and inadmissible in court.

Original proposals for the expansion of permanency mediation called for gradual growth using Permanency Operational Districts (PODs), which would divide the state along judicial district lines. The implementation plan anticipated that approximately fifty mediators statewide would expand mediation gradually into every judicial district, with each mediator conducting permanency mediation sessions primarily within his or her POD. The implementation plan also established procedures to guide the development of the program by identifying the types of cases to be mediated, designating parties to be present at mediation, establishing the use of a co-mediation model, and prescribing mediator qualifications.

The AOC first focused its attention on establishing mediator standards and on training mediators. To be considered for the training, candidates had to have a juris doctorate or bachelor of arts degree in law, or at least a master's degree in psychology, social work, family counseling, or comparable human relations discipline. While having experience related to juvenile dependence or family relations was preferred, candidates had to demonstrate at least three year's experience as an attorney, a judicial officer, a mediator, or a therapist. Because only the State of Florida offered a certification program for permanency mediation, a Florida trainer provided a comprehensive, forty-hour training session, first in 2006 and again in 2008. Once trained, the candidates were required to complete several hours of observation, co-mediation, and mentoring requirements.

Permanency mediation has expanded slowly across the state. Varying from the Mecklenburg model, the Buncombe County program refers to mediation only those cases that were not resolved at the pretrial conference. The Wake County program started in 2007; Cumberland County followed in 2008. In both of these programs, A/N/D cases that present challenges in service provision (or have other unresolved issues) are referred to mediation. The most recent program initiated is Guilford County, which was granted authorization in 2010.

Implementing the mandate to expand permanency mediation has been challenging. There is some confusion for courts regarding the use of such processes as Child Planning Conferences, Family Team meetings, and Family Group Conferencing as they relate to or compete with the permanency mediation process. Another challenge is gaining the collaboration necessary for districts to agree on how local rules, policies, and procedures for a permanency program should be written, what they should say, and who should be involved. Devoting significant time to educating the stakeholders before the program begins and during the first six to twelve months of program implementation is key to developing the "buy-in" that leads to collaboration. Since the funding provides for paying mediator-contractors for time spent in the mediation sessions only, identifying local court personnel willing to coordinate appointment schedules and communication between parties is necessary for a program to be operational.

Program Procedures

Initially, a judge orders a case to permanency mediation depending on the needs and preferences of the particular judicial district. The time to permanency is a factor taken into consideration when ordering a case to mediation as well. Often a case is referred to mediation by one of the stakeholders, usually the guardian ad litem or DSS. The judge speaks plainly and strongly about the importance and opportunity of permanency mediation. The date for the mediation session is set, and the judge and the attorneys stress that parents must attend. The coordinator's work is key, as this individual often provides follow-up information and documentation to all of the parties involved, communicates with the mediators about the calendar and necessary case specifics, and makes room arrangements for the mediation session. On the day of the mediation session, the coordinator often ensures that all parties are present and passes the case file to the mediators.

Permanency mediation does not flourish without adequate support and motivated participants. The fifteen to twenty people who typically attend the session include parents and extended family, foster parents, DSS agents and attorneys, parents' attorneys, a guardian ad litem volunteer, and the guardian ad litem attorney for the child. Occasionally other professionals, such as therapists, counselors, or psychologists, are also invited (or required) to participate to provide information or assessments. If the mediation involves the termination of parental rights, the adoptive parents may attend. Children are rarely present in a permanency mediation setting, although there are times when their input may be requested.

In all North Carolina permanency mediation programs, a co-mediation model is followed. This provides mediators more ability to observe, facilitate, and prepare draft agreements at the session. Mediators start with an orientation for the parent or parents and any professionals that may be new to the process. Once a consensus is reached, the mediators draft the agreement at the table, print copies for all participants, and allow everyone to review the agreement. If changes are needed, the parties can renegotiate or change wording in the agreement until all parties are satisfied and willing to sign. All parties receive copies of the signed agreement. Allowing parties to leave with a copy of the agreement provides a level of certainty and accountability that helps parties, especially parents, move forward toward compliance with the terms of the agreement. If parties are negotiating the terms of the petition and case plan, a copy of any signed mediated agreement is given to the DSS attorney to present at the next adjudication hearing.

Challenges for the Future of Permanency Mediation in North Carolina

Those with experience initiating or managing permanency mediation programs agree that the challenges faced by North Carolina in implementing its programs are not unique. Experts in the field acknowledge that there generally are four components to a successful permanency mediation program.

1. **A strong judicial advocate.** It is imperative to have support from a judge who believes strongly in the power of mediation as a better solution for A/N/D cases and who is willing to spend the time and energy to gain support. A judge must be willing to refer cases and maintain a commitment to influence others to attempt mediation in good faith. While lawyers, social workers, or others may not fully support permanency mediation initially, they are often won over by the process once they participate in it a few times. Without a court referral to mediation, stakeholders will never comprehend personally the power or possibility of the mediation process in this setting.

2. **A community willing to participate in mediation and work in good faith toward a mediated solution.** Getting "buy-in" from the child welfare community and local attorneys can be challenging, but it is fundamentally important to starting and maintaining a mediation program. Obtaining input, including concerns and challenges from potential participants, should be a first step in the planning stages of a permanency mediation program. To foster strong participation, most mediation programs create committees or workgroups comprised of the same stakeholders normally around the mediation table: DSS agents and DSS attorneys, parents' attorneys, guardians ad litem, judges, and court staff. These committees can discuss concerns as they arise, create policies, and air disputes over implementation early on, before they have a chance to result in discouragement with the process. After the mediation program is in place, these committees should continue in order to address concerns as they arise.

3. **Competent and well-trained mediators.** One challenge of all mediation programs is maintaining a cadre of trained, competent, independent, committed, and experienced mediators to work contractually. The work done in A/N/D cases is challenging, involving sensitive and painful issues and strong personalities. This specialized type of mediation can strain the mediators' confidence as they maintain balance between tough impartiality, objectivity, and sincere empathy in an atmosphere of institutionalized professionalism and sometimes appalling abuse or neglect of an innocent child. The challenge of dealing with multi-party dynamics and sometimes sporadic assignments may dissuade well-qualified mediators from participating.

4. **Stable funding.** The success of a permanency mediation program is heavily dependent on stable funding to sustain the initiation and

program implementation process. Such resources were available during the development of the Mecklenburg and Gaston programs. As a result, the mediation process is institutionalized in those districts. While many programs depend solely on grant funding, which requires annual reporting and application, North Carolina is fortunate to have a legislated mandate and a continuing budget as authorized by the AOC. However, limits and delays in the funding stream due to the current state budget deficit place stress on the stakeholders dependent on the process, as well as on the coordinators and managers of these programs. Confidence in the program waned in 2008 when there was a delay in issuing mediator contracts. Rebuilding support and generating referrals was challenging. Some mediators chose not to renew contracts in the uncertain financial climate. If the funding cannot be maintained, stakeholders and mediators can lose interest in and commitment to the program.

Conclusion

North Carolina's Permanency Mediation Program is considered a success and continues to gain support in operational districts. Other districts have expressed interest and hope to move forward with the program if mediators and funding become available. For those who started the movement and continue to depend on the mediation process, there is no doubt that it decreases the number of court hearings, thereby freeing valuable judicial and court resources, and reduces the time to adjudication. It has increased communication, which has led to better professional relationships and a more effective provision of services. Most important, the program has helped the courts meet the ASFA standard of placing children more quickly into safe, stable homes.

NOTES

1. "Concept and History of Permanency in U.S. Child Welfare," U.S. Department of Health & Human Services, Administration for Children & Families, www.childwelfare.gov/permanency/overview/history.cfm.

2. *Id.*

3. *Id.*

4. *See* Judge Lewis A. Trosch, Jr. and Erin Mack Stack, "The Success of Permanency Mediation in Mecklenburg County, NC," *The Judges' Page,* Newsletter of the National Court Appointed Special Advocate (CASA) for Children website (October 2008), http://www.casaforchildren.org/atf/cf/%7B9928CF18-EDE9-4AEB-9B1B-3FAA416A6C7B%7D/0810-Alternative_Dispute_Resolution_Programs-0019.pdf.

CHAPTER TWENTY-ONE

Voluntary Alternative Dispute Resolution in Family Matters

"People who fight fire with fire usually end up with ashes."
—Advice columnist Abigail Van Buren

Voluntary mediation and collaborative law are increasingly common alternatives to traditional litigation for North Carolina families in crisis. As with court-mandated programs, such as mediation under the Family Financial Settlement Program or the Child Custody and Visitation Mediation Program, voluntary methods of alternative dispute resolution (ADR) use professional neutral facilitators to guide the process and allow the parties to be active problem solvers. The neutrals help foster agreement, reduce the acrimony and stress of conflict, and place the children's best interests at the heart of the proceedings.

Voluntary mediation also may be used to address a range of issues related to elder law, especially in disputes within families about the care of aging parents and management of their assets. The mediation process can help adult children work through decisions in a cooperative way, easing the difficult process associated with transitions near the end of life.

Voluntary Mediation in the Process of Separation and Divorce

Many couples going through separation and divorce choose to participate voluntarily in mediation to resolve all of the issues that need to be addressed. The mediated agreement may include a parenting agreement (custody and support), a division of assets and debts, post-separation support, alimony, and language specifying how the family will communicate and solve future problems. The family can move forward with the mediated agreement and decide whether or not it is necessary for them to transform the agreement into a court order. Voluntary family mediation is offered by many community dispute settlement centers on a sliding scale fee system.

In addition, there are many private family mediators who are available for party selection.

Voluntary mediations can be structured to meet the needs of the parties. The mediator may be transformative, directive, evaluative, or a combination of these styles. Meetings can include both joint and breakout sessions. The parties may schedule their mediation in two-hour increments over a period of time, or they may choose a single session that can last for hours, continuing until they finalize an agreement. The single session option has the advantage of getting the agreement done and allowing parties to move on more quickly. Multiple sessions allow parties more time to think and to evaluate their options and preferences. They hear proposals and then go home and "sleep on it" before making any final decisions.

Parties engaged in voluntary mediation also may choose to mediate with or without attorneys. It is common for attorneys to appear at the first session but to be consulted between sessions only when a party needs further legal advice or consultation on specific issues. The attorneys then re-engage in the drafting and review of the final settlement agreement.

Voluntary mediation has proven to be a viable and beneficial process for many families. It facilitates communication, problem solving, and future planning while preparing a foundation for families to move forward without suffering through a difficult and contentious adversarial process.

Collaborative Divorce Proceedings

A growing number of divorcing couples want the assistance of an attorney to resolve conflicts but do not want to engage in adversarial behavior or litigation. This goal can be accomplished through the use of collaborative law proceedings. In 2003, the General Assembly established the validity and requirements of collaborative law in actions for divorce by enacting North Carolina General Statutes Sections 50-70 through 50-79. The State Bar of North Carolina subsequently issued Ethics Opinion 2002 FEO 1, approving the creation of "collaborative law organizations" (also known as practice groups). Through these groups, attorneys may refer spouses of clients to other members of the group without a conflict of interest. As a result, a growing number of family lawyers in North Carolina advocate for their clients in a collaborative manner outside of the courtroom instead of in an adversarial manner inside the courtroom.

The collaborative law process anticipates that parties and their attorneys will use their best efforts and make a good faith attempt to resolve all of the family's issues by consensus. The procedure includes an agreement that if the dispute does not settle and moves into the courtroom, the collaborative attorneys must withdraw from the case and will not represent the parties. (This typically is called the "Four-Way Agreement" because it is between the two parties and their two attorneys.) Any work product of attorneys or other advisors developed during the collaborative process is not admissible in court except upon agreement.

After committing to the collaborative process and signing the agreement, the parties and their attorneys attend a number of "four-way conferences." During the conferences, the parties, with the guidance of their attorneys, compile and share all information necessary to make decisions about assets, debts, post-separation support, alimony, child custody, and child support. The parties use the conferences to explore the future needs of the family. Professional advisors may be brought in to assist, including financial advisors, tax advisors, child specialists, mental health professionals, or others. With the collaborative process, all parties are using the same advisors, thus saving money and eliminating "battling experts."

The collaborative process gives parties more control over their lives, allows communication to be private, is more efficient, and saves money by keeping the family conflict out of court. For many parties, the process is transformative. It puts them in a position to move forward with their lives in a positive fashion, with improved communication and problem-solving skills.[1]

The Use of ADR with Elder Issues

While most ADR programs for families in conflict center on divorce, separation, and child custody, there is also a role for mediation in family disputes involving elderly or incapacitated parents. Adult children often are faced with difficult decisions regarding an aging parent's care. Issues such as where the parent will live, who will provide transportation, who will make medical decisions, and who will handle the finances may become sources of significant conflict. Mediation can help foster a spirit of cooperation among family members and encourage them to make decisions based on the best interests of the elderly parent.

Disputes also may arise when a parent dies and leaves an estate to family members. There may be a need to establish new working relationships among the heirs, especially if the deceased parent was the one who typically held the family together and managed conflicts. For example, perhaps for many years the adult siblings have enjoyed vacationing with mom at her mountain home; but now that the siblings have inherited the home, they may need the assistance of a neutral facilitator to help them determine how to share the joys and the responsibilities of owning it.

Finally, as more elders move into assisted living or other care facilities, there also may be conflicts that arise regarding institutional care and management. Mediation can provide a positive opportunity for resolution of disputes among staff, elder residents, and family members.

NOTE

1. Kerry Burleigh, "Collaborative Family Law," *The Peacemaker* 25, no. 2 (February 18, 2011): 3, also available at http://disputeresolution.ncbar.org/media/11269980/drfeb11.pdf.

MEDIATION CENTERS

CHAPTER TWENTY-TWO

Community Dispute Settlement Centers in North Carolina

"Good fences make good neighbors."
—Robert Frost, "Mending Wall," *North of Boston* (1914).

Community mediation is in many ways the foundation of alternative dispute resolution (ADR) processes in North Carolina. Its effectiveness as a non-adversarial means of conflict resolution is amply demonstrated in programs offered by the state's twenty-three dispute settlement centers, which stretch from Wilmington in the east to Murphy in the west. The success of these centers over the years has resulted largely from the focus that each places on local needs. Each center has developed programs tailored to its community and has devised procedures unique to its setting. Consequently, it is impossible to give a single description of center operations. This chapter summarizes some of the most frequently utilized programs offered by dispute settlement centers across the state, including criminal district court mediation, mediation of civil disputes, mediation in appeals of Medicaid decisions, and community-based public dispute resolution. The chapter concludes with a more detailed description of one center, Carolina Dispute Settlement Services (CDSS), as an example of the range and scope of ADR programs that can be employed at the local and state levels.

Overview of the Community Mediation Process in North Carolina

The following is a typical scenario of a mediation at a dispute settlement center. Two parties meet in an informal setting with two mediators. First, the mediators guide the discussion to clarify issues and to create a common understanding of what each person wants to accomplish in mediation. Then, to help the participants decide for themselves how to resolve their problem, the mediators encourage the parties to explore possible solutions. The mediators are not decision makers: they do not decide who is right or wrong, they do not tell the parties what to do, and they do not provide legal or financial advice.

All participants in a mediation sign a "Consent to Mediate" agreement that stipulates: (1) that the discussion is confidential; (2) that the center has no opinion as to the legal effect of any agreement that arises out of mediation; and (3) that parties are present of their own free will. Community mediators undergo a minimum of twenty-four hours of training. Centers attempt to maintain a pool of mediators that represents the kind of diversity present in the local community.

District Criminal Court Mediation

Instead of proceeding with a court disposition, parties in district criminal court have an option to resolve problems with the help of trained neutral mediators. (For a description of North Carolina's optional, statewide program for certification and regulation of district criminal court mediators, see Chapter 23.) Sitting down with mediators in the courthouse (outside of the courtroom), parties talk about the situation and solve it themselves in a way that both sides think is fair. Mediation can lead to dismissal of the charges through an arrangement with the district attorney's office prior to a court hearing in the case. Agreements are based on a mutual understanding of the events and can include payment of money, apologies, and rules for future interactions. Although in the past court costs have not been charged in mediated cases, a $60 fee is now assessed for all "successfully mediated" district criminal court cases referred to community mediation centers. The fee must be paid by the defendant to the clerk of superior court before the center can provide the district attorney with a dismissal form in the case. The fee is then distributed to and shared by the center that conducted the mediation and the Mediation Network of North Carolina.

Cases can be referred to mediation in several ways: (1) by self-referral; (2) by the district attorney or defense attorney; or (3) by recommendation of the judge. In court settings where an officer has taken out a warrant, mediators are present on the day of court to assist if needed. In some districts, magistrates have been instructed to set the court date for citizen-generated warrants for a specific day where all the cases are initially referred at the calendar call to the mediators for screening and/or intake.

Mediation is not appropriate in certain situations: (1) where either party is concerned for his or her personal safety; (2) in cases of ongoing domestic violence; (3) for crimes involving dangerous weapons or severe injury; or (4) for felonies. Appropriateness is determined through pre-screening by an assistant district attorney (in all domestic cases) and by a mediator's assessment, both in talking with the parties before and throughout the mediation. A mediator may at any time declare the situation inappropriate for mediation and refer the case back to the court system.

Mediations are always voluntary and held confidential from the court. A party in mediation can decide at any time that he or she would prefer to take the case back into court. If this occurs, the mediation discussion will not be part of the court hearing. At the beginning of the mediation, parties sign consent forms in which they agree to refrain from involving mediators or the center in any future court action.

Any case where an agreement is reached and restitution in the form of future performance or payment of money is involved will be continued by the court system to allow for compliance. If the agreement is not fulfilled, the case will come back to court, and parties will proceed in court. If the case has been dismissed, the complainant can only file new charges for *new* incidents that allegedly have occurred.

Civil Mediation

Dispute settlement centers provide mediation in a wide variety of civil disputes. Cases where the court system is not the referral source typically involve issues between neighbors, roommates, and co-workers, and issues involving families, landlords and tenants, customers and merchants, and the like. When the referral is made by a supervisor, police officer, or animal control officer, the mediation coordinator discusses the matter with the official to determine appropriateness and to work out contact with the parties. Usually a referral source (e.g., a supervisor) will then talk to the parties about mediation. If a matter is self-referred, the coordinator usually talks to the other party after the initial interview. In all cases, the mediation coordinator will discuss the issues and the process of mediation with *both* parties before the mediation occurs. Such informed consent is necessary to ensure that all parties are freely participating in the mediation and know what to expect from the process.

The mediation takes place in a daytime or evening session within a two-hour time frame. Mediators help individuals talk about the problem and solve it themselves in a way that both sides think is acceptable. This type of mediation can be an efficient way to resolve many types of personal disputes between family members, friends, or neighbors because it is quick, free, private, and less stressful than court. Any decisions that are jointly created can be written down in a memorandum, but the parties do not sign this memorandum. It is expected that the parties will take this memorandum to an attorney or other source to complete the necessary process to create a binding agreement, if needed.

Couples who are separating are often referred to centers by their individual attorneys to draft the basics of a separation agreement. The mediation coordinator conducts extensive interviews with the parties, informing them about the process while looking for any signs of domestic violence in the relationship. Only mediators who have taken additional hours of family mediation training are eligible to conduct these mediations. Issues of property, parenting, and finances may be discussed in these sessions, along with spousal and child support issues. Although attorneys are not usually present in the mediation, parties are encouraged to consult with their attorneys before and throughout the mediation process, which often lasts from two to six sessions. If an agreement is reached, a draft memorandum is taken by the parties to give to their respective attorneys for review and further action. Fees for separation/divorce mediation are determined on a sliding scale, based on the parties' ability to pay.

Truancy Mediation

Dispute settlement centers also mediate truancy cases referred by local school systems. When a center's mediation coordinator receives a referral from a school social worker, he or she schedules a mediation time with school personnel and writes a letter to the parent(s) of the truant child, giving notification of the mediation time and date. The coordinator also usually contacts the parent(s) prior to mediation to explain the process and answer questions. Typically the parent(s), a school social worker, and one or two administrators from the school attend the mediation session. In special circumstances, the child also may attend. When an agreement is reached, the school personnel and the parent(s) receive a written copy of the agreement.

Medicaid Appeals Mediation

In October 2008, the North Carolina General Assembly established a procedure for Medicaid recipients to appeal the denial or modification of Medicaid services. A key part of the procedure is voluntary mediation of the dispute by a community mediation center prior to hearing of the appeal.

The appeals process is initiated by submitting a hearing request to the state's Office of Administrative Hearings (OAH). OAH immediately notifies the Mediation Network of North Carolina of all appeals, and the Network distributes them to the most appropriate community mediation center within twenty-four hours. When a petitioner agrees to mediation, the local mediation center schedules and mediates the case within twenty-five days from the date that OAH received the request for hearing.

Medicaid appeals are mediated by telephone with the petitioner and representatives of the North Carolina Department of Health and Human Services (and, on occasion, representatives of the Attorney General's Office). If the mediation results in resolution or if the appeal is withdrawn, then the case does not advance to an administrative hearing. During the first two and a half years of the program, approximately 12,500 appeals were filed. Mediation resolved more than 80 percent of these disputes, saving the State of North Carolina millions of dollars and garnering praise from participants. It seems likely that this effective use of mediation and of community mediation centers could be replicated with success in other appeals processes within state or local government.

Educational Efforts of Dispute Settlement Centers

Dispute Settlement Centers also offer a number of skill-building workshops to members of the community. They promote their mission through education by offering training programs in the following areas to individuals and interested organizations: arbitration; med-arb; mediation; facilitation; interpersonal skills; diversity; and adventure-based team building, problem solving, and workplace conflict resolution. They also offer training for school-based programs in peer mediation, conflict resolution, and problem solving, and for employment and workplace mediation.

Community-Based Public Disputes Resolution
in North Carolina

Local elected officials, homeowner and business association leaders, citizen activists, and members of government advisory boards and nonprofit agency boards receive assistance from local mediation centers in designing and managing public meetings, conducting multiparty negotiations and problem-solving sessions, and improving meeting design and facilitation skills. Recognized as a major trend in community mediation, no discussion of local dispute settlement centers today would be complete without reference to public disputes resolution.[1]

Examples of Community-Based Public
Disputes Resolution in North Carolina

- A North Carolina community mediation center designed and facilitated a series of successful work sessions through which residents living near a regional landfill and representatives of local governments negotiated the conditions of an agreement. The governments agreed to obtain soil from adjoining tracts for use in landfill operations while minimizing adverse impacts on residents and the local environment.

- A community mediation center facilitated a series of meetings through which representatives of the University of North Carolina at Chapel Hill and neighborhoods surrounding the campus power plant reached understandings and agreements for minimizing the impacts of a coal silo demolition and reconstruction project.

- A community mediation center facilitated an innovative community problem-solving process sponsored by the Winston-Salem/Forsyth County Coalition on Drug and Alcohol Problems. Through the process, more than sixty organizations in the public, private, and civic sectors reached a consensus on improvements to local substance abuse treatment services.

- A community mediation center in North Carolina designed and facilitated a year-long community consensus-building process through which residents of about two dozen neighborhoods and crossroad communities within a town's extraterritorial jurisdiction met with staff and elected officials from the town and adjoining jurisdictions to resolve a long agenda of land use planning issues.

- A town manager, planning director, and planning department staff in a North Carolina town saw that downtown merchants and developers were disgruntled, but they were uncertain as to what exactly the dissatisfaction was about. Rather than let the situation fester, they decided to organize a meeting with the business community to learn about its concerns. They conferred with staff at the local mediation center and asked a neutral facilitator to develop a meeting agenda and to help run the meeting. The facilitator agreed to conduct the meeting, freeing the planning staff and town manager to participate fully in the discussion.

- A regional planning agency in North Carolina saw the need for better coordination among local departments of planning, public works, transportation, and engineering. An agency staff member contacted a local dispute settlement center for help in organizing a land use and infrastructure workshop. Individuals from the mediation center assisted workshop participants in developing recommendations to municipal and county managers in the region on opportunities for collaboration among land use planners and infrastructure departments. The mediation center also helped by providing instruction in collaborative problem solving during the workshop.

- Planning boards often face off with angry citizens at public meetings. A regional council of governments in North Carolina organized a workshop for area planning board chairs and planning department directors and invited a speaker from a local mediation center to describe effective ways to address citizen concerns and manage public participation at planning board meetings.

- A county task force on AIDS in North Carolina called a public meeting to begin a dialogue between residents of a neighborhood and local advocates for AIDS patients who were considering renting a home in the neighborhood. No public permits were required, but media reports on the proposed care facility helped ignite a public debate on the project. Prior to the meeting, a representative of the local dispute settlement center advised members of the task force on how to manage the meeting. The representative also sat in on the meeting as an observer and provided a report on the meeting to the task force chair.

- A North Carolina planning department provided staff support to a task force charged with making recommendations on a local tree protection ordinance. The task force, chaired by a town council member, was comprised of environmentalists, home builders, and representatives of other interest groups. The local mediation center gave a presentation on collaborative problem solving at the task force's orientation meeting.

- A town manager, planning director, and planning department staff in North Carolina asked their local mediation center to design a "mini-retreat" to help improve communication and conflict management skills. They found that the skills learned were as useful in their own workplace as they were in working with the public.

- Residents in a North Carolina neighborhood petitioned their town council to take measures to discourage through-traffic on a neighborhood street. The petition was opposed by residents on neighboring streets. A citizen from the first group contacted the local mediation center for advice on ways to encourage the two neighborhood groups and the town staff to collaborate. A mediation center staff person met with the citizen and explained principles and techniques of collaborative problem solving.

Assistance Available

Through the training provided by local centers in meeting facilitation skills, group consensus building, problem-solving skills, and skills in large-scale process design and management, residents and officials are introduced to new ways of looking at community-wide and large group conflicts. They improve their understanding of conflict management concepts and build skills that are needed for preventing and intervening in large-scale disputes.

Community leaders have consulted with local mediation centers, getting advice on ways to overcome obstacles to multiparty consensus building. These leaders have generated new ideas and insights on how to approach large-scale conflicts by conferring with their local mediation centers.

Sometimes a more extensive consultation is needed. For example, a local center can conduct a conflict assessment at the request of a planning department that is facing a potential dispute. In a conflict assessment, the mediation center reviews relevant documents and interviews people in the community who are affected by or knowledgeable about the dispute. The purposes of the assessment are: (1) to determine whether there is sufficient motivation among the affected individuals and interest groups for a collaborative problem-solving process to be successful; and (2) to gather information needed for designing a consensus-building process. Community-based dispute settlement centers have worked with public agencies, citizen groups, and local business associations to design collaborative public participation and problem-solving processes.

Local centers have provided trained, experienced meeting facilitators to manage forums at which community-wide issues are being considered. Such facilitators can be helpful either when an issue has already proven contentious or as a preventive measure. In either event, the facilitators first work with the meeting organizers to see that the meeting's objectives, agenda, structure, and list of attendees are sound and well thought out. During the meeting, the facilitators refrain from addressing the content of the group's discussions. Instead, they assure that the agenda is acceptable to the group and is followed; that the ground rules for discussion and decision making are clear, acceptable to all, and enforced fairly; that discussions are balanced and free from personal attacks; and that the group uses problem-solving skills that are appropriate for their tasks. With a neutral facilitator taking care of these considerations, meeting participants are able to concentrate more fully on the issues under discussion.

Community-based dispute settlement centers in North Carolina also are providing trained mediators for local multiparty disputes. The mediators help begin and maintain negotiations on behalf of all sides in a dispute. The parties retain whatever decision-making authority they had when they entered the process. They also retain their right to pursue courses of action outside of mediation (political, legal, self-help, etc.). Participation is voluntary and motivated by the parties' mutual interests in terminating the dispute. An informal agreement developed by the parties in a mediation can form the basis of a formal recommendation or proposal to decision makers.

Process

Before accepting a complex case, a public disputes mediator conducts a conflict assessment. The mediator speaks separately with the parties (and with others in the community, if needed) to gain different views of the conflict and to learn about the interests of the affected parties and their ability and willingness to negotiate on the issues of concern. If a case is accepted, mediators work with the parties to tailor the process to the specifics of the situation.

The scope of a mediation in a public dispute is determined through discussions between the mediator and the parties. For example, in a particular rezoning dispute, the first tasks of the local mediation center were to determine whether any kind of intervention could help the parties, and, if so, to identify representatives from the neighborhood and the agency who would be willing to confer. The mediator spent more than thirty hours interviewing neighborhood residents, staff, and board members of the local human services agency, members of the planning board, and planning staff. These interviews helped the mediator become familiar with the parties and their concerns and helped the parties understand the mediator's role and the mediation process. The mediation center then designed a meeting based on what was learned in the interviews. The meeting was held to provide a safe setting (i.e., no commitments would be solicited) in which a small group of people from both sides of the dispute could explain their own concerns and listen to others' concerns.

Carolina Dispute Settlement Services

History

In 1983, Mediation Services of Wake County was created to serve the local community by providing mediation and conciliation services to citizens who were in need of a process to resolve conflict fairly, peacefully, and expeditiously. One of the first community dispute settlement centers established in the state, Mediation Services mediated two-party, group, neighborhood, city, and county-wide disputes, both in and out of the criminal district court setting, utilizing trained staff and volunteers. It also created educational programs for the general population on conflict resolution and the peaceful resolution of disputes. In 2000, Mediation Services of Wake County became Carolina Dispute Settlement Services (CDSS). The name change better reflects the wider array of services that CDSS offers locally and throughout North Carolina.

Mission

CDSS is a nonprofit, private organization dedicated to the process of cooperative conflict resolution through the use of alternative dispute resolution methods. To promote this purpose, one of the primary functions of CDSS is to educate citizens in resolving disputes by means of positive communication skills, cooperative decision making, collaborative law, and mediation. CDSS provides services to the private sector and government entities, especially the courts, with the intent to offer cost-effective resolution of conflict, financial and administrative efficiency for the courts, and enhanced quality of life for the community through improved social relations and communication.

District Court Services

CDSS provides mediation in district criminal court in two judicial districts—the 9th (covering Granville, Vance, Franklin, and Warren counties) and the 10th (Wake County). Mediation is appropriate in many criminal cases where the parties have an ongoing relationship, where there are damages similar to those found in a civil case, and where the public is not best served by a traditional prosecution and/or conviction. Mediation allows victim and offender to understand their problem better and to create their own solution. Mediations save valuable and limited resources by freeing up the prosecutor, clerk, and judge to handle more pressing criminal matters. In 2007, when the General Assembly created the District Criminal Court mediator certification program, administered by the North Carolina Dispute Resolution Commission (DRC), CDSS took the necessary steps to become a certified center, utilizing mediators certified under the program. The program, which is voluntary, establishes professional standards, requires training, and specifies how the mediations should be conducted. (For a more complete description of the voluntary, statewide district criminal court mediation program, please see Chapter 23.)

In Wake County, at the request of the judges, CDSS created programs within district civil court where mediation is a tool for resolution of conflict. For several years, mediation has been available in actions requesting a civil "no contact" order under Chapter 50C of the North Carolina General Statutes, in domestic violence cases filed pursuant to Chapter 50B of the General Statutes (where appropriate), and in child support cases involving extraordinary expenses (usually unreimbursed medical expenses). Currently, CDSS is operating a pilot program at the request of the family court judges to mediate issues that are being raised through show cause hearings.

Family Services

CDSS offers a variety of services to families in conflict. Mediation is provided for families working with and without attorneys, utilizing a sliding-scale rate based on income. Mediation occurs both before and after cases are filed in family court.

File It Yourself Clinic

Several years ago, CDSS created the File It Yourself Clinic, a program which offers unbundled legal services to members of the public who wish to file their own actions for divorce, custody, and emergency custody. Attorneys who work with the clinic set their fees on a sliding scale based on the client's income and the level of services provided. The attorneys consult, advise, and prepare paperwork for filing, but they do not go to court with the clients. The attorneys also discuss mediation as an option that clients may wish to consider.

Separating Together

In 1999, CDSS created the Separating Together program. This collaborative law initiative uses the services of attorneys who are committed to working together to resolve all of the issues facing a family going through separation and divorce. The two parties and their lawyers enter into a four-way agreement whereby they agree to: work collaboratively, share information, utilize the same experts, and decline to litigate the case. Most of the hard work takes place in a four-way conference. By avoiding litigation, the parties reduce both the emotional toll and the financial devastation that often occurs during separation and divorce proceedings. The Separating Together group, which now has eight lawyers, functions independently but continues to share office space with CDSS.

ADR Program Design

CDSS works with both private and public entities to create grievance and disciplinary systems that utilize mediation, arbitration, or other ADR systems. CDSS was instrumental in developing the grievance systems currently used by the North Carolina Office of State Personnel, Guilford County, and UNC Health Care. (For more information on these processes, see Chapter 26.)

CDSS also helped the Office of Administrative Hearings and the North Carolina Department of Health and Human Services to create the mediation program that is a part of the Medicaid appeal process for recipients of Medicaid who receive notice that their benefits are either reduced or eliminated. (For more information on the Medicaid program, see Chapter 24.)

Mediation and Conflict Resolution Training

Mediation and ADR training is a vital part of the CDSS mission. CDSS is certified by the DRC to provide mediation training in the superior court, family financial, district criminal court, and clerk of court programs. CDSS provides employment mediation training for the North Carolina Office of State Personnel, UNC Health Care, and Guilford County. The Office of Administrative Hearings utilizes CDSS to train mediators throughout the state who work with the Medicaid mediation program. At the community level, CDSS is available to work with local partners, such as Habitat for Humanity and the Wake County Domestic Violence Task Force, to teach conflict resolution skills to a wide range of community members.

The ADR Clinic at the North Carolina Central University School of Law

Alternative dispute resolution has become a permanent part of the legal landscape. This is particularly true in North Carolina, which has one of the most comprehensive court-based alternative dispute resolution systems in the country. Other chapters in this volume detail the breadth and depth of changes that the ADR movement has brought to legal institutions in North Carolina and to the practice of law in the state. These changes have had important implications for legal education. The modern lawyer must be aware of the range of processes available for resolving disputes and must be prepared to operate effectively within them, both as an advocate and as a neutral.

The North Carolina Central University (NCCU) School of Law, like many law schools, has for several years offered a basic survey course in alternative dispute resolution, focusing on negotiation as well as mediation theory and practice. But in 1999, the Law School entered into a partnership with CDSS to begin the first clinical course in alternative dispute resolution offered by a North Carolina law school. The arrangement between CDSS and NCCU offered immediate benefits for both partners. For NCCU, the primary obstacle to providing a clinical experience in ADR for law students had been the problem of developing or locating a consistent source of suitable cases. CDSS has had a longstanding in-court mediation program in Wake County, where it provides free mediation services in criminal district court. Mediations are conducted by unpaid volunteers from CDSS, who are trained and supervised by CDSS staff. By joining forces with CDSS, the NCCU Law School gained a reliable source of suitable cases for students to mediate, and CDSS quickly and substantially increased its pool of volunteer mediators. In addition to district court mediations, clinic students observe superior court and Court of Appeals mediations and observe and co-mediate Medicaid mediations.

THE EDUCATIONAL GOALS OF THE NCCU ADR CLINIC

The NCCU ADR Clinic aims to: (1) provide law students with an understanding that most legal disputes are best resolved outside the courtroom;

(2) introduce students to the range of available dispute resolution processes, particularly within North Carolina's court-based ADR programs; and (3) teach them how to determine what processes may be most appropriate for resolving different kinds of cases.

More specifically, the Clinic provides opportunities—through role-playing and actual cases—to learn basic negotiation and mediation techniques, communication skills, problem-solving approaches to legal disputes, and other skills necessary to effectively function in the lawyer's historical role as advisor and counselor. The cases mediated by the students over the course of a semester provide a rich source of opportunities to confront the special ethical problems facing attorney-mediators, as well as an opportunity to examine and reflect upon the sources and dynamics of conflict and the ways in which individuals from different cultures perceive and deal with conflicts. Often the clinic experience reinforces what students have learned in courses in evidence, remedies, criminal law, and procedure.

THE COURSE OF INSTRUCTION

Students who enroll in the ADR Clinic program arrive on the NCCU campus a week before classes officially begin for an intensive, forty-hour training program in superior court mediation, arbitration, collaborative law, and related subjects. The class is a mix of law students, lawyers, and other professionals interested in mediation. The training is provided by the NCCU Law School faculty, the staff of CDSS, and practicing attorneys in the Research Triangle area. Students also meet for a one-hour class each week during the semester. Each student is required to keep a journal of his or her clinical experiences throughout the course and present it for evaluation at the end of the semester.

THE EXPERIENCE IN THE FIELD

After the forty-hour training period is over, students rotate through the district court mediation programs in Wake County. Initially, students act as observers or co-mediators in district court criminal matters, under the supervision of attorney-mediators or experienced non-attorney volunteer mediators. Each student attends multiple sessions of district court, participating in several mediations. The goal is to teach the student to be the "lead" mediator in a co-mediator model. Another goal is to bring students to a level of competence that will permit them to be certified by CDSS to serve as volunteer mediators in district court.

Sessions of criminal district court are held in Wake County on Mondays. After the calendar call that begins each court session, the assistant district attorney or the presiding judge refers cases for mediation to the student volunteers present in the courtroom. Mediations are conducted in rooms adjoining the courtroom. Typically, students observe a case, act as co-mediators in their next two or three cases, and then serve as lead mediators thereafter.

After each session of court, students and mediators meet for debriefing. Much of the best instruction and learning takes place during these sessions. The format provides a non-threatening environment in which senior mediators can give students constructive evaluations of their performances, and where students can ask questions and reflect on their experiences during the mediations.

CDSS provides a number of other ADR programs and handles a broad range of cases in its Raleigh office. These programs include: mediation in felony and juvenile drug treatment courts; family mediation; mediation of matters involving consumer complaints filed with the Office of the Attorney General of North Carolina; district court arbitration; family and divorce cases; and superior court mediations. Students are required to observe one session of district court arbitration and one session of drug treatment court. After each session, students meet with the arbitrator, the judge, and court personnel to discuss the process they have observed and the role of legal professionals within that context. Students are encouraged to observe or to participate in other programs and ADR activities as caseloads and scheduling permit. The program has proven to be a great success by giving students the tools they need to assist their future clients with conflict resolution.

Presentations and Participation
in Professional Groups

CDSS has made presentations to the Eleventh United Nations Congress on Crime Prevention and Criminal Justice, the American Bar Association Dispute Resolution Section (in New York, Los Angeles, and Boulder), and the North Carolina Bar Association Dispute Resolution Section. CDSS staff have served on both the DRC and the State Bar Council.

Conclusion

Communities may need many different types of assistance in building a consensus on local issues. Community-based dispute settlement centers are accessible sources of assistance in conflict-management training, consulting, facilitation, and mediation. Citizen groups, business organizations, elected officials, advisory commissions, and local government staff can benefit by learning about and applying consensus-building skills offered to better manage existing community disputes and to head off potential conflicts.

NOTE

1. *See* Daniel McGillis, *Community Mediation Programs: Developments and Challenges* (U.S. Dep't of Justice, Office of Justice Programs, National Institute of Justice, July 1997).

CHAPTER TWENTY-THREE

The District Criminal Court Mediation Program

"We are all formed of frailty and error;
let us pardon reciprocally each other's folly—
that is the first law of nature."

—François Marie Arouet (pen name Voltaire),
"Tolerance," *The Philosophical Dictionary* (1764).

Introduction

During the past thirty years, many of North Carolina's community mediation centers have offered mediation services to parties involved in misdemeanor criminal matters. These programs have been provided in partnership with local district attorneys and judges and have successfully resolved many cases that otherwise might have gone to trial. But because each mediation center developed its own procedures over time to meet local needs, the training and standards that evolved for district criminal court mediators were not uniform across the state.

In 2006, the directors of three community mediation centers approached the North Carolina Dispute Resolution Commission (DRC or Commission) about creating a system for the certification and regulation of district criminal court mediators. Their goal was to develop a system that would have statewide application and that would be modeled on the rules and certification requirements for mediators in the state's other court-based programs. It was hoped that these measures would result in additional program credibility and would enhance the status of the mediators engaged in this important work. DRC Chair Judge Sanford L. Steelman, Jr. asked Frank C. Laney to chair an ad hoc committee to consider the proposal.

The Ad Hoc Committee sought input from multiple community mediation centers, district attorneys, and district court judges. After extensive study and review, the Committee's recommendations to the DRC included the enactment of legislation and the adoption of rules to govern an optional, statewide certification program for district criminal court mediators. The

Committee suggested that uniform program rules would provide consistent standards for existing programs and could give more structured guidance to centers that might wish to offer this type of mediation in the future.

Legislation providing for statewide certification of district criminal court mediators was enacted in July 2007 as North Carolina General Statutes Section 7A-38.3D. In November 2007, the North Carolina Supreme Court adopted Rules Implementing Mediation in Matters Pending in District Criminal Court. The new statute and rules did not require judicial districts to offer mediation in district criminal court matters or to follow the program rules. Instead, they provided an option for those districts that desired uniformity in certification, regulation, and program operations.

At the time of publication, twenty-one of the twenty-two community mediation centers in the Mediation Network of North Carolina provide criminal district court mediation. Four of the twenty-one centers, and Wake County's mediation center, have opted to participate in the DRC's certification program and to operate pursuant to the program's rules. Participating centers follow standardized operations and, through the DRC and its website, provide their mediators with statewide recognition similar to that given for certified mediators in the superior court's Mediated Settlement Conference (MSC) Program and the district court's Family Financial Settlement (FFS) Program. Non-participating centers follow certification requirements set by the Mediation Network of North Carolina.

Program Procedures and Rules

Overview

District criminal court mediation certification is subject to the provisions set forth in North Carolina General Statutes Section 7A-38.3D and is governed by the North Carolina Supreme Court's Rules Implementing Mediation in Matters Pending in District Criminal Court (Rules). The statute's stated purpose is to promote high mediator standards through certification, and the mediation procedures it outlines are closely modeled after the process that has been used for decades in various mediation centers across the state.

A court may encourage voluntary mediation for any pending district criminal court action, and the district attorney may delay prosecution to accommodate mediation. Multiple charges against a single defendant and charges pending in multiple courts may be consolidated for mediation by court consent.

Referral to mediation is based on a number of factors, including the parties' likely willingness to mediate, whether prosecution is in the best interest of the parties, if a continuing relationship between the parties is expected, whether cross-warrants were filed, and whether voluntary dismissal might otherwise occur. Community mediation centers assist in screening cases for appropriateness, scheduling mediations, and providing certified volunteer or staff mediators. To support the voluntary nature of criminal district court mediations, a party's willingness or refusal to participate in mediation is not revealed to the court or the district attorney. This confidence is maintained to protect the party from any potential prejudice.

Pursuant to the statute and Rules, courts are to encourage parties to try mediation as soon as practicable. Mediation may occur prior to assigning a defense attorney, because a mediated agreement will not result in jail time for any participant. Once parties agree to mediation, the court assigns a community mediation center or a specific mediator to conduct the mediation. For good cause shown, the complainant or defendant may move the court to disqualify the mediator. Nothing in the statute or Rules prohibits assigned mediators from disqualifying themselves.

Mediations may occur at the courthouse, at the community mediation center, or at any other place agreed upon by the parties and mediator. Complainants and defendants must physically attend unless they and the mediator agree that one may participate by telephone, or unless an order of the court imposes an alternative. Other participants approved by the mediator may attend but later may be excluded from further participation if the mediator finds their contribution to be counterproductive. Attorneys may physically attend and participate, or they may provide advice before, during, or after the mediation.

Agreements must be written and signed to be enforceable. If no agreement is reached, the mediator declares an impasse, and the case goes to hearing.

Mediations must be scheduled to occur before any court deadlines. For good cause, a mediator may request a deadline extension to complete the mediation, if a delay or recess is necessary.

Mediator Certification

To take part in the statewide mediator certification process, the chief district court judge, the district attorney, and the director of the local mediation center must agree to participate in the District Criminal Court Program. The center then applies to the DRC, citing the court's agreement and laying out its training curriculum for the Commission's approval. Once the center is accepted into the program, the DRC receives and approves applications for district criminal court mediators. Applicants must be affiliated with a community mediation center, either as a volunteer or staff mediator. There are two tracks for certification. An applicant must be: (1) DRC-certified as a mediator in the MSC or FFS Program or an Advanced Practitioner member of the Association for Conflict Resolution; or (2) he or she must have either a four-year college degree or a two-year degree plus mediation/work experience, in addition to a twenty-four-hour district criminal court training course. Trainees must observe and co-mediate district criminal court mediations, demonstrate certain competencies, commit to mediating cases, comply with continuing education or training, and submit proof of qualifications. Certification must be renewed every two years.

Mediator Authority

Mediators have discretion to allow participation in a mediation session by any person likely to assist resolution of the dispute. Similarly, mediators have discretion to exclude any person, except the parties or their attorneys, whose presence the mediator deems counterproductive.

Mediators may communicate privately with any party or parties' counsel prior to and during the mediation. That a prior conversation took place must be disclosed to all participants at the beginning of the mediation, although the substance of the conversation may be held in confidence.

It is the mediator's duty to explain to the parties the process and purpose of mediation, the role of the mediator as a neutral, how communications may take place during mediation, the inadmissibility of evidence at a subsequent hearing, the requirement of mutual consent to any written agreement, and that an impasse will result in the case going to court. Mediators have the authority and responsibility to determine when parties reach an impasse.

Mediator Immunity

Mediators have judicial immunity to the same extent as a judge, except that they may be disciplined pursuant to rules of mediator conduct adopted by the North Carolina Supreme Court. Mediation centers and staff who supply mediators are immune from suit in any subsequent civil action, except in actions for willful or wanton misconduct.

Confidentiality and Inadmissibility

Memoranda, work notes, or work products of the mediator are confidential. The case files maintained by community mediation centers are confidential.

Statements and conduct that occur during mediation are not discoverable and are inadmissible if the case proceeds to a hearing. Any threat to the safety of a person or property made during mediation may be reported to law enforcement by mediators, but such reporting is not required. Mediators have discretion to warn a person against whom a threat has been made.

Discoverable evidence in a case does not become inadmissible by being discussed in mediation. The protection of statements made in mediation from discovery and from their admission as evidence does not provide a shield for evidence that can be discovered and admitted on its own terms, outside of the mediation.

No mediator or observer (such as an ADR student or mediator trainee) may be compelled to testify in any subsequent proceeding in the action that was mediated unless any one of four exceptions applies: (1) a statutory duty to report exists, as in proceedings for abuse, neglect, or dependency of a juvenile or for abuse, neglect, or exploitation of an adult; (2) in disciplinary proceedings before the North Carolina State Bar or to enforce standards of mediator conduct; (3) in proceedings about which the mediator (now a witness) exercised discretion and reported a threat of harm made during mediation; or (4) in felony trials, where the evidence cannot be obtained otherwise, and the presiding judge determines that disclosure is necessary to effectuate justice.

Program Statistics

The Mediation Network of North Carolina consists of twenty-two community mediation centers across three regions of the state: Western, Central, and Eastern North Carolina. In addition, Wake County is served by Carolina Dispute Settlement Services which, while not a Mediation Network affiliate, is one of the five mediation centers that have opted for certification of its district criminal court mediation program. In 2010, the five certified centers provided mediation for approximately 2,700 district criminal court cases, and the remaining centers provided mediation for approximately 5,700 district criminal court cases.

Program Fees and Funding

If agreement is reached by the parties, the defendant must pay a $60 dismissal fee for the district attorney to dismiss the case. Alternately, the parties may agree that someone other than the defendant will pay some, or all, of the dismissal fee. The judge has discretion to waive the fee due to indigence, unemployment, full-time student status, receipt of public assistance, or other compelling factors.

Prior to June 2011, the $60 dismissal fees went to support the General Court of Justice, and mediation centers received a set amount of pass-through funding from the state's general fund, regardless of caseload. In 2010, state funding to community mediation centers was approximately $1,100,000. Effective July 1, 2011, the General Assembly eliminated the pass-through funding and replaced it with a fee-for-service model. The $60 dismissal fee continues to be paid by the defendant to the clerk of court, and $57 of that fee goes to the mediation center providing the service. However, this change has resulted in a significant decrease in program funding. Centers were authorized under the budget act to assess and collect additional mediation fees in district court programs; but there were no guidelines provided, and the clerk of court is prohibited from assisting with the collection of fees. District courts are not compelled to offer mediation services, so individual centers can weigh the costs and benefits of the fee-for-service structure and proceed or withdraw accordingly.

Conclusion

The District Criminal Court Mediation Program provides an opportunity for parties involved in a misdemeanor case to sit down with a mediator to try and talk through and resolve their disagreements without the negative consequences that often result from a court hearing and disposition. The program continues many of the traditional practices followed by community mediation centers in providing such services, but it also helps participating judicial districts to assure both the quality of mediators and consistency in procedures. Because participation is optional, each district can determine whether the program meets the needs of its local community. It is hoped that the rules and standards established by the program will continue to strengthen the process of mediation in district criminal courts across the state.

CHAPTER TWENTY-FOUR

The North Carolina Medicaid Mediation Program

"Don't find fault. Find a remedy."
—American industrialist Henry Ford

Prior to 2008, the Medicaid program in North Carolina was in crisis. The state was at risk of losing millions of dollars in Medicaid funds because officials were having difficulty processing recipient appeals within the time requirements established by federal law. To avert catastrophe, innovative leaders and interested individuals within the state created a first-of-its-kind program offering voluntary pre-hearing mediation as a crucial step in the appeal process. The results have been remarkably successful.

The Collaboration

The backlog of Medicaid appeals in North Carolina was a problem that needed to be remedied quickly, but getting the necessary and appropriate people to the table to craft a solution was challenging. A variety of interests needed to be represented. Administrative law judges from the North Carolina Office of Administrative Hearings (OAH), staff from Carolina Dispute Settlement Services (CDSS), employees from the state's Department of Health and Human Services (DHHS), members of the North Carolina General Assembly, representatives of the North Carolina Attorney General's Office, attorneys from Legal Aid of North Carolina, and representatives of community mediation centers around the state collaborated on the project. One of the primary objectives was to maintain Medicaid funding adequate to provide authorized medical care to recipients. Another critical objective was to create a process for appeals of adverse rulings that would be timely, efficient, cost-effective, and workable for the many parties who had a role within an appeal. The program adopted by the General Assembly in October 2008[1] has succeeded in accomplishing each of those objectives.

Overview of the Appeal Process

An appeal from an adverse Medicaid ruling, from the giving of notice by the recipient to the final decision by the DHHS, must be completed within ninety days to comply with federal law. This "rocket docket," as it is called, requires that all participants within the appeal process be attentive, prepared, and willing and able to use technology.

An appeal begins with a denial, reduction, suspension, or termination of Medicaid services by DHHS. Within thirty days of the mailing date of the notice (mailing date and notice date must be the same), the recipient must file a request for hearing with the OAH. Staff at OAH notifies the Department of Justice (DOJ) and DHHS that the hearing request has been received. DHHS, through its Division of Medicaid Assistance (DMA), notifies the appropriate medical service vendor of the appeal. OAH sends a notice to the recipient with a tentative date for the hearing in the event the case is not disposed of before hearing.

Upon receipt of a request for hearing, OAH immediately notifies the Mediation Network of North Carolina (the Network) that an appeal has been made. The Network assigns the case to a participating community mediation center. The statute authorizes only community mediation centers, as defined by law, to conduct the Medicaid mediations. Private mediators may not conduct them. The mediation center must contact the recipient regarding the availability of mediation services within five days of OAH receiving the appeal. If the recipient elects to go to mediation, which is voluntary and not mandatory for the recipient, then the mediation center must schedule and conduct the mediation within twenty-five days from the date OAH received the notice of appeal. If mediation is rejected or is unsuccessful, OAH will send a hearing date to the recipient. The hearing must be within forty-five days of the date notice of appeal was received by OAH, ensuring that the recipient had at least fifteen days notice of the hearing date. The hearing is conducted at OAH before an administrative law judge. The state is represented by the Attorney General's Office (DOJ). The recipient may or may not be represented by an attorney. Within five days of the hearing, an audiotape of the hearing is provided to DHHS/DMA, and within twenty days of the hearing, OAH sends a copy of the written decision to the parties and to DHHS/DMA, which also receives the record. DHHS/DMA makes a final agency decision within twenty days of receiving the OAH decision and notifies the recipient and the Medicaid service vendor. The appeal process up to this point satisfies the federal time requirements. The recipient has thirty days to pursue appellate review through the superior court, but this time is beyond the federal time requirements imposed on the State. As long as the recipient has an active appeal, services will continue.

How Mediation Is Conducted

It is important that each mediation center participating in the Medicaid Program have an excellent case management system in place. Steps must be in place to ensure that the recipient is contacted within five days from giving notice of appeal. The initial telephone conversation with the recipient is critical because this is the first, and often the only, opportunity to educate the recipient about the availability of mediation, how the process works, and when the mediation can be scheduled. This is the time to begin building a trust relationship. The case manager also will communicate with the respondent (DHHS/DMA or its representative) to confirm the mediation date.

The majority of mediations are conducted by telephone, and they usually are concluded within one hour. The first responsibility of the mediator is to review the Agreement to Mediate and acquire authorization from the parties to continue with the mediation process. The Medicaid recipient often is assisted by a case manager or qualified provider who can be permitted to speak on behalf of the recipient. The respondent is represented by a staff member (of DHHS/DMA) who is familiar with the recipient's file and has authority to negotiate and make decisions within the criteria established by Medicaid.

When the mediation is concluded, the mediator has a responsibility to notify OAH and DOJ about the results. If the issue is resolved, the appeal needs to be removed from the court docket. Likewise, if the case is going to move forward to hearing, DOJ staff must prepare. If there is resolution, which occurs in more than 80 percent of the cases, the mediator will craft an agreement, review the agreement with the parties, and receive authorization to sign on behalf of the parties. The mediator provides a copy of the agreement to the recipient (or his or her representative) and to the respondent and gives a Report of Mediator and the agreement to OAH. DOJ also receives a copy of the Report of Mediator. The mediator uploads the Report of Mediator and the agreement into the DHHS electronic file system for Medicaid recipients. Mediators have twenty-four hours to prepare and file the records. Mediation centers are paid a set fee for each case mediated.

Why Training and Education Are Crucial to the Program

Education was a critical part of the Medicaid Mediation Program's success. Informal training took place with staff at the state agencies involved in the Program so that they could become familiar with the new roles and responsibilities involved. At the request of OAH, Carolina Dispute Settlement Services and DMA provided training to both respondents and mediators. The respondents in each mediation are vendors with whom DHHS has contracted to evaluate and authorize Medicaid services. It is the respondent who has conducted an assessment, evaluated a recipient's medical needs, and reviewed established Medicaid guidelines and criteria to determine whether services are authorized and appropriate. The assessment may be conducted as a part of a regular or periodic review or as a result of a recipient requesting new or different services. If the respondent denies or reduces services, then the recipient is notified and has the authority to request a hearing. If mediation is selected by the recipient, as it usually is, the respondent will participate in the mediation. Respondents are required to participate while recipients may choose.

So that respondents could better understand their role at mediation, training was offered to explain: the purpose of mediation; the six stages of a mediation (Beginning, Acquire Information, Define the Main Concerns, Generate Alternatives, Evaluate Alternatives, Resolution); the forms used in the Medicaid Mediation Program; introduction of the participants; and tips to help the respondents prepare for the mediation.

Training also was provided to the community mediation centers and their mediators. While the basics of mediation were already understood by this group, it was necessary to discuss the particulars of the Medicaid program, with emphasis on the forms and the very strict time frames within which the mediators had to perform their duties. An overview of how Medicaid works and its particular vocabulary and an introduction to the many agencies that work within the system was provided. Mediators had to understand that the mediation absolutely had to take place within twenty-five days of the notice of appeal. Of equal importance was the necessity of reporting the results of the mediation within twenty-four hours to everyone who needed to know the result. Continuing education and information sharing are coordinated through e-mail, with updates from OAH and the Mediation Network.

The Results of the Mediation Program

Since the appeals process went into effect on October 1, 2008, most recipients have voluntarily chosen to use mediation. Statewide, more than 80 percent of the cases referred to mediation have been resolved successfully. When an appeal ends at mediation, no resources are expended to prepare for or hold a formal hearing in the case. The recipient and respondent understand each other better because they have had an opportunity to communicate more effectively, to share information, and to reach a solution to their conflict in a respectful environment, with the assistance of a mediator utilizing a structured process. As a result, authorized and appropriate services can be provided, and unauthorized or inappropriate services can be stopped.

NOTE

1. *See* N.C. Session Law 2008-107 § 10.15A(h2) (3), as amended by N.C. Session Law 2009-550 §1.1(b)(3).

CHAPTER TWENTY-FIVE

The Prisoner Re-Entry Mediation Program

> *"Whenever you're in conflict with someone,*
> *there is one factor that can make the difference*
> *between damaging your relationship and deepening it.*
> *That factor is attitude."*
> —American psychologist and philosopher William James

One of the newest mediation programs in North Carolina is the Prisoner Re-Entry Mediation Program launched in early 2011. The program is an example of how alternative dispute resolution can be used, not just to prevent trials but also to prevent crime by reducing recidivism. The re-entry mediation process offers an opportunity for inmates who are within one year of release from prison to mediate issues related to re-entry into society with an outside participant who they have identified as potentially playing a significant role in their successful re-entry. The outside participant might include a family member, a member of the inmate's faith community, an adult child, the person caring for the inmate's children during incarceration, a girlfriend or boyfriend, or a past employer or landlord.

Re-entry topics often include housing, employment, sobriety, personal responsibility, independence, and family reintegration. Issues concerning forgiveness, acceptance, self-confidence, trust, and uncertainty surface and are examined by the parties in the confidential, voluntary, facilitated structure of mediation. Detailed plans are developed by the parties that identify and delegate specific tasks to accomplish goals associated with each topic. The final agreement provides a self-designed re-entry road map that establishes firm guidelines and mutual expectations between the parties, paving the way for a productive, supported transition from incarceration to community.

The Re-Entry Mediation Method

The re-entry mediation method provides for up to three two-hour mediation sessions between the parties. The first two sessions are held at the prison, and the third session is offered in the community after release. Each session is co-mediated by two mediators. Experienced mediators from community mediation centers, the Dispute Resolution Institute at the North Carolina Central University School of Law, and private practice mediators receive an additional sixteen hours of re-entry mediation training that builds on their existing skills and introduces principles of deep listening, acceptance of the parties' contributions, and techniques for controlling the emotional intensity that often is present during these mediation sessions.

Unlike court-ordered mediation, which begins with the mediator setting out ground rules for civility, re-entry mediators avoid imposing norms. A general tone of acceptance can help prevent a party's retreat into defensiveness, which often is a trigger for anger. Deep-listening techniques allow mediators to continuously reflect a party's meaning, giving voice in a calm and reasonable way to fears and emotions that the prisoner may not be able to express appropriately. This process serves two purposes. First, it prevents a party from practicing the kind of manipulation that may have helped him or her to cope or survive in the past. If a mediator stays with the party's true meaning and demonstrates it through reflection, the party is less likely to become sidetracked or limited by emotions or preconceived ideas; and if the speaker is unable to lead the listener astray, manipulation is defeated. Second, deep listening allows the mediator to prevent a heated discussion from spiraling out of control. This result is achieved when the mediator interposes at appropriate times with names for the feelings, values, and topics that are at the core of the heated messages. The succinct reflection process offers proof to the speaker that he or she has been heard and mitigates the need to escalate, shout, and repeat oneself in an attempt to be understood. By harnessing and redirecting the emotional intensity often present in these situations, the mediator avoids halting the flow of information, allowing the parties to reach understandings about themselves and each other that might not be achieved if the process was prematurely truncated by normal rules of civility.

Offering the Program in Prisons

Eligibility criteria for re-entry mediation include release from state prison within twelve months or participation in the Community-Based Corrections Program through the Durham Criminal Justice Resource Center. Inmates are invited to attend an orientation session that includes an hour of interactive conflict resolution activities followed by one-on-one discussions with intake staff to explore outside participant options. The purpose of the intake session is twofold. First, it provides nonviolent tools to inmates to foster beneficial participation during mediation. Second, it helps them begin imagining their own re-entry and the interpersonal challenges that lie ahead, increasing their likelihood of participating in the program.

After an inmate signs up for mediation, the intake staff contacts the outside participant and invites him or her into the program. Thorough background checks are run with the outside party's permission to ensure the safety of both parties. Funds are available to defray the outside participant's transportation costs, if necessary. No prison guards or other Department of Corrections staff are present in the mediation room.

The standard measurement for recidivism reduction is an ex-offender staying out of prison for three years. General statistics are being collected for evaluation to monitor the program's effectiveness. Because an analysis of the program's effect on recidivism requires three years of data, results will not be available until 2014.

Contributors to the Program

There have been a number of outstanding contributors to the Prisoner Re-Entry Mediation Program. First, inmates at the Orange Correctional Center in Hillsborough shared their concerns with prison volunteers about reuniting with family after decades of incarceration, thus prompting the search for a solution. Second, Lorig Charkoudian, Executive Director of Community Mediation Maryland, developed this model and has been conducting re-entry mediation in eleven Maryland prisons for the past several years. When contacted about sharing her experience and materials, Dr. Charkoudian responded generously and conducted the initial training for seventeen North Carolina mediators in late 2010. Finally, the inaugural year for the North Carolina Prisoner Re-Entry Mediation Program was made possible by a JAMS Foundation grant administered through the Elna B. Spaulding Conflict Resolution Center in Durham, North Carolina.

Conclusion

The final chapter of this book ends with the encouragement that "[t]he unfinished business [of the ADR profession] is to expand beyond the courts and to help fashion a society that weaves the philosophy and spirit of ADR into its very fabric." The North Carolina Prisoner Re-entry Mediation Program is one example of how progress is being made to help achieve this important goal.

ADR IN GOVERNMENT AGENCIES

CHAPTER TWENTY-SIX

Governmental Dispute Resolution in North Carolina

"All government, indeed every human benefit and enjoyment, every virtue, and every prudent act, is founded on compromise and barter."
—Anglo-Irish statesman, political theorist, and philosopher
Edmund Burke, Speech on Conciliation with America (March 22, 1775).

The stakes are high when government and the citizens it serves come into conflict. Dispute resolution in the public sector provides processes that are critical to maintaining a fair and efficient government. More importantly, however, the availability of alternative approaches to resolving public disputes can strengthen the confidence of the people in government and public institutions through the clarification of issues, the disclosure of pertinent information, and the opportunity to develop options. This chapter outlines a range of governmental dispute resolution models in North Carolina and describes the ways that mediators and other neutrals facilitate the resolution of public conflicts. It also provides examples of ways that alternative dispute resolution (ADR) methods have been utilized to improve the handling of workplace conflicts involving governmental employees.

Overview of Public Disputes Resolution

Public disputes resolution is the application of ADR principles in civic affairs. The development or evaluation of a local or state government policy, program, or plan; the progression of an enforcement action; or the allocation of a public resource are just some of the ways that the use of ADR affects governmental functions and private interests.

The purpose of public disputes resolution is to facilitate collaboration among one or more government decision makers and (often) a combination of other affected stakeholders—such as citizen groups, nonprofit organizations, private businesses, or property owners—thus allowing them to work together to clarify and, if possible and desired, to reconcile each other's interests.

Even when conflict is not intense, the resolution of a public issue can be complicated by the presence of multiple parties, a diversity of perspectives, diffuse stakeholders who may be hard to represent (e.g., taxpayers, future generations, the elderly), and different levels of familiarity with the relevant technical or institutional facets of the issue (such as fiscal details, various mandates or regulations imposed by a variety of agencies, and, in the case of environmental issues, the scientific aspects).

The public disputes resolution process requires a substantively neutral mediator or facilitator. As in other mediation processes, the neutral helps the parties work effectively with the conflict and/or with the complexity that is present in the situation. The neutral does not provide his or her own ideas about the parties' options or render a decision.

There are varied types of neutral assistance available to stakeholders within the arena of public disputes resolution. This is not surprising given the many different contexts in which public disputes take place. Public disputes can occur at the neighborhood, municipal, county, regional, state, or federal levels. They address public health, environmental, transportation, budgetary, fiscal, and human services issues, and/or intergroup relations. In addition, public disputes resolution processes may be initiated either voluntarily by stakeholders at the urging of decision makers, their staffs, or advisory boards, or through one of North Carolina's mandatory court-related programs.

Examples of Public Disputes Resolution in North Carolina

The following examples of public disputes resolution in North Carolina illustrate the various contexts in which ADR techniques have been applied, as well as the options that exist for structuring a process to avoid litigation.

ENVIRONMENTAL, HEALTH, AND LAND USE DISPUTES

- The New Hill Community Association (NHCA) in Wake County dropped a five-year battle, including a lawsuit, against a plan to build a $327 million wastewater treatment plant after two court-ordered mediation sessions generated a settlement among the following parties: NHCA, the North Carolina Department of Environmental and Natural Resources, the towns of Cary, Apex, and Morrisville, and Research Triangle Park (RTP) South.

- The Protect the Catawba Coalition and the Catawba Riverkeeper Foundation, Inc. reached a mediated settlement agreement with the cities of Concord and Kannapolis to resolve the appeal of an Interbasin Transfer Certificate granted to Concord and Kannapolis by the North Carolina Environmental Management Commission.

- The Facilitated Small Area Plan for Carrboro's Northern Study Area resulted from an innovative year-long community involvement process convened by the Town of Carrboro. The Plan was devised to help create consensus among municipal and county residents, property owners, and elected officials in Orange County on how development would be managed in its extraterritorial jurisdiction. The land use plan later was selected by the North Carolina Chapter of the American Planning Association as the recipient of the Brian Benson Award for Small Community Comprehensive Planning.

- Dobson, Elkin, Mount Airy, Pilot Mountain, and Surry County formed an ad hoc Water Partnership Working Group (WPWG) to examine opportunities for creating an inter-local water services partnership. The WPWG met multiple times over the course of a year, developed a set of partnership principles, and established a standing Advisory Committee on water partnerships that may, among other things, seek joint funding for infrastructure projects and coordinate service area plans.

- When residents of four surrounding neighborhoods began lobbying in opposition to a proposed group home for people living with HIV/AIDS, the Town of Carrboro encouraged neighborhood representatives and the project proponents to use community mediation to resolve their conflict. Through mediation, representatives from the two sides jointly organized a facilitated public forum at which the proposal and neighborhood concerns were discussed openly. Opposition to the group home subsided after information was shared, relationships were established, and lines of communication were opened between the two groups.

SCHOOL AND EDUCATION-RELATED DISPUTES

• According to the UNC School of Government, twenty-eight successful mediations between school boards and county commissioners took place between 1997 and 2009. These mediations took place pursuant to North Carolina General Statutes Section 115C-431, which provides counties and boards of education with a process for settling differences and avoiding litigation over county appropriations for local public education.

• Facilitated study circles for faculty, staff, and students at North Carolina State University increased understanding and appreciation of different races and cultures and provided practical recommendations for actions that individuals can take to promote equality on campus. These study circles were an outgrowth of a wider off-campus initiative on race relations begun in 1998 by the League of Women Voters of Wake County, the YWCA, the North Carolina Coalition for Indian Affairs, and eight local churches. The Study Circles program assigned participants to racially mixed groups who engaged in small, democratic, peer-led discussions regarding their racial attitudes. Trained impartial facilitators managed the deliberation process.

HEALTHCARE DISPUTES

• In December 2010, after an extensive facilitated public engagement process, the Fayetteville City Council established a Hospital Area Plan Overlay Ordinance, which helped to resolve conflicts over the encroachment of a high-density development associated with the Cape Fear Valley Hospital into surrounding residential neighborhoods. A series of community meetings enabled local residents and property and business owners to participate meaningfully in the development of a plan and an ordinance designed to manage development in the area.

BUDGETARY DISPUTES

• "Get Real 2011" (GR 2011) was a facilitated community dialogue process that invited participants from all over Mecklenburg County to envision the future and generate consensus on community priorities. Its goal was to help guide local leaders in making budgetary decisions based on clearly articulated community values. The facilitated dialogue was designed in part to address tension that surfaced around the question of whether or not race was a factor influencing decisions about funding cuts made to various local programs. Organizers of the GR2011 dialogue also hoped to use the process to build consensus on such topics as affordable housing and access to education and community services for the county's immigrant population.

LEGISLATIVE DISPUTES

• In the traditional legislative process, bills and amendments are often presented on behalf of specific interest groups. This process frequently provokes controversy and does not necessarily produce a coherent bill. The "605 process,"—named for the room in the State Legislative Building where interest group meetings often take place—is used to facilitate the drafting of bills and rules related to environmental protection and natural resources conservation. It accomplishes this aim by promoting collaboration among representatives of the regulated community, environmental advocacy groups, state agencies, and local governments. These representatives gather as a working group and meet with staff members of the North Carolina General Assembly to raise and resolve concerns about environmental legislation. Consensus amendments or bills that emerge from the process go back through the normal legislative process to become law. For example, in a matter involving ground water contamination that had state and county people at loggerheads for weeks, a resolution was reached in one afternoon through the "605 process."

INFRASTRUCTURE DISPUTES

• Long-time conflict over the City and County of Durham's urban loop highway project (known as "Eno Drive") was resolved through a process that utilized input from a citizens committee and a city/county elected officials committee. Facilitated by the Triangle J Council of Governments, the process resulted in most of the freeway loop being replaced by a series of five individual road projects designed to serve the travel needs of Northern and Eastern Durham County.

- The Topsail Beach Board of Commissioners sponsored a facilitated roundtable discussion of a controversial beach nourishment project in Pender County. Over the course of two meetings, a citizens committee composed of sixteen individuals—balanced among those who were initially in favor of the project, those initially opposed, and those initially undecided—heard presentations from leading experts, local officials (both former officeholders and those currently serving), and members of the general public. The citizens group then generated a consensus recommendation that the Board continue with an interim project to protect the town's eroding shoreline.

Human Relations and Public Safety

- The Buncombe County District Attorney's Office, the Asheville Public Defender's Office, local law enforcement officers, community activists, local ministers, and others in Asheville and Buncombe County participated in a facilitated meeting after a popular anti-gang educator was given what some considered an excessively harsh prison sentence for an armed robbery conviction. The resulting discussions brought certain tensions and concerns in the community to the surface in a healthy way, including: leniency and accountability; second chances and public safety; gang violence; early intervention; mandatory sentencing; and the needs in Asheville's low-income neighborhoods for better opportunities for recreation, education, and employment. Several additional facilitated meetings followed, creating a real conversation among the community, law enforcement officers, and service providers on the subjects of gang prevention, intervention, and suppression.

Public Disputes Resolution Services in North Carolina

Many public disputes are mediated by certified mediators in private practice through the superior court's Mediated Settlement Conference (MSC) Program. (For example, Mediation, Inc. was the neutral for the New Hill and Catawba cases cited above.) In addition, public disputes resolution mediators and facilitators operate from some of North Carolina's local community mediation centers, especially the ADR Center based in Wilmington, the Elna B. Spaulding Conflict Resolution Center in Durham, the Dispute Settlement Center's Public Disputes Program based in Carrboro (which facilitated in the AIDS and Carrboro Northern Study Area examples provided above), the Center for Dialogue in Brevard, the Dispute Settlement Center of Henderson County, and The Mediation Center (TMC) in Asheville. (TMC facilitated the anti-gang process described above.) The earliest and perhaps most developed of these efforts, the Dispute Settlement Center's Public Disputes Program in Carrboro, started with a grant from the Mary Reynolds Babcock Foundation and has maintained a full-time position devoted to public disputes resolution since 1987.

Public disputes resolution services also are made available by some of North Carolina's public universities. The North Carolina State University Natural Resources Leadership Institute (NRLI) convenes business and industry leaders, public interest groups, and government agencies to jointly explore environmental and natural resource public policy issues. For example, NRLI facilitated a panel of environmental organizations, timber industry representatives, and others to guide a statewide study of the impacts of wood chip production in North Carolina. In another case, NRLI helped whitewater outfitters, wildlife interests, lakeshore homeowners, and power company executives reach agreement on water use and allocation in the Nantahala and Tuckasegee watersheds in western North Carolina.

The work of the University of North Carolina School of Government (SOG) in the area of community problem solving and collaboration includes special courses, consultative services, and publications designed to help government officials and employees work effectively with citizens and other government and community leaders to address complex public problems. The SOG's Public Dispute Resolution Program provides consulting on public disputes and helps stakeholders across the state in locating mediators and facilitators, including faculty from the SOG itself. (The Public Dispute Resolution Program facilitated the Topsail Beach example noted above. The SOG's Strategic Public Leadership Initiative facilitated the ad hoc Water Partnership Working Group, also discussed above.) In addition, the SOG's Public Intersection Project assists governments, nonprofits, businesses, faith-based groups, and philanthropic organizations in recognizing shared concerns and acting as partners to solve public problems.

North Carolina's regional Councils of Government facilitate problem solving across their local jurisdictions (such as the Triangle J Council of Governments' Eno Drive project referenced above). In addition, some private land use, engineering, and organizational management consultancies combine their technical expertise with public involvement facilitation. For example, Glenn Harbeck Associates facilitated the Cape Fear Valley Hospital

Area planning process described above. Leading and Governing Associates, Inc. assisted the Inter-Faith Council for Social Service in conducting public listening sessions to help in managing controversy over a proposed residential facility for homeless men in Chapel Hill.

Finally, broad community initiatives such as Crossroads Charlotte (which organized the GR2011 project mentioned above) are convening and facilitating across sectors to address local and regional public issues. After a national study in 2001 ranked the Charlotte-Mecklenburg area as being high in faith-based giving and volunteerism but low in social and interracial trust, the Foundation for the Carolinas convened a diverse group of some twenty community leaders to grapple with the root causes of distrust in the community, especially between people of different races and ethnicities. Crossroads Charlotte was created from that initiative.

Methods and Process of Public Disputes Resolution

Stakeholders and decision makers can consult directly with public disputes resolution service providers and obtain advice on ways to overcome obstacles to multiparty consensus building. These consultations can provide a civic leader with new ideas and insights on how to approach a controversial issue.

Before agreeing to serve as a mediator or a facilitator in a public dispute, a neutral's best practice would be to conduct a conflict assessment. The neutral should speak separately with the directly affected parties (and with other interested stakeholders, as needed) to learn about their interests and their ability and willingness to collaborate with other participants. If the neutral determines that the situation is appropriate, he or she then can work with the parties to tailor the process to the circumstances.

The scope of an intervention in a public dispute is determined through discussions between the mediator and the parties. For example, in a prelitigation rezoning dispute in which a nonprofit human services agency's proposal to locate its offices in a residentially zoned area was met with strong neighborhood opposition, the mediator's first task was to identify representatives from the neighborhood and the agency who would be willing to confer with each other about the proposal. The mediator spent over thirty hours interviewing neighborhood residents, staff, and board members of the local human services agency, members of the planning board, and planning staff. These interviews helped the mediator become familiar with the parties and their concerns and helped the parties understand the mediator's role and the mediation process. The mediator then designed a series of meetings based on what was learned in the interviews. In contrast, when a case is referred to mandatory mediation in the context of litigation, the neutral might work only with the litigants and have no role in identifying parties.

Public disputes resolution mediators help initiate and maintain collaborative problem solving on behalf of all sides in a public dispute. The parties retain whatever decision-making authority they had when they entered the process. They also retain their right to pursue courses of action outside of mediation (political, legal, self-help, etc.). Most proponents of ADR would agree that the best mediation cases are those in which participation, even if mandated, is motivated by each of the parties' interest in truly resolving the dispute. An agreement developed by the parties in public disputes mediation can form the basis of a more formal recommendation or a proposal to the appropriate government decision makers.

Training Collaborative Civic Leaders

Civic leaders in North Carolina have developed new skill sets and supportive networks of collaborative colleagues through training programs and conferences focused on public disputes resolution, community consensus building, collaborative problem solving, and facilitative leadership. Examples include the following:

- In 2010, the Wildacres Leadership Initiative, American Leadership Forum, Charlotte Arts and Science Council's Leadership Program, Leadership Development Institute, Leadership Charlotte, Innovation Institute, and Whitehead & Associates (collectively called the Leadership Workgroup) convened 130 participants at a conference called "Leadership and Civility: Navigating Complex Conversations with Passion and Courage." Among other things, attendees were instructed in and practiced using tools for greater civility in public leadership.

- Every two years, the Natural Resources Leadership Institute selects a diverse group of about twenty North Carolinians for education and support in collaboration around natural resources and environmental quality.

- The Charlotte Region Chapter of the American Leadership Forum, the flagship program of The Lee Institute, draws about twenty-five individuals from business, government, academia, and nonprofits promoting collaborative problem solving within and among communities in that region.

- The School of Government at UNC-Chapel Hill offers three annual courses in resolving public disputes. Training in related skill sets is provided by some of the local dispute settlement centers. For example, at least once a year the Orange County Dispute Settlement Center offers a two-day workshop on how to facilitate a meeting.

As concerns have been raised about the lack of civility in public discourse, the value of using trained and experienced meeting facilitators to manage public discussion forums has become more apparent. Facilitators can be helpful when a public issue has already proved contentious, but they also can assist in preventing conflicts. As in public disputes mediation, the best practice in public issues meeting facilitation is for the neutral to work with the meeting organizers—and a larger cross section of the stakeholders, if possible—to ensure that the forum's real-world relevance, objectives, agenda, resources, and invitees are well integrated. During a well-facilitated forum, the neutral refrains from influencing the content of the group's discussions. Instead, he or she assures that the agenda is acceptable to the group and is followed; that the ground rules for discussion and decision making are clear, acceptable to all, and enforced fairly; that discussions are balanced and free from personal attacks; and that the group uses problem-solving skills that are appropriate for the task at hand. With a neutral facilitator focusing on these considerations, meeting participants are able to concentrate more fully on the issues under discussion.

Mediation of Employment Disputes
Involving Public Employees

North Carolina Office of State Personnel: Employee Mediation and Grievance Process

In 2005, the State of North Carolina renewed a commitment to the fair and efficient resolution of employee appeals and grievances by adopting a statewide Employee Mediation and Grievance Process (the Process). It was designed and implemented by the North Carolina Office of State Personnel (OSP), working in collaboration with Carolina Dispute Settlement Services. The Process gives state agencies the flexibility to adopt a policy that offers mediation as the first step of an appeal or grievance procedure. With the inclusion of mediation, an agency's internal grievance procedure is reduced from a three-step process to one with just two steps. In creating the Employee Mediation and Grievance Process, the State sought to facilitate the efficient and effective resolution of workplace issues, while at the same time helping to contain costs and provide its employees with a non-adversarial method for settling grievances.

STEP 1: MEDIATION

When workplace disputes arise, supervisors and employees are encouraged to communicate directly with each other in the spirit of cooperation and compromise. If this communication does not resolve the dispute, mediation is the first step in the two-step internal grievance process. An employee must file a grievance within fifteen calendar days of the incident triggering the grievance or the attempt to resolve the issue. Upon request from the agency (i.e., the agency of state government for which the grievant works), OSP is responsible for assigning a mediator in a timely manner to ensure that the mediation process can be concluded within forty-five calendar days of the time the grievance is filed.

The grievant and a designated agency respondent with authority to reach an agreement attend the mediation. Other representatives, including attorneys, are not permitted to attend the mediation. However, either party may request a brief recess during the mediation to obtain legal counsel or other needed advice.

At the end of the mediation, the mediator prepares either a statement of impasse or a written mediation agreement that is signed by both parties. The mediation agreement is legally binding and is maintained for at least three years. A mediation agreement may not include any provision that is contrary to OSP policies or rules or is in violation of state or federal law. Because any resolution achieved through mediation is a settlement agreement, it is subject to the rules that require the approval of certain agreements by the State Personnel Director and/or the State Personnel Commission. If a mediation agreement requires a personnel transaction to be processed, the approval of the State Personnel Director is required, except where a resignation is substituted for a dismissal. If a mediation agreement involves an exception to any State Personnel Commission policy, the approval of the State Personnel Commission is required.

STEP 2: HEARING OFFICER/HEARING PANEL

If mediation does not result in an agreement between the employee and the agency (and thus reaches an impasse), the employee is entitled to proceed to the second step of the internal grievance process. Within ten days of the unsuccessful mediation, the agency will notify the employee of his or her option to present the grievance orally to a reviewer or reviewers outside the employee's chain of command (such as a hearing officer or a hearing panel). The employee has the right to challenge whether the reviewer(s) can render an unbiased recommendation. Agency procedure establishes a process for the challenge as well as for the procedure to select a replacement reviewer, when necessary. Once the case has been presented to a hearing officer or hearing panel, a recommended decision will be provided to the agency head. The agency head will render a final agency decision (FAD).

Step 3: Office of Administrative Hearings

Contested case issues, which are defined in the State Personnel Act as appealable, allow the grievant to appeal the FAD to the Office of Administrative Hearings. An administrative law judge (ALJ) hears the appeal, taking sworn testimony and other evidence, and makes findings of fact and conclusions of law. For cases filed prior to January 1, 2012, the ALJ's decision is then referred to the State Personnel Commission for review of the record, the findings of fact, and the conclusions of law. The Commission then makes a final decision, which may be appealed via a petition for judicial review to the Superior Court Division of the General Court of Justice.

For cases filed after January 1, 2012, the ALJ creates a record in the same manner, but renders a final decision, which may be appealed via a petition for judicial review to the Superior Court Division of the General Court of Justice.

Volunteer Mediators

The mediator's role is to guide the mediation process, facilitate communication, and help the parties to generate and evaluate mutually satisfactory outcomes. The mediator does not act as a judge, does not give advice, and does not render decisions. State employees are given the opportunity to volunteer to serve as mediators. The OSP mediation pool is further augmented by professional mediators, who also volunteer to serve. Only OSP-approved mediators mediate grievances presented by state agency employees. OSP periodically sponsors forty-hour employment mediation trainings for state employees interested in becoming mediators. An interested employee must be approved by and be in good standing with his or her agency, must successfully complete the forty-hour training course, and must serve as an apprentice for a minimum of four mediations under the guidance of an experienced senior mediator. All mediators must agree to adhere to OSP's Mediator Code of Conduct.

SUMMARY OF EXPERIENCE

The Employee Mediation and Grievance Process has achieved its goal of providing a cost-effective and non-adversarial method for resolving employee grievances. Overall, the inclusion of mediation in the grievance process has met with great success. Many disputes are settled at mediation. In other cases, although mediation has resulted in an impasse, tangible and intangible benefits have still been realized from open discussion of the dispute. Grievants in such cases often decide not to proceed to the next step of the process. Rather, the parties apparently agree to disagree, and the grievants conclude that no further action on their part would be productive. As a result, the overall cost of the grievance process is reduced.

Feedback from questionnaires provided at the close of mediations reveals that, in many cases, grievants appreciate the mediation forum and feel that they have had an opportunity to be heard in a respectful environment. Agency respondents report that the mediation forum offers them an opportunity to better understand the issues raised by the grievant and to reach an appropriate resolution of the grievant's concerns. At the same time, the process provides the grievant with a better understanding of the rationale behind actions taken by the agency. Thus, mediation often works to improve the workplace atmosphere, regardless of whether or not the grievance at issue is settled.

Conflict Resolution with Local Government Employees: The Use of Mediation in Guilford County's Disciplinary and Grievance/Complaint Procedures

Guilford County has a program that is an excellent example of local government's use of conflict resolution. The County revised its personnel regulations to incorporate mediation as an option within both its disciplinary policy and its grievance/complaint resolution policy for employees. The program's goal is to offer a mediation service to employees, teams, supervisors, and managers to help resolve workplace disputes before they result in lost productivity, decreased morale, disciplinary action, or lawsuits. The mediation process is voluntary and can be requested by either an employee or a supervisor. It emphasizes personal responsibility and encourages individuals to move from an adversarial mode to a problem-solving mode, with the goal of forging lasting resolution of conflicts. Working with Carolina Dispute Settlement Services, Guilford County created the program, provided mediation training to selected employees, and implemented the mediation options.

THE DISCIPLINARY POLICY

Guilford County's disciplinary policy sets out the responsibilities of County management and supervisory staff. It specifies that a progressive disciplinary process is designed to assist supervisors in facilitating the professional growth and development of employees. Supervisors and employees are encouraged to work together to establish and communicate reasonable job expectations, to encourage employees to rely on supervisors for assistance, to empower supervisors to address issues as they arise, to handle problems as informally as possible, and to promote open communication.

Supervisors in Guilford County government are encouraged to coach an employee as a first step in addressing unsatisfactory job performance or unacceptable personal conduct. But coaching is not considered disciplinary action. Disciplinary action can be taken only with just cause, which is defined as unsatisfactory job performance or unacceptable personal conduct. When an incident arises that could result in a finding of just cause, the supervisor must investigate and take appropriate disciplinary action. For a serious incident of unacceptable personal conduct, a supervisor has the authority to move directly to any level of disciplinary action that is appropriate, up to and including dismissal.

The first step of disciplinary action is a written warning, and guidance is provided on how to craft and administer an effective warning. If a supervisor determines that severe disciplinary action is warranted, the available options are: disciplinary suspension without pay for a minimum of one and a maximum of five calendar days; disciplinary demotion; or dismissal. There are conditions that must be met prior to issuing severe disciplinary action, depending on whether the problem involves personal conduct or job performance. A supervisor must always discuss the recommendation for discipline with each person in the chain of command. If management determines that severe disciplinary action is warranted, the Guilford County Director of Human Resources is notified to discuss whether the employee will be offered an opportunity to utilize the mediation process.

If the supervisor, the appointing authority (typically the employing agency), and the Human Resources Director determine that the matter could be resolved in mediation, the supervisor offers the employee the opportunity to request mediation prior to the Pre-Disciplinary Conference. The employee is provided with a written description of how mediation works. If the mediation produces resolution, a mediation agreement is written and signed by the parties. If there is no resolution, management proceeds with the Pre-Disciplinary Conference. If discipline is implemented, an eligible employee has access to an appeal process that utilizes a three-member review panel. The panel conducts a hearing and submits findings to the Human Resources Director, who then forwards the recommendation to the appointing authority. The appointing authority makes a final decision on behalf of the County. Further appeal rests with the Superior Court.

THE GRIEVANCE/COMPLAINT RESOLUTION POLICY

Guilford County wanted to provide a grievance process through which any employee could request mediation to discuss an employment matter. An "employment matter" is defined as a condition of employment, working conditions, pay administration, and training. It does not include disciplinary action or performance appraisal ratings.

The employee initiates the process by completing a complaint resolution form describing the particular grievance and indicating whether the employee is willing to participate in mediation. The Human Resources Director reviews the complaint to determine if the matter is eligible for resolution under the grievance procedure and if it is appropriate for mediation. If mediation is an option, the employee is notified, and the supervisor has five days to decide if he or she is willing to participate in mediation. If both parties are willing to mediate, the Human Resources Director schedules the mediation. After the mediation process is complete, both parties are provided with written documentation of the outcome.

If the parties decline to participate in mediation or if mediation is deemed not appropriate, the supervisor reviews the complaint, meets with the employee, and attempts to resolve the issue at the lowest practical level.

The Use of ADR in the University of North Carolina Health Care System

In 1999, the University of North Carolina Health Care System (UNC Health Care), in collaboration with Carolina Dispute Settlement Services, created two programs that can be utilized by employees to resolve conflict within the workplace. When problems or conflicts arise, UNC Health Care encourages employees to find informal means to resolve matters as quickly as possible. Mediation is available and is encouraged as a viable option for all. All employees, regardless of role, have the right to participate in the procedure without interference, coercion, restraint, discrimination, or reprisal.

THE MEDIATION PROGRAM

The mediation program was established to provide for the expeditious and orderly resolution of workplace conflicts. Mediation is an optional process available to all full-time and part-time permanent employees, including probationary employees. A Mediation Coordinator, who works within UNC Health Care's Employee Relations Office, administers the program. Either party to a dispute may initiate access to the mediation program with the other party or through the Mediation Coordinator. Administrators, managers, supervisors, employee relations staff, employee assistance program representatives, or the Equal Employment Opportunity officer may also make a referral to mediation when an employee raises a concern. The Mediation Coordinator selects one or more mediators from a group of trained mediators employed by UNC Health Care. The mediators may not work in the same department or division as the disputants and may not be friends or acquaintances of either party.

Mediations are scheduled by the Mediation Coordinator and are to be conducted as quickly as possible. The mediation is confidential. Although the mediation team may make notes during the process, at the end of the mediation all notes are to be destroyed. Either party may withdraw from the mediation process at any time, for any reason. The mediator has the authority to discontinue the mediation and declare an impasse, after assuring that the parties have had an opportunity to discuss the issues and after determining that further discussion would not be productive.

If the parties reach resolution, a written agreement is made and signed by the parties to serve as a written record of the mediation. The agreement may not contain provisions contrary to UNC Health Care policy or any state law or policy. It may not bind UNC Health Care to anything beyond its authority or control. It cannot be transferred to another state agency and cannot provide any benefit that would constitute preferential treatment of the employee. The Mediation Coordinator reviews the agreement prior to signing to assure conformity with relevant policies and law, and he or she keeps a copy of the document. The agreement is considered binding. Breach of an agreement by either party can result in corrective action, including termination from employment, pursuant to UNC Health Care System policies and procedures. If the mediation does not result in resolution, the Mediation Coordinator notifies the Director of Employee Relations.

THE GRIEVANCE RESOLUTION PROCEDURE

The Grievance Resolution Procedure involves a three-step process that utilizes multiple conflict resolution models. The UNC Health Care Employee Relations Department administers the grievance procedure with the assistance of Carolina Dispute Settlement Services, which provides administrative services. The goal is to offer a fair, orderly, and prompt resolution of conflicts that arise between employees, or between employees and anyone who is in a position of authority.

All UNC Health Care System employees who have completed their probationary period and are not employees "at will" are eligible to use the procedure. Probationary employees have only limited access to the procedure, depending on the nature of their grievance. All employees may utilize the process for employment discrimination or harassment claims based on any of the following grounds: protected and defined status; retaliation for protesting alleged violations of equal opportunity employment; retaliation for reporting violations of hospital policy; and violations of employment opportunity posting requirements. Non-probationary employees may also use the process to contest dismissal, demotion, suspension without pay, failure to post a job vacancy, alleged inaccurate or misleading personnel file information (but only if connected with a dismissal), demotion or suspension without pay, and denial of employee priority consideration and veteran's preference.

The Process

Step 1: Department Review. The grievant must file the grievance in writing within ten business days of the triggering event. The most senior division executive (or his or her designee) has fifteen business days to meet with and respond to the grievant in writing. The grievant has ten business days from the day of the mailing of the response to file an appeal in writing with the Employee Relations office. The Employee Relations office provides the necessary forms—as well as consultation and interpretation of policies—for both the grievant and the management team. Either party may request a support person for assistance in the process.

Step 2: Investigating Officer and Employee Panel. After the grievant files an appeal, a trained employee is designated as the investigating officer. The investigating officer has five business days to meet with the grievant and then begin an investigation. Within twenty business days, the investigating officer must complete the investigation and submit a fact-finding report to the three-member employee review panel. The employee panel has fifteen business days to meet, to review the information provided, and to present a recommendation to the President of the UNC Health Care System (or to the President's designee). Within twenty days, the President submits a decision to the employee panel and the disputants. Most grievances end at this point.

Step 3: Internal Hearing. The Step 3 internal hearing is limited to terminations, demotions, suspensions without pay, and Equal Employment Opportunity-related issues that are integral to the termination, demotion, or suspension without pay that is the subject of the grievance. The grievant has ten business days from the date of mailing of the President's Step 2 decision to file a written appeal requesting the Step 3 hearing. The issue is limited to the grievance and the relief requested in Step 1. The Step 3 hearing is held before a three-member panel. Two of the panelists are trained employees. The third panelist, who serves as chair, is an arbitrator selected by the parties from a panel provided by Carolina Dispute Settlement Services. The Step 3 hearing is the only step that allows the grievant to be represented by an attorney. If the grievant chooses to be represented by counsel, then UNC Health Care System may also be represented by an attorney. Likewise, if the grievant proceeds without an attorney, then so does the UNC Health Care System. The Step 3 process provides for a pre-hearing conference, discovery orders, an adversarial hearing, and a court reporter. Witnesses may be subpoenaed and sequestered during the hearing. Each party is given an opportunity to give an opening statement, present evidence, cross-examine witnesses, and make a closing statement. There are time limitations built into the process. After the hearing concludes, the panel deliberates privately. The panel chair will prepare a recommended decision that is provided to the Chief Executive Officer of UNC Health Care System within ten business days. The Chief Executive Officer (or that person's designee) must make a final decision within twenty business days.

Strengths of the Program

As designed, the process contemplates that mediation is continuously available during the life of a grievance prior to the final decision of the Chief Executive Officer (or his or her designee) for those issues proceeding to Step 3. In Step 1 and Step 2, the mediation is conducted using a single mediator or a co-mediation model. The mediator or mediators may include an employee of the Human Resources Department and/or an employee trained in mediation from a department different from that of the employee involved in the grievance. If the grievance reaches Step 3, and the grievant requests mediation, then Carolina Dispute Settlement Services will retain a mediator certified by the North Carolina Dispute Resolution Commission to conduct mediated settlement conferences.

One of the strengths of the UNC Health Care System's process is that employees are an integral part of each step. At any step in the process an employee may serve as support person for the grievant or management representative (unless an attorney participates in Step 3). In Step 1, employees serve as co-mediators. In Step 2, the grievance is investigated, and a report is presented to a three-employee panel for review. In Step 3, employees serve as two of the three panel members who hear evidence in the adversarial proceeding, deliberate, and make a recommended decision for consideration. Employees participate in a three-day training program provided by Carolina Dispute Settlement Services and UNC Health Care Human Resources after joining the program. The training teaches basic mediation skills, covers the grievance and mediation procedures, and explores roles and responsibilities.

The North Carolina Agricultural Mediation Program: A Federal ADR Model

Farmers may face a wide array of issues that can give rise to disputes, including problems with credit denials and finance; zoning, land use, and land access; pesticides, pollution, and degradation of land; fish and wildlife protection; and complex matters related to access to resources management through federal aid and assistance. The North Carolina Agricultural Mediation Program (NCAMP), based at the Western Carolina University School of Business, was created to meet the needs of farmers and to help fulfill the school's mission, as announced by then Chancellor John Bardo: to become a "seriously 'engaged university' that works with our region and the state to improve the quality of life for the people we serve—the people of North Carolina."

In August 2006, the United States Department of Agriculture (USDA) certified NCAMP as the mediation service provider in North Carolina to assist in the resolution of disputes between participating USDA agencies and their program participants. Program operations began in 2007, when North Carolina became the thirty-third state to adopt an agricultural mediation program. NCAMP offers convenient, customized, and readily available mediation services to assist North Carolina USDA agencies and their customers in resolving disputes. NCAMP also provides mediators with agricultural and natural resources training to work with North Carolina agencies, farmers, producers, homeowners, and businesses to provide workable alternatives in the resolution of farm-related disputes.

The Mediation of Public Records Disputes

The policy of the State of North Carolina is that documents compiled by the State or its subdivisions are the property of the people and that the people may obtain access to them, unless otherwise specified or provided by law.[1] Conflicts often arise when documents are withheld because of concerns about confidentiality, the sensitive nature of the material included, or some other matter. The 2009 General Assembly adopted mediation as a means of resolving public records controversies. Effective October 2010, North Carolina General Statutes Section 7A-38.3E established that parties embroiled in disputes under the Public Records Laws[2] have the option of agreeing to pre-litigation mediation. This process provides private citizens, journalists, businesses, organizations, and the State and local government entities who seek to resolve public records disputes with an alternative to expensive and time-consuming litigation. After commencement of a civil action to compel disclosure, the law requires that the parties participate in mediation.

Requests for mediation in public records disputes are filed with the clerk of superior court in the county in which the underlying civil action may be brought. Voluntary, pre-litigation mediation may be requested at any time before an action is filed if the parties agree to it. The Administrative Office of the Courts is charged with prescribing the request for mediation form. The party filing the request must mail a copy of the form by certified mail, return-receipt requested, to each party to the dispute. In the case of mandatory mediation, the plaintiff initiates the process by filing a request with the clerk of court no later than thirty days from the filing of responsive pleadings. This time frame affords the parties an opportunity to achieve a speedy resolution of the conflict. In both voluntary and mandatory mediations, the clerk starts the mediator selection process by supplying each party to the litigation with a list of mediators certified by the North Carolina Dispute Resolution Commission.

If the parties agree on a mediator, the clerk appoints the person selected. If they do not agree, the party who filed the request for mediation form has the responsibility of reporting the disagreement to the clerk of superior court. The senior resident superior court judge then selects the mediator. The clerk notifies the parties of the appointment. The statutory provisions for mediated settlement conferences (MSCs) in superior court[3] and the rules and standards adopted pursuant to those statutes control the public records mediation process, except as otherwise expressly provided by law.[4]

The North Carolina Supreme Court may adopt additional rules and standards to implement the mediation process, including an exemption from MSC procedures, for situations in which mediation has already been attempted voluntarily. Waiver of mediation is permitted when the parties inform the mediator in writing. Costs will not be assessed to any party if all parties waive mediation before an initial mediation meeting occurs.[5]

The mediator is required to prepare a certification stating the date on which the mediation was concluded and the general results, including whether the parties waived mediation, whether an agreement was negotiated, whether mediation was attempted but an agreement was not reached, or that one or more parties (to be specified in the certification) failed or refused without good cause to attend the process. The mediator must file the original certification with the clerk and provide a copy to each party.[6]

Alternative dispute resolution to resolve controversies involving access to public records advances the "mandate for open government" and reinforces that the public must have "liberal access" to those records.[7] The General Assembly has entrusted mediators with a crucial role in this area of public disputes resolution and has afforded them an opportunity to improve the efficiency of the civil justice system by promoting more options and better outcomes.

Conclusion

The State of North Carolina has embraced a wide range of ADR procedures to assist in resolving conflicts with its citizens and employees. Many state-run institutions and local governments have followed suit. These procedures allow groups and individuals to take an active role in resolving conflicts and effecting change without resort to costly and time-consuming litigation. They also help foster more openness in government and a more active and involved citizenry, essential components of our democracy.

NOTES

1. N.C. Gen. Stat. § 132-1.

2. *Id.* § 132-1 et seq.

3. *Id.* §§ 7A-38.1 and 7A-38.2.

4. *Id.* § 7A-38.3E.

5. *Id.* § 7A-38.3E(e).

6. *Id.* § 7A-38.3E(f).

7. News & Observer Publishing Co. v. Poole, 330 N.C. 465, 471 (1992) (quoting News & Observer v. State ex. rel. Starling, 312 N.C. 276, 281 (1984)).

CHAPTER TWENTY-SEVEN

North Carolina Public School Systems and Alternative Dispute Resolution Programs

"We all, the most unbelieving of us, walk by faith. We do our work and live our lives not merely to vent and realize our inner force, but with a blind faith and trembling hope that somehow the world will be a little better for our striving."
— United States Supreme Court Justice Oliver Wendell Holmes, Jr., Address at Ipswich, Massachusetts (July 31, 1902).

In recent years, North Carolina lawmakers have amended state laws governing methods by which local public school systems resolve disputes to include alternative dispute resolution (ADR) processes. The legislature has specified that mediation be used in budget disputes between local boards of county commissioners and boards of education, and in the resolution of disagreements concerning special education services provided by local school systems. In 2010, the legislature added provisions mandating the use of mediation in disputes under the Public Records Laws.

This chapter provides a brief explanation of the procedures required by statute and a summary of the various ADR programs employed in school systems across the state. It also describes the development of peer-mediation and conflict-resolution programs in a number of North Carolina schools, colleges, and universities. Many of these programs, developed through the joint efforts of dispute settlement centers and local schools beginning in the early 1980s, continue to serve communities around the state.

Use of Mediation in Funding Disputes Between Local School Systems and County Commissioners

Disputes over funds for public schools are inevitable, given the large sums of money devoted to public education in North Carolina. Nearly all of the funding for public schools in the state comes from two sources: (1) allocations made at the state level by the General Assembly, and (2) funds made available at the local level by boards of county commissioners. State law requires that the superintendent of each local school system prepare a budget sufficient to operate a system of free public education in the county.[1] The budget must be submitted to the local board of education by May 1 of each year. The board of education must formally adopt a budget and present it to the local board of county commissioners by May 15 of each year. The board of county commissioners is required to adopt a budget by July 1 and to determine the amount of county revenues to be appropriated to the school unit for the budget year. The fiscal year for public schools runs from July 1 to June 30.

For several decades prior to 1996, state law allowed any local school board dissatisfied with the county appropriation for the school system to sue the local board of county commissioners in superior court. Under the statute, the parties were required to present their case to the clerk of court before trial. The clerk would issue a ruling, which, in essence, served as a non-binding arbitration award. From that non-binding decision, the parties could proceed to a jury trial, if they desired.

With the advent of the Mediated Settlement Conference Program in superior court in 1992, such funding disputes were diverted to mediation once they reached superior court. In 1993, three such county budget disputes were ordered to be resolved through mediated settlement conferences. Two of them were settled as a result of the mediation process, and the third was later tried and appealed. In 1996, however, the statute setting out the process was changed, taking it out of the normal superior court mediated settlement conference program. The change eliminated the clerk's hearing and set out a mediation procedure required of the parties prior to filing a lawsuit. The statute was modified again in 1997, in large part to redefine the mediator's role.

The Two-Step Mediation Process

Under current law, if a local board of education determines that the amount of money appropriated by the board of county commissioners is insufficient, the chairman of the board of education and the chairman of the board of county commissioners must arrange a joint public meeting of the two boards, to be held within seven days after the board of county commissioners' decision on school appropriations. Before the joint meeting, the boards can agree to select a mediator jointly. If they fail to agree, the senior resident superior court judge must appoint one. There are no restrictions on who can serve as an agreed-upon mediator. The mediator is to preside at the joint meeting and act as a "neutral facilitator of disclosures of factual information, statements of positions and contentions, and efforts to negotiate an agreement settling the boards' differences."[2] The two boards split the cost of the mediator's fees and expenses.

If no agreement is reached at the joint meeting, the mediator must commence mediation within a reasonable period of time, upon request of either board. Members of "working groups" represent the boards in the mediation. These groups include the board chairpersons, attorneys, finance officers, the county manager, and the superintendent of the board of education. State law specifies that the mediation proceedings involving the working groups must be conducted in private. Information disclosed during the proceedings is privileged and confidential. The mediator may not divulge any information about the mediation and may not make any recommendations or a statement of findings.

The mediation must end no later than August 1, unless the boards agree to continue it beyond that date. However, the mediator is empowered to declare an impasse. If no agreement is reached, the mediator must notify the resident superior court judge immediately. Upon a declaration of an impasse, the school board may file an action in the superior court against the board of county commissioners.

Mediator Training

In May 1997, the Institute of Government of the University of North Carolina at Chapel Hill (now the School of Government) held a training session for mediators interested in mediating local public school budget disputes. The training session was co-sponsored by the North Carolina Association of County Commissioners and the North Carolina School Boards Association. The list of mediators who have received such training in public school budget disputes is available from the School of Government, the North Carolina Association of County Commissioners, and the North Carolina School Boards Association.

Success of the Budget Dispute Mediation Program

The public school budget dispute mediation process has led to pre-litigation settlement of disputes in a number of cases. While in the past only a few disputes arose each year, the disputes that did occur were often contentious and always expensive. Since mediation became available, however, some threatened litigation has been resolved through the mediation process. For example, in the summer of 1997, two counties that used the statutory pre-litigation mediation process—Pamlico and Wake—were able to reach agreements. In 1998, Burke, Moore, and Union counties used the budget dispute mediation process to reach settlements in their school funding cases.

The failure of the mediation process in a budget dispute between the county commissioners and the school board in Guilford County in 2000, however, points out some problems with the current program. First, state law does not set forth guidelines as to what constitutes "a free public education." Thus, counties can (and do) spend vastly different sums of money per student, leaving county commissioners free to contend that they are, indeed, providing a free public education to their students. A second problem is that any tentative agreement reached in the private negotiations of the "working groups" must be approved by board members on both sides of the dispute. In counties with a large number of board members, gaining approval can become an unwieldy and time-consuming process, which, at times, can sidetrack or destroy a negotiated settlement. Despite the limited number of disputes resolved and the existence of some impediments to success, the budget dispute mediation program has been beneficial for county governments. The program has been effective in allowing boards of education and boards of county commissioners to resolve differences without the expense of litigation and without jeopardizing the working relationships they must maintain in order to fulfill their duties. According to the School of Government, since 2001, mediation has been scheduled or used under the statute to address budget disputes in the following counties: Beaufort, Bladen, Burke, Cabarrus, Cumberland, Duplin, Graham, Halifax, Iredell, Madison, Moore, Northampton, Pamlico, Pender, Person, Scotland, Union, and Wayne.

Even when a budget dispute is not resolved through mediation it can, in some instances, result in better communication and improved working relationships between the stakeholders. This process can ultimately facilitate the achievement of important goals. Such an outcome was demonstrated in at least two cases mediated in 2004. Following mediation of a budget dispute in Cabarrus County, a bond referendum was submitted and passed to obtain needed funding. In Iredell County, mediation led to the creation of a Joint Facilities Task Force, which helped to improve communication between the Iredell County Board of Commissioners and the Iredell-Statesville Board of Education in developing a facilities plan for the local school district. In both cases, working relationships improved through the mediation process. A study of these 2004 mediations conducted by the School of Government indicates that the parties felt their boards benefited from one-on-one sessions between the stakeholders, with and without the mediator, during the course of the mediation.

Mediation Processes for Special Education

Under federal law, parents of children with special needs have a right to contest the appropriateness of the educational services being provided to their child through a due process action against their local school district. To bring such an action, the child must have a disability identified under the federal Individuals with Disabilities Education Act (IDEA). In North Carolina these due process cases are heard by the Office of Administrative Hearings.

Special education cases are very complex, legally and factually. They inevitably cost a lot of money. Attorneys' fees, expert witness fees, and other expenses tend to add up quickly, resulting in a costly trial. The cases are also emotionally charged on both sides, which can make it very difficult for school systems and parents to work together, as they must, to ensure that the child is educated appropriately.

The Mediation Process

The IDEA, passed by Congress in 2004, requires that mediation be made available to parents challenging decisions related to their child's identification, evaluation, educational placement, or provision of a Free Appropriate Public Education (FAPE). Mediation is strictly voluntary, however, and a school system cannot require a parent to participate. A pre-litigation mediation alternative has long been available to parents of special needs children. In this context, "pre-litigation" means that the mediation occurs before the request for a due process hearing is filed. Prior to 1997, however, this pre-litigation proceeding was limited to mediations conducted by the superintendent (or, by delegation, one of his associate or assistant superintendents). This type of mediation was rarely used, presumably because the mediation was conducted by a school system administrator, who was perceived by parents to be biased.

In 1997, the North Carolina special education mediation provisions were revised to make pre-litigation mediation more attractive to parents, providing that before a request for administrative review of a challenge, the matter could be mediated at the request of either party, if both parties consented and agreed to the selection of a mediator. School systems were required to notify parents of the right to mediation and to pay for the first mediation session. The parties could agree to additional mediation sessions and, unless agreed otherwise, the mediation fees were to be paid by the school system. Parties could also participate in mediation after a request for administrative review was filed, or could agree to use other ADR methods.

The mediation provisions were again modified in 2006 to conform to changes in federal law.[3] The revised statutes provided that special education disputes be mediated before or after a request for formal administrative review if the parties voluntarily agree to the mediation and the mediation is not used to deny or delay the parents' right to a due process hearing. Under the current procedure, upon request for mediation, the Exceptional Children's Division of the North Carolina Department of Public Instruction (DPI) assigns a mediator from its list of qualified individuals who are knowledgeable about special education law. Mediation is free to both parties, provided that they accept the mediator assigned by DPI. If the parties reach an accord through mediation, they must sign a legally enforceable agreement setting forth the terms of their settlement. They may also agree to use other dispute resolution methods.

The federal IDEA regulations issued in 2006 mandated that a resolution session between the parties be held within fifteen days of receipt by the school of the petition for a due process hearing. The parties may waive this requirement (in writing) and go directly to mediation.

Special Education Mediators

In January 1998, the Institute of Government conducted a two-day training session for fifty-three mediators affiliated with the statewide network of dispute settlement centers. With the exception of only a few people, these mediators were not attorneys. The Exceptional Children Division of the North Carolina Department of Public Instruction (DPI) maintains a roster of qualified mediators who are knowledgeable in the law and regulations related to special education and who are trained in resolving special education disputes. DPI provides copies of this list to all school systems in the state. There is a mandatory fifteen-hour training process required for these mediators, which includes instruction in both special education law and the mediation process. There is nothing to prohibit parties from selecting mediators at their own cost who are not on the list.

Results of the Special Education Mediation Program

In recent years, the special education mediation program at DPI has been used more extensively, resulting in earlier resolution of claims to the benefit of all parties. According to published reports from DPI, there were a total of 581 mediation requests received by the agency during the school years 2004–2010. Three hundred and thirty mediations were held. The remaining requests were declined, withdrawn, or pending at the end of a school year. Between 68 and 84 percent of mediations resulted in an agreement during the period. DPI further reports that when mediation is requested in the early stages of a dispute, the settlement success rate is dramatically higher than when mediation is requested after a request for a due process hearing is filed.

Mediation of Anti-Discrimination and Civil Rights Claims for Children with Special Needs

Children with special needs may have claims outside the due process hearing provided by IDEA. Section 504 of the Rehabilitation Act (504) and the Americans with Disabilities Act (ADA) are federal anti-discrimination civil rights statutes that require the needs of students with disabilities to be met as adequately as the needs of the non-disabled. These federal laws sometimes provide an alternate cause of action for children who may not be covered under IDEA. For example, 2009 amendments to this federal legislation expand the definition of disability to be significantly wider than the definition of disability under IDEA. Section 504 claims are pursued through the Local Education Agency (LEA) or through the Office for Civil Rights (OCR). It is worth noting that mediation processes could be sought to help resolve these disputes. However, neither the statutes nor regulations provide for mediation. Therefore, if such a process is voluntarily used, parties must decide on fees and cover their own costs.

Mediation of Public Records Disputes in Public Schools

Two Opportunities for Mediation

The North Carolina General Assembly has provided that, as of October 2010, disputes under the Public Records Laws may be resolved through mediation.[4] Because public schools may receive requests for public records, this new mediation process is worthy of brief consideration in the context of this chapter. (The topic is covered in greater detail in Chapter 26.)

Under the new law, parties have two opportunities to mediate a dispute. Prior to the initiation of a lawsuit, voluntary mediation is available to any party by filing a request for mediation with the clerk of superior court in the county where the lawsuit could be brought. Once a lawsuit is filed, mandatory mediation must be initiated within thirty days of the filing of responsive pleadings. However, even mandatory mediation may be waived if all parties agree and provide the mediator with written notice.

Procedure for Mediations

In both the voluntary pre-litigation mediation and for those subject to the mandatory mediation requirement imposed by the new legislation, the procedure to follow will be established by the rules already in place for the mediated settlement conference in superior court civil actions. A mediation request is filed with the clerk's office in the county in which the underlying civil action may be or already has been brought. The process for selection of a mediator will be the same in both voluntary and mandatory mediations. The clerk supplies a list of certified mediators.

Conflict-Resolution Instruction and Mediation Programs in Public Schools

Today, many public school students are learning an important life skill in America's classrooms: how to resolve disagreements peacefully. They are part of an expanding effort to introduce the concept of nonviolent conflict resolution to public school students across the country. The idea of using alternative means of conflict resolution in schools, which began in 1981, continues to grow.

The North Carolina School Boards Association Policy Manual now includes a policy providing for the development of programs for conflict resolution in schools. The North Carolina General Assembly also recognizes the value of peer mediation and instruction programs as part of a school's basic education program.[5] In addition, the Department of Public Instruction has a lesson plan available on its website for teachers wishing to incorporate mediation skills into the curriculum.

Some History

Elementary schools led the way in the development of conflict-resolution and mediation programs for students and teachers. Such programs now exist in middle schools, high schools, and colleges. These programs typically include instruction and skill-building activities in areas such as anger management, cultural diversity, communication skills, and violence prevention.

In North Carolina, school conflict-resolution instruction and mediation programs were initiated in 1985 by community dispute settlement centers in three counties: Chatham, Buncombe, and Orange. These programs involved schools at a variety of levels: elementary, middle, and high schools in Chatham; a high school in Asheville (Buncombe); and the University of North

Carolina at Chapel Hill (Orange). The remaining sections of this chapter examine the development of these programs and their operations and provide a brief overview of some recent programs making a difference in North Carolina's schools.

Chatham County: Young Conflict Managers

In January 1985, the Chatham County Dispute Settlement Center in Pittsboro, now the Deep River Mediation Center, began an innovative program to train elementary and middle school students to become conflict managers. The program was modeled on a successful initiative by the Community Boards Center for Policy and Training in San Francisco. Its goals were to improve students' communication, problem-solving, and conflict-resolution skills; to improve the social and learning environment of local schools; and to decrease hostility, violence, bullying, and other antisocial behaviors.

Chatham County Dispute Settlement Center Director Alice Phalan made a special effort to include "troublemakers" and "problem kids" in the program and sought to train them to use their capabilities to become decision makers and problem solvers. Participants also represented the demographic composition of the student body in terms of gender, racial, and ethnic identity.

Each student mediator in grades four through eight received twelve hours of training in the skills required to help other students peacefully express and resolve disputes as they occurred on the playground, at lunch, or between classes. After the training, these students—wearing "Conflict Managers" T-shirts or buttons—paired up and patrolled the playground, hallways, and cafeterias to offer their services. The other students were free to accept or reject the assistance.

For example, if a fight broke out during a break, the designated conflict managers asked whether the combatants wished to try to resolve their differences or if they wanted their teacher to intervene. If the combatants were willing to talk over their differences, then the peer mediators would let them each give their side of the story and offer ideas for possible solutions.

The conflict managers were viewed as leaders in the school community in helping others resolve their disputes and stay out of trouble. Anecdotal evidence also showed that the student conflict managers sometimes used their new skills at home as well, when disagreements flared up in the family.

According to Phalan, the conflict managers, when compared to their nontrained peers, were able to communicate their wants and needs far more effectively to parents, teachers, siblings, and friends. The Chatham County director felt they had greater confidence and a more positive self-image.

A follow-up survey showed that most teachers in the Chatham County schools felt they had been able to give students more responsibility and had sent fewer students to the office. The students surveyed said that they noticed an improvement in the atmosphere on the playground and in the classroom and felt a sense of pride in resolving conflicts without adult intervention.

The conflict managers program was funded by grants from the Z. Smith Reynolds Foundation and from the North Carolina Governor's Crime Commission. Similar programs were established in Guilford County and in the Durham city schools in the ensuing years.

"Fuss Busters" in Asheville

In 1986, the Mediation Center in Asheville initiated "Fuss Busters," a program in which all students in grades four through six received training in conflict resolution. Some students then volunteered to continue as peer mediators, working in pairs, as in the Chatham County program. The benefit of extending training to all students soon became evident. Carol Bennett, a teacher in what had been a highly conflicted fourth grade classroom in Asheville, observed that after the students received the training, their major complaint was that there were not enough "fusses to bust." Bennett attributed this lack of conflict to the fact that many students had learned how to better communicate their needs and to work together for a "win-win" outcome.

Asheville and Chatham County: Training Teenage Mediators

Both The Mediation Center in Asheville and the Chatham County Dispute Settlement Center in Pittsboro launched programs to turn high school students into full-fledged volunteer mediators. In Chatham County, the idea was to expand upon the conflict manager program developed for the elementary and middle schools. In these programs, students received more extensive training (fifteen to twenty hours), with additional support provided through classroom presentations on conflict resolution and in-service workshops for teachers and administrators. After receiving training, peer mediators usually worked in pairs for scheduled mediation sessions between students—or between a student and a teacher—rather than patrolling the playground.

With funding from the Asheville City School System, The Mediation Center in Asheville hired Paul Godfrey in September 1985 to work part time to start a mediation program at Asheville High School. The program, called Peers Addressing Conflict Together (PACT), trained sixteen students and five teachers in mediation in its first year and averaged six to ten cases per month. Most of the cases came from in-school suspension. These were kids who had been getting into trouble. Barbara A. Davis, Director of The Mediation Center in Asheville, noted that suspension gives consequences for inappropriate behavior; however, it does not address the underlying conflicts. If two students have a fight, get suspended, and return to school without clearing up the reason they argued in the first place, tensions will continue to boil and the problem will, in all likelihood, escalate. The program gave them an opportunity to talk through their differences and put the conflict to rest. But Paul Godfrey was quick to note that the program's success had not happened overnight. A successful program takes more than two or three months to get going and requires legwork and administrative support.

The Education Committee of the Mediation Network of North Carolina helped community dispute settlement centers provide information about school mediation and has supported the development of programs across the state. In 1990 and 1991, the Committee held week-long symposiums for teachers, principals, and school counselors interested in starting peer counseling and mediation programs in their schools. The Governor's Crime Commission also took a strong interest in peer mediation programs as a way of addressing the growing problem of violence in the schools. Many schools in North Carolina now have peer mediation and/or conflict-resolution programs for students in kindergarten through grade twelve. The twenty-two member centers of the Mediation Network of North Carolina continue to collaborate with school social workers, teachers, and principals to support these programs.

Orange County: Mediating Campus Conflicts

The Orange County Dispute Settlement Center in Chapel Hill began working with students and administrators at the University of North Carolina at Chapel Hill (UNC) to initiate a special conflict-resolution program for students at the university. The idea began in the Office of Student Affairs when Associate Dean Annie Bowden began noticing that the student judicial system was increasingly being asked to rule on personal disputes between students, including a number of roommate squabbles. She began looking for a way to resolve matters that should not be included in the judicial system. Bowden learned that the Orange County Dispute Settlement Center had been working with the Campus YMCA (now the Campus Y) to train students as volunteer community mediators. She thought expanding the program to train more student mediators and to educate the student body about mediation would be valuable in resolving conflicts.

In the summer of 1985, Bowden met with Roy J. Baroff, at the time a trained volunteer mediator and a UNC law student. Together they began working out a plan that eventually grew into a viable campus project. Although the program at UNC is currently less active, it helped spawn a number of other programs across the state that continue to promote collaborative problem solving on campuses.

In the early 1990s, several North Carolina law schools—including Wake Forest, Duke, and UNC—began offering mediation and conflict resolution courses and workshops. There are now campus mediation programs with coursework and internship options for undergraduates and graduate students at a number of North Carolina colleges and universities, including Guilford College, Wake Forest University, Duke University, the University of North Carolina at Asheville, Fayetteville State University, the University of North Carolina at Greensboro, North Carolina Central University, and North Carolina A&T State University. UNC-Greensboro offers both a master's degree and a certificate in Conflict and Peace Studies.

Recent Developments

BUNCOMBE COUNTY PROGRAMS

Several new youth programs are now available in Buncombe County to resolve conflicts and teach problem-solving skills to students. There are also new training opportunities for school faculty and community youth workers in mediation. Local social services, law enforcement, and state agencies in the county have begun a youth program called "Changing Together" to help prevent gang violence. "Life Skills" is another conflict-resolution and communication-skills program helping teens and their parents solve problems. Staff at R. J. Reynolds High School are partnering with the Buncombe County Mediation Center to train up to twenty-five students and ten interested staff members in mediation during the summer. This program is supported by a Paddison Grant from the Buncombe County Schools Foundation. The goals of the program are to reduce the number of out-of-school and in-school suspensions and to create an alternative to detention. It would seem that conflict resolution is now a way of life in Buncombe County.

GUILFORD COUNTY SCHOOLS

In the spring of 2009, the Guilford County School District established peer mediation programs in nine middle schools as part of its strategic plan and character education initiative. One of the goals of the program is to de-escalate rumor-fueled arguments before they turn into fights. The program also aims to develop leadership and conflict-resolution skills in these young students. About 270 students throughout the school district have been trained as mediators. Guilford College's Department of Peace and Conflict Studies assisted with their training. Hairston Middle School in Greensboro started with seventeen trained mediators. By the fall of 2010, administrators at the school attributed a drop in suspensions to the program.

Charlotte-Mecklenburg Schools: Character Education and Peer Mediation

In 2010 the North Carolina Department of Public Instruction sent representatives to observe a character-education and peer-mediation program at work in one Charlotte-Mecklenburg School. At Beverly Elementary School, fourth and fifth graders are learning to be peer mediators. The mediators listen to each side of a dispute, help students resolve the problem, and shred their materials at the end of each session. The young mediators indicated that they want school to be a better place to learn and to help put an end to bullying, which some had experienced themselves. One day the program might serve as a model for a statewide initiative by the Department of Public Instruction.

Success of Peer Mediation

Since 1985, hundreds of students and teachers across North Carolina have received instruction in peer mediation and/or conflict resolution. In the last decade, such programs have expanded to include conflict-resolution games and activities for children in the lower elementary grades, as well as in-depth courses and internships for graduate and professional students in business, law, and related fields. As a result of the groundwork laid by dispute settlement centers in Durham, Brevard, Asheville, Chapel Hill, Pittsboro, Alamance County, and Guilford County, many school districts have launched district-wide programs and have undertaken the ongoing development of school mediation instruction. The recent development of the programs in Buncombe, Charlotte-Mecklenburg, and Guilford counties confirms that mediation continues to make a difference in schools and communities around the state. Students fortunate enough to receive mediation instruction have learned lessons not found in textbooks and have acquired skills that will serve them well in their homes, workplaces, and communities. North Carolina schools and communities continue to benefit from the efforts of these young mediators to make school a better place to learn.

NOTES

1. N.C. Gen Stat. § 115C-427.
2. *Id.* § 115C-431.
3. *Id.* § 115C-109.4.
4. *Id.* § 7A-38.3E.
5. *Id.* § 115C-81.

CHAPTER TWENTY-EIGHT

ADR in the North Carolina State Bar Attorney-Client Fee Dispute Resolution Programs

"The [North Carolina] State Bar, pursuant to its authority to 'formulate and adopt rules of professional ethics and conduct' and to 'arbitrate disputes concerning legal fees,' clearly had the authority to adopt rules requiring members of the legal profession to participate in good faith in a fee dispute resolution program as a precondition for initiating litigation against clients for the purpose of attempting to collect unpaid legal fees...."
—Cunningham v. Selman, 325 N.C. 699 (2009).

According to the North Carolina State Bar Rules of Professional Conduct, Rule 1.5(f), any lawyer having a dispute with a client regarding a fee for legal services must "(1) make reasonable efforts to advise his or her client of the existence of the North Carolina State Bar's program of fee dispute resolution at least thirty days prior to initiating legal proceedings to collect the disputed fee; and (2) participate in good faith in the fee dispute process if the client submits a proper request." The rule creates an affirmative duty, imposed upon all attorneys licensed to practice law in the State of North Carolina.

Fee Dispute Resolution Program of the North Carolina State Bar

The North Carolina State Bar, a regulatory body authorized to govern the conduct of all licensed attorneys within the state, has utilized alternative dispute resolution (ADR) since 1993, when the State Bar Council approved rules instituting non-binding arbitration as a means to resolve fee disputes between attorneys and their clients. In 2000, the program was amended to provide for mediation of these disputes.

In the following years, staff representing the Attorney-Client Assistance Program—Fee Dispute Resolution (ACAP) followed a dispute resolution procedure that was actually a hybrid between mediation and neutral evaluation. They facilitated negotiations, conducted independent investigations, and made recommendations about how the disputes might be resolved. Due to limitations on personnel and time, mediations often were carried out by telephone with individual parties rather than in person, as originally contemplated by the program rules. In October 2009, a subcommittee of the State Bar's Program Evaluation Committee recommended approval for publication of proposed amendments to clarify the functions and operations of the fee dispute program.

New rules amended the program in March 2010 to provide for a "facilitation" process whereby North Carolina State Bar staff "assist the parties to resolve a fee dispute to the satisfaction of the parties involved." Not all fee disputes justify selection for the facilitation process.[1]

Petition and Response

Once a complainant contacts the North Carolina State Bar's Fee Dispute Resolution Program, he or she receives a written notice that the program is "limited in nature" and deals only with issues involving fees charged for the legal services provided. In cases in which the legal fees appear to the facilitator to be "excessive for the legal services provided" or if "the fees appear to have been earned but are not paid, an attempt at resolution will be made." The complainant is provided with a form, "Petition for Resolution of a Disputed Fee." The existence and content of the petition, including the lawyer's responses, are confidential. After a screening process, the case is assigned to a facilitator, who is an employee of the North Carolina State Bar. The facilitator notifies the attorney and provides a copy of the petition to the attorney, who must respond within fifteen days.

Facilitation Process

After an investigation, the facilitator conducts a settlement conference between the parties. Importantly, the facilitator is authorized to carry out the settlement conference by separate telephone calls with each of the parties or by conference call, depending upon which method the facilitator believes has the greatest likelihood of success. Among other things, the facilitator is required to inform the parties of the differences between a facilitated settlement conference and other forms of conflict resolution, that he or she is not a judge, and that the procedure is not a trial. The parties are also informed that the conference does not deprive them of any right they would otherwise have to pursue resolution through the court system if they do not reach a settlement. The facilitator has a duty to be impartial and to advise all participants of any circumstance that might cause either party to conclude that the facilitator has a possible bias, prejudice, or partiality.

The conference ends if a settlement is reached or if the facilitator determines that the dispute cannot be resolved by settlement and that an impasse has been reached. The facilitator must prepare a disposition letter to be sent to all parties. The letter contains the terms of the settlement or explains that the conference resulted in an impasse.

The Vice-Chairperson of the State Bar Grievance Committee reviews the facilitator's disposition letter. The Vice-Chairperson determines whether there is probable cause to believe that the respondent/attorney is guilty of misconduct justifying disciplinary action and, if so, refers it to the full Grievance Committee for a determination. If the facilitator believes that legal fees appear to have been earned and do not appear to be clearly excessive for the legal services provided, the facilitator refers the matter to the Vice-Chairperson for review and dismissal. If the Vice-Chairperson agrees that the fee dispute should be dismissed, the facilitator prepares a letter for the Vice-Chairperson's signature informing the parties that the fee dispute petition is dismissed.

District Bar Fee Dispute Resolution Programs

The State Bar Rules permit local judicial district bars to establish a different District Bar Fee Dispute Resolution Program, subject to the approval of the North Carolina State Bar Council.[2] An approved "judicial district bar fee dispute resolution program has jurisdiction over disputes that would otherwise be addressed by the State Bar's ACAP department."[3] These local programs must be offered without cost and must comply with the jurisdictional requirements set out in the rules for the State Bar program.[4] The district judicial bar programs are specifically authorized to use arbitration to resolve fee disputes and may accommodate local conditions provided they comply with the jurisdiction rules. The lawyer named in the petition must "attend a settlement conference." There is a requirement that any agreement be reduced to writing and signed by the parties (and their counsel, if any) if they reach an agreement.[5]

Conclusion

The North Carolina State Bar was formed to regulate the legal profession, to promote reform in the law and in judicial procedure, and to promote the spirit of cordiality and unity among members of the Bar. Considering these goals and the role of North Carolina attorneys in making alternative dispute resolution a reality in our legal system, it is entirely appropriate for members of the bar to use ADR tools to settle their own disputes with clients.

NOTES
1. 27 N. C. Admin. Code § 01D.0700 *et seq.*
2. *Id.*§ 01D.0710.
3. *Id.*
4. *See Id.* § 01D.0702.
5. *Id.* § 01D.0711.

ADR IN NORTH CAROLINA'S FEDERAL COURTS

CHAPTER TWENTY-NINE

Mediation in the United States Bankruptcy Courts of North Carolina

"Parties who must or wish to interact on a regular basis in the future benefit greatly from consensual conflict resolution."
—Note, *Mandatory Mediation and Summary Jury Trial: Guidelines for Ensuring Fair and Effective Processes,* 103 Harv. L. Rev. 1086, 1092 (1990).

Formal mediated settlement procedures have been used in North Carolina's bankruptcy courts since the mid-1990s. The implementation of the mediation process has proceeded more slowly in bankruptcy courts than in other court systems, largely because the economic realities of bankruptcy lead attorneys to favor informal negotiation over litigation, resulting in a higher rate of settlements. Nevertheless, mediation has proven to be most helpful in resolving certain types of bankruptcy cases, particularly those cases involving multiple competing claims or situations in which clients have been unwilling to negotiate.

Authority for the Use of Mediation in Bankruptcy Court

In recent years, the bankruptcy courts' authority to promulgate mediation procedures and require litigants to use them has been recognized. Such authority derives most directly from Federal Rule of Bankruptcy Procedure 7016, which, by incorporating Federal Rule of Civil Procedure 16, authorizes bankruptcy courts to use "special procedures to assist in resolving . . . dispute[s] when authorized by statute or local rule."[1] Drawing on Rule 7016, the bankruptcy courts for the Eastern and Middle Districts of North Carolina have adopted local rules establishing mediation procedures in their respective districts.

Other sources of authority are available to support the bankruptcy courts' requirement that parties engage in mediation, even in districts that have yet to adopt a local rule addressing the issue. These include: (1) the inherent authority of courts to manage their own dockets; (2) statutes encouraging and expressly authorizing the federal district courts to use methods of alternative dispute resolution; and (3) the broad equitable powers recognized by Section 105 of the Bankruptcy Code.

Under the doctrine of inherent authority, federal courts are allowed to control their caseloads by promulgating mandatory pretrial procedures, including forms of non-binding alternative dispute resolution. The courts' use of this power is limited, however, by the litigants' own constitutional rights, including the right to due process of law. These constitutional limits prevent the court from coercing a settlement through binding alternative dispute resolution, or from adopting procedures that would impose undue burdens or delays on the parties.

The inherent authority assumed by the bankruptcy courts is bolstered by provisions in the Bankruptcy Code granting the courts the equitable power to "issue any order, process or judgment that is necessary or appropriate to carry out the provisions" of the Code and to prescribe "such limitations and conditions as the court deems appropriate to ensure that the case is handled expeditiously and economically."[2] These statutes implicitly authorize bankruptcy courts to submit disputes to mediation and to promulgate procedures for doing so.

Finally, the power of the federal court to establish and employ mediation procedures has been recognized by Congress. The Alternative Dispute Resolution Act of 1998 (ADR Act)[3] authorizes the federal district courts to implement alternative dispute resolution procedures. Bankruptcy courts are given passing mention in the ADR Act and, as units of the district courts, arguably have derivative authority to act in accordance with the policies expressed in the statute.

Current Procedures in North Carolina's Bankruptcy Courts

Eastern District of North Carolina

In 1997, the United States Bankruptcy Court for the Eastern District of North Carolina adopted Local Rule 9019-2, which allows the court to require parties to attend a pretrial mediated settlement conference in any adversary proceeding pending before the court. Before adopting Local Rule 9019-2, the Eastern District had implemented an experimental mediation program based on the Rules of the North Carolina Supreme Court Implementing Statewide Mediated Settlement Conferences in Superior Court Civil Actions (MSC Rules). The experimental program authorized the bankruptcy administrator (or a qualified member of his or her staff) to conduct mediated settlement conferences at no charge to the parties. Under the Guidelines Governing Mediated Settlement Conferences in Bankruptcy Court Actions for the Eastern District of North Carolina (Guidelines), two mediation scenarios were possible: the parties could request a mediated settlement conference, or the bankruptcy judge could recommend that the parties attempt mediation before trial. The Guidelines did not provide that mediation could be ordered by the court, but the court found other sources for this authority in certain cases.[4] The experimental program and its Guidelines were supplanted by the mediation process codified in Local Rule 9019-2.

Like the experimental program in the bankruptcy court, Eastern District Local Rule 9019-2 is modeled on the mediated settlement conference program used in North Carolina's state superior courts. The court may, by written order, require parties to attend a pretrial mediated settlement conference in any adversary proceeding or contested matter. If a mediated settlement conference is ordered, the parties have fourteen days to file a motion asking the court to dispense with the conference. If mediation is not ordered by the court, any party may file a motion requesting a mediated settlement conference.

To select a mediator, the plaintiff (or movant in a contested matter) must file a notice within fourteen days after the order referring the case to mediation. The bankruptcy court does not currently provide its own form for this purpose; thus, most parties base their submission on the corresponding Designation of Mediator form used in state court. If the parties are unable to agree on a mediator, the plaintiff (or movant in a contested matter) must file a motion for court appointment of a mediator indicating the parties' inability to designate a mediator. A mediator will be appointed by the court if the parties are unable to agree or if the notice indicating the selection of a mediator is not received within fourteen days after the court's order.

The mediated settlement conference may be held in any United States bankruptcy courthouse (or in any other public building) in the Eastern District. The order directing the case to mediation will set a date for the completion of the conference, which will generally fall well before trial but after the parties have had a reasonable time to conduct discovery. The court may extend the date for completion of the conference. The mediator may also call a recess in the conference and set the date on which it will reconvene.

The actual procedure for conducting a mediated settlement conference under Local Rule 9019-2 is virtually identical to the procedure used in the North Carolina superior courts. The role and functions of the mediator, as well as the duties imposed on parties and attorneys, are similarly modeled on the state court procedure.

As in state court, if the parties cannot reach a settlement, the mediator declares an impasse and the matter proceeds to trial. If the conference results in a settlement, the parties are required to reduce its terms immediately to a signed, written agreement. The mediator is to file a Report of Mediator with the court within two weeks of the conclusion of the conference or upon receipt of a copy of a written settlement agreement, whichever occurs first. Unless the agreement is confidential, the mediator shall attach the written settlement agreement to the Report. Currently the Eastern District's local rule is displaced by Bankruptcy Rule 9019, which provides that settlements involving the estate must be approved by the bankruptcy judge after a hearing and notice to the bankruptcy administrator, all creditors, and the debtor.[5] For this reason, the parties' agreement cannot be self-executing, but must be placed before the bankruptcy judge in conjunction with a formal motion to compromise the controversy.

In the absence of a contrary agreement or order, the costs of mediation—including the mediator's compensation—are paid in equal shares by the parties. If the mediator was selected by the parties, Local Rule 9019-2 allows the parties to fix the mediator's compensation. The mediator's fee will be set by the court if the mediator was appointed by the court.

Middle District of North Carolina

In August 2000, the United States Bankruptcy Court for the Middle District of North Carolina added a formal mediation procedure to its local rules, using the same standard numbering convention used by the Eastern District to add a new Local Rule 9019-2 for the Middle District. Before the adoption of the Middle District's Local Rule 9019-2, the bankruptcy judges in the Middle District had relied on other sources of authority to refer a few selected cases to mediation (with the consent of the parties).

Like the Eastern District, the Middle District used the MSC Rules as the model for its Local Rule 9019-2. As a result, the structure and contents of the Middle District's local rule are similar to the Eastern District's local rule. In the Middle District, however, the parties may, within fourteen days of the court's mediation order, move the court to authorize some other settlement procedure in lieu of a mediated settlement conference, as long as all parties consent. Another difference in the Middle District is that when the parties select a mediator, the mediator must be certified under the MSC Rules, whereas in the Eastern District this is no longer required. The parties do have the right to nominate a non-certified mediator, but such a candidate must be approved by the court. To select a mediator, the plaintiff must file a written Designation of Mediator form within twenty-one days after the order referring the case to mediation.

A significant difference between mediation practice in the two districts is found in Local Rule 9019-2(d)(3), which, in the Middle District, requires the mediator to prepare a written draft of any settlement terms before the conclusion of the conference and requires the parties, within seven days, to submit a formal, executed, written settlement agreement to the mediator. The mediator is to attach a copy of the agreement to the Report of Mediator.

The clerk of the court is directed to maintain a directory of state-certified mediators available for mediation in the Middle District bankruptcy court. To safeguard the neutrality of the bankruptcy judge, communications concerning mediated settlement conferences are to be addressed to the bankruptcy administrator, not to the court itself. If the mediator fails to fulfill the duties outlined in Local Rule 9019-2(f), the court may withhold future appointments.

Western District of North Carolina

At the time of publication, the United States Bankruptcy Court for the Western District of North Carolina has not adopted a local rule establishing formal procedures for mediation. However, the Western District has referred cases to mediation on a few occasions, relying on sources of authority other than local rules. In these cases, the proceedings have been governed by the procedures adopted by the United States District Court for the Western District of North Carolina pursuant to the ADR Act. Like the local rules adopted in the Eastern and Middle District bankruptcy courts, the Western District court's mediation procedures are modeled on the MSC Rules.

Conclusion

By allowing parties to voice their concerns and participate in reaching a solution, mediation can help resolve otherwise intractable disputes in bankruptcy cases. Mediation is particularly useful when the parties must continue working together after a case is closed. Recognizing these advantages, the bankruptcy courts in North Carolina, particularly in the Eastern and Middle Districts, have begun to encourage the use of mediation in certain cases.

NOTES

1. Fed. R. Civ. P. 16(c)(2)(I).

2. 11 U.S.C. § 105(a), (d).

3. 28 U.S.C. §§ 651–658.

4. *See* In re Rose's Stores, Inc., No. 93-01365-5-ATS (Bankr. E.D.N.C. April 11, 1994) (Section 105(d) of the Bankruptcy Code used to order mandatory mediation).

5. Fed. R. Bankr. P. 9019.

CHAPTER THIRTY

United States District Court ADR Programs in North Carolina

"The law must be stable, but it must not stand still."
—Distinguished American legal scholar and educator Roscoe Pound,
An Introduction to the Philosophy of Law (1922).

ADR in the Eastern District of North Carolina

Since the early 1980s, litigants and court personnel of the United States District Court for the Eastern District of North Carolina have experimented with various alternatives to traditional litigation. These alternate approaches to resolving disputes have been many and varied. The Local Rules of Practice and Procedure of the United States District Court for the Eastern District of North Carolina (adopted in 1993 and later amended) contain a section devoted to alternative dispute resolution (ADR),[1] developed in response to the Civil Justice Reform Act of 1990 (CJRA).[2]

History

Faced with heavy civil and criminal dockets by the early 1980s, the Eastern District began to seriously consider various alternative dispute resolution processes. The criminal docket took precedence because of the Speedy Trial Act of 1974, which establishes time limits for completing the various stages of a federal criminal prosecution. The civil docket was reduced with a combination of firm trial dates and assignment of civil cases to United States magistrate judges. Motions, pretrial conferences, and trials frequently were assigned to magistrate judges. The district judges encouraged the magistrate judges to discuss settlement with counsel at pretrial conferences and motion hearings. Attorneys liked the opportunity for early settlement intervention and soon began requesting settlement conferences. In addition, in the late 1980s, the Eastern District experimented with summary jury trials in several large and complex cases, building on the work of federal district courts in Ohio and California.

In 1993, the court codified the practice for conducting court-hosted settlement conferences in the Eastern District's Local Rules as part of a Civil Justice Expense and Delay Reduction Plan. Responding to the CJRA, the court formed a Civil Justice Reform Advisory Group consisting primarily of attorneys practicing in federal court. The Advisory Group considered six methods of alternative dispute resolution: early neutral evaluation, mediation, arbitration, court-hosted settlement conferences, mini-trials, and summary trials. As part of the Advisory Group's Report and Recommended Plan, the Advisory Group recommended three forms of alternative dispute resolution: court-hosted settlement conferences, summary trials (jury and non-jury), and mediated settlement conferences. The court adopted the Advisory Committee's alternative dispute resolution recommendations as part of the Local Rules. The Local Rules adopted provided for court-hosted settlement conferences, mediation, and summary jury trials.

Effective June 27, 2008, the court adopted a revised set of local ADR rules. The revisions were prepared by the ADR Subcommittee of the court's Local Rules Committee. The most significant change in the 2008 amendments was to make mediation mandatory in most civil cases. The rules continued to provide for court-hosted settlement conferences and summary trials, although the terms relating to them were updated and otherwise revised. The Rules make clear that the express provision for these three ADR techniques is not intended to exclude the use of other ADR procedures, as appropriate, that the parties or the court may suggest.

Mediated Settlement Conferences

The mediation program in the Eastern District is based on that in the Middle District of North Carolina. The Eastern District used the program in the Middle District of North Carolina as a model because doing so promoted uniformity between the districts and the Middle District program has proven itself to be successful.

In the Eastern District (as in the Middle District), mediations are conducted much as they are in the Superior Courts of North Carolina, and the related court procedures are similar. There are, however, notable differences reflecting unique attributes of the federal forum and other factors. For example, mediations in the Eastern District must be held during the discovery period unless the court specifically orders otherwise. As a further example, while the parties are encouraged to select their own mediators, if they cannot agree on a selection, the clerk in the Eastern District appoints the mediator from a list of certified mediators the clerk maintains.

Because it is usually mandatory, mediation is the most frequently used formal ADR procedure in the Eastern District. And it has proven successful. Close to 50 percent of mediated cases settle at or immediately after the mediated settlement conference.

Court-Hosted Settlement Conferences

Court-hosted settlement conferences may be requested by the parties or ordered by the court on its own initiative. They are generally to be held after discovery and the ruling on any motions for summary judgment. The rationale for this timing is to reserve court-hosted settlement conferences for those cases in which any mediation has proven unsuccessful and the direct involvement of a judge in the settlement process is warranted. But there can be reasons to hold a court-hosted settlement conference earlier, including, in pro se cases, the need to avoid the expense of a mediator.

Court-hosted settlement conferences in the Eastern District proceed much like mediations, except that the neutral is a judge, typically a magistrate judge not otherwise assigned to the case. Advantages that a court-hosted settlement conference can offer include the absence of the cost of a mediator, as previously mentioned, and the judge's familiarity with federal procedure and federal causes of action. In addition, a judge has greater freedom than a mediator to express his or her opinions regarding the merits of a case, and the opinions of a judge can, in the eyes of some parties and some attorneys, be uniquely persuasive.

Further, as former Magistrate Judge Alexander B. Denson of the Eastern District has observed, having the opportunity to tell a judge about their case, as at a settlement conference, can be a critical factor in the willingness of some litigants to settle:

> The thing that you have to be aware of for ADR to be effective is a very real need that parties have for their day in court, particularly in a tort or employment discrimination case. People who have been wronged in their view have a need to tell the judge about that. They do not want . . . their case . . . [to] go away until they tell the judge. During Court-hosted settlement conferences, particularly in ex parte conferences, I encourage the litigants themselves to say anything they want to tell me, get it off their chest. It is amazing to me how often they just have a need to pour out their hearts about how they have been wronged, and they just have to say that to the judge.[3]

While mandatory mediation has supplanted the court-hosted settlement conference as the most frequently used formal ADR procedure in the Eastern District, the court-hosted settlement conference continues to be used extensively, both at the request of the parties and on the court's initiative. The continued use of this procedure is testament to its continued effectiveness in resolving cases.

Summary Trials

The distinguishing feature of the summary trial is that evidence is presented not by live witnesses, but by counsel who summarize the testimony their witnesses would present. Strict time limits are also an important feature of most summary trials. The results of summary trials in the Eastern District are not binding unless the parties agree to it. The Local Civil Rules provide detailed procedures for summary jury trials and authorize summary non-jury trials employing procedures to be developed on a case-by-case basis.

With Magistrate Judge Denson presiding, the Eastern District made history by hosting the first two summary jury trials in North Carolina. (Former Magistrate Judge Charles K. McCotter of the Eastern District conducted the third.) Magistrate Judge Denson has noted that each of his summary jury trials would have taken four to six weeks to try in the traditional manner, but that each summary jury trial took only a day and a half.[4]

Summary trials have not been used regularly in the Eastern District. Nevertheless, they remain a viable, cost-effective alternative to traditional litigation in appropriate cases.[5] (For a discussion of summary jury trials in North Carolina's state courts, please see Chapter 36.)

Conclusion

The Eastern District pioneered court-hosted settlement conferences as a form of alternative dispute resolution. The process assisted the court in becoming a national leader among federal courts in civil case disposition. In recent years, the Eastern District has implemented a more aggressive and comprehensive ADR program. The Eastern District's tradition of flexibility, individuality, and choice in avenues of dispute resolution should help guide its ADR programs in the future.

ADR in the Middle District of North Carolina: From Court-Annexed Arbitration to Mandatory Mediation

Examining Court-Annexed Arbitration

By 1990, the United States District Court for the Middle District of North Carolina had for more than five years successfully operated a program of non-binding, mandatory arbitration for a portion of the civil cases on its docket. The judges of the court were convinced that the bar and the public accepted court-annexed arbitration as a useful tool in resolving some disputes in lieu of a traditional trial. In 1988, however, the United States Congress began to place limitations on arbitration within the federal courts, setting a $100,000 cap on the size of cases that could be referred to arbitration. It also enacted a provision that certain civil rights cases cannot be included in an arbitration program and established a requirement that all summary judgment motions be ruled upon by the court before arbitration is conducted.[6] The judges of the Middle District concluded that these limitations made court-annexed arbitration less effective in saving time and/or money for litigants. Arbitration had become, in the view of the Middle District, an ADR procedure that was too limited in scope to be of major benefit to the federal courts. The judges, under the leadership of Chief Judge Frank W. Bullock, Jr., began to look at other ADR techniques, particularly mediation.

Civil Justice Reform Act Advisory Group

The Civil Justice Reform Act (CJRA) required the federal district courts to examine their dockets and their procedures for conducting civil and criminal proceedings to determine if costs and delays could be reduced. The Middle District organized a CJRA Advisory Group, chaired by Winston-Salem attorney William K. Davis, to study the court's procedures and to make recommendations. One of the topics addressed by the Advisory Group Report (issued in December 1992) was the matter of alternative dispute resolution procedures. The Advisory Group recommended that the court should continue its arbitration program, but also suggested that the court draft mediation rules modeled on the North Carolina state superior court rules for the pilot mediated settlement conference program. Chairman Davis's group recommended that the mediation rules not be implemented, however, until the state courts had more experience with mediation.

In response to the Report of the Advisory Group, the court issued its own CJRA Plan in November 1993. The court discontinued its arbitration program due to the recently enacted legislative limits on court-annexed arbitration in the federal courts. But, at the same time, the court expressed its belief that mandatory mediation in nearly all civil cases on the docket would be of great benefit to the bar and the public and would reduce costs and delays in federal litigation, just as it had in the pilot mediated settlement conference program in state superior court. The Middle District therefore adopted mediation rules modeled on the state rules.

Mediation

Development

Mediation replaced court-annexed arbitration in 1993 as the court-sponsored alternative dispute resolution program in the Middle District. The court considered, but rejected, a proposal that it become a "multi-door" court, offering an array of procedures ranging from early neutral evaluation to summary jury trials. Instead, the court focused on the most promising dispute resolution technique it had found—mediation—and worked to develop a high level of expertise in that process. Since 1993, the Middle District has offered only one ADR program: mediation.

Since the outset of its program in 1993, the Middle District court has been strongly committed to mediation. The court's motivation in implementing its mediation program was not just to produce more settlements in civil cases, although that clearly has been an important objective. Rather, the court saw mediation as an alternative dispute resolution method that had benefits not available in traditional litigation. These benefits include: (1) enhancing each litigant's sense of participation and self-determination; (2) providing a forum for remedies that could be more creative than those available at trial; and (3) fostering earlier resolutions that could save litigants the expense of full summary judgment briefing or a lengthy trial. The court saw itself as contributing to a beneficial change in the legal culture in North Carolina. In its view mediation was a natural complement to traditional litigation, one that could temper the all-or-nothing risk taking that is a part of a civil trial. (The court also recognized, of course, that some cases cannot be resolved under any procedure short of trial.)

The challenge for the court in 1993 was to ensure that its court-ordered mediation would be of the highest quality. The Middle District intended to implement a large, comprehensive program covering nearly all of its civil cases. The court considered that the mediator would be seen by many litigants, at least in some sense, as a representative of the court. Although this is not strictly true, the court nonetheless would act as sponsor of the mediation program, and the court would order the parties to appear before the mediator. It would be necessary, therefore, for mediators to foster respect for the court as an institution and display attributes that the court would ask of its own judges: courtesy, objectivity, fairness, honesty, and integrity. Clearly, the court's challenge would be considerable in meeting such a high standard.

Quality in mediation can be said to start with the mediator. The court first authorized its existing panel of arbitrators to serve as mediators, in recognition of the outstanding service these attorneys had provided to the court during the arbitration years. Magistrate Judge P. Trevor Sharp and Clerk Joseph "Joe" P. Creekmore attended North Carolina Bar Association programs on mediation in the North Carolina superior courts to assess the level of training and expertise required for state-certified mediators. Magistrate Judge Sharp also attended national mediation seminars to learn more about alternative approaches to mediation. Ultimately, the Middle District adopted mediation rules closely modeled on the state rules, but with particular points of emphasis.[7] To ensure high-quality mediators, the rules of the court emphasize the parties' voluntary selection of a mediator by agreement at an agreed-upon fee. To facilitate subject matter expertise in appropriate cases, the parties may select a mediator who is not on the court's list.

EVALUATION OF THE MEDIATION PROGRAM

The local rules of the Middle District court require periodic evaluation of the mediation program. Mediator surveys conducted since 1993 have shown 99 percent *mediator* satisfaction with the program. An early concern with court-ordered mediation had been that it might be used inappropriately by some attorneys as a discovery tool. But mediator surveys have shown that more than 90 percent of mediators believe that counsel participated in good faith with the objective of obtaining a settlement. Of the *lawyers* who have participated, more than 96 percent approved of the court's mediation program and procedures. Client surveys have shown that more than 80 percent of clients believed that mediation was very helpful or somewhat helpful in resolving their cases, and 94 percent of clients approved or strongly approved of court-ordered mediation in principle.[8] The court closely evaluated the mediation program for a three-year period after its adoption, concluding that not only had the program been well received by the bar and the public, but also that it had strongly contributed to the administration of civil justice in the Middle District.

STATISTICS

In the years since 1993, mediation has proven to be a successful settlement tool under the Middle District's program. Statistics compiled by the court during the two-year period 2009–2010 show that 317 civil cases were assigned to mediation. Of these cases, 124 were settled at mediation, and 51 were settled prior to the scheduled mediation. Eleven mediation cases resulted in civil trials. The remaining mediated cases were resolved on dispositive motions. Thus, approximately 55 percent of the cases assigned to mediation were settled at or prior to the mediated settlement conference.

These statistics confirm that the Middle District's mediation program significantly enhances the court's ability to effectively adjudicate its civil docket.

Conclusion

ADR in the Middle District grew from small beginnings—arbitration of diversity cases under $150,000—to a comprehensive program of mediation of most cases on the civil docket. Arbitration established a foothold for ADR within the court, and its early promise played a critical role in informing lawyers and litigants of the potential benefits of alternative dispute resolution programs. When Congress severely limited the scope of arbitration that could be conducted in the federal courts in 1988, the Middle District began to look for an ADR technique that could have much broader application. The judges selected mediation as the most promising ADR program for the court and focused the resources of the court on creating the highest quality mediation program possible. The result has been a resounding success, and today, after nearly twenty years of experience, the Middle District's mediation program enjoys widespread support from the bench, the bar, and the public.

ADR in the Western District of North Carolina

Early History

In response to the Civil Justice Reform Act of 1990, the United States District Court for the Western District of North Carolina appointed a committee of experienced litigators, law clerks, and clerk of court staff to study the use of ADR in various jurisdictions across the state and around the nation. The committee met in Statesville, Asheville, Charlotte, and other communities in western North Carolina over a period of eighteen months to gather information. The committee also solicited information from the North Carolina Bar Association's Dispute Resolution Committee, which had developed a reputation as a leader in the design and implementation of ADR techniques. By the time the Western District committee was drafting its report to the court, expansion of the federal arbitration program in North Carolina seemed questionable. Meanwhile, the Mediated Settlement Conference (MSC) Program in North Carolina's superior courts was showing positive results. Thus, the committee recommended that the Western District implement an ADR process modeled on the state MSC program. The court moved quickly and, in 1993, adopted an MSC program, one which—with some modifications—remains in place today.

Rules for Proceeding with Alternative Dispute Resolution

The Western District encourages the use of alternative dispute resolution, ordinarily in the form of a mediated settlement conference, for the efficient and orderly resolution of civil cases. Under the Rules of Practice of the United States District Court for the Western District of North Carolina (Western District Local Rules), an MSC is a pretrial, court-ordered conference of the parties to a civil action and their representatives, conducted by a mediator. All parties are required to attend the MSC, unless otherwise ordered by the Court.

The use of alternative dispute resolution in the Western District does not apply to habeas corpus proceedings or other actions for extraordinary writs, appeals from rulings of administrative agencies, forfeitures of seized property, or bankruptcy appeals. The judicial officer may determine, either sua sponte or on application of any party, that any other action is not suitable for ADR, in which case no ADR procedure will be ordered.

The parties file a form, Certification and Report of Initial Attorneys' Conference, indicating their assessment of the usefulness of ADR, their preferred method of ADR, and their opinion of the most advantageous time at which to commence ADR. If the parties fail to submit, or are unable to agree on, a proposed method of ADR, an MSC becomes the default procedure. The parties may select a mediator from a list of mediators certified by the Western District. The parties should be prepared to offer that name to the court at the initial pretrial conference. If the parties do not select or cannot agree on a mediator, the presiding judge or other judicial officer will select the mediator. The presiding judge or other judicial officer will specify the selected ADR method in a Pretrial Order and Case Management Plan, or in an Order for Alternative Dispute Resolution issued shortly thereafter, and order it to begin on a schedule consistent with the responses given by counsel in the Certification and Report.

After entry of the Pretrial Order and Case Management Plan or the Order for Alternative Dispute Resolution, the case proceeds in one of several ways. If an MSC is ordered, it is governed by the Rules Governing Mediated Settlement Conferences in Superior Court Civil Actions promulgated by the North Carolina Supreme Court pursuant to North Carolina General Statutes Section 7A-38 (MSC Rules), and by the supplemental rules set forth in Western District Local Rule 16.3. The Local Rule modifies Rule 3(a) of the MSC Rules, permitting the MSC to be held in an appropriate facility anywhere in the division in which the case is pending.

If an alternative ADR procedure is ordered, it is governed by the Western District Local Rules and by any other procedural rules submitted by the parties and approved by the judicial officer. Rules submitted by the parties must include, in addition to rules regarding the actual proceeding, the following elements: (1) provisions setting a deadline for completion of the proceeding; (2) the location for the proceeding; (3) pre-proceeding submissions; and (4) the method for selection and compensation of a mediator, evaluator, or other neutral to preside over the proceeding. The judicial officer, either sua sponte or on application of any party, may permit exceptions or deviations from the Local Rules.

Supplemental Rules for Mediated Settlement Conferences

In addition to the MSC Rules, the supplemental rules set forth in the Local Rules apply to MSCs in the Western District. Under these rules, no record may be made of any mediation proceedings. Furthermore, all mediated settlement conferences shall be conducted in person, unless leave is otherwise granted by the mediator. Also, the mediator's report required by the MSC Rules must be issued within seven days of the conclusion of the MSC. The mediator may submit his or her report on a form provided by the Western District Clerk of Court (and also available on the Court's website), or by a mediation report form of his or her own devising.

Certified Mediator Database

Mediators are selected in accordance with the MSC Rules. All mediators must have North Carolina certification or, if they are otherwise qualified to mediate by training or experience, may be approved by the presiding judge or other judicial officer. A non-exclusive list of mediators certified to mediate in the Western District is maintained by the Western District clerk's office. Parties should be prepared to select a mediator at the time of the initial pretrial conference. If the parties cannot agree on a mediator, the court will appoint one.

A current list of mediators certified to mediate in the Western District is also available on the court's website. Mediators may obtain a certification form from the court's website, or by contacting the clerk's office.

Judicial Settlement Conference

In the Western District, a judicial officer to whom a case is assigned may at any time order the parties to participate in a judicial settlement conference to be convened by the court. Any party also may file a request for a judicial settlement conference. Except for government attorneys and federal agency parties, attorneys for all parties must be present at the conference, along with the party or a person with full authority to settle all pending claims. Government attorneys are required to bring as much binding authority as is feasible. A knowledgeable representative of a federal agency party who has authority to recommend any contemplated settlement is required to attend the conference, except for good cause shown prior to the date of the conference. Any judicial officer of the district other than the judicial officer to whom the case is assigned for disposition may preside over a judicial settlement conference convened by the court.

Conclusion

Since its inception in 1993, the ADR program in the Western District has helped promote the efficient resolution of many civil cases. Through the years, the Western District has modified its program as the potential for improvement presented itself. Although the parties may select from different forms of ADR, the mediated settlement conference has, in most cases, been the ADR technique of choice in the Western District.

NOTES

1. Local Civil Rules 101-101.3a, EDNC.

2. 28 U.S.C. §§ 471–482.

3. James E. Gates, "ADR in the Eastern District of North Carolina: An Interview with Magistrate Judge Alexander B. Denson," *Dispute Resolution* 2, no. 3 (June/July 1995): 8, also published at http://disputeresolution.ncbar.org/media/5588585/06_1995.pdf.

4. *Id.*

5. For a particularly informative article on summary jury trials, *see* Alexander B. Denson, "The Summary Jury Trial: A Proposal from the Bench," 1995 *Journal of Dispute Resolution* 303.

6. 28 U. S. C. §§ 651–658.

7. *See* LR83.10a–.10g.

8. *See generally CJRA Annual Assessment for the MDNC* (1995).

CHAPTER THIRTY-ONE

The Pre-Argument Mediation Program of the United States Court of Appeals for the Fourth Circuit

"Constitutional guarantees of human rights ring hollow if there is no forum available in fact for their vindication. Statutory rights become empty promises if adjudication is too long delayed to make them meaningful or the value of a claim is consumed by the expense of asserting it. Only if our courts are functioning smoothly can equal justice become a reality for all."

—American Bar Association, *Report of the Pound Conference Follow-Up Task Force*, 74 F.R.D. 159, 167 (1976).

The federal courts of appeals are authorized by Federal Rule of Appellate Procedure 33 to conduct pre-argument mediation conferences to explore settlement prospects, to narrow issues, and to consider other matters that may aid in the disposition of an appeal. The United States Court of Appeals for the Fourth Circuit (Fourth Circuit) established a pre-argument mediation program on August 1, 1994, pursuant to that federal rule and Local Rule 33. The Fourth Circuit program applies to most civil and agency cases in which all parties are represented by counsel on appeal.

If a case is selected for mediation by the Office of the Circuit Mediator, participation is mandatory, but all settlement agreements reached are voluntary. The mediation sessions are conducted by circuit mediators who are trained neutrals employed by the Fourth Circuit. The sessions are usually conducted by telephone, although some sessions may be in person, when beneficial.

In many civil appeals, the court schedules mediation sessions with the attorneys for all parties involved in the case. Although attention may be given to procedural questions and problems raised by counsel, the main purpose of the mediation is to offer participants a confidential, risk-free opportunity to candidly evaluate their case with an informed neutral and to explore possibilities for voluntary disposition of the appeal.

The Office of the Circuit Mediator

The Pre-Argument Mediation Program is administered through the Office of the Circuit Mediator. The Chief Circuit Mediator is Thomas F. Ball of Charlottesville, Virginia. He is assisted by three circuit mediators: Donna Slawson Hart in Durham, North Carolina; Frank C. Laney in Cary, North Carolina; and Edward G. Smith in Duncan, South Carolina. All of the circuit mediators, who are employees of the Fourth Circuit court, are experienced attorneys with special training in alternative dispute resolution techniques.

Case Selection

There are several ways in which cases in the Fourth Circuit are selected for pre-argument mediation. Most civil appeals in which the parties are represented by counsel are automatically referred to a circuit mediator for a conference. Excepted from the screening process are habeas corpus cases and certain agency cases. The mediator may screen out other cases that do not appear amenable to settlement, such as voting district cases or certain types of agency appeals.

Cases may be scheduled for a mediation conference at the request of one or more of the parties. Such requests are kept confidential by the court, but may be disclosed by the requesting party. Requests for a mediation usually are granted in any civil appeal where all parties are represented by counsel. Cases occasionally are referred for mediation by hearing panels just before or after oral argument.

Mediation Scheduling and Format

Nearly all pre-argument mediations are scheduled before briefs are submitted and a case is set for oral argument. Written notice from the court is mailed to each party's representative in advance of the mediation date. Most mediations are conducted by telephone, with the court initiating the calls, but they may be conducted in person with the parties and their representatives present if the circuit mediator determines that it would be convenient and beneficial for everyone.

Most mediations begin with the mediator briefly explaining the mediation process. The focus of discussion usually moves fairly quickly to an explication of the issues on appeal. The purpose of this discussion is not to decide the case or to reach conclusions about the issues, but to understand what the issues are and to evaluate the risks on appeal. The mediator will also inquire whether there are any procedural questions or problems that can be resolved by agreement, such as issues relating to the joint appendix to the briefs or the need for a specially tailored briefing schedule.

Initial mediations typically last an hour or longer. In many cases the discussions go no further. Often proposals are generated that require additional review; thus, it is not uncommon for follow-up discussions to continue for days or weeks. If negotiations continue productively and all parties and the circuit mediator agree, briefing may be postponed for a reasonable time, until negotiations are completed. Follow-up telephone or in-person mediations may be scheduled as necessary, with or without participation by the parties, in order to pursue all chances for a negotiated settlement.

What Participants Can Expect

Participants can expect the circuit mediator to facilitate or lead a thoughtful and sometimes detailed exploration of the case on appeal. The extent of the mediator's preparation varies with the amount of information available at the time of the mediation. The circuit mediator has usually read the district court's opinion, as well as the docketing statement. The circuit mediator typically inquires about settlement and seeks to determine each party's interests (if they are not self-evident). This is usually done in private caucuses with each party. Every effort is made to generate offers and counteroffers until the parties either settle or know that the case cannot be settled. While mediations are relatively informal, they are official proceedings of the court.

What the Court Expects

Court staff attempts to identify lead counsel for all parties when scheduling mediations. This is not always possible, so those notified of the mediation conference are asked to advise the court in advance if other counsel will be attending the mediation.

Mediation demands considerable time and effort from counsel, both in preparation and during the mediation process itself. Attitudes and perceptions of participants often change during the process. Time and effort may be wasted and opportunities for settlement lost if the lawyers participating in the mediation are not the lawyers on whose judgment the client will rely when making decisions. Any perceived tactical advantage in sending an attorney with limited knowledge or authority to the mediation is more than offset by losing the opportunity to influence—or be influenced by—this informed settlement discussion. For this reason lead counsel are asked to attend the mediation and to be prepared to articulate their view of the merits of the case, as well as their clients' interests and needs.

While attorneys should have authority to make and respond to offers, the circuit mediators do not necessarily expect counsel to have absolute settlement authority. In most cases, there is more movement from prior settlement positions than is expected, and further consultation with clients is often required. Counsel may therefore wish to have clients present or available by phone at the time of the mediation.

Mandatory Participation–Voluntary Settlement

Rule 33 of the Fourth Circuit's Local Rules of Procedure requires participation of all parties in scheduled mediations, usually through their counsel and by telephone. Clients are not required to be present at most initial mediation conferences, although the circuit mediator has the authority to compel the physical presence of each party. Sometimes the purposes of the mediation cannot be achieved without the involvement of individuals or groups who are not parties to the appeal. Such parties may be invited to participate.

Under Local Rule 33, counsel must attend (in most cases via telephone) "any scheduled conference." However, mediators are careful not to require participation in multiple conferences where the parties do not appear open to the possibility of settlement, or where there is no other purpose to be served. Follow-up conferences can be conducted by a telephone call to one or more parties, or by a joint conference involving all counsel.

Upon failure of a party or attorney to comply with the provisions of the mediation conference program rules, the court may assess reasonable expenses (including attorneys' fees) caused by the failure to appear. The court may assess all or a portion of appellate costs, dismiss the appeal, or take other appropriate action.

Confidentiality

By rule, nothing said during the mediation by any participants (including the circuit mediator) may be disclosed to anyone in the Fourth Circuit court or any other court that might ever deal with the case. Disclosure to any person other than those participating in the mediation process, either directly or indirectly, is also prohibited. This rule of confidentiality is broader than that employed in most mediation settings, since it prohibits disclosure—even by the parties—to anyone outside the mediation. The only exception to this prohibition is in Local Rule 33, which allows disclosure only upon approval of the Standing Panel on Attorney Discipline.[1] All proceedings before the Standing Panel involving the disclosure of information are kept confidential.

The confidentiality rule applies in all cases, including those referred for mediation by the court. The rule does not apply to settlement agreements. However, this fact in no way prohibits the parties from separately deciding that the terms of their own settlement agreement must remain confidential.

Program Statistics

Each circuit mediator averages more than two hundred mediations per year. In the program's first sixteen years, mediation conferences were held in 9,693 cases. Of these, 3,361, or 35 percent, settled. Clearly, the Fourth Circuit Pre-Argument Mediation Program has helped to expedite resolution of cases in the appellate process.

NOTE

1. *See* In re Anonymous, 283 F.3d 627 (4th Cir. 2002).

ARBITRATION

CHAPTER THIRTY-TWO

Court-Ordered Arbitration in North Carolina's Courts

"The State can point with pride to this program. Against every measure, court-ordered, non-binding arbitration is a success, enhancing government's responsiveness to its citizens."

—*Interim Report of the North Carolina Supreme Court Dispute Resolution Committee to the Supreme Court of North Carolina and the Administrative Office of the Courts* (April 8, 1994).

The court-ordered, non-binding arbitration program is a district court program that seeks to resolve contested monetary claims. The program's goals are to reduce case disposition time and to promote litigant satisfaction with the court system. It began in 1987 as a pilot program in the district court division of Judicial Districts 3, 14, and 29. In 1989, the program was authorized statewide. However, the program has been implemented in only thirty-two judicial districts. The program may be implemented if the Director of the Administrative Office of the Courts and chief district court judge of any district determine that arbitration may improve efficiency in that district.

Overview of Court-Ordered Arbitration

"An arbitration hearing is an informal legal proceeding held before a neutral court official. . . [It] is intended to be a simple, inexpensive, and quick way to resolve disputes."[1]

Arbitration is an informal hearing that is held before a neutral court official. The rules of evidence do not apply in an arbitration hearing, but rather, serve as a guide. The goal of arbitration is to provide a cost-effective manner to resolve civil disputes. Parties must pay a $100 arbitration fee for each arbitration hearing. This amount is divided equally among the parties and is used to offset the cost of providing the arbitrator. The North Carolina Rules for Court-Ordered Arbitration, promulgated by the North Carolina Supreme Court, prescribe the case types that are eligible for the court-ordered arbitration program. Eligible civil case types include those district court cases not assigned to a magistrate and all appeals from magistrates involving a claim for monetary relief, with the exception of certain types of cases, such as those involving family law issues, title to real estate, wills, special proceedings, or summary ejectment. In any case not ordered by the district court to arbitration, the parties may request arbitration under this program by joint written motion. The parties may also agree in writing that the award in any arbitration under this program will be binding and final.[2]

Procedures Prior to Arbitration Hearing

The clerk of superior court makes the initial determination if a case is eligible for arbitration at the time a complaint or an appeal from a magistrate's judgment is filed. The parties then receive notice that the case has been selected for arbitration and are given the name of the arbitrator appointed by the court to hear the case. The arbitration hearing date is scheduled by the court and should be conducted within sixty days of the filing of the last responsive pleading, the docketing of an appeal from a magistrate's judgment, or the expiration of the time allowed for the filing of responsive pleadings. The parties may, however, request that the hearing be held earlier than the date set by the court, subject to approval by the court.

Under the Rules for Court-Ordered Arbitration, the parties must exchange the following items at least ten days before the date set for the hearing: (1) lists of witnesses expected to testify; (2) copies of documents or exhibits expected to be offered as evidence; and (3) a brief statement of the issues and contentions. Parties may agree to rely on stipulations and/or statements (sworn or unsworn), rather than a formal presentation of witnesses and documents, for all or part of the arbitration hearing.

Arbitrators

An arbitrator must be licensed to practice law for at least five years and must have been a member of the North Carolina State Bar for at least the last two years of the five-year period. Arbitrators have the same immunity as judges from civil liability for their official conduct in an arbitration hearing.

The court appoints an arbitrator from an approved list. To receive court appointments, an arbitrator must meet the eligibility requirements noted above and also complete the arbitrator training course prescribed by the North Carolina Administrative Office of the Courts (AOC) and observe an arbitration conducted by a certified arbitrator. The arbitrator must also take an oath of office and must be approved by the chief district court judge in each judicial district that he or she wishes to serve.

Upon the filing of an award with the court and an application for payment to the AOC, the arbitrator is paid $100 by the court for each arbitration hearing. The rate of compensation increased in 2003 from $75 to $100 dollars per arbitration hearing after several requests were made to the General Assembly. Arbitration hearings are limited to one hour.[3] However, because arbitrators typically spend almost two hours[4] plus travel time on each arbitration, work as an arbitrator is essentially viewed as pro bono work. It is a tribute to the bar that so many attorneys agree to serve in this capacity.

A key ingredient to the ultimate success of the arbitration program has been the quality of the arbitrators. Significant efforts were made in the development of the program to ensure arbitrator competence and impartiality.[5] An AOC publication has noted the crucial role of the arbitrator in the state's legal system:

> Attorneys who offer their services to the court as arbitrators assume a great responsibility. The success of court-ordered arbitration depends to a large degree upon the abilities and dedication of the arbitrators. An arbitrator acts as an arm of the Court by judicial appointment, bound by an oath similar to that of a judge. Arbitrators are empowered with the authority of a trial judge to conduct hearings and to decide their outcome. Acting as sole juror in finding the facts, as judge in applying the law, and as arbitrator in rendering an award, the trial lawyers who participate as arbitrators have found the role to be a challenging and rewarding one. Because serving as a neutral gives them a new perspective on the litigation process, many also find their service as an arbitrator makes them a better advocate.[6]

Arbitration Hearings

Arbitration hearings are scheduled by the court and are held in a courtroom or in any other public room suitable for conducting judicial proceedings.

The hearings are open to the public. Arbitration hearings are limited to one hour unless the arbitrator determines at the hearing that more time is necessary to ensure fairness and justice to the parties. If a party would like substantially more time, written application must be filed with the court and the arbitrator and must be served on opposing parties no later than the date for the pre-hearing exchange of information.

The arbitrator is empowered and authorized to administer oaths and affirmations in arbitration hearings. Hearings are to be conducted with decorum but are more informal than a trial in the sense that the Rules of Evidence apply only as a guideline. There is no official transcript of the hearings. Witnesses can be called, but their testimony is usually brief. Evidence presented during the hearing is returned to the party that submitted it and is not retained in the court file in the clerk of superior court's office. The arbitrator has discretion to receive post-hearing briefs—but not evidence—if submitted within three days after the conclusion of the hearing. Ex parte communications with the arbitrator are not allowed.

If a party fails to appear without good cause, the hearing may proceed, and an award may be made by the arbitrator against the absent party upon the evidence offered by the parties present. However, an entry of a default judgment or dismissal of the case is not permissible according to the Rules of Court-Ordered Arbitration. The court may order another arbitration hearing in any case in which an award was made against a party who failed to obtain a continuance of a hearing and failed to appear for reasons beyond the party's control. All motions for another arbitration hearing must be filed with the court within the time allowed for demanding a trial de novo. Parties may appear pro se as permitted by law at an arbitration hearing. However, corporations may not represent themselves in arbitration hearings.[7]

The Award

Once an arbitration hearing has concluded, the arbitrator has three days after the hearing or the receipt of post-hearing briefs, whichever is later, to file an award with the court. The arbitrator may also issue the award at the conclusion of the hearing. If the arbitrator does not issue the award at the conclusion of the hearing, the court must serve copies of the award on the parties or their counsel and document the manner of service. No findings of fact or conclusions of law or opinions are required, but the award must resolve all issues. The arbitrator may include in an award court costs accruing through the arbitration proceedings in favor of the prevailing party. However, the arbitration fee, which is paid at the conclusion of the hearing, must be divided equally among all parties. Parties have thirty days from the date the arbitration award is served to file a request for trial de novo. If a request for trial de novo, consent judgment, or dismissal is not filed during the thirty-day period following the service of the award, the award is entered as a judgment of the court by the clerk of superior court. A copy of the judgment is mailed to all parties or their counsel.

Trial De Novo

A party dissatisfied with the arbitrator's award may seek a trial de novo by filing a written request with the court within thirty days of the service of the award on all parties. The date that the award is served may be either the date that the award was mailed to the parties or the date the arbitrator gave the award to the parties, if the award was made at the conclusion of the hearing. The filing of a request for a trial de novo preserves the rights of all parties; therefore, no judgment will be entered against any party pending the resolution of the trial de novo. The filing fee for demanding a trial de novo is equivalent to the arbitration fee. It is held by the court until the case is completed. The fee may be returned to the party that requested the trial de novo if its position improved at trial from that awarded by the arbitrator. If a jury trial was requested in the original pleadings, the trial de novo will be held before a jury. Otherwise, a judge conducts the trial. The arbitration hearing may not be referenced in the presence of a jury.

Administration

During the court-ordered arbitration pilot program, a staff person was provided to each participating judicial district. A study of the pilot program noted that "[i]n this respect, the North Carolina program clearly benefitted from careful attention to the importance of administration."[8] Once the program was expanded beyond the original districts, however, staff was not always provided. Staffing was based on the number of case filings. As a result, many districts started offering arbitration without adding additional staff.

In districts where court-ordered arbitration currently is implemented, a judicial support-staff person, often referred to as the "arbitration coordinator," administers the program and manages the case process. The arbitration coordinator reviews the cases that have been determined eligible by the clerk of superior court. Once the time for responsive pleadings has expired, the coordinator sends notices to the parties that the case has been selected for arbitration. At that time, the arbitration coordinator appoints an arbitrator from the list of court-approved arbitrators. The arbitration coordinator schedules the arbitration hearing, prepares paperwork for the arbitrator prior to the hearing, and notifies the arbitrator, attorneys, and parties of the date and time of the arbitration hearing. Arbitration coordinators also track the timeline for paperwork, the award, requests for a trial de novo, and dismissals. They work closely with the parties, attorneys, and arbitrators to answer questions and to ensure that cases are resolved efficiently and within the established timelines. Arbitration coordinators also submit statistics on arbitration and trial de novo cases to the AOC Court Programs and Management Services Division.

Conclusion

Court-ordered, non-binding arbitration has proven to be an economical and efficient procedure to resolve certain civil cases. The conclusions of a study of the arbitration program conducted by the Institute of Government at the University of North Carolina at Chapel Hill in 1989 still resonate:

> *The arbitration program disposed of eligible civil cases faster than standard procedures. It reduced trials and out-of-court settlements, replacing them with promptly scheduled adversarial hearings before specially-trained arbitrators. The program improved litigants' satisfaction with the outcome and procedure used in their cases.*[9]

NOTES

1. *A Guide to Court-Ordered Arbitration in North Carolina*, N.C. Administrative Office of the Courts (1997), p. 1.

2. There are a number of arbitration resources available for both pro se litigants and arbitrators on the website of the North Carolina Court System at http://www.nccourts.org/Citizens/CPrograms/Arbitration/Default.asp. The following information concerning court-ordered arbitration is available:

- History of the Program;
- The Rules for Court-Ordered Arbitration;
- Arbitrator Benchbook;

- The enabling legislation;
- Arbitrator oath;
- Canons of Ethics for Arbitrators;
- AOC Arbitration forms; and
- Frequently Asked Questions (FAQs).

3. *Rules for Court-Ordered Arbitration in North Carolina,* Rule 6(q), http://www
.nccourts.org/Citizens/CPrograms/Arbitration/Documents/arbitrationrules_
withdisclaimer.pdf.

4. Stevens H. Clarke et al., *Court-Ordered Arbitration in North Carolina: An
Evaluation of Its Effects* (Institute of Government, The University of North Carolina at Chapel Hill, 1989), p. 73.

5. *Court-Ordered Arbitration, Report to the Supreme Court of North Carolina by
the North Carolina Bar Association* (March 1989), p. 3.

6. *Benchbook for Arbitrators,* (N.C. Administrative Office of the Courts,
July 1997), p. 2, available at http://www.nccourts.org/Citizens/CPrograms/
Arbitration/Documents/benchbook.pdf.

7. N.C. Gen.Stat. §84-4; LexisNexis v. Travishan Corp., 155 N.C.App. 205, 573
S.E.2d 547 (2002).

8. *Court-Ordered Arbitration, supra* note 5.

9. Stevens H. Clarke et al., *supra* note 4 at xiii.

CHAPTER THIRTY-THREE

Arbitrating Disputes by Agreement

"As the work of the courts increases, delays and costs will rise and the well-developed forms of arbitration should have wider use. Lawyers, judges and social scientists of other countries cannot understand our failure to make greater use of the arbitration process to settle disputes. I submit a reappraisal of the values of the arbitration process is in order, to determine whether . . . arbitration can divert litigation to other channels."

—United States Supreme Court Chief Justice Warren E. Burger, *Agenda for 2000 A.D.—A Need for Systematic Anticipation*, Address Delivered at the National Conference on the Causes of Popular Dissatisfaction with the Administration of Justice, 70 F.R.D. 79, 94 (1976).

Introduction

Agreeing to arbitrate matters, at times even before a controversy arises, has been a feature of conflict resolution in North Carolina for nearly a century, long before the advent of the modern dispute resolution movement. Some professions, businesses, and organizations have used agreements to arbitrate disputes for many years, including architects, labor unions, the construction industry, and the maritime transportation industry. Advocates for the procedure note its relative efficiency, flexibility, lower cost, and privacy compared with litigation. Critics argue that arbitration can be slower than litigation, less effective, and more expensive.

Unlike court-ordered arbitration or mediation, arbitration by agreement is completely voluntary. Parties are not bound until they sign an agreement to arbitrate. Once an agreement is signed, the parties are committed; so anyone considering arbitration must be thoroughly familiar with its procedures and implications before signing.

Governing Statutes

Arbitration by agreement in North Carolina may be subject to one of several statutory provisions. The Federal Arbitration Act (FAA), 9 U.S.C. Sections

1–16, has governed arbitration of disputes involving interstate commerce or maritime matters for more than seventy-five years. In North Carolina, arbitration agreements not within the purview of the FAA generally are subject to the state's Revised Uniform Arbitration Act (RUAA), North Carolina General Statutes Sections 1-569.1 to 1-569.31, enacted in 2003. Older agreements may be subject to the former Uniform Arbitration Act, North Carolina General Statutes Sections 1-567.1 to 1-567.20, no longer published in the General Statutes but available in Volume III of the North Carolina Bar Association (NCBA) Family Law Section's *2006 Revised Handbook: Arbitrating Family Law Cases Under the North Carolina Family Law Arbitration Act as Amended in 2005 (Arbitration Handbook)*. (The text of the *Arbitration Handbook* is available on the North Carolina Bar Association's website.[1]) Agreements involving international arbitrations may be subject to the federal laws implementing certain treaties (9 U.S.C. Sections 201–307) or state law, as provided in the North Carolina International Commercial Arbitration and Conciliation Act (ICACA), North Carolina General Statutes Sections 1-567.30 to 1-567.87. Arbitration of family law disputes is generally governed by North Carolina's Family Law Arbitration Act (FLAA), North Carolina General Statutes Sections 50-41 to 50-62. Since its initial enactment, the FLAA has been amended to conform to the RUAA. The former version of the FLAA, which may apply in older family law arbitration agreements, is available in Volume III of the NCBA Family Law Section's *Arbitration Handbook*.[2]

Common Features of Arbitration by Agreement

Validity of Arbitration Agreements

A central principle governing all arbitrations by agreement in North Carolina is that they are valid, irrevocable, and enforceable by the courts. Absent a waiver or other reason for granting relief, agreements to arbitrate bind those who sign them. Statutory provisions permit courts to stay or to compel arbitration in appropriate circumstances, or to stay litigation pending arbitration.

Scope of Agreement to Arbitrate

The scope clause of the agreement to arbitrate, which describes what matters the parties want to submit to arbitration, probably is the single most important standard provision. Generally, the parties are free to determine the scope of their agreement. Arbitration form books can be a helpful source for standard clauses, but these provisions must be reviewed carefully to ensure that they fit what the parties want the arbitration to cover. In addition, some statutes exclude certain matters from arbitration. For example, the North Carolina UAA provides that the parties can submit to arbitration "any controversy" that exists between them at the time an agreement is entered, or include in the written contract a provision for the settlement by arbitration of "any controversy" that may arise between them relating to the contract. However, it excludes agreements between employers and employees, unless the agreement provides that the UAA will apply to it. In addition, case law sometimes holds that certain issues are not arbitrable.

Rules Established by Agreement

Except as state statutes limit or require it, arbitration by agreement allows parties to chart their own course in settling a dispute. The parties are free to establish their own rules of procedure and evidence, as well as their own standards for arbitrator conduct. This differs from court-ordered arbitration, where the Supreme Court of North Carolina has promulgated both Rules for Court-Ordered Arbitration and Canons of Ethics for Arbitrators.

Agreements to arbitrate may be part of a contract regulating substantive matters, such as construction agreements and prenuptial agreements. Although parties may devise their own procedural rules for arbitrating disputes that arise under the agreement, most parties incorporate standard rules by reference, with any modifications expressly stated in the agreement. Institutions that offer arbitration services or other dispute resolution techniques, such as the American Arbitration Association (AAA), publish standard rules. The North Carolina Bar Association Family Law Section has developed special rules for FLAA-governed cases.

North Carolina's Canons of Ethics for Arbitrators, in force for court-ordered arbitration, also may be incorporated into an agreement to govern arbitrator conduct. The American Bar Association (ABA) and the AAA jointly publish a revised Code of Ethics for Arbitrators in Commercial Disputes (ABA-AAA Code). Older agreements may be subject to the 1977 Code version. Other published ethics rules for arbitrations exist, and the revised FLAA and RUAA have arbitrator disclosure requirements that must be consulted. The standard FLAA arbitration rules, published in Volume II of the NCBA Family Law Section's *Arbitration Handbook* incorporate the North Carolina Canons by reference. Other agreements may refer to these standards as well but must comply with applicable legislation.

The ABA-AAA Code was developed for disputes involving commerce. This is common for arbitration rules; often they are tailored for particular kinds of matters and may not be suitable, in whole or in part, for other disputes. Before North Carolina enacted the FLAA, some family law practitioners tried to arbitrate marital disputes using the ABA-AAA Code. In so doing, they sometimes omitted provisions that can be very helpful in family law cases and that appear in other, more appropriate rules, while including rules that were not relevant. Volume II of the NCBA Family Law Section's *Arbitration Handbook* publishes suggested forms and rules for FLAA-governed cases. While these tools may fit the purpose of a family law case, they may not be suitable for other matters, such as commercial disputes. There are few one-size-fits-all sets of arbitration rules or standards for arbitrator ethics, and drafters of arbitration agreements must be aware of this. The North Carolina Canons of Ethics for Arbitrators are an exception, because they were drafted to be used in many cases besides court-ordered arbitration. Nevertheless, the drafters of an arbitration agreement should ensure that the Canons fit a particular transaction before incorporating them.

In matters governed by the ICACA, the arbitrator(s) may select the rules if parties cannot agree on them. In family law matters, the FLAA permits an arbitrator or a court to select rules for an arbitration if the parties cannot agree.

Selection of Arbitrator

Agreements to arbitrate typically include a method for selecting arbitrators. If the agreed method fails or cannot be followed, a court will appoint the arbitrator(s). If an agreement to arbitrate is signed long before a dispute arises, it generally will not name the arbitrator(s) but will say how many must be chosen. Under most rules in multi-arbitrator cases, the party-chosen arbitrators will select the last (or neutral) arbitrator.

Parties often name an institution that provides dispute resolution services (such as the AAA) as manager of the arbitration and agree that they will be bound by that institution's rules. In such cases, the institution supplies a list of institution-qualified arbitrators. Parties select the arbitrator(s) from those names. There is nothing to stop parties from incorporating institutional rules in an agreement without naming the institution as the manager, but an institution like AAA often assures more experienced administration and management than the parties and independently chosen arbitrators may be able to provide. However, arbitration institutions charge fees and expenses that can be higher than party-negotiated fees and expenses.

In family law matters, the FLAA provides that if parties cannot agree on arbitrators, a court may appoint an established arbitration institution that it considers qualified in family law arbitration to handle the dispute. North

Carolina's ICACA has a similar provision for disputes involving international commercial agreements.

Parties and arbitrators hearing matters under the RUAA or the FLAA must comply with those statutes' disclosure rules; they also may be subject to arbitrator ethics rules that the parties choose in an agreement.

The Arbitration Site and Choice of Law Provisions

Another element common in agreements to arbitrate is the arbitration site, including a choice of law provision. This is important for two reasons. First, without such a provision in an agreement to arbitrate, common law conflict of laws principles govern. If parties choose a North Carolina site for arbitration, this state's conflict of laws rules govern, unless there is an express agreement to apply the laws of a different state.

The second reason relates to the expense of arbitrating a dispute. Any proffered draft contract to arbitrate must be examined closely. Often a proponent of a draft will want arbitration close to home, or perhaps close to the location of the law firm that represents it. Even if a suggested geographic location is satisfactory, arbitrating in an opponent's business or lawyers' offices can be intimidating. Parties may agree to hold the hearing at a neutral site, such as a conference room in a public building. If parties choose an arbitration institution to conduct the arbitration hearing, its rules often provide that the institution will name the site. Most arbitration institutions are cognizant of costs and are willing to move the site to a less expensive place. Most standard rules allow arbitrators to move the site after arbitration begins if it is reasonable to do so, as in cases where a change in site will simplify document examination. If the parties have any doubt about the site, they should specify the site or sites for the hearing in the agreement.

With respect to international agreements, the ICACA provides for the arbitration site and the choice of law. Other statutes, such as North Carolina General Statutes Section 22B-3, which identifies certain contracts that contain forum selection provisions as being against public policy, may impact the choice of law and the arbitration site.

Common Procedural Features in Statutes and Rules Governing Arbitration

Except as statutes may require, the parties in an arbitration can "write their own ticket" on the procedures to be followed in arbitration by agreement. The Rules of Civil Procedure and the Rules of Evidence do not apply in arbitrations unless incorporated by reference. However, courts may scrutinize an agreement to ensure procedural fairness, particularly if the two sides did not have equal bargaining power at the time the agreement was signed. Certain issues may not be modified even by agreement of the parties; for example, agreements not to have attorneys present, or not to record the arbitration hearings, would not be enforceable.

Initiating Arbitration and Pre-Hearing Procedures

Most arbitration rules establish procedures for initiating a hearing, for submitting statements of claims and defenses, and for amending such statements. Rules may also provide for an administrative conference, a proceeding similar to a pretrial conference.

Other pre-hearing matters are governed by statute, but there is a lack of uniformity as to several important issues. For example, consolidation of arbitration cases is permitted under the RUAA and the FLAA. Prejudgment or interim remedies, like attachment of a party's property, are available in family law arbitrations under the FLAA, arbitrations under the RUAA, and in international disputes subject to the ICACA. The FAA provides for arresting ships or cargo, or subjecting them to maritime attachment and garnishment in admiralty cases. Parties may agree on arbitration rules for pre-award or interim relief and for consolidation. However, the ICACA, the RUAA, and the FLAA, all of which allow such forms of relief, must be consulted for exceptions to the parties' choice. The RUAA and the FLAA permit an award of punitive damages, but only if the law provides for them or if the parties agree to them. The RUAA and the FLAA allow consolidation of cases; the ICACA does not. Arbitration rules may provide for consolidating ICACA-governed cases, however.

All North Carolina arbitration statutes permit discovery, but parties must keep in mind that a goal of arbitration is minimizing pre-hearing fact-finding costs. The RUAA, ICACA, and the FLAA expressly provide for depositions, witnesses, and subpoenas in connection with arbitration hearings. Parties can, of course, modify procedural rules in the agreement, subject to statutory limits.

Hearings

Unless the arbitration agreement provides otherwise, the arbitrator sets the date, time, and place for the hearing. The RUAA also permits an early hearing, like an initial pretrial conference. There may be representation by counsel in arbitrations if a party has a lawyer. Statutes declare that parties cannot waive this right. Since a court reporter does not automatically attend arbitration hearings, parties must agree on how to record the proceedings and how to pay for them. Some arbitration rules address the use of a court reporter. For example, Rule 28 of the AAA Commercial Dispute Resolution Procedures states that a party desiring a stenographic record must make arrangements directly with the stenographer and should notify the other parties of the arrangements at least three days in advance of the hearing. The requesting party or parties must pay the cost of the record under Rule 28.

Like a trial judge, an arbitrator may grant postponements. Rules may set out standards for communications between arbitrators and parties and, as discussed earlier, may include ethical requirements. (In some instances, statutes or rules set standards for arbitrator ethics or disclosure.)

Arbitration rules often provide for use of hearsay (which would be inadmissible in court), allowing an arbitrator to consider it for what it is worth. This parallels court-ordered arbitration principles. If parties want arbitrators to use the laws of evidence, the parties must agree to it.

The Arbitration Award

Unless legislation or a rule provides for it, arbitrators in the United States do not deliver reasoned awards like a judge's Rule 52 findings of fact and conclusions of law. The parties can usually agree that an award must state the reasons on which it is based, but they should adhere to the requirements of applicable statutes and rules. For example, the ICACA follows the federal rule for international commercial arbitrations, providing that the award does not state the reasons on which it is based unless the parties agree otherwise. However, family law arbitration awards must be reasoned unless otherwise agreed. Parties wanting a reasoned award should be prepared to pay for the additional time that the arbitrator will need to draft it.

Costs and Sanctions

Both the ICACA and the FLAA provide for payment of costs and for sanctions in appropriate cases. If statutes do not regulate costs and sanctions, as with the North Carolina RUAA, or, if parties want different allocations of costs or sanctions, a rule should be included to specify the parties' agreement on these issues.

Confirmation of Award

Statutes governing arbitration by agreement provide for a court's confirmation of an award, upon application by a party. In all cases, a confirmed award becomes a judgment and is enforceable like any other judgment.

However, there is no obligation to apply to a court for confirmation in disputes resolved through arbitration by agreement. As with other contractual agreements, if parties comply with an award, it remains private. If there is noncompliance, parties can apply to a court. Counsel must be aware of statutes of limitation for enforcing contract obligations.

Setting Aside, Modifying, or Correcting an Award

The statutes governing arbitrations by agreement provide for setting aside, modifying, or correcting arbitral awards. These statutes vary, and counsel should review them carefully to determine appropriate procedures and requirements.

Appeal of Awards

Issues for appeal of awards confirmed as judgments are limited. The FLAA allows appeal for review of errors of law if parties so agree. Other governing statutes do not address the issue.

Unlike the situation in court-ordered arbitration, where a request for a trial de novo in the district or superior court may be made, appeals of judgments confirming awards in arbitrations by agreement follow the usual path to the Court of Appeals and the Supreme Court. A district or superior court has roles in confirming, setting aside, modifying, or correcting these awards, but appellate review is outside trial court jurisdiction.

Particular Features of Statutory Schemes

Proceedings Governed by the Federal Arbitration Act

The Federal Arbitration Act (FAA) applies to maritime transactions as defined in the Act and to transactions in interstate and foreign commerce. The scope of interstate commerce extends to the limits embodied in the Constitution's Commerce Clause. The FAA also applies in international transactions if treaties and special enabling legislation do not apply.

The basic FAA does not confer subject matter jurisdiction on the federal courts. If there is no admiralty, diversity, or federal question jurisdiction, state courts must hear matters arising under the FAA and must enforce the Act and the parties' agreements to arbitrate. There is a broad federal policy favoring arbitration under the Act.

To the extent that the FAA does not govern a transaction, state legislation or the parties' agreement may supply rules for arbitration. FAA-governed litigation in state court and arbitrations under it must pay heed to appropriate state legislation and to what the parties contract for in agreements.

The North Carolina Revised Uniform Arbitration Act

The RUAA generally governs arbitrations by agreement in North Carolina if neither the FAA, the ICACA, nor the FLAA governs a dispute.

Arbitrating Family Law Matters

North Carolina's FLAA supersedes in part the common law principle that holds that arbitration by agreement cannot result in a binding award for child custody and child support. The FLAA accomplishes this by a special provision allowing modification of awards for alimony, post-separation support, child support, or child custody based on a substantial change of circumstances.

The FLAA attempts to give the parties maximum flexibility. If an award has not been confirmed as a judgment, parties may ask the arbitrator for modification. They may get an award confirmed and move the court for modification. If an award has been confirmed as a judgment, they may move the court for modification or agree to submit the modification to arbitration upon court order. The same standards apply to such modifications as would apply in litigated cases.

Parties may agree on the FLAA procedure at any time, but they cannot agree in a prenuptial agreement to arbitrate child custody, child support, or the divorce itself. Child custody and support may be subjects of a postnuptial agreement (e.g., a contract modifying a prenuptial agreement). However, the divorce itself cannot be the subject of a postnuptial agreement.

Because prenuptial or other agreements to arbitrate may involve interspousal business arrangements, including businesses or partnerships in interstate or international commerce, the FAA and other state arbitration legislation (like the ICACA) may be implicated. If parties want to exclude application of the FLAA, they must opt out of its coverage when they sign an agreement to arbitrate a marital dispute.

The NCBA Family Law Section's *Arbitration Handbook* includes comments on each section of the FLAA and the suggested forms and rules for arbitration under the Act.

International Commercial Arbitration and Conciliation

Parties drafting agreements to arbitrate with international implications must consider any treaty applying to the transaction, as well as federal and state legislation and rules they wish to use. Federal policy favoring arbitration is even stronger in situations involving foreign commerce.

The FAA implements two treaties of the United States dealing with international commercial arbitration. This special legislation incorporates the basic FAA to the extent that it is not inconsistent. For example, the FAA provides that the "act of state doctrine," a defense in most international cases, does not apply to enforcing arbitral agreements. This provision is incorporated in the special legislation by reference, but it also applies to arbitrations under the basic FAA.

The special FAA legislation for international agreements incorporates treaty rules by reference, but under the "later in time" rule of construction, the legislation may apply if it is inconsistent with a treaty provision. Unlike the basic FAA, which depends on other, substantive legislation to create subject matter jurisdiction, provisions governing international commercial arbitrations deem a case involving arbitration under these treaties a federal question, providing an automatic ticket to federal court.

North Carolina's ICACA in general follows the older version of the United Nations Commission on International Trade Law (UNCITRAL) Model Law for international arbitrations as it is in force in several states and other countries. The Act applies where federal arbitration legislation does not and thus supplements the federal procedures. ICACA provisions that may be important in arbitrations otherwise governed by federal law include: (1) authority to obtain interim relief; (2) power to consolidate arbitrations; (3) expanded discovery procedures; and (4) specific performance, costs, and interest. The ICACA lists commercial transactions defined as "international" that may be broader than the scope of federal legislation. If parties want to exclude application of the Act, they must opt out of ICACA coverage in their agreement to arbitrate.

The ICACA provides for conciliation, an alternative dispute resolution procedure favored in Asian countries. This option allows a trusted neutral (who may be the arbitrator) to proceed as he or she thinks appropriate to help settle a dispute first brought to arbitration. Conciliation is, in effect, a hybrid of arbitration and mediation. A conciliator may prepare a non-binding conciliation agreement for the parties' consideration as a settlement agreement. If they accept the agreement or if conciliation otherwise settles the dispute, any written agreement is treated as an arbitral award, with the same force and effect as any arbitral award. Parties in other arbitrations might consider adopting the ICACA procedures by stipulation and court order.

In some international transactions, these laws will not apply. An example would be a family law dispute having no international commercial implications. In such a case, a dispute subject to arbitration would be governed by North Carolina's FLAA.

Conclusion

Arbitration by agreement can be valuable for resolving disputes if (1) the parties understand the procedure, and (2) they draft clauses and rules to suit a particular dispute *before signing an agreement to arbitrate*. However, this ADR procedure may not be suitable for every dispute or problem. Failure to understand and properly apply clauses and rules as permitted or required by arbitration statutes (and in the international context by treaties) is a sure recipe for disaster.

Contracts with clauses requiring arbitration are becoming more universal. Scrolling through terms and conditions of an Internet sale contract often reveals an agreement to arbitrate, maybe at a site far from a buyer and much more convenient to the seller. These contracts, and their paper cousins, have not escaped the attention of Congress, state legislatures, and the courts. Perhaps to head off adverse legislative or court action, some institutional users of arbitration (for example, the securities industry) often agree to move arbitrations to more mutually convenient sites, rather than hold them in an expensive city stipulated in the contract. Administrators of arbitration (for example, the AAA) have also moved arbitrations to more convenient sites. Nevertheless, with increasing use of the procedure for small consumer-level claims, there is a possibility of protective legislation and/or court decisions. Those drafting agreements to arbitrate, and parties to these agreements, must be aware of such developments.

NOTES

1. *2006 Family Law Arbitration Handbook: Volume III—Former Statutes and Rules*, online publication of the North Carolina Bar Association's Family Law Section, http://familylaw.ncbar.org/media/1633058/2006FamilyLaw HandbookVol3.pdf.

2. *See Id.*

CHAPTER THIRTY-FOUR

International Arbitration

*"When will Mankind be convinced . . . and agree
to settle their difficulties by Arbitration?"*
—Benjamin Franklin,
Letter to Mary Hewson (January 27, 1783).

The global economy of the twenty-first century requires participation in foreign markets. In fact, international contracts have become the norm for many businesses. This increase in cross-border activity naturally leads to an increase in cross-border disputes. Because judicial processes vary widely from country to country, parties entering into international commercial contracts should consider alternatives to the local courts. International arbitration is widely regarded as the most effective alternative method for resolving such disputes, and its availability (or lack thereof) in a given country can have a major impact on the willingness of companies to do business there. Accordingly, as the economies of formerly undeveloped countries mature, those countries find it prudent to adopt a commercial arbitration infrastructure that will enable companies to turn to neutral private decision makers to resolve the substance of any disputes that may arise. Since 2007, international arbitration providers have reported a substantial increase in the number of new cases filed with them, and many providers have established new operations outside the United States and Europe, particularly in the Middle East and Far East, to handle the disputes that are increasingly arising in that part of the world.

This chapter is not intended to be a comprehensive description of international arbitration but to provide an overview of the history of international arbitration and a description of selected international arbitration providers. It also highlights some of the practical differences a North Carolina practitioner may encounter in international arbitration.

History

The modern form of arbitration is often said to have its roots in the Treaty of London of 1794 (the Jay Treaty) between the United States and Great Britain. This treaty created commissions to decide outstanding issues between the two countries. Throughout the nineteenth century, forms of arbitration were increasingly used to resolve disputes between countries. Ultimately, companies doing business internationally came to realize the practical benefits of avoiding foreign courts by agreeing to arbitrate contract issues using private decision makers. In 1925, Congress enacted the Federal Arbitration Act (FAA),[1] which was intended to lay to rest arguments that contracts to arbitrate were inimical to the American system of justice.[2] As more recently stated, the FAA was enacted to "reverse the longstanding judicial hostility to arbitration agreements . . . and to place arbitration agreements upon the same footing as other contracts."[3]

International commercial arbitration did not come into common use, however, until after World War II. In 1958, a United Nations diplomatic conference adopted the Convention on the Recognition and Enforcement of Foreign Arbitral Awards (New York Convention). The New York Convention is widely considered to be the foundation of international commercial arbitration. The United States adopted the New York Convention in 1970.[4] As of January 2011, the New York Convention had been adopted or ratified by approximately 150 countries.[5] The Convention requires courts in countries that have adopted it to compel arbitration where the parties have so agreed and provides for the courts to recognize and enforce awards issued following the completion of the arbitral process. Often, these countries have legislatively adopted the Model Law promulgated by the United Nations Commission on International Trade Law (UNCITRAL). The United States has not adopted the UNCITRAL Model Law, although it is the basis for international arbitration statutes often adopted at the state legislative level, including in North Carolina.

The New York Convention is not the only vehicle for enforcement of arbitration agreements in the international context. For example, the Inter-American Convention on International Commercial Arbitration was completed in Panama City, Panama, on January 30, 1975 (Panama Convention). The enforcement provisions of the Panama Convention are similar to the provisions of the New York Convention. The Panama Convention takes precedence over the New York Convention if the majority of parties to an arbitration agreement are from ratifying countries. Nineteen countries have adopted the Panama Convention. All of the signatories are members of the Organization of American States. The United States adopted the Panama Convention in 1986.[6] Similarly, for trade agreements between parties located in European countries, the European Convention of 1961 may aid in enforcement.[7]

Choosing the Situs and Enforcement

The conduct of an international arbitration is governed by the rules of the selected arbitral provider, but is also guided by the law of the country where the arbitration takes place. This is why businesses often choose New York or London as the situs of the arbitration, even if the contract in dispute involves performance thousands of miles away and even if it greatly constrains the ability to compel witness attendance. In addition, once the arbitration is concluded, the courts of the situs country will handle any challenges to the award. For example, if parties arbitrate a dispute in Paris, then challenges to the award should be brought in the courts of France.[8] After the French courts resolve the challenges, the award may then be enforced in other countries.

Time limits for challenging an award may vary depending on the applicable rules, but may be short. For example, under the Model Law, a party has three months to serve a motion to vacate, modify, or correct an award.[9] In the United States, an award must be confirmed within three years.[10]

Enforcement of an award is typically a two-step process, with initial confirmation taking place in the courts of the country where the hearing occurred and the award was rendered, followed by enforcement in the country where the losing party has assets. If the award survives challenge or is not challenged in a timely fashion in the courts where the arbitration took place, the prevailing party may then enforce the award in that country or take the award to another country that has adopted the Convention.

Under the New York Convention, a court should enforce an award unless the court finds that the award fails for one of the specific reasons listed in Article V. These reasons are: (1) that the arbitration agreement was not valid under its governing law; (2) a party was not given notice of the appointment of the arbitrator or of the arbitration proceedings, or was otherwise unable to present its case; (3) the award contains matters beyond the scope of the arbitration; (4) the composition of the tribunal was not in accordance with the arbitration agreement; (5) the award is not yet binding or has been set aside by a competent authority; (6) the subject matter of the award was not capable of resolution by the arbitration; or (7) enforcement would be contrary to public policy.[11] A court may also decline to recognize the award if the subject matter is not capable of settlement by arbitration under the law of the enforcing country or the recognition of the award would be contrary to the public policy of the enforcing country.[12]

When a party seeks to enforce an arbitration award in the United States, the matter is a federal question under the FAA and the above-listed treaties and therefore should be filed in federal court.[13]

Selecting the Provider and the Process

The selection of an arbitration provider requires consideration of a number of practical and legal factors such that it is best to consult attorneys with experience with international arbitration before making your choice. Issues to be considered include convenience of the venue and the familiarity of the situs courts with the arbitral provider and arbitration generally, including appeals from and review and enforcement of awards.

The rules of arbitral providers may vary or even be silent on expected ethical practices, rules of evidence, number of arbitrators, selection of arbitrators, confidentiality, interim relief, availability of different types of damages or remedies, fees and costs, and form of decision and award. In addition, parties may need to consider the type of currency in which they prefer the award be rendered.

Arbitration Providers

The International Chamber of Commerce (ICC), the London Court of International Arbitration (LCIA), and the International Centre for Dispute Resolution (ICDR) are generally recognized as the major international commercial arbitration institutions. Regional or local arbitral institutions, such as the Belgian Center for Arbitration and Mediation (CEPANI) may be appropriate as well. These regional and local providers often model their rules on the rules of the larger providers or the UNCITRAL rules described above. A comprehensive list of arbitral providers and a complete analysis of the differences in their rules and practices is beyond the scope of this chapter. The brief descriptions of the following three providers illustrate the range of provider services available.

The ICC International Court of Arbitration, which was created in 1923, is one of the oldest of the international providers. Since then it has handled more than 16,500 cases, including 817 new cases in 2009 alone. The ICC is highly regarded, and its practices are widely copied by regional and local arbitration providers.

The LCIA promotes itself as a modern and forward-looking institution that provides an efficient, flexible, and impartial administration of arbitration. The LCIA consists of arbitration professionals from the major trading nations, including China and Japan. The LCIA has a fairly comprehensive set of arbitration rules, but is flexible enough to implement ad hoc procedures agreed to by the parties.

The ICDR, the international arm of the American Arbitration Association, states that it is "premised on its ability to move matters forward, facilitate communications, ensure that qualified arbitrators and mediators are appointed, control costs, understand cultural sensitivities, resolve procedural impasses, and properly interpret and apply its international Arbitration and Mediation Rules." The ICDR is headquartered in New York and has offices in Dublin and Mexico City. The ICDR also has cooperative agreements with sixty-two arbitration institutions in forty-three countries, enabling it to administer arbitrations around the world.

How International Arbitration Is Different from North Carolina Litigation Practice

Conducting an international arbitration is not the same as litigating a case in state or federal court in North Carolina. A lawyer who attempts to apply the same approach to both arbitration and litigation jeopardizes the case.

In the past, the international arbitration bar was relatively small and the arbitrators conducting international arbitrations came from a shared background. As a result, there were implicit understandings and universal norms as to ethics and hearing practice. However, counsel and arbitrators now come from many geographic and legal backgrounds with different expectations as to the correct practices to follow. Expected practice and ethical norms may vary depending on the location of the arbitration, whether the arbitrators come from a civil or common law jurisdiction, and the common experience of the counsel. Is witness preparation and coaching acceptable? What about witness sequestration? These are just two of many issues that can trip up the unsuspecting practitioner. Failure to agree on practices in advance can lead to serious setbacks for a new international practitioner.

As to ethics and hearing practice, there is no uniform ethical code of conduct and one is not likely to be enacted in the immediate future. Attorneys must therefore be cognizant of potential ethical differences. Although they are not binding absent agreement or application through the arbitral provider chosen by the parties, the American Bar Association Model Rules of

Professional Conduct, the new International Bar Association (IBA) Rules, and the Council of Bars and Law Societies of Europe's Code of Conduct (CCBE Code) are potential sources of ethical guidance. These codes have differences in approach, a fact that counsel should address at the outset of the arbitration.

In addition, most international provider rules simply refer to conducting a hearing and do not direct the arbitrators as to standards for how that hearing should be conducted. This gap should be filled by reaching agreement early on to use the IBA or another standard set of rules.

In international arbitration, much of the case will be presented in writing. Communications with the arbitrators may include preliminary written submissions. The purpose of such submissions is to identify the scope of the arbitration and help the arbitrators devise the appropriate procedure for the case. A schedule will then be set, which may include additional written submissions as needed. Typically, there will be page limits on written submissions and the time limits for exchanging pleadings may be short.

The arbitrators will likely be well educated and well trained. They will have read the evidentiary submissions of the parties. They are likely to expect a style of advocacy that is less aggressive and contains less rhetoric than is customary in American courts. In many cases, the arbitrators will set time limits for presentations. This softer approach and the limited discovery are intended to streamline the proceedings, leading to shorter hearings and faster resolution.

The discovery process in international arbitration is limited. The expectation is that the parties will exchange the evidence they intend to rely on. Depositions are typically not permitted, and requests for document production are usually curtailed. Discovery is another area where expectations may be widely divergent, and counsel should reach agreement as early in the process as possible. Guidance for discovery can be found from several sources, including the protocols from the International Institute for Conflict Prevention and Resolution (CPR), guidelines from the International Centre for Dispute Resolution, and the new IBA Rules. In addition, the parties may choose to craft their own process and should consider utilization of a document exchange process often referred to as the Redfern Schedule. A Redfern Schedule is a four-column chart that (1) identifies each document or category of documents; (2) describes the reason for each request; (3) summarizes any objection to producing the document; and (4) lists the decision of the arbitral tribunal on each request.[14]

The examination of witnesses is another example of the more streamlined proceedings in arbitration. The direct examination of witnesses will likely be limited. Indeed, the parties may be expected to submit all direct evidence in the form of written statements. The cross-examination of witnesses is similarly limited both by time period and subject matter. Some arbitration tribunals are increasingly using witness conferencing, an approach that originated with expert witnesses. Witness conferencing essentially involves identifying, usually through submission of written witness statements, the areas on which the witnesses disagree. The two witnesses are then placed across the table from one another with the arbitral panel controlling the examination. This is considered by arbitrators to be a highly effective form of confronting witnesses that focuses on getting to the truth. Arbitrators, not counsel, control the process. Witness preparation must take a very different form for this type of examination.

In sum, the conduct of an arbitration can vary by provider, by the geographic and legal background of the panel and counsel, and by the ethics and typical practice in the seat of the arbitration. Counsel should make no assumptions about expected practice and must inquire early on to avoid missteps that could adversely affect the outcome of the matter.

Controlling Costs

Parties choose international arbitration to ensure a fair and impartial forum and to increase the chance of award enforcement. The cost of international arbitration, however, has skyrocketed in recent years, particularly since U.S. practitioners increasingly attempt to bring costly U.S. litigation practices—including discovery and dispositive motions—into arbitration.

As a result, arbitrators are becoming more willing to control the process. Arbitrators, who usually have the ability to award fees and costs to the prevailing party, may seek additional authority to sanction a party, prevailing or not, for excessive document requests, dilatory tactics, exaggerated claims, baseless dispositive motions, and the like. Guidance in these matters has been developed by the ICC and ICDR, as well as the IBA.

American attorneys must resist the urge to "judicialize" the arbitration procedures. Judicial procedures are inimical to the cost savings and efficiency of arbitration.

Additional Resources

Attorneys may wish to consult the following resources for additional information:

www.iccwbo.org   www.sccam.org   www.ccbe.org
www.lcia.org   www.uncitral.org   www.americanbar.org
www.adr.org/icdr   www.cpradr.org

Catherine A. Rogers, *Fit and Function in Legal Ethics: Developing a Code of Conduct for International Arbitration*, 23 Mich. J. Int'l L. 341 (2002).
Catherine A. Rogers et al., *Restating the U.S. Law of International Commercial Arbitration*, 113 Penn St. L. Rev. 1333 (2009).
Stacie I. Strong, *Research in International Commercial Arbitration: Special Skills, Special Sources*, 20 Am. Rev. of Int'l Arb. 119 (2010).
Nigel Blackaby et al., *Redfern and Hunter on International Arbitration* (5th ed. 2009).
James M. Gaitus et al., *The College of Commercial Arbitrators Guide to Best Practices in Commercial Arbitration 2nd Ed.* (2010).

NOTES

1. 9 USC § 1 *et seq.*
2. *See The New Federal Arbitration Law*, 12 Va. L. Rev. 265 (1925–1926).
3. Green Tree Financial Corp. v. Randolph, 531 U.S. 79, 89 (2000).
4. 9 USC § 201 *et seq.*
5. The current list of signatories is available on the website of the New York Arbitration Convention, http://www.newyorkconvention.org/new-york-convention-countries/contracting-states.
6. 9 USC § 301 *et seq.*
7. European Convention on International Commercial Arbitration, April 21, 1961, 484 U.N.T.S. 7041, at 349, also published at http://treaties.un.org/doc/publication/UNTS/Volume%20484/v484.pdf.
8. *See* International Trading and Industrial Investment Company v. Dyncorp Aerospace Technologies et al., Civil Action No. 09-791(RBW) (D. D. C. January 21, 2011) (U.S. court was required to recognize and enforce arbitral award rendered in Paris despite order vacating award issued by Qatari court; although Qatari law governed the interpretation of the contract, Qatari court was not a competent authority under the Convention to set aside the award as Paris was the seat of the arbitration).

9. UNCITRAL Model Law on International Arbitration, Art. 34(3).

10. 9 U.S.C. § 207.

11. *See Id. See also* United Nations Conference on International Commercial Arbitration, Convention on the Recognition and Enforcement of Foreign Arbitral Awards, 1958 [New York Convention], Article V(1).

12. 9 U.S.C. § 207; New York Convention, *supra* note 11, Article V(2).

13. 9 U.S.C. § 203.

14. *See* Nigel Blackaby et al., *Redfern and Hunter on International Arbitration* § 6.115 (5th ed. 2009).

OTHER USES OF ADR

CHAPTER THIRTY-FIVE

Pre-Litigation Dispute Resolution Programs

*"The great thing in this world
is not so much where we stand, as in
what direction we are moving."*
—Poet, physician, and essayist Oliver Wendell Holmes, Sr.,
The Autocrat of the Breakfast Table, Chapter IV (ca. 1857).

The General Assembly has turned to mediation on several occasions when confronted with the need to resolve a large class of problems. Its choice of mediation was a testament to the broad public appeal of the process, spawned largely by the success in North Carolina of the Mediated Settlement Conference (MSC) Program. In 1995, the same year that the MSC Program was established as a permanent part of the superior court process, there was considerable public outcry over air and water pollution emanating from large production farms, particularly hog farms in eastern North Carolina. To deal with the threat of massive litigation, the legislature mandated that aggrieved parties participate in mediation prior to filing suit. In 1999, the legislature implemented a similar pre-litigation mediation program to deal with the losses and massive disruptions that many feared would occur when the year 2000 arrived if computers could no longer read dates properly, and key business, transportation, and other systems failed as a result. A third program, adopted in 2003, permitted insurance companies to seek mediation of claims before litigation simply by disclosing the limits of the applicable coverage. A fourth program, the Electrical Supplier Territorial Dispute Mediation Program, was established by the legislature in 2005, but was repealed in 2007.

All of these programs have certain features in common. First, they cover a specific class of claims that (at the time) threatened to overwhelm either the courts or a particular industry. In an effort to divert these claims from time-consuming and potentially expensive litigation, the legislature provided for mediation. A second common element of these programs is that each one required pre-litigation mediation, as opposed to the prevalent model, used in the MSC Program and most others—i.e., referring cases to mediation after suit is filed.[1] Finally, as described below, these programs have, in practice, been used very little, if at all.

The Pre-Litigation Farm Nuisance Mediation Program

> *"Litigation: a machine which you go*
> *into as a pig and come out as a sausage."*
> —American writer and satirist Ambrose Bierce,
> *The Cynic's Word Book* (1906).

Program History

The statewide Pre-Litigation Farm Nuisance Mediation Program was established by North Carolina General Statutes Section 7A-38.3 on October 1, 1995, to promote early resolution of disputes over the existence of alleged "agricultural nuisances." The law defines an agricultural nuisance as farming or livestock-raising activity that is injurious to health, indecent, offensive to the senses, or an obstruction to the free use of property. Most cases mediated pursuant to this statute involved hog farm operations in the eastern coastal plain and sandhills regions of the state. In some cases, public outcry led to citizen groups becoming involved in such disputes and alleging, among other things, offensive odors and ground water contamination.

Program Summary

North Carolina's Pre-Litigation Farm Nuisance Mediation Program differs from most other statewide dispute resolution programs in its preemptive approach. Mediation of farm nuisance disputes is mandatory before a civil action can be brought in either superior or district court alleging the existence of such a nuisance. Any case filed prior to a pre-litigation mediation can be dismissed upon motion of either party.

Pre-litigation mediation is initiated by the filing of a Request for Mediation form with the clerk of superior court in the local judicial district. (The form is available from the North Carolina Dispute Resolution Commission and from clerks of superior court.) Once a copy of the Request for Mediation has been served on all parties to the dispute, the parties may select their mediator. If the parties cannot agree on a mediator, the senior resident superior court judge in the district will appoint one.

A waiver of the requirement for mandatory pre-litigation mediation of farm nuisance disputes is allowed if the parties agree to waive mediation and notify the mediator of their waiver in writing. Upon either receipt of a waiver or the conclusion of a pre-litigation mediation, the mediator issues a certificate indicating what took place. If the parties apply for a waiver or if mediation results in an impasse, then the parties may use the certificate issued by the mediator to proceed with filing their dispute in court.

Pre-litigation mediations are conducted in accordance with the Rules of the North Carolina Supreme Court Implementing Statewide Mediated Settlement Conferences in Superior Court Civil Actions and with Rules Implementing the Pre-Litigation Farm Nuisance Mediation Program (Rules). Other than the pre-litigation aspects, the program operates similarly to the MSC Program. Program forms and copies of the Rules for the farm nuisance program are available from the Dispute Resolution Commission (DRC) and are posted on its website.

Program Impact

Although a few cases have been mediated under the Pre-Litigation Farm Nuisance Program (including some high-profile class-action suits), at the time of publication, the Program has not had a significant impact on the resolution of such disputes. In many instances, parties have elected to waive pre-litigation mediation.

The Year 2000 (Y2K) Pre-Litigation Mediation Program

"Failing to plan is planning to fail."
—American educator and civil rights activist
Effie Neal Jones (1919–2002).

Program History

The Year 2000 Pre-Litigation Mediation Program was established as a statewide program by North Carolina General Statutes Section 66-298 on July 14, 1999. The statute was adopted in response to concerns that surfaced in the business community near the beginning of the new millennium. At that time, there were widespread fears that some computers would not recognize the entry of the Year 2000 (Y2K), and that they would cease to function or not function properly, resulting in massive delays and losses to the business community. The direst predictions included dysfunctional transportation/delivery systems, disabled banks, downed power grids, and massive hardships for ordinary citizens. Authors of the legislation wanted to establish a framework for addressing the disputes that might accompany such widespread computer failures. The legislation and Supreme Court rules that authorized this Program were modeled on the Pre-Litigation Farm Nuisance Mediation Program established in 1995.

Program Summary

In this program, mediation was mandatory before a civil action could be brought in either superior or district court alleging the existence of a Year 2000 Problem, and any case filed prior to a pre-litigation mediation would be dismissed by the court. A Year 2000 Problem is defined by statute as any computing, physical, enterprise, or distribution system complication that has occurred or may occur as a result of the change of the year from 1999 to 2000 in any person's technology system.[2]

Pre-litigation Y2K mediation was initiated by the filing of a Request for Mediation with the clerk of superior court. A copy of the Request was served on all parties to the dispute. A waiver of the requirement for mandatory pre-litigation mediation of a Year 2000 dispute was allowed if the parties agreed and notified the mediator of their waiver in writing. A party with an affirmative defense could also refuse to participate in mediation. Upon receipt of a waiver or refusal to participate, or at the conclusion of a pre-litigation Y2K mediation, the mediator would issue a certification. If the parties applied for a waiver, a party refused to participate, or a mediation resulted in an impasse, then the parties could use the certificate issued by the mediator to proceed with filing their dispute in court. Time periods relating to the filing of a claim for damages resulting from a Y2K Problem were tolled upon the filing of the Request for Mediation until thirty days after the date on which the mediation was concluded, as set forth in the mediator's certification.

Pre-litigation mediations were to be conducted in accordance with the Rules of the North Carolina Supreme Court Implementing Statewide Mediated Settlement Conferences in Superior Court Civil Actions and with Rules Implementing the Year 2000 Pre-Litigation Mediation Program. They were to be completed within sixty days after the date of the mediator's selection or appointment. Other than the pre-litigation aspects of the program, it operated similarly to the MSC Program.

Program Impact

Fortunately, the disasters that were predicted with the coming of the Year 2000 did not occur. The DRC is not aware of any use of the program. Nonetheless, the procedures are described above to provide guidance if a similar model is needed in the future.

Pre-Litigation Mediation of Insurance Claims

"Let us never negotiate out of fear,
but let us never fear to negotiate."
—President John F. Kennedy, Inaugural Address (January 20, 1961).

Program History

In 2003, the legislature passed North Carolina General Statutes Section 7A-38.3A, providing for pre-litigation mediation of insurance claims. The purpose was to allow an insurer to forestall litigation by disclosing the limits of any applicable insurance policy. The thought was that if claimants understood the limits of insurance coverage, they would be more likely in certain situations to try to negotiate a settlement than to engage in potentially costly litigation, especially if the claim readily exceeded the policy limits.

Program Summary

An insurance carrier may initiate mediation of a claim by disclosing the policy limits to the claimant and then filing a request for mediation with the clerk of superior court in a county in which an action may be brought. The statute provides that the mediation is to be conducted in accordance with the rules and policies of the MSC Program, under North Carolina General Statutes Sections 7A-38.1 and 7A-38.2.[3] After the mediation has occurred, the mediator is required to file with the clerk a report stating the date of the mediation, who failed or refused to attend without good cause, and if a settlement was reached. Time periods, such as statutes of limitation, are tolled from the date of the request for mediation until thirty days after the filing of the certificate by the mediator.

Program Impact

This procedure has been used very little, if ever. If an insurance carrier wants to negotiate or mediate, they most likely do so without the formalities of this program. Also, plaintiff's attorneys have not seen the "carrot" of learning the limits of an insurance policy as sufficient incentive to alter the usual process of negotiating and litigating insured claims. This is particularly true when considering the plaintiff's disclosure requirements set forth in North Carolina General Statutes Section 58-3-33 and the fact that policy limits must be disclosed under Rule of Civil Procedure 26(b)(2).

Electrical Supplier Territorial Dispute Mediation Program

"It seemed like a good idea at the time."
—English writer and intellectual Dame Rebecca West (1892–1983).

Program History

In 2005, the General Assembly established a mediation program to handle territorial disputes between suppliers of electrical power throughout North Carolina, including large power companies and smaller, locally owned cooperatives and corporations. Among the various entities, all of the state has been divided into territories, with one provider for each specific territory. This structure is designed to prevent more than one provider from having to build an electrical distribution grid to serve any one location. Having more than one provider build poles and string power lines down the same road is expensive and extremely inefficient. In many parts of the state, the boundary lines between the electrical service providers run across undeveloped farms or woodlands and may not follow property boundary lines. Thus, some parcels may lie within two territories. When the parcels on these boundaries are subdivided and developed, disputes may arise as to which provider has the right (or in some cases the duty) to provide power to the homes or businesses located in the new development. To resolve such disputes, the legislature passed North Carolina General Statutes Section 7A-38.3C, establishing the Electrical Supplier Territorial Dispute (ESTD) Mediation Program.

Program Summary

Under the ESTD Program mediation was not required, but rather was initiated by a party filing a request with the clerk of superior court. The clerk opened a special proceeding file. Once the request was filed, the process became mandatory. All parties were required to participate, except that if all parties agreed, mediation could be waived. The rules for this program closely tracked the MSC Program Rules, with certain exceptions. The ESTD process was much quicker, giving the parties only seven days to select a certified mediator before one was appointed by the court. Once the mediator was selected or appointed, the parties had thirty days to complete the mediation process. The court could grant an extension of the thirty-day period, but for no more than another thirty days. Once the mediation was completed, the mediator was required to file a certification with the clerk. However, under Rule ESTD 8.B, if the dispute was not resolved in the mediation, then the mediator was required to also file copies of the certification with the Clerk of the North Carolina Utilities Commission and the Executive Director of the Public Staff. ESTD Rule 9 outlined a post-mediation hearing process to be conducted within the North Carolina Utilities Commission. The hearing was in the nature of an arbitration, and the hearing officer's opinion was binding on the participants.

Program Impact

In December 2005, the North Carolina Supreme Court adopted rules implementing the ESTD Mediation Program. In 2007, however, before any cases were mediated, the legislature passed a law repealing North Carolina General Statutes Section 7A-38.3C.

Conclusion

Although pre-litigation mediation programs have not played a large role in dispute resolution in North Carolina, the fact that the General Assembly strongly favored mediation indicates that it is perceived as a superior alternative to the standard litigation process. The choice of mediation as the preferred remedy in times of distress serves as high praise for the entire mediation community.

Notes

1. There is debate within the mediation community as to whether pre-suit mediation is the preferred model that should be pursued—as opposed to waiting for a lawsuit to be filed and then referring the parties to mediation.

2. N.C. Gen. Stat. § 66-296.

3. The statute also allows the North Carolina Supreme Court to adopt additional implementing rules or standards. At the time of publication of this book, however, none have been adopted.

CHAPTER THIRTY-SIX

Summary Jury Trials

"The summary jury is the means by which the final settlement figure is ascertained. Having established the settlement parameters, the parties are more willing to simplify the case and shorten the trial, which results in the saving of time and money, especially for the court system."
—Thomas B. Metzloff, The Summary Jury Trial in the North
Carolina Courts, 38 N.C.B.Q. No. 3, 8, at 12 (1991).

Overview

The summary jury trial is a specialized dispute resolution technique. Unlike mediation and arbitration, which can be used in a wide variety of situations, the summary jury trial is appropriate only in certain kinds of cases. In general, a summary jury trial makes sense only in complex civil cases involving substantial sums of money, where the outcome of the case at trial is particularly difficult to predict.

Like many other types of dispute resolution, the specific attributes of a summary jury trial are often modified to suit the needs and interests of the parties. However, the core of the summary jury trial technique consists of condensed presentations by counsel to a jury. The jury—usually drawn from the court's own pool of eligible jurors—then renders a non-binding verdict. A typical summary jury trial can be completed in a single day.

A number of techniques are used to shorten the presentations to the jury. Live testimony is severely curtailed or eliminated altogether. Instead, the attorneys offer the jury summaries of what their key witnesses would say. Evidentiary objections are discouraged, and the traditional questioning of potential jurors during voir dire is either restricted or dispensed with completely. Evidence of marginal value is omitted.

Like most other dispute resolution techniques, the summary jury trial seeks to reach a settlement. Properly conducted, a summary jury trial promotes settlement by showing the parties how a "real" jury evaluates the evidence presented, and by forcing each side to realistically view both the strengths of the opponent's case and the weaknesses of its own case.

Advantages and Disadvantages

The summary jury trial is a powerful settlement technique, particularly when the presentations to the jury accurately depict the evidence that would be introduced at trial. Obviously, if the summary jury trial leads to a settlement, the time and expense of an actual trial can be saved. In addition, the summary jury trial offers the parties a chance to have their case determined by a jury in a setting similar to a civil trial.

Yet the very fact that a summary jury trial approximates a conventional civil trial suggests that it holds similar disadvantages. A summary jury trial usually will not be feasible until after discovery has been completed and the case is close to being ready for trial. Thus, a large part of the time and expense associated with civil litigation cannot be saved. Also, if the case turns on the credibility of one or more witnesses, the summary jury trial may not provide a meaningful preview of likely jury behavior, since live testimony will be limited and cross-examination probably will be unavailable.

The summary jury trial is, on balance, a "niche" dispute resolution technique. It makes sense in complex civil cases where forecasting the outcome at trial is particularly difficult—for instance, when the parties hold widely disparate views of the case. It is important to keep in mind, however, that like most other dispute resolution techniques, the summary jury trial is flexible in nature and can be adapted to suit the needs and wishes of the parties.

The North Carolina Experience

In 1987, the North Carolina Supreme Court authorized the use of summary jury trials in Wake County, Mecklenburg County, and Buncombe County on a provisional basis. (See Chapter 30 for a discussion of the use of summary jury trials in the United States District Court for the Eastern District of North Carolina.) At the end of the pilot program, an evaluation was conducted by the Private Adjudication Center of the Duke University School of Law, which issued a favorable report in early 1991.[1] Later that year, on the recommendation of the Dispute Resolution Committee of the North Carolina Bar Association, the Supreme Court adopted a rule authorizing the use of summary jury trials in superior courts. Rule 23 of the General Rules of Practice for the Superior and District Courts permits the senior resident superior court judge to order the use of a summary jury trial, upon joint motion of the parties.

The most important feature of Rule 23 is that it makes the use of the summary jury trial technique voluntary. The trial judge may suggest its use, but cannot order the parties to conduct a summary jury trial without their consent. Rule 23 also grants the parties considerable leeway in shaping the summary jury trial to fit their needs. For example, the proceeding can be made binding or non-binding. Time limitations for the presentation of evidence can be set in advance, restrictions on voir dire can be imposed, and a referee to preside over the process can be appointed. Nevertheless, the superior court retains jurisdiction over the case at all times, and, where appropriate, may rule on pending motions. In December 2002, summary jury trials were incorporated into a range of settlement procedures available in superior court, pursuant to revised rules implementing statewide mediated settlement conferences and other settlement procedures.

The voluntary nature of the summary jury trial perhaps explains why the technique has not been widely employed in the North Carolina state courts. In those cases where the summary jury trial has been used, the results have been positive. Still, it remains a dispute resolution technique whose potential has not been fully realized.

NOTE
1. Thomas B. Metzloff et al., *Summary Jury Trials in the North Carolina State Court System*, Duke Private Adjudication Center (1991).

CHAPTER THIRTY-SEVEN

ADR and Employment Law Cases

*"Over the next generation, . . . society's greatest opportunities will lie
in tapping human inclinations toward collaboration and compromise
rather than stirring our proclivities for competition and rivalry.
If lawyers are not leaders in marshaling cooperation and designing
mechanisms which allow it to flourish, they will not be at the
center of the most creative social experiments of our time."*

—Former Harvard University President Derek C. Bok,
Law and Its Discontents: A Critical Look at Our Legal System,
38 Record of the Association of the Bar of the
City of New York 12, 20 (1983).

Introduction

In the last two decades, the field of employment law has witnessed an increase in the use of alternative dispute resolution (ADR) processes, particularly pre-litigation private mediation and court-ordered mediation. Many
participants involved in employment law cases are finding that early mediation gives the employee an opportunity to be heard at a time in the process
before each side has amassed considerable fees and expenses, and before
each side has become entrenched in its position.

Parties are privately engaging in pre-litigation ADR, and many employers and employees are also engaging voluntarily in mediation offered by
the Equal Employment Opportunity Commission (EEOC). While employees
have generally been receptive to mediation, employers are becoming more
willing to mediate at an early stage of the parties' dispute as they gain additional experience with the mediation process. In fact, many employers
have embraced ADR in the workplace by creating internal (or "in-house")
organizational systems for conflict resolution.

Although in the past arbitration has been a primary means of resolving
employment disputes, this chapter examines recent changes in the employment law landscape, focusing on the shift toward mediation and in-house
dispute resolution programs. The chapter first discusses the EEOC Mediation Program—how it was established and how it works. Next, private

pre-litigation mediation in employment law cases (particularly sexual harassment cases) is covered. Finally, in-house ADR systems used in private and public organizations for the resolution of employee complaints are explained.

EEOC Mediation Program

Background

The EEOC began its alternative dispute resolution program in 1991 with pilot mediation programs in field offices in Philadelphia, New Orleans, Houston, and Washington, D.C. An evaluation of the pilot programs concluded that they were successful in resolving claims and found a high level of satisfaction among participants.

Because of the pilot programs' success, an ADR Task Force was formed to determine whether the EEOC should use mediation more widely. The Task Force found that mediation was consistent with the agency's goals and recommended expanding the program. As a result of this recommendation, the EEOC issued an ADR policy statement stating that any such program must not only further the mission of the agency, but also that it must be fair, voluntary, neutral, confidential, and enforceable. The policy statement also suggested that any ADR program should take into account the differing priorities and caseloads in EEOC district offices, and that it must have adequate training and evaluation components.[1]

After Congress reenacted the Administrative Dispute Resolution Act (ADRA) in 1996, more funds were made available for agency-sponsored mediations. EEOC field offices began using pro bono mediators, and at the same time the agency entered into its first contract with the Federal Mediation and Conciliation Service (FMCS) to provide outside (external) mediators. By 1997, all EEOC field offices had viable pilot mediation programs in place.

Because of the continued success of the pilot programs, in fiscal year 1999 Congress provided funding specifically for EEOC's mediation program. Field offices hired and trained staff (internal) mediators and entered into contracts with external mediators, who also were carefully selected and trained. While the funding for contract mediators has declined, the agency continues to enter into contracts with skilled external mediators. Since its full implementation in April 1999, the EEOC's ADR Program has been remarkably successful, as indicated by the results of both a 2000 independent evaluation and annual agency ADR program evaluations.[2] Since 2001, the agency has resolved more than 80,000 charges of discrimination through its mediation program.[3]

How the Program Works

Obtaining Agreement to Mediate

Mediation is a pre-investigation procedure in the EEOC setting. When a charge is filed with the EEOC, an intake officer reviews it and determines if the claim is appropriate for mediation. The charging party is then informed that voluntary mediation is available. If the charging party agrees to participate in the mediation process, an internal mediator will contact the employer (by letter, telephone, or e-mail) about participating in the voluntary program. Employers are encouraged to participate, and it is in their interest to take part, since participation in voluntary mediation allows them to stay the preparation of a formal position statement and response to an EEOC Request for Information.

Scheduling and Costs

If both parties consent to mediation, a mediation session is scheduled. The EEOC's ADR Coordinator assigns a mediator (internal or external) to the charge. There is no cost to the parties for the mediation, and it is not necessary to have an attorney or other representative present in order to participate. However, the parties have the right to be represented, if they so choose. If a party retains a representative to take part in the mediation, the party is responsible for payment of any fees and other expenses charged by his or her representative. Once the parties have consented to the mediation, the mediation session generally is scheduled to occur within forty-five days.

The EEOC Mediators

Mediators are either EEOC employees or external mediators who serve under contract with the agency or who serve on a pro bono basis. The external mediators are all experienced mediators who have some experience mediating EEO matters. At one time, the EEOC used the Federal Mediation and Conciliation Service (FMCS); however, FMCS is used only sparingly because of the increase in internal mediators.

The Mediation Session

Prior to the start of the mediation session, the participants (parties and their representatives) are required to sign an agreement to mediate and a confidentiality agreement. In addition, it is crucial to the success of the mediation that the persons attending have the authority to settle the dispute.

EEOC mediation sessions generally last three to four hours and are conducted in the same manner as mediation conferences in other settings. The mediator begins the mediation with a joint session and then may convene the parties in private caucuses. If the parties reach an accord, they will execute an EEOC agreement. However, if the agreement reached references terms over which the EEOC has no jurisdiction or contains terms to which the EEOC cannot be a party (e.g., complete waiver of all claims that could arise during employment) the parties will execute a separate agreement. If the EEOC is a party to the executed agreement and the agreement is breached, it may seek to enforce the agreement in court, just like any other settlement agreement involving a charge of discrimination filed with the EEOC.

Since fiscal year 2005, more than 70 percent of the charges mediated by EEOC have resulted in resolution.[4] In cases not resolved, the charge is sent to the EEOC enforcement unit for investigation. Information revealed during the mediation may not be disclosed to anyone, including members of the enforcement unit. Investigators have been instructed to suspend any line of inquiry with a charging party or respondent who begins to discuss what took place in mediation.

Private Pre-Litigation Mediation of Employment Law Cases[5]

For many years, the public policy of the United States encouraged ADR for certain types of employment-related cases. Yet, until the late 1990s, ADR had not achieved prominence outside the area of labor relations, and no single dispute resolution process had assumed a preferred position. Many employers and some legal scholars pressed for arbitration as the primary means of resolving employment disputes. In the last few years, however, as many questions about arbitrating statutory employment disputes have remained unresolved, mediation has emerged as a preferred means for resolving workplace claims (and in particular, sexual harassment claims).

Although the evidence is still largely anecdotal and somewhat inconclusive, mediation appears to have the inside track among ADR alternatives as a favored form of dispute resolution in the federal courts, at the EEOC, and among private counsel and their clients involved in employment discrimination disputes. Both employers and employees are understandably looking for relief from the high cost of discovery-driven litigation, a phenomenon only likely to become more costly as social media and electronically stored information (ESI) issues come to the fore. Utilizing an appropriate dispute resolution method without engaging in full discovery can result in significant cost savings for all parties and can reduce caseloads for the judiciary. Mediation appears well suited for this task.

The Advantages and Disadvantages of Mediating Employment Discrimination Disputes

Although mediation may not be a panacea for all problems besetting the American judicial system, when applied to employment discrimination disputes (and particularly to claims of sexual harassment), the advantages of mediation appear to outweigh its disadvantages. What follows is a summary of the pluses and minuses of mediation as it relates to sexual harassment claims. This summary can also be applied more generally to other workplace discrimination claims as well.

ADVANTAGES OF MEDIATION

Safe forum

Mediation provides a comfortable forum for all parties. Thus, it is more likely to facilitate a workable resolution to a dispute than a more adversarial process involving adjudication in a formal setting under a fixed set of rules. In cases alleging sexual harassment, the mediated settlement conference is a safe and confidential setting that permits the employee to assert his or her claims and to confront the employer with less apprehension. It also provides some protection against retaliation by the accused. For the alleged harasser, the mediated settlement conference is also a safe forum for trying to explain (if not deny) the conduct at issue. For the employer, mediation offers an opportunity to address a problem directly and to obtain feedback without fear of having its position misconstrued by either the victim or the alleged harasser, both of whom may be productive and valued employees. Despite some legitimate criticism that victims may find it uncomfortable to face their harassers, the safeguards of the mediated settlement conference, under the guidance of experienced mediators, should alleviate most concerns about compounding any wrongdoing.

Confidential forum

Mediation provides a confidential forum for resolving disputes without revealing publicly the intimate and embarrassing details of conduct that might otherwise have to be disclosed in adjudication. While this feature of mediation may seem troublesome in a judicial system that our society generally regards as public and transparent (a disadvantage discussed below), both employers and employees generally seem to appreciate the opportunity to air their differences in private. Anecdotal reports indicate that the privacy of mediated negotiations appears to make resolution of those differences more likely.

Early resolution

The prospect of settlement at an early stage offers substantial advantages to all parties, especially in cases where acts constituting sexual harassment are admitted or otherwise verified in the course of mediation. The victim, who may be quite traumatized, will be permitted to obtain appropriate redress, including counseling or other treatment that he or she otherwise might not have been able to afford, and will generally be able to move beyond the incident more quickly. The alleged harasser can be held accountable (or absolved from wrongdoing) more quickly and, if appropriate, trained or sensitized more effectively through early intervention. From the standpoint of the employer, early settlement offers the obvious advantages of both cost savings and minimal distraction from the ordinary course of business. Finally, given the cost of litigation—and particularly the financial, emotional, and lost opportunity costs associated with discovery—early settlement through mediation offers all parties a significant incentive to participate in good faith.

Dealing with emotions

Mediation provides an opportunity to redirect emotions in a more productive manner. In contrast to the courtroom or the arbitral forum, where a rule-bound adversarial process subjects parties to the stress of cross-examination, mediation is designed to put the parties at ease in a setting where their own interests and needs are more adequately addressed. This is not to say that emotions in a sexual harassment case are left outside the door of the conference room. Both the general session and the private caucuses may involve displays of emotion on all sides. Indeed, such displays are sometimes therapeutic and may ultimately be useful to mediators in ferreting out a victim's true concerns and interests. Particularly in a sexual harassment case, the unhealthy aspects of these emotions can best be managed in a setting where the parties are in control of the proceeding and are made to feel that way. Among the commonly used ADR alternatives, only mediation offers this opportunity.

Flexibility

Adaptability of procedures and flexibility of outcomes are among mediation's primary advantages in employment discrimination cases. Standard mediation procedures can be adjusted to meet the physical and emotional needs of the parties, and the range of other remedies available to the parties is bounded only by their own creativity. In contrast to the judicial or arbitral forums, mediation allows parties to craft remedies without regard to the confines of Title VII of the Civil Rights Act of 1964 (which prohibits employment discrimination based on race, color, religion, sex, or national origin) or other statutes. Mediators who seize this advantage of flexibility can engage in creative ways to help the parties resolve their differences.

Financial benefits

Although there does not appear to be any hard evidence to affirm or deny it, there is considerable anecdotal evidence to suggest that both victims and their employers in gender discrimination cases can benefit financially from mediating these disputes. Available evidence suggests that while employers can often avoid liability at the high end of the damage scale through mediated settlements, they are also more likely to pay something in a greater number of cases. On the other hand, victims of discrimination, particularly sexual harassment, can expect a more certain recovery through mediation. They must balance this likelihood against the prospect of receiving the maximum relief available—though rarely attainable—at trial.

Precedential value

The avoidance of troublesome precedent is a positive consequence of mediation's inherent privacy. Some victims, of course, may not care about the effect of their own settlements on other situations, but there is often a desire to change an employer's practices in order to discourage future instances of harassment. On the other hand, employers are understandably concerned about the precedential effect of any disposition of an employment discrimination claim, particularly in the area of sexual harassment, where valuing a claim is so case specific. That is why confidentiality, for good or ill, is such a common element in mediated settlements of employment claims.

Preserving relationships

One of the principal values of mediation—the resolution of a dispute in a manner conducive to the continuance of a business, professional, or personal relationship—gives it an advantage over other adjudicatory forms of dispute resolution. Judicial litigation and private arbitration, with their emphasis on adversary procedures, tend to drive parties further apart, thus endangering the future of the employer-employee relationship. If the promise of Title VII—to make the nation's workplaces equitable and more hospitable for all workers—is to be fully vindicated, non-adjudicatory ADR devices like mediation are the most promising means of handling workplace discrimination cases.

Avoiding legal uncertainty

Another of mediation's advantages has a special meaning in the field of sexual harassment. The shift of focus in mediation away from the technical legal merits of a dispute lessens the impact that undecided legal issues may have on resolving the dispute. By directing the parties' attention to their interests instead of to their legal positions, a mediator can sidestep the uncertainties in Title VII law to a far greater extent than is possible with other ADR techniques. Although the Unites States Supreme Court has attempted to settle most recurring issues in employment discrimination law, the net result has been to raise as many questions as it has resolved. Mediation thus remains advantageous in navigating through legal waters that are still uncertain or uncharted.

Personal autonomy

Perhaps the most significant advantage mediation has to offer in sexual harassment cases is the greater chance for a victim to heal from emotional injuries and to recover a sense of self-determination. After all, in mediation it is the party—not some outside agent such as a jury, a judge, or an arbitrator—who decides whether or not and on what terms to resolve the claim. Particularly for victims of sexual harassment, the prospect of controlling a situation—instead of being controlled by it—may be critical to recovering self-esteem, continuing gainful employment, and stabilizing fraught personal situations. In this regard, personal autonomy is recognized and validated through the mediation process. The recognition of individual dignity and equality before the law is, of course, at the heart of Title VII's promise. Self-resolution through mediation thus advances Title VII's goal of systematically ending discrimination in the workplaces of America.

DISADVANTAGES OF MEDIATION

Jurisprudence not advanced

Mediation may impair the orderly development of a coherent employment discrimination jurisprudence. To the extent that mediation is successful in resolving large numbers of disputes, the cases left for the courts to decide may involve such unique factual situations that the resulting body of case law will be shaped (and possibly distorted) by mediation's "leftovers."

Lack of public vindication

The absence of public vindication—and thus the possible recovery of a party's reputation—is a distinct disadvantage of mediation from the standpoint of an employee. However, most employees confronted with this reality still opt to agree to confidentiality in order to gain other benefits offered by employers.

Appearance of weakness

Some parties—typically employers, but occasionally employees—believe that proposing or even agreeing to mediation is a sign of weakness or an admission of responsibility. Whatever disadvantage may be associated with that perception, the increased use of court-ordered mediation as an ADR device has greatly diminished its force. Indeed, in North Carolina, mediation is the norm for employment cases in all federal districts, and neither side has anything to fear from embracing this process fully.

Revealing evidence

Disclosure of unrevealed information that may be used at trial is another perceived disadvantage of mediation. Mediators often hear experienced trial counsel lament the prospect of having to deal with "trial secret" type of information during a mediation. Sexual harassment cases appear no different in this regard. Indeed, the kind of intimate, personal, and potentially embarrassing information about parties that is often revealed in the mediation of a sexual harassment dispute magnifies the disadvantage that some parties and trial lawyers perceive. Responsible mediators, however, have been able to minimize much of the worry about secret information and trial strategies through scrupulous adherence to their duty of confidentiality under the Standards of Professional Conduct for Mediators adopted by the North Carolina Dispute Resolution Commission. Nevertheless, the parties themselves must ultimately decide whether revealing undisclosed material information in the hope of resolving the dispute outweighs the risk that mediation might fail, with the attendant possibility that such sensitive information might become a matter of public record at trial.

Lack of deterrence

Mediated settlements may not fully serve the deterrence objective of Title VII. The lack of public disapproval, the prospect of cheaper and quicker settlements, and other perceived advantages of privately negotiated and confidentially performed settlements may result in fewer incentives for employers to control the conduct of their supervisors, managers, and other employees. As the jurisprudence of employer liability has matured and a body of settlements has grown under the regime of mandatory mediation of employment suits, confidentiality has been the rule. The inability of the bar and the public to assess whether mediated settlements reflect the merits of cases in rough economic terms has made it more difficult to convince employers of their exposure to liability for employment discrimination.

Obscuring what the law requires

The confidential nature of most mediated employment settlements deprives the community of information about what the law actually is, who is violating the law, and what the costs of illegal conduct are. Some prominent members of the academic community see this aspect of mediation—and of settlement in general—as a substantial departure from sound public policy. Congress may eventually examine the consequences of private resolution of employment discrimination disputes. Until that time, however, confidentiality appears to be the norm.

Public policy concerns

The absence of public scrutiny of how sexual harassment law is being developed and applied may be a significant disadvantage of this trend toward the "privatization" of justice in the workplace. Not only is there little assurance about how the careful framework of employer liability is being construed and applied at the negotiating table, but the lack of oversight and the absence of a public record of negotiations and outcomes make it unlikely that the law can be applied in any uniform way across the country. Moreover, justice achieved in private may be regarded by some as an abdication of public authority by the judiciary to a private group of professionals (mediators). Whatever force these arguments about public oversight may have in other areas, Congress long ago expressed in Title VII a legislative preference for methods of conference, conciliation, and persuasion to resolve employment discrimination disputes. And, most importantly, the fact that resolution by mediation is both entirely consensual and backed up by a court system which handles disputes that do not settle is some assurance that privatization is not being pursued in a way that offends either our system of public justice or the manner in which Congress said Title VII should be enforced.

Internal Organizational Systems for Conflict Resolution

Both public and private organizations in the United States have relied upon use of internally administered (in-house) ADR systems for the prevention and resolution of internal organizational disputes. These internal systems are formal procedures designed and administered by an organization for the systematic and uniform resolution of internal grievances and conflicts.[6]

Advantages of Internal Dispute Resolution Systems

Increasingly, public and private organizations are incorporating internal processes that utilize ADR for many of the same reasons private parties use mediation or arbitration in lieu of litigation. In the experience of many Fortune 1000 companies, ADR and internal systems for dispute resolution share the following advantages over litigation or administrative hearings: time savings, monetary savings, preservation of confidentiality, avoidance of legal precedents, more satisfactory settlements, more satisfactory processes, and more durable resolutions.

From the perspective of the individuals involved, many internal organizational disputes lend themselves to the outcomes most frequently produced by mediation, namely: the parties retain some control over the process; remedies can be broadly structured to allow parties to address numerous and varied concerns; relationships can be restored and preserved; and parties can feel they have had the opportunity to be heard, recognized, and empowered.

From the perspective of the organization, internal systems for the resolution of disputes provide a "safety valve" to address problems at the earliest stage of grievance, preventing them from escalating to the point where the parties become more entrenched in their positions and eventually resort to litigation. Such a system keeps the organization's problems inside the organization, thus preserving confidentiality, offering substantial savings in both time and money, providing disputants with faster resolution, and avoiding the dual costs to the organization of both lost productivity and escalating legal fees.

Global and domestic economic conditions have created greater pressure on both private and public organizations to control costs and increase productivity in order to remain economically viable. Not surprisingly, organizations have learned from experience that protracted litigation and unresolved workplace conflict decrease productivity and increase costs.

A survey conducted by the Cornell Institute of Conflict Resolution of Fortune 1000 companies located in the United States found that 78 percent of the companies reported using mediation and 62 percent reported using arbitration for the resolution of internal employment-based disputes.[7] Many corporations, such as Motorola and NCR (formerly the National Cash Register Company), as well as governmental organizations, such as the United States Air Force, the Department of Veterans Affairs, and the United States Postal Service, have implemented highly successful internal systems for the resolution of disputes that rely heavily on ADR processes.[8]

Design of Internal System

Many of these organizational models for internal dispute resolution follow a similar design. A system is created that provides for the resolution of employee grievances or internal disputes through a series of escalating interventions ranging from training, to coaching, to mediation, and finally, to arbitration. The system is generally operated and administered by and through the human resources or employee relations office of the organization, in consultation with the training and development department and office of legal counsel. In the broadest sense, these systems are designed to operate at the preventive level through programs offering skills training in conflict resolution, communication, and coaching for managers and supervisors.

These internal ADR programs also work at the remedial level by creating a structure of escalating interventions, allowing an aggrieved party to access multiple forums in which to seek redress. In the first of such opportunities, a party in conflict may elect to file a complaint describing the situation with an appropriate officer in human resources or employee relations, or with a program administrator external to the organization. The filing of this grievance triggers the filing party's right to seek coaching and consultation from a neutral third party, who may be either an internal member of the company from human resources or employee relations, or an external consultant/coach retained for this purpose.

If an individual consultation does not result in resolution, the complaining party has the option to request a form of mediated settlement conference, in which a mediator facilitates a dialogue between the parties in dispute. Again, depending upon the model, this mediator can be an employee of the organization from a department neutral to the dispute (typically the human resources or employee relations department), or the mediator may be an external contractor retained for this purpose. Organizations determine how they want to structure this role, bearing in mind that the perceived neutrality of the mediator and confidentiality of the proceedings are essential contributing factors to the success of the mediation session. For this reason, many organizations choose to have the mediator be an independent outside party.

If the mediated settlement conference fails to produce a resolution, the parties may then elect to proceed to arbitration, choosing arbitrators from a panel pre-screened and selected by the organization. These individuals come from an outside source, either as private ADR providers, or as individuals offered through a commercial panel such as JAMS (formerly Judicial Arbitration & Mediation Services)/Endispute or the American Arbitration Association. The arbitration may be conducted by a single arbitrator chosen by consent of both parties, or by a panel of three arbitrators, with one selected by each party and the third selected by the two arbitrators. Arbitration in this context may be binding or non-binding.

Success of Programs

Such programs have proven successful at reducing costs and restoring productivity. For example, over a six-year period, Motorola reported a 75 percent reduction in employment-related litigation costs after implementation of a mediation option for employees to resolve their disputes. Over a seven-year period, NCR reported a 50 percent reduction in employment-related litigation costs and a corresponding drop of pending lawsuits from 263 to twenty-eight. The United States Air Force estimated savings of 50 percent per claim in one hundred EEO complaints through routine use of mediation.[9]

Cost savings to organizations can be measured in both tangible and intangible ways. Easily quantified savings can be measured through reduced legal costs resulting from a reduction in EEO complaints and lawsuits filed. Costs eliminated or reduced include the fees associated with inside and outside counsel, as well as the reduced productivity of managers, executives, and workers engaged (either directly or indirectly) in the litigation or hearing process through testimony, deposition, and discovery-related activities. Cost savings may also be measured through reduction in potentially substantial monetary judgments against the organization.

Equally compelling to the human resource and employee relations departments are the potential savings that result from more intangible factors, such as increased individual and group productivity, increased employee morale, and lowered attrition. Organizations also benefit by avoiding the damage to reputation and morale that can come from highly publicized organizational disputes. Organizations that embrace ADR systems may also help foster a culture of innovation reflecting larger organizational values such as collaboration, creativity, recognition, and empowerment.

While many organizations have found such systems to be effective, not all organizations have embraced ADR or internal ADR systems, nor are all attempts to create these internal systems successful. Key components of success include strong executive and management support for the effort and the commitment of mid-level and frontline managers to such initiatives. In some instances, senior management has recognized the potential cost savings and benefits to the organization of such systems, but the effort failed because mid-level and first-line management resisted implementation, feeling a threat to their power and authority.

Other key components of a successful internal system include the perception of fairness and neutrality of the system. If its use is voluntary, those entering the system must perceive its value. If its use is mandated, then effectiveness for the participants depends largely on the ability of the process to deliver a satisfactory result. Positive results often depend upon the level of participation that the parties are willing to exhibit. The level of participation and commitment to the process is higher when all parties perceive it to be fair, consistent, reliable, confidential, and administered by competent neutrals.[10]

Summary of Internal ADR Programs

As organizations seek ways to increase efficiency and productivity while decreasing costs, many have examined ways to reduce the expenses associated with internal conflict. A significant percentage of private, public, commercial, and governmental organizations have turned to some form of ADR to handle disputes and to avoid the costs, delay, and other perceived disadvantages of litigation or administrative hearings as a mechanism to resolve conflict. Some of these organizations have taken the additional step of designing their own internal process for the resolution of disputes, which typically involves some combination of training, coaching, mediation, and arbitration. The general structure and mechanism of these programs follows a consistent pattern. Parties with a grievance file a complaint, which triggers access to an escalating series of opportunities designed by the organization to address the grievance. These programs begin, in some instances, with individual consultation with a neutral third-party consultant, coach, or mediator and advance through internal mediation and arbitration involving all parties to the dispute. Cost savings reported from such internal systems can be significant and may include tangible savings in litigation costs and monetary judgments as well as other less tangible benefits, such as increased employee retention, morale, and productivity.

NOTES

1. *EEOC's Alternative Dispute Resolution Policy Statement*, EEOC Notice No. 915.002 (July 17, 1995).

2. E. Patrick McDermott et al., *An Evaluation of the Equal Employment Opportunity Commission Mediation Program*, EEOC Order No. 9/0900/7632/2 (Sept. 20, 2000).

3. *See* "EEOC Mediation Statistics FY 1999 through FY 2010," U.S. Equal Employment Opportunity Commission, http://www.eeoc.gov/eeoc/mediation/mediation_stats.cfm.

4. *Id.*

5. Much of this section consists of excerpts from (or is based on) material contained in Jonathan R. Harkavy's article *Privatizing Workplace Justice: The Advent of Mediation in Resolving Sexual Harassment Disputes*, 34 Wake Forest L. Rev. 135 (1999) (citations omitted).

6. *See* Cathy A. Constantino and Christina Sickles Merchant, *Designing Conflict Management Systems* (Jossey-Bass 1996), for detailed definitions of conflict management systems.

7. David Lipsky and Ron Seeber, *The Appropriate Resolution of Corporate Disputes: A Report on the Growing Use of ADR by U.S. Corporations*, Cornell/PERC Institute on Conflict Resolution (Ithaca, N.Y., 1998).

8. Administrative Dispute Resolution Act of 1996, Pub. L. No. 104-320 (encourages use of ADR methods to resolve controversies relating to administrative programs).

9. Karl A. Slaikeu and Ralph H. Hasson, *Controlling the Costs of Conflict: How to Design a System for Your Organization* (Jossey-Bass 1998), pp. 14–15.

10. John P. Conbere, "Theory Building for Conflict Management System Design," *Conflict Resolution Quarterly* 19, no. 2 (Winter 2001): 215–35.

CHAPTER THIRTY-EIGHT

The IACT Program:
Using Collaborative Law
to Resolve Medical Malpractice Claims

*"As an attorney and judge, I have been involved in many cases arising
out of the medical care of patients. I have concluded that our system
for resolving many of these cases fails the patient and the health care
provider. As an alternative to litigation, the IACT Program offers
an efficient option that addresses the needs of the parties
through a collaborative process."*

—Judge Ralph A. Walker, retired Superior Court and
North Carolina Court of Appeals judge and first chair of
the North Carolina Dispute Resolution Commission.

Introduction

Research shows that the three things patients want most when faced with a
medical error are information about what happened, a sincere apology, and
measures to prevent the error from happening to someone else. Financial
compensation is a lower priority.[1] Frequently, however, information about
the patient's medical treatment is withheld. Patients often pursue litigation
simply to obtain answers, seeking help from an attorney out of a sense of
anger and frustration.

When unanticipated adverse medical outcomes occur—whether due to
error or not—physicians and other health care providers tend to distance
themselves from patients and their families due to feelings of guilt and/or
fear of malpractice litigation.[2] This defensive response only fuels specula-
tion that something went wrong—that otherwise, information would not
have been withheld.

Physicians often want the opportunity to answer a patient's questions
when there is an adverse medical outcome, and health care organizations
would like the chance to design or modify systems to prevent future incidents. Both want to repair relationships with patients and families and to
maintain a good reputation within their community. However, these opportunities are often denied.

Lawsuits strongly affect doctors. Among physicians who have been sued for malpractice, 97 percent experience significant physical or emotional reactions. They often feel unfairly targeted. Although actual rates of medical error are high, doctors overestimate the rate of malpractice claims brought in response to those errors, perhaps because the impact is so devastating to them.[3] In August 2011, a study published in the *New England Journal of Medicine* found that 75 to 99 percent of physicians, depending on their specialty, are sued during their careers.[4] Even seeing a colleague endure the process of litigation is quite painful and anxiety provoking. As a result, physician tolerance for uncertainty about medical outcomes is pushed to very low levels, and they tend to practice medicine more defensively. After unanticipated adverse outcomes, whether there has been an error or not, patients often become "potential plaintiffs" in the minds of physicians. In reality, only 2–3 percent of patients injured by medical mistakes actually file lawsuits, and only half of those who bring a suit ever receive compensation.[5]

Most Americans are becoming increasingly aware of the frequency of medical errors. A landmark report published in 2000 by the Institute of Medicine[6] showed that medical errors were the eighth leading cause of death in the United States, exceeding the number of deaths from motor vehicle accidents and breast cancer combined. (This statistic did not include the number of errors resulting in permanent injuries that did not involve death.) Recent estimates, according to U.S. Department of Health and Human Services Secretary Kathleen Sebelius, are that one in three hospitalizations results in a medical error.[7] Tremendous efforts to increase patient safety have been directed at encouraging disclosure of medical errors and near misses, in order to understand why they occurred and how to design safer systems. Patient safety improvements depend on the ability of health care providers to learn from errors and near misses, yet disclosure is far from the norm. Fear of litigation creates secrecy and mistrust; lack of disclosure creates frustrated, angry patients and families.

Though appropriate for some cases, our tort system provides only one remedy—financial compensation. Yet, medical malpractice claims are about so much more than money. Doctors, patients, and families need to resolve conflicts early on through a process that brings them together to work through conflicts and restore relationships. Medical disclosure and transparency through a safe, supportive, and highly effective dispute resolution process can address both the individual needs of patients and physicians and the broader goals of disclosure and patient safety.

The Tort System/Litigation Model

When medical care or treatment results in an unexpected adverse outcome, health care providers and organizations customarily notify their medical malpractice insurers of a possible claim. Lawyers are routinely engaged at this stage, even if no lawsuit has been initiated. Health care providers and organizations generally follow the advice of counsel and decline to discuss the patient's care with the patient or his or her family. While this result is logical in the context of potential or actual litigation, it may prompt a lawsuit, as patients and families seek information and answers. Although lawsuits *may* result in monetary payments, they often fail to address the deeper needs of those involved and do little to foster quality-improvement efforts. Unfortunately, very few patients injured from medical error ever receive compensation. Research shows that only 2 percent of those harmed ever file a lawsuit and far fewer ever receive compensation.[8] Moreover, patients actually receive less than 50 percent of each dollar awarded in compensation, as the rest is used to cover costs and attorney fees.[9]

The IACT Program

The Integrated Accountability & Collaborative Transparency Program (IACT Program) is a pilot dispute resolution program sponsored by Carolina Dispute Settlement Services in Raleigh. Under the leadership of Jessica S. Scott, M.D., J.D., it offers an entirely new approach for addressing claims that could result in medical malpractice litigation. The IACT Program combines two innovative and successful models for early dispute resolution and learning: (1) the disclosure-and-offer model, as employed most notably by the University of Michigan Health System; and (2) collaborative law, an alternative dispute resolution method used primarily in the family law arena. The result is a safe and supportive conflict resolution process that emphasizes transparency and early disclosure of medical errors when they occur in order to minimize the physical, emotional, and financial stress for patients, doctors, and health care organizations. Even when there is no medical error associated with an unanticipated adverse outcome, transparency allows for increased understanding of the event and often improves health care quality and safety.

The IACT model serves as an alternative to our current tort system and is more effective than litigation in satisfying many of the needs that result from adverse medical outcomes, including the following:

- Patients receive full disclosure, an understanding of what occurred, and, in appropriate cases, an apology and timely compensation.

- Physicians are allowed to proactively address issues and communicate with their patients in a safe and effective way, so that both physicians and patients can gain closure.

- Health care organizations can learn from errors (and near misses) to improve systems and processes in health care delivery.

- Society as a whole benefits through an increase in patient safety and reduced costs.

Rex Hospital in Raleigh, part of the UNC Health Care System, was the first health care facility in the state to begin implementing the IACT Program, starting January 1, 2012. At the time of this book's publication, several other hospital systems in North Carolina have also expressed interest in implementing the Program.

How the IACT Program Works

Overview

The IACT Program uses specially trained collaborative law attorneys, coaches, and neutral medical experts who are committed to the peaceful, non-adversarial, and cooperative resolution of conflict. The model focuses on conflict resolution through transparency and full disclosure with interest-based (rather than positional) negotiations to promote healing and closure for both patient and doctor (or other health care provider). Participation is voluntary, and patients never give up their right to pursue remedies in the court system.

Collaborative law is not mediation. When parties mediate, discovery typically has been largely completed. When the parties are together, the attorneys do most of the talking, but much of the process takes place with the parties separated. In collaborative law, the parties sit together, face-to-face, and engage in difficult but very necessary conversations. They explore the problem together. The collaborative law attorneys help to structure the conversation and guide each party to better understand and communicate underlying needs and interests to the other party. For example, patients will often need information and empathy, and perhaps forgiveness of medical charges; provision of follow-up treatment; or compensation for future care resulting from medical error. Physicians may need to provide information about what happened and share their feelings about the adverse outcome, especially when they have made an error. Physicians also may feel the need to apologize, which may help them gain closure. Even when they have not made an error, physicians may still feel remorse regarding a poor outcome. The therapeutic doctor-patient relationship has been harmed, and both parties may have an interest in repairing it. Doctors will want to avoid the stress of litigation, and if patients feel that their needs have been addressed and adequately met, most will also want to avoid the long and stressful process of litigation. Health care organizations may want to resolve conflict, avoid negative publicity, and, most importantly, learn about poor outcomes and near misses so that they can improve quality of care in an effective and efficient manner. The collaborative law approach helps to achieve all of these results.

To begin the process, the parties meet with their respective collaborative law attorneys to prepare for an upcoming collaborative conference, when all parties meet together. Most cases involve between one and three conferences, each lasting two to three hours. The conference is designed to allow the parties to work toward the creation of a resolution that most adequately meets their collective needs. Collaborative law coaches, who are licensed psychotherapists specially trained for their unique role as coaches in the IACT Program, assist the parties separately in understanding their needs and communicating effectively in the conference. Based upon the information gained from their clients in the pre-conference meetings, the collaborative law attorneys then assist the parties during the collaborative conference. Each party is able to ask questions and share information that he or she believes is important for the other to know.

The IACT Program requires all parties to sign a participation agreement with a confidentiality clause at the beginning of the conference to protect the information that is discussed during the collaborative conference. In preparation for the conference, a neutral medical expert with subject matter expertise reviews the related medical records and then provides information to both parties about the medical care or treatment at issue. The expert determines whether the medical care provided was reasonable or unreasonable, and he or she is available to answer any questions the parties may have as they prepare for the conference. The parties will have the benefit of this information and the neutral expert's opinion for use during the conference.

If a resolution is reached during the conference, the attorneys draft a Health Care Settlement Agreement. If the parties are not able to reach a mutually satisfactory resolution and wish to pursue litigation, the collaborative law attorneys must withdraw, since they are barred from litigating the case. Upon request, however, they may refer the parties to other counsel to pursue litigation.

The Three Stages of IACT's Collaborative Law Model

Patients at medical facilities participating in the IACT Program are automatically eligible to utilize this dispute resolution process. If they experience an unanticipated adverse outcome, a patient (or his or her family) may elect to participate. No patient is ever required to take part, however, and patients do not give up their rights to pursue remedies through the court system. The three stages of the IACT Program are described below:

BEGINNING STAGE—TRANSPARENCY AND DISCLOSURE

Once a patient elects to participate in the IACT Program, each party selects an attorney from a list of several IACT Program collaborative law attorneys provided to them by the IACT Program case manager. The IACT Program attorneys alternate representing patients, doctors, and hospitals to avoid being locked into one point of view.

As a first step, the participating facility gathers all relevant medical records and provides them to the IACT Program case manager. The case manager makes copies for the attorneys and the neutral medical expert, who is selected through the IACT Program to review the records and render an opinion about the case. (In some cases, there may be more than one neutral medical expert.) The neutral medical expert reviews the records, forms an opinion, and communicates with each party's attorney. The expert notifies the collaborative lawyers of all opinions with respect to the case. Thereafter, the attorneys have an opportunity to consult the expert to gain a better understanding of the facts of the case and the basis for the physician expert's opinions.

To prepare for the collaborative conference, the parties meet with their respective IACT Program collaborative law attorneys. Each collaborative law attorney helps his or her client to identify underlying needs and interests, as well as the goals and objectives for the conference. During this pre-conference meeting, the attorney also shares the medical expert opinions with the client. If necessary, the lawyer can seek clarification as to any additional questions the client may have. Attorneys communicate with one another closely to facilitate the collaborative process and to prepare for the collaborative conference. Each collaborative law attorney assesses whether his or her client might benefit from one or more sessions with a collaborative coach. The role of the coach is to assist in preparing the client for the collaborative conference by helping that party to clearly articulate his or her perspective, feelings, and needs and to actively listen to the other parties involved.

MIDDLE STAGE—THE COLLABORATIVE CONFERENCE

After the parties have had an opportunity to gather information, and to meet with their respective attorneys and coaches, they proceed to the collaborative conference. The collaborative conference takes place at a neutral location. Together, the parties and collaborative lawyers: (1) review the program's participation agreement, including the confidentiality clause; (2) assure clear understanding of the terms; and (3) and sign the agreement. At this point, the substantive part of the collaborative conference begins.

The collaborative conference allows patients and/or families to ask questions about all aspects of patient care before, during, and after the salient event. Of particular focus are the acts (or omissions) that resulted in the adverse outcome. The patient and/or family often have specific questions that they want answered. It is critically important that they are able to ask these questions of the individuals who were directly involved in the medical care or treatment that led to the adverse outcome. Each medical professional has the opportunity to answer questions and to explain what happened and why, to the best of his or her knowledge. Also, the face-to-face meeting allows for a heartfelt communication from one human being to another, which often has a powerful impact on forgiveness, especially if accusations and defensiveness can be minimized.

The neutral medical review allows all of the parties to place what happened in context. Whether or not medical error is found, the patient and family may begin to understand why the outcome was poor. They may feel relieved to have answers to their questions, and where there was an error, an apology can be quite powerful. On the other hand, when there is no error, this independent review will offer consolation and reassurance to the physician, who may be second-guessing himself or herself and feeling significant guilt. The physician may even be feeling anxious or depressed as a result of having delivered what he or she believes was suboptimal care. Physicians, nurses, and hospital administrators may be questioning one another's actions, and all may feel on the defensive. Thus, there is a genuine need for an open forum with a neutral expert opinion, allowing for increased understanding for all involved. The collaborative conference also may result in identification of health care systems issues that can be targeted for improvement.

END STAGE—RESOLUTION

If the parties are able to resolve their differences through the IACT Program, they will enter into a Health Care Settlement Agreement. This settlement agreement will include the resolution to which the parties have collectively agreed. It also will routinely include a waiver of malpractice claims arising from the care at issue, unless the parties agree otherwise. For example, such an agreement could include an obligation for the hospital to improve or redesign any procedures or systems that may have contributed to the adverse outcome. Similarly, physicians feel supported and less stressed through improved relationships with hospitals and patients.

Where successful, the IACT Program enables doctors and hospitals to save time and resources that would otherwise have been devoted to defending a lawsuit. Instead, it allows them to focus on quality improvements and patient safety. In addition to increasing patient safety, the hospital may improve its relationship with the patient and/or family and avoid the negative attention of a lawsuit. The collaborative process may also strengthen the hospital's relationship, not only with the physicians involved in a particular event, but also with the medical staff generally.

For patients and families, it can be truly transformative to have open communication with their medical care providers, to understand what happened, and to have their needs met quickly and responsively. Early resolution of a dispute over medical care or treatment can eliminate the years of anger and emotional turmoil that a lawsuit may bring and may provide for compensation within months of a medical error's occurrence. The parties are able to create an agreement that works for them as individuals, with their particular needs and interests in mind, rather than having a result imposed on them by a judge or jury, whether in the tort system or administrative tribunals (such as health courts).

Conclusion

When unexpected adverse outcomes occur, the IACT Program provides a safe and effective process for understanding and resolving complex issues, whether there has been a medical error or merely an unanticipated poor outcome. The Program offers the opportunity to share information and to compensate a greater number of patients than in the traditional tort system, while at the same time enhancing quality of care and reducing overall legal expenses.

Transparency also allows medical professionals and health care organizations to learn from errors, near misses, and adverse outcomes. Specifically, health care organizations obtain the benefit of this information to improve systems and processes in health care delivery. Improved systems will assume inevitable human error but will incorporate procedures to reduce the risk of catastrophic injury, based on experience. When health care professionals work in a culture that encourages disclosure and learning from errors, near misses, and adverse outcomes, patient safety improves and legal and health care costs decrease.[10]

The IACT Program also offers an opportunity to address the human side of health care when poor outcomes occur. The Program's transparency allows patients, families, doctors, and hospitals to have conversations when care does not go as planned. Patients and families gain information about what happened and will know that measures are being taken to prevent the same error from happening to someone else. Doctors can explain the facts surrounding patient care and express their thoughts and feelings about those facts. These difficult conversations will help those involved to gain closure.

Like all ADR techniques, the IACT Program provides an option other than adjudication by trial. A court proceeding may seem to hold promise of vindication or exoneration, yet in most cases the patient-plaintiff who "wins" in court receives a verdict less than his or her total economic loss, and the defendant-physician who "wins" still feels traumatized by the process. The IACT Program can offer a greater sense of resolution for both parties. It also holds appeal for judges and all those in the justice system who are struggling with busy court dockets. When disputes are resolved through the IACT process, there is a savings of time and resources, not only for the parties, but for the court system as a whole.

NOTES

1. Thomas H. Gallagher et al., "Patients' and Physicians' Attitudes Regarding the Disclosure of Medical Errors," *Journal of the American Medical Association* 289, no. 8 (February 26, 2003): 1001–1007.

2. Kathleen M. Mazor, Steven R. Simon, and Jerry H. Gurwitz, "Communicating With Patients About Medical Errors," *Archives of Internal Medicine* 164, no. 15 (August 9/23, 2004): 1690–1697.

3. Office of Technology Assessment, U.S. Congress, *Defensive Medicine and Medical Malpractice* (1994).

4. Anupam B. Jena et al., "Malpractice Risk According to Physician Specialty," *New England Journal of Medicine* 365 (August 18, 2011): 629–636.

5. David M. Studdert, Michelle M. Mello, and Troyen A. Brennan, "Medical Malpractice," *New England Journal of Medicine* 350 (January 15, 2004): 283–292.

6. Committee on Quality Health Care in America, Institute of Medicine, *To Err Is Human: Building a Safer Health System* (L. Kohn, J. Corrigan, & M. Donaldson, eds. 2000).

7. David C. Classen et al., "'Global Trigger Tool' Shows That Adverse Events In Hospitals May Be Ten Times Greater Than Previously Measured," *Health Affairs* 30, no. 4 (April 2011): 581–589.

8. Studdert et al., *supra* note 5.

9. Richard C. Boothman et al., "A Better Approach to Medical Malpractice Claims? The University of Michigan Experience," *Journal of Health & Life Sciences Law* 2, no. 2 (January 2009): 125–159.

10. The Joint Commission on Accreditation of Healthcare Organizations, *Health Care at the Crossroads: Strategies for Improving the Medical Liability System and Preventing Patient Injury* (2005).

CHAPTER THIRTY-NINE

Other Alternative Dispute Resolution Programs in North Carolina

"The condition of our survival in any but the meagerest existence is our willingness to accommodate ourselves to the conflicting interests of others, to learn to live in a social world."

—Judge Learned Hand, "Democracy: Its Presumptions and Realities," *The Spirit of Liberty* (1932).

Various uses of alternative dispute resolution (ADR) are regularly explored and developed in different settings throughout North Carolina. This book describes the most prevalent forms of ADR in North Carolina, but it does not provide an exhaustive review of all programs. In order to alert readers to additional uses of ADR, this chapter lists some legislatively sanctioned programs that have not been discussed elsewhere in this book. There are also other ADR programs outside the purview of the North Carolina General Assembly that have not been examined in this book. However, the information in this book—and in this chapter—should provide a useful foundation if the reader is called upon to participate in such programs or forums.

Mediation

Programs with Specialized Applications

PARTITION SALES OF REAL PROPERTY
Statutory Authority: North Carolina General Statutes Section 46-22.1.
Oversight: The clerk of superior court or the court.
Function: The statute permits mediation of a partition dispute at any time. After a partition sale has been requested, but before it has been ordered, the clerk or the court may order a mediated settlement conference.

MEDIATION OF EMERGENCY OR DISASTER-RELATED PROPERTY INSURANCE CLAIMS
Statutory Authority: North Carolina General Statutes Sections 58-44-70 through 58-44-120.

Oversight: The Commissioner of Insurance.

Function: The statute gives insured parties the right to mediate disputes arising from emergency- or disaster-related property insurance claims.

LABOR DISPUTES—CONCILIATION THROUGH THE COMMISSIONER OF LABOR

Statutory Authority: North Carolina General Statutes Section 95-36.

Oversight: None stated.

Function: The Commissioner of Labor may order a conciliator from the state Department of Labor to attempt settlement of a labor dispute via mediation.

DISPUTES INVOLVING THE CHARTERING OF CHARTER SCHOOLS

Statutory Authority: North Carolina General Statutes Section 115C-238.29G.

Oversight: None stated, but the mediation is to be conducted in accordance with "rules and standards of conduct adopted under Chapter 7A of the General Statutes."

Function: Disputes arising between a charter school and the State Board of Education may be mediated, if both sides agree.

REGULATION OF SURFACE WATER TRANSFERS

Statutory Authority: North Carolina General Statutes Section 143-215.22L(h).

Oversight: Department of Environment and Natural Resources.

Function: North Carolina General Statutes Section 143-215.22L(a) requires a certificate from the Environmental Management Commission of the Department of Environment and Natural Resources for any large-scale transfer of surface waters. If a dispute arises, upon request of any interested party, the applicant, or on its own motion the Department of Environment and Natural Resources, may appoint a mediation officer, for the purpose of initiating settlement discussions.

PRISON INMATE GRIEVANCES

Statutory Authority: North Carolina General Statutes Section 148-118.8.

Oversight: None stated.

Function: The statute authorizes the appointment of grievance examiners by the Grievance Resolution Board in the Department of Corrections. Grievance examiners are directed to investigate inmate grievances and are to attempt to resolve grievances through mediation with all parties.

ADMINISTRATIVE HEARINGS
Statutory Authority: North Carolina General Statutes Section 150B-23.1.
Oversight: Office of Administrative Hearings.
Function: The statute authorizes the Office of Administrative Hearings to establish a mediated settlement conference program. The chief administrative law judge may order the parties in a contested case to attend a pre-hearing mediated settlement conference.

Official Encouragement of the Use of Mediation

VICTIM-OFFENDER MEDIATION
Statutory Mention: North Carolina General Statutes Section 7B-1706(4).
Oversight: None stated.
Function: Victim-offender mediation is one of the diversion options that juvenile offender intake counselors may invoke.

DISPUTES BETWEEN MANAGED CARE ENTITIES AND INSUREDS
Statutory Authority: North Carolina General Statutes Section 90-21.56.
Oversight: None stated.
Function: North Carolina General Statutes Section 90-21.56 creates a cause of action for enrollees or insured parties for damages caused by a managed care entity's failure to exercise ordinary care. The statute expressly provides that arbitration or mediation may be used to settle such disputes, but only pursuant to an agreement to do so after the dispute has arisen.

Arbitration

Programs of Specialized Application

PUBLIC UTILITIES COMMISSION
Statutory Authority: North Carolina General Statutes Section 62-40.
Oversight: None stated.
Function: If the parties agree, the Public Utilities Commission may arbitrate disputes between a public utility and "another person." The award is binding and has the same effect as a judgment of the superior court.

NURSE LICENSURE INTERSTATE COMPACT
Statutory Authority: North Carolina General Statutes Section 90-171.92.
Oversight: None stated.
Function: Disputes between states that are parties to the Nurse Licensure Compact are to be resolved by binding arbitration.

Voluntary Arbitration of Labor Disputes

Statutory Authority: North Carolina General Statutes Sections 95-36.1 through 95-36.9.

Oversight: The North Carolina Department of Labor.

Function: Written agreements to arbitrate labor disputes are enforceable, as are the awards subsequently rendered. The Commissioner of Labor is authorized to adopt appropriate rules of procedure for the arbitration of labor disputes.

Multi-County School Districts: Selection of School Location

Statutory Authority: North Carolina General Statutes Section 115C-510.

Oversight: None stated.

Function: Arbitration is to be used in the event a disagreement arises between two or more county school boards as to the location of a schoolhouse, after a multi-county school district has been approved by the voters.

Compensation of County Employees

Statutory Authority: North Carolina General Statutes Section 153A-92(b) (3).

Oversight: None stated.

Function: If the board of county commissioners reduces the compensation of employees assigned to an elected official, and the reduction does not apply to all county departments, the elected official must consent to the reduction in compensation. If the elected official does not consent, the dispute may be referred to arbitration by either the board of county commissioners or the elected official. Arbitration is to be conducted by the senior resident superior court judge of the superior court district.

Other Statutory Uses of Arbitration

Precautionary Safety Arrangements for Overhead High-Voltage Lines

Statutory Authority: North Carolina General Statutes Section 95-229.10(c).

Oversight: None stated.

Function: In the event of a dispute over the amount of payment due between the owner or operator of high-voltage lines and the person or entity responsible for installing the required precautionary safety arrangements, "arbitration or other legal means" may be invoked to resolve the dispute.

OFF-PREMISES OUTDOOR ADVERTISING (BILLBOARDS)
Statutory Authority: North Carolina General Statutes Sections 153A-143 (counties) and 160A-199 (cities).
Oversight: None stated.
Function: The statute provides for the arbitration of relocation disputes of off-premises outdoor signs when a local government requires the removal of an outdoor sign from its present location. However, the arbitrator is not permitted to determine compensation for the removal of the sign.

Ombudsman Programs

INDUSTRIAL COMMISSION OMBUDSMAN PROGRAM
Statutory Authority: North Carolina General Statutes Section 97-79(f).
Oversight: The North Carolina Industrial Commission.
Function: The North Carolina Industrial Commission is directed to establish an ombudsman program to assist pro se claimants and employers. The assistance provided includes, at the claimant's request, communicating with the employer's insurance carrier and physicians, but does not include representation at workers' compensation hearings.

LONG-TERM CARE OMBUDSMAN PROGRAM
Statutory Authority: North Carolina General Statutes Sections 143B-181.15 to 181.25.
Oversight: The Department of Health and Human Services, Division of Aging.
Function: The State Long-Term Care Ombudsman is directed to promote community involvement with long-term care providers and residents; to serve as a liaison between residents, their families, and facility staff; to certify Regional Long-Term Care Ombudsmen; and to attempt to resolve complaints using mediation, conciliation, and persuasion whenever possible.

AIR QUALITY COMPLIANCE PANEL—OMBUDSMAN FOR THE SMALL BUSINESS STATIONARY SOURCE TECHNICAL AND ENVIRONMENTAL COMPLIANCE ASSISTANCE PROGRAM
Statutory Authority: North Carolina General Statutes Section 143B-318(g).
Oversight: Department of Environment and Natural Resources.
Function: The Secretary of Environment and Natural Resources is directed to establish an office in the Department to serve as ombudsman

for the Small Business Stationary Source Technical and Environmental Compliance Assistance Program.

SMALL BUSINESS OMBUDSMAN
Statutory Authority: North Carolina General Statutes Section 143B-432.1.
Oversight: Department of Commerce.
Function: The Small Business Ombudsman is directed to work with small businesses "to ensure they receive timely answers to questions and timely resolution of issues involving state government."

Fact Finding

DISMISSAL OR DEMOTION OF CAREER TEACHERS AND ADMINISTRATORS: HEARING OFFICERS
Statutory Authority: North Carolina General Statutes Sections
    115C-325(h1)–325(i1).
Oversight: State Superintendent of Public Instruction.
Function: Hearing officers (who are required to be members of the NC State Bar and have demonstrated experience and expertise in relevant areas of the law within the last five years and have completed a special training course) are authorized to conduct a fact-finding hearing in contested dismissal or demotion cases. The decision whether to use a hearing officer is the career teacher/administrator's to make.

Other Dispute Resolution Techniques

POWERS OF A TRUSTEE
Statutory Authority: North Carolina General Statutes Section
    36C-8-816(23).
Oversight: None stated.
Function: Included among the specific powers of a trustee under a trust, a trustee is authorized to resolve a dispute concerning the interpretation of the trust or its administration by mediation, arbitration, or other ADR procedure.

DISPUTES BETWEEN INSURERS AND INDEPENDENT CERTIFIED PUBLIC ACCOUNTANTS
Statutory Authority: North Carolina General Statutes Section 58-10-210.
Oversight: None stated.

Function: An independent certified public accountant may enter into an agreement with an insurer to have disputes relating to an audit resolved by mediation or arbitration.

PUBLIC BUILDING CONTRACTS
Statutory Authority: North Carolina General Statutes Section 143-126(f1).
Oversight: None stated.
Function: The statute directs public entities to use the dispute resolution process adopted by the State Building Commission, pursuant to General Statutes Section 143-135.26(11) for specified public building contracts. The dispute resolution process must include mediation.

RESIDENTIAL SCHOOLS
Statutory Authority: North Carolina General Statutes Section 143B-146.14.
Oversight: None stated.
Function: The statute directs the Secretary of Health and Human Services to establish a procedure for the resolution of disputes between parents and residential schools.

HUMAN RELATIONS PROGRAMS
Statutory Authority: North Carolina General Statutes Section 160A-492.
Oversight: None stated.
Function: Local governments may establish and fund human relations programs, which are defined to include programs devoted to dispute resolution.

PART III
The Future Development of ADR
in North Carolina

CHAPTER FORTY

Technology and the Future of ADR in North Carolina

"The new electronic independence re-creates the world in the image of a global village."
—Canadian educator, philosopher, and scholar Marshall McLuhan
The Gutenberg Galaxy (1962).

The field of alternative dispute resolution (ADR) has its roots in the last decades of the twentieth century, but ADR processes and procedures have evolved and expanded significantly in the current global age of information technology. Advances in technology have influenced almost every aspect of ADR practice, allowing instant access to information, enhanced communications, and greater productivity. This chapter examines some of the ways in which technology aids North Carolina's ADR professionals and will continue to impact their work in the future.

Access to ADR Information

One of the most significant aspects of technological innovation over the past twenty years has been the growth of the Internet and the proliferation of Internet websites that provide quick and easy access to information for the general public. Among the best websites for North Carolina's ADR professionals and participants at all levels is the one maintained by the North Carolina Dispute Resolution Commission (DRC).[1] In addition to providing information on the certification and regulation of mediators who serve the courts of this state, the DRC uses its website to serve as a clearinghouse for information about court-based mediation programs; to assist other State agencies that are interested in or are currently providing dispute resolution services to their constituencies; and to publish a newsletter on dispute resolution. The DRC's website also provides the public with an online guide to selecting a mediator and with a composite listing of certified Superior Court Mediated Settlement Conference (MSC) mediators, District Court Family

Financial Settlement mediators, and Clerk Program mediators. Information about the education, professional experience, and dispute resolution training of certified mediators is available through the DRC's website.

Various private mediation groups and other organizations of neutrals, mediators, and arbitrators provide access to their respective organizations and members through a myriad of websites available on the Internet. These portals allow participants an opportunity to more closely examine and vet the selection of neutrals as to interests, education, professional experience, and mediation training. Some even provide virtual calendars where participants can reserve specific dates and times with mediators online. Mediators often provide information about their qualifications, availability, and scheduling through their individual websites as well.

Additional access to information has developed in the form of several types of social media. Mediators, arbitrators, and other neutrals network with colleagues and ADR participants and make their profiles transparent to the public through such sites as Facebook and LinkedIn. Use of such networking sites can facilitate the process of selecting and scheduling an appropriate neutral in the ADR process.

Sharing of Information

The process of sharing information in the field of ADR has followed the general trend in other fields and continues to develop through e-mail, e-newsletters, Listservs, blogs, and social media. The North Carolina Bar Association's Dispute Resolution Section publishes *The Peacemaker* newsletter online and provides access to it for its members.[2] Several commentators run active blogs and e-newsletters facilitating the dissemination and discussion of developing news and trends in the field of ADR. The effectiveness of this type of communication has enhanced the skills and professionalism of neutrals, which in turn has increased the acceptance and utilization of ADR throughout the state.

Increasing Productivity

Most mediators already recognize the value of technology in managing their practices. The use of e-mail for communication and scheduling is a standard tool. But the wave of smart phones and tablet computers has taken these tools to a higher level of productivity. Mediators no longer have to wait to return to the office to read and respond to e-mail. These devices include calendars, so scheduling can be accomplished no matter where one might be. Tablet computers allow professionals to keep up with their reading, have access to files, download forms or entire books, and conduct research on the Internet without having to load up a briefcase with files, legal pads, books, or a laptop computer. Given the rapid progress of technology, there probably will be newer, faster, and more convenient hardware available before the ink is dry on the pages of this book.

New Tools for Traditional ADR

Although most mediators still prefer face-to-face meetings between all participants in order to explore, communicate, and understand the interests, needs, motives, and emotions of the parties, technology can be an essential tool for developing a successful mediation when not all of the parties can be physically present during the session. The absence of a party may result from a variety of acceptable reasons, including a last-minute conflict in scheduling; the existence of international parties; the distance, cost, or hardship of travel; or the time constraints placed on particular individuals within an organization, such as insurance company representatives who must be in different locations for mediations on the same day. The ability to teleconference or videoconference with these persons can be the difference between having a successful mediation and not having a mediation at all. The consolidation of claims offices into national locations, the sometimes distant location of the national headquarters of a business, the international location of parties in many business transactions, and the high cost of travel increasingly have caused mediators to combine telephone and videoconferencing technology with more traditional face-to-face mediations.

In these scenarios, local attorneys may be present along with their clients and local representatives while the business executive with the power of the purse may participate from a distant location via telephone conference call or videoconferencing. People working for large national and international corporations are accustomed to using teleconferencing and videoconferencing effectively and expect to be able to use it in ADR to avoid expensive and time-consuming travel. Without the use of these tools, mediation in some cases would not be successful due to rescheduling issues, the inability to gather many parties in the same location at the same time, and the opportunity to have meaningful participation by key, upper-level management. Similarly, the use of ADR in multi-district litigation many times cannot be successful without the ability of the parties to participate via teleconferencing or videoconferencing due to scheduling and distance constraints.

Technology also can be essential in preserving the momentum of multi-session or continued mediations in complex cases. In situations where the mediation comes to the end of the day without either impasse or settlement, but is adjourned for another date, the mediator is able to continue the momentum gained in the face-to-face session by having private sessions through videoconferencing and teleconferencing, sharing complex data and information through e-mail, and communicating changes in position to all parties without having to physically reconnect. The written e-mail communications by the mediator can document progress made by the parties and prevent them from settling back into pre-mediation postures. Hard-won moves by both sides are thus preserved and energy retained by employing communications technology. When successful mediations require the exchange of information beyond the time allotted for the conference, the mediator can use e-mail and telephone communication to facilitate the exchange and help accelerate the pace at which settlement may be reached.

Online Mediation

During the first decade of this century, online mediation services have proliferated, suggesting a need for and acceptance of quick, low-cost ADR in many consumer transactions and other types of claims. Online dispute-resolution (ODR) services generally are of two types: (1) blind bidding and (2) discussion-based resolution of disputes. These procedures are distinctly different from face-to-face ADR processes but can be effective in reaching swift and successful settlements. They usually are available twenty-four hours a day, seven days a week, and fees typically are low, often a small percentage of the value of the claim.

In the blind-bidding model, a claimant initiates the dispute resolution process by logging into the settlement service website (usually password protected) indicating a desire to attempt to resolve a claim. The service's software allows the claimant to make a confidential settlement demand (or bid). It then contacts the other party to the dispute by e-mail, advising the party that a settlement offer has been made. The respondent can log onto the website and submit an offer of its own. The software protects each party's bid from disclosure to the other, so that neither party loses any bargaining advantage if the claim does not settle. When a bid is greater than or equal to the opposition's demand or is within a pre-agreed dollar range or percentage, the claim automatically settles. Some websites offer unlimited rounds of bidding, but most only permit a designated number of offers and counteroffers. If the case does not settle after the authorized number of rounds, then either party can resubmit the dispute with different bids, or they can agree to telephone facilitation. This model is particularly well suited to disputes in consumer and commercial matters where the amount of the dispute is the true issue involved. If facilitation is requested, then the model becomes more like traditional mediation with a facilitator standing in the place of the computer, helping to reduce the time it takes to bring both parties to a mutually agreeable number.

In the discussion-based resolution model, the settlement service website assists participants in more complex disputes involving issues other than just dollar value. Such services allow communication among parties located anywhere in the world, using standard browser software (such as Google, Firefox, Safari, or Microsoft Internet Explorer). Generally the communication systems are text based, but some of these websites are developing videoconferencing capabilities. The text-based systems attempt to eliminate bias (by the parties or by the neutral) based on race, age, gender, or disability. However, they do not capture as effectively the interests, needs, motives, and emotions of the parties—factors believed to be important by most mediators in face-to-face mediation. The growth of online videoconferencing capabilities may help to alleviate this concern.

A number of online mediation services have come and gone on the Internet in the last fifteen years. However, an example of the blind-bidding model that has survived is CyberSettle,[3] which has been in operation since 1998. An example of a discussion-based model that has survived is Resolution Forum, Inc.,[4] a Texas nonprofit organization that has been in existence for more than thirteen years. The perseverance of these two online services indicates the broad increase in acceptance of ADR by the general public and a willingness to use technology to engage in dispute resolution processes.

Software

There are several software applications that allow ADR professionals to conduct mediations over the Internet.[5] Typically the software will have at least two conference "chat rooms" available for break-out sessions. Parties in one conference room may not communicate with parties in the other, but the mediator may communicate with both rooms simultaneously. Participants on one side of a dispute who are in different locations may communicate privately within the chat rooms in the system during an online session, allowing them to have private discussions before their responses are transmitted to all participants. The private messaging capability also allows participants to communicate with the mediator in a similar fashion. The software thus mirrors the traditional process of private session caucusing and "shuttle diplomacy" employed in face-to-face mediation. The cost of such software probably is prohibitive for most individual mediators, but may decrease sufficiently over time to make it a more viable ADR tool.

In the meantime, individual mediators are using less expensive solutions than dedicated mediation software where time and distance prohibit traditional face-to-face mediation. Many mediators are building on the fact that they and most participants have access to the Internet at home, at work, and on the road. They are using a growing technology application known as the Web conference, a real-time, online meeting that offers many different options, depending on which service provider is selected.[6] These services offer document collaboration, desktop sharing, presentations, voice and video communication, and whiteboards. The cost of Web conferencing varies depending on how many people need to be connected, whether an operator is required, and pre-scheduling and availability requirements.

Conclusion

Technological innovation will continue to expand the availability of ADR services to the citizens of North Carolina. The increasing use of the Internet and computer software applications will enhance the effectiveness of traditional, face-to-face mediation and will provide additional tools to encourage settlement when circumstances prevent resolution during an initial mediated settlement conference. In addition, the role of online dispute resolution is well established, often providing an efficient, low-cost alternative to parties seeking to avoid legal action. ADR and technology will continue to go hand-in-hand through the twenty-first century, with new approaches likely to offer simpler, more effective techniques for collaboration in mediation via the Internet.

NOTES

1. *See* http://www.ncdrc.org. This URL is automatically redirected to the website of the North Carolina Court System, http://www.nccourts.org/courts/crs/councils/drc/.

2. *See* North Carolina Bar Association, Dispute Resolution Section, "Newsletters," http://disputeresolution.ncbar.org/newsletters.aspx.

3. *See* http://www.cybersettle.com.

4. *See* http://www.resolutionforum.org.

5. An example of software that can be used for online mediations is Sonexis, available at http://www.sonexis.com.

6. For example, Adobe offers Acrobat Connect, which allows for real-time collaboration on a document via the Internet. The tool is free for up to three people and can be accessed at www.acrobat.com. Use can be as simple as hammering out the mediated settlement agreement or working from a predetermined set of issues and responses. There are other popular services available to creative mediators, including Webex (http://www.webex.com), Meeting Bridge (http://www.meetingbridge.com), and GoToMeeting (http://www.GoToMeeting.com).

CHAPTER FORTY-ONE

Learning from the Past and Looking Ahead: The Future of ADR in North Carolina

"It's tough to make predictions, especially about the future."

—Yogi Berra

Learning from the Past

In predicting the future of alternative dispute resolution (ADR) in North Carolina, one can look at the past and (1) recall what was originally conceived, (2) examine what was accomplished, and (3) assess what has yet to be done. The future may yet be the rest of the "to do" list—a list that has accumulated over time as the understanding of ADR has grown, as more possibilities have been imagined, and as the first tasks in developing ADR in North Carolina have been accomplished.

One can only hope that the future of ADR in North Carolina will be as bright as its beginning. As this book demonstrates, its development over the last three decades has been remarkably successful. Some of the early heroes and heroines of the ADR movement raised public awareness of the crisis in the court system, saw new possibilities and better ways of resolving disputes, and challenged society to create new structures of dispute resolution in North Carolina. An initially skeptical legal profession has embraced it; the judicial system is better because of it; and the legislature has seen fit to prescribe it and support it with appropriations in a variety of circumstances. Community dispute settlement centers, operating mostly independently of the courts and lawyers, have flourished in locations statewide. But what has been accomplished in North Carolina so far is only the beginning, and a promising future lies ahead.

The North Carolina Bar Association

The North Carolina Bar Association (NCBA) took up the initial challenge of creating new structures and began to explore the many facets of ADR.

Its Dispute Resolution Task Force identified two basic ways that the subject could be explored: through court-based options and community-based options. At the conclusion of its efforts, the Task Force made a fateful decision that determined the course of ADR development in North Carolina: to engage in an experiment with court-ordered arbitration in the state court system (a system that was also being explored in the United States District Court for the Middle District of North Carolina). In essence, the NCBA began with what its members knew best, the courts of North Carolina.

This was an understandable decision. The Task Force was an NCBA project. It was conceived by lawyers, headed by lawyers, and comprised largely of lawyers, all of whom were involved with and committed to the courts. If there was a "better way" of doing things, if the courts were overcrowded, if alternatives to traditional approaches needed to be found, it was natural that lawyers would be interested in exploring those problems and opportunities. And so, the Task Force (later the Dispute Resolution Committee, and still later the Dispute Resolution Section) focused its attention on studying the ways ADR could affect what was most dear to its members—the courts of North Carolina.

A New Civil Procedure

For the past thirty years, the NCBA has investigated how ADR could influence the courts for the better; but it has largely overlooked how ADR may affect the world beyond the courts. In the process, something odd has happened in the understanding of what ADR is and what it can accomplish. As the reader now knows from earlier chapters, some form of ADR has been engrafted onto the life of every civil case in the state and federal trial and appellate forums in North Carolina. Lawyers handling non-criminal cases in North Carolina will, by court rule, discuss ADR options with their clients at the beginning of the case and will participate with their clients by court order in some form of ADR before trial is conducted.

In 1985, the Dispute Resolution Task Force proposed its first ADR pilot program, a program of court-ordered arbitration for simple monetary claims. The decision to propose and implement an ADR pilot project in the court system has been replicated in program after program through the years. The use of pilot programs in which proposed changes are tested and professionally evaluated has been a hallmark of the ADR revolution that occurred in the courts of North Carolina over the past three decades.

The North Carolina court system is now thoroughly infected with the

ADR "bug," so much so that North Carolina lawyers now talk about how the court's civil procedure has been changed. ADR is no longer an oddity nor an alternative. It has been so completely incorporated into the court system in North Carolina that it has become part of the life of every civil case. It has become part of North Carolina's civil procedure.

Even though the ADR programs in North Carolina's courts are authorized and governed by statutes found in Chapter 7A of the North Carolina General Statutes, the ADR programs are more truly revisions to Chapter 1A of the General Statutes, the North Carolina Rules of Civil Procedure. ADR has revolutionized the court system in an unexpected way. It has provided a set of settlement procedures in the courts that were not imaginable as the ADR movement began. ADR was conceived of as an alternative to the courts, but its first major impact in North Carolina occurred within the courts.

ADR Professionals

The implementation of these settlement procedures has brought about major changes and benefits to the many constituents of the court system. Most of these changes have been chronicled in previous chapters. What has not been captured in these chapters is the dramatic change that settlement procedures have had on the practicing bar. The most obvious one is the creation of a cadre of professional mediators and arbitrators who make their livings as neutrals within the court system. More than a thousand lawyers arbitrate small civil cases for a small fee. The Dispute Resolution Commission has certified more than 1,900 superior court and family financial mediators. Many of these are attorneys who continue to practice law, but a smaller group of them now devote their entire professional lives to the settlement of, rather than the trial of, civil litigation. In addition, there are professional mediators working outside of the courts in such areas as divorce, child custody, land use planning, and public policy disputes.

The Practicing Bar

Less dramatic, but as important, is the impact that court-ordered ADR processes have had on the members of the practicing bar. The implementation of court-ordered ADR in the courts of North Carolina has created mechanisms for lawyers to settle their cases earlier, with less stress, with a greater degree of client interaction, and without the duplication of effort and trial preparation that characterized law practice before the advent of these programs. Trial lawyers no longer have to wait until they reach the courthouse steps to have a realistic chance of getting their cases settled. They no longer have to "sell" the notion of settlement discussions to their adversaries because the system has court-ordered mechanisms to bring about those negotiations. Court-ordered ADR has improved the working relationships of attorneys and their clients, because clients are more involved in the discussions that lead to the settlement of their cases. Simply put, court-ordered ADR procedures have made the practice of law a more satisfying and rewarding experience.

Legal Education

The widespread use of ADR also has brought a change in the education of lawyers in North Carolina. Settlement used to be conducted totally in private, between attorneys outside the presence of their clients. It involved techniques that were rarely visible or subject to critique. Mandatory ADR processes brought the settlement of civil litigation into the light, however, and revealed a glaring weakness in the training and education of many lawyers. Attorneys not schooled in the art and science of negotiations and settlement had to scramble to learn more about this aspect of practice. They attended courses in negotiation and mediation offered by private providers and began "retooling" to meet the demands that court-ordered ADR placed upon them.

As the need for additional training for lawyers became better known, law schools began to investigate whether ADR in general, and negotiation in particular, should be offered as part of the law school experience. To some law schools, ADR is still a curiosity or fad that is not worthy of integration into the curriculum. However, the law schools in North Carolina are moving in a different direction. Most of them now offer ADR and negotiation coursework, and some provide opportunities for students to work as interns along with ADR neutrals in nonprofits and other settings. Educational partnerships between law schools and nonprofit ADR providers offer an exciting opportunity for aspiring lawyers to learn about and practice the skills involved in settling disputes.

It still is not a generally accepted norm that learning how to settle cases is as important as learning how to try them. ADR is most often taught as an elective subject or in limited-seating seminars. Expanding the range and focus of law school course offerings was never envisioned when the ADR Task Force issued its first report in 1985. Legal education remains one of the new frontiers for ADR, however, and is one of the territories that ADR pioneers will move to and settle in the coming years. Surely, the fundamental principles of ADR will be taught in more and more schools, colleges, and law schools in order to prepare students for the work of collaboration and problem solving required for settlement of legal disputes.

ADR Menu

As court-related ADR matures, it seems certain that dispute resolution increasingly will be offered to litigants in a "menu" of settlement procedures. The menu format is currently used in the settlement procedures program for district court equitable distribution cases and for superior court cases. The vision of a "multi-door" courthouse where litigants are offered several dispute resolution programs in addition to formal litigation is fundamentally sound, and it allows the litigants maximum discretion in choosing which procedure they want in order to "fit the forum to the fuss."

ADR Governance

The governance of court-related ADR will probably need to be addressed as the system continues to grow and mature. Responsibility for court-annexed ADR is currently divided among the State Judicial Council of the Supreme Court of North Carolina, the Administrative Office of the Courts, and the legislatively established Dispute Resolution Commission. (See Chapter 7, The Governance of North Carolina's Court-Based ADR Programs.) Some believe this system has not worked well and advocate for a single body to oversee both program development and the certification and regulation of neutrals. This issue will be carefully watched in the coming years.

Better Communication

Timely and effective communication between neutrals and the courts to which they report will be needed as part of ADR's continued maturation. The neutrals who provide ADR services are largely private providers who do not work in courthouses and who are not under the direct supervision of judicial officials. Tension between the two groups has sometimes been caused by poor communication and differing responsibilities. Relationships can be improved with increased understanding of the needs and constraints of each group and with optimal utilization of advanced telecommunications to share information.

The Future of the Court System

As North Carolina incorporated ADR into the court system by creating mandatory settlement procedures, two philosophies provided good, albeit different, rationales for embracing ADR. One approach emphasized that ADR would improve the way the court system resolved disputes, in terms of both the quality and the efficiency of the resolution. The other philosophy focused on the need of disputants—whether or not in the context of litigation—to have methods of resolution other than litigation available to them. This second idea was embodied in the creation of several community dispute resolution centers, which pre-dated the introduction of court-annexed ADR in the state.

Since lawyers and judges spearheaded court-annexed ADR (now more commonly referred to as "court-ordered" ADR) in North Carolina, it was natural that many, if not most, of the early pioneers thought in terms of court improvement. Even among the "court improvement school," however, there were two different approaches, or emphases: one focused on how to make the courts better instruments for resolving disputes; the other focused on how to make the courts better serve the needs of litigants. In a way, this was a classic two-sides-of-the-same-coin situation.

Those who have formally studied court-ordered ADR in North Carolina have found mixed results as to whether ADR significantly improved court efficiency. Although it generally has been accepted that ADR procedures significantly reduce the time spent in resolving litigation, other conclusions seemed to vary depending on the type of alternative being studied, the nature of the dispute being resolved, and the trial division in which the case is found. One finding, however, was consistent across the board: there was a high degree of satisfaction among the users of ADR. The disputants liked it, and, when they were represented by counsel, their lawyers liked it, too.[1]

These findings are significant. They will help to ensure that ADR has a future in North Carolina, and they say something about what that future may be. They suggest that those who saw in the beginning that ADR's principal reason for being was to serve the needs of disputants probably had the best argument. Only secondarily would ADR also serve the needs of the courts.

Most of the history of ADR in the courts of North Carolina has concentrated on creating improvements within the courts. Does ADR, and the principles of cooperation and conciliation that underpin much of it, have the potential of altering jurisprudence in more fundamental ways than simply providing earlier settlement procedures?

One of the ways that has been suggested as a means to achieve that goal is to redefine what it takes to be eligible to file a lawsuit in the first place. The "get your ADR ticket punched first" theory advocated by some is just such an approach and has been embodied in such programs as Pre-Litigation Farm Nuisance Mediation, Year 2000 (Y2K) Pre-Litigation Mediation, Pre-litigation Mediation of Insurance Claims, and Electrical Supplier Territorial Dispute Mediation. (See Chapter 35.) Is that something lawyers and the courts should be proposing and working toward? That question will be debated frequently in the future to address the issue of how to make the courts a place of last, rather than first, resort.

Former North Carolina Supreme Court Chief Justice James G. Exum, Jr., clearly the most influential figure in the early development of ADR in the courts of North Carolina, once speculated on the ways that the structure of the court system itself might be affected and shaped by the philosophy underpinning alternative dispute resolution. His thoughts are both interesting and provocative:

> ADR will become a specialty not only for neutrals but for what we call today "advocates." It will become a discipline and a course of study for which degrees will be offered. ADR specialists will work not only as neutrals, but also as advocates for clients in dispute. These specialists will not litigate in court. Litigators will continue to be trained in schools of law for this purpose. They will not participate in ADR. ADR will be conducted not in the context of litigation, but independently of the courts in community ADR centers and by private providers. This could create a bifurcated bar a bit like the English system of solicitors and barristers.

> Most of the disputes that are now litigated in courts will be resolved through community ADR. The courts will be reserved for resolving serious criminal disputes, large civil disputes like present-day class actions involving multiple parties, some international disputes involving treaty interpretations (most international disputes will be resolved through ADR), and important constitutional questions. Probably the courts will no longer be involved in sentencing those convicted of less serious crimes. Sentencing may even be determined using ADR techniques, with the victims and perpetrators participating with neutrals. Sentencing may also become an administrative matter accomplished through some administrative agency closely connected with the agency where sentences will be carried out.

There probably will be several phases where the definitiveness of ADR resolutions will gradually increase until ADR is the only definitive dispute resolution mechanism for most disputes. These phases might happen like this. The first phase will be similar to what exists today. The courts will require that ADR be a prerequisite to litigation, but the ADR will be conducted separately from the courts in community ADR centers or with private providers. Dissatisfied participants may then invoke court-conducted litigation. The second phase will be one in which the parties will choose whether to engage in ADR or whether to litigate. Parties who choose ADR will be bound by it and will not have access to the courts. The third phase will be one in which ADR is the only available resolution mechanism for most disputes.

New forms of ADR will evolve in addition to those that exist today. Neutral evaluators will become popular as will experts in fields relevant to the dispute. Many disputes simply will be submitted to these evaluators and experts for resolution. The disputants will submit them not in a combative or adversarial spirit but, being guided by their ADR specialists, in a spirit of collaboration, cooperation, and reconciliation.

It will be this collaborative spirit, this spirit of cooperation and reconciliation, that will be the hallmark of almost all dispute resolution in the not too distant future. Young people are being taught the superiority of this method. Its precepts are the foundation upon which the ADR movement rests. They are what inspired the movement's founders in North Carolina. ADR, not litigation, will be the way of the future.

Is this the future of ADR in North Carolina? One cannot know, obviously, but Justice Exum's words are a reminder of the vision that originally inspired the ADR movement in North Carolina, and they evoke the original work of the Dispute Resolution Task Force and the way in which the task of investigating ADR was first conceived.

The Future: Unfinished Business

From 1983 to 1985, the NCBA's Dispute Resolution Task Force divided its investigations into two separate areas of focus: one court-based and one community-based. Although the work of the NCBA has brought successes in the courts, its efforts in the community arena have lain dormant. There has not been a concentrated focus on how to keep disputes from going to court in the first place. For many of the leaders of the early ADR movement this was the goal, to divert cases from the courts and provide a "better way" of settling disputes in communities so that they never have to be handled by the courts.

It is often said that as society has grown more industrialized and complex, the days of intimacy and community have been lost and, as a result, so have the informal dispute resolution mechanisms that were inherent in family and community structures. Some have suggested that because the old structures have disappeared, courts have been called upon to shoulder an ever-increasing dispute resolution function, something they were not intended to do originally. The ADR movement is often seen as part of an attempt to rebuild dispute resolution capabilities throughout society, so that people in conflict draw first on their own resources to resolve their differences, rather than on the resources of the state through its courts. In fact, some bar leaders have seen the entire court-based ADR movement not as a way to improve the courts, but rather as using the courts to teach self-reliance and self-determination.

The ADR movement, and mediation in particular, is also seen as part of a wider effort to bring about a new and "higher vision of self and society, one based on moral development and interpersonal relations rather than on satisfaction and individual autonomy."[2] This quote is from *The Promise of Mediation* by Robert A. Baruch Bush and Joseph P. Folger, who go on to say:

> Scholars and thinkers in many fields have begun to articulate and advocate a major shift in moral and political vision—a paradigm shift—from an individualistic to a relational conception. They argue that, although the individualistic ethic of modern Western culture was a great advance over the preceding caste-oriented feudal order, it is now possible and necessary to go still further and to achieve a full integration of individual freedom and social conscience, in a relational social order enacted through new forms of social processes and institutions. Mediation . . . represents an opportunity to express this new relational vision in concrete form.[3]

The future development of ADR may not lie within the courts, where its growth has been most evident over the past three decades. The future of ADR may lie in the larger society, in the building of new structures of dispute resolution in all segments of culture. It may lie in curriculum development in which dispute resolution is added to the three Rs, in the crafting of grievance procedures for business and professional organizations, and in the invention of new language and expectations that permeate the speech of our religious and political leaders.

Some see the teaching of ADR skills and concepts in public schools as a significant contribution to this societal change. More and more elementary schools are including conflict resolution as a part of their core curriculum. In middle and high schools, student-led mediation clubs or teams provide peer mediation to fellow students in conflict. A hoped for outgrowth of this educational effort will be an awakening in society that individuals in conflict can resolve their problems on their own; but if they cannot, there are other avenues that may be explored prior to going to the courts.

If this is the future of ADR—the unfinished business in the larger society—then what role will legal professionals play as a group? Lawyers have done what comes naturally so far by improving and reforming the court system. Is there a desire on the part of attorneys to step out of the familiar and to move into work that carries ADR into the larger community?

Lawyers in North Carolina have much to offer. They have taken their own corner of the world—the court system and attorney-client fee disputes—and have worked hard to build dispute-resolution mechanisms within it. The publishing of this volume also demonstrates the success of their efforts. The bar clearly has something to offer the world beyond the judicial system. It is hoped that other jurisdictions and institutions can learn from what has been done in North Carolina and work to improve their own systems of resolving disputes through use of appropriate settlement procedures.

Finally, as revealed throughout this volume, attorneys have something to offer other professionals who struggle with the litigation process and are conscious of deteriorating relationships with both their clients and their colleagues. Experience gained in court-based ADR programs can form the basis for looking beyond the professional and business worlds and working to promote the building of new structures for dispute resolution in other institutions—religious, educational, and nonprofit organizations of all kinds.

The original Dispute Resolution Task Force of the NCBA set out a blueprint for study and action many years ago. As this book demonstrates, much has been accomplished to further the goals of the established ADR programs. The unfinished business is to expand beyond the courts and to help fashion a society that weaves the philosophy and spirit of ADR into its very fabric. Then those involved in the development of ADR might look back and say with great pride that now the courts are truly a place of last rather than first resort. That future is not so much something to predict as it is something to choose and strive to create.

NOTES

1. *See* Laura F. Donnelly and Rebecca G. Ebron, *The Child Custody and Visitation Mediation Program in North Carolina—An Evaluation of Its Implementation and Effects*, N.C. Administrative Office of the Courts (Jan. 2000); Stevens H. Clarke et al., *Court-Ordered Civil Case Mediation in North Carolina: An Evaluation of Its Effects* (Institute of Government, The University of North Carolina at Chapel Hill, 1995); and Stevens H. Clarke et al., *Court-Ordered Arbitration in North Carolina: An Evaluation of Its Effects* (Institute of Government, The University of North Carolina at Chapel Hill, 1989).

2. Robert A. Baruch Bush and Joseph P. Folger, *The Promise of Mediation: Responding to Conflict Through Empowerment and Recognition* (Jossey-Bass 1994), p. 3.

3. *Id.* at 3–4.

North Carolina's Dispute Resolution Leaders

Past and Present Chairs of the Groups That Have Led North Carolina's Dispute Resolution Efforts

Mediation Network Executive Directors

Dee Reid	1985–1989	Scott Bradley	1992–2001
Frank C. Laney	1990	Don McKee	2001–2004
John Fenner	1991	Jody Minor	2005–Present

Mediation Network Board Chairs

Mike Wendt (acting)	1985	Melissa Johnson	1998–1999
Alice Phalan	1985–1986	Tammy Wilcox	2000
Clair Millar	1987–1989	Kirsten Atkinson	2001
Barbara Davis	1990–1991	Ann Flynn	2002–2005
John Fenner	1992–1996	Tony Gibbons	2006
Frances Henderson	1997	Janice Almond	2007–Present

North Carolina Bar Association
Alternatives to Litigation Task Force Chair

Wade Barbour, Jr.   1983–1985

North Carolina Bar Association
Dispute Resolution Committee Chairs

Larry B. Sitton	1985–1987
H. C. "Jack" Roemer	1987–1989
Horace R. Kornegay	1989–1991
J. Anderson Little	1991–1993

North Carolina Bar Association Dispute Resolution Section Chairs

J. Anderson Little	1993–1994	Elizabeth G. McCrodden	2003–2004
Reagan H. Weaver	1994–1995	Frank C. Laney	2004–2005
Rosemary G. Kenyon	1995–1996	Jonathan R. Harkavy	2005–2006
J. Dickson Phillips III	1996–1997	M. Ann Anderson	2006–2007
Dorothy C. Bernholz	1997–1998	Lynn G. Gullick	2007–2008
James E. Gates	1998–1999	Ellen R. Gelbin	2008–2009
John C. Schafer	1999–2000	Kenneth P. Carlson, Jr.	2009–2010
Kenneth J. Gumbiner	2000–2001	Zebulon E. Barnhardt, Jr.	2010–2011
Roy J. Baroff	2001–2002	George P. Doyle	2011–2012
Jacqueline R. Clare	2002–2003	Rene S. Ellis	2012–2013

Dispute Resolution Commission Chairs

Judge Ralph A. Walker	1995–2002
J. Anderson Little	2002–2004
Judge Sanford L. Steelman, Jr.	2004–2008
Judge W. David Lee	2008–2012

State Judicial Council Dispute Resolution Committee Chairs

Randy S. Gregory	2000–2001
Judge Kenneth C. Titus	2001–2003
Judge Ralph A. Walker	2003–2005
Frank C. Laney	2005–Present

The Peace Award

Each year the North Carolina Bar Association Dispute Resolution Section, pursuant to its Bylaws, recognizes one or more individuals in North Carolina who have made a special contribution or commitment to the peaceful resolution of disputes. Nominations are restricted to North Carolina residents who are selected by the Section's Nominating Committee. Nominations may be solicited from Council and Section members, court administrators, dispute resolution providers, judges, lawyers and other individuals.

The nominee(s) are considered in accordance with the criteria listed below. Recipients are named the Peace Award winner(s) for a particular fiscal year, announced when the award is presented.

Criteria for Selecting Recipients of the Peace Award
Overall contribution and commitment to the field of alternative dispute resolution, including but not limited to the following:

- Development of new or innovative programs;
- Demonstrated improvements in service;
- Demonstrated improvements in efficiency;
- Research and writings in the area of dispute resolution;
- Development of continuing education programs;
- Leadership with local, state, and national boards and legislative bodies.

Peace Award Recipients

Carmon J. Stuart	2002	Beth Okun, Tan Schwab	
Scott Bradley	2003	and Charlotte Adams	2008
Frank C. Laney	2004	Justice James G. Exum	2009
Jacqueline R. Clare	2005	Judge James M. Long	2010
J. Anderson Little	2006	John C. Schafer	2011
Judge Ralph A. Walker	2007	Judge James G. Gates	2012

Images of ADR's History

NC BAR ASSOCIATION DISPUTE RESOLUTION COMMITTEE, 1992.

Wade Barber, initial chair *(left)*; Andy Little *(standing)*; Horace Kornegay *(right)* at the last meeting of the NC Bar Association Dispute Resolution Committee, 1992.

Justice Henry Frye *(left)* and Andy Little *(right)* at the last Committee meeting, 1992.

Andy Little, Chair *(left)*; Horace Kornegay *(standing)*; Larry Sitton, past chair *(right)*.

Photos courtesy of Andy Little.

Carmon J. Stuart
(1914–2004)

2003 celebration of the publication of the
first edition of *Alternative Dispute Resolution
in North Carolina. (Back row)* Judge Ralph
Walker, Frank Laney, Andy Little; *(front row)*
Jackie Clare, John Schafer. Photo courtesy of
Frank Laney.

NORTH CAROLINA DISPUTE RESOLUTION COMMISSION MEETING IN 2005,
BLOWING ROCK, NC.

Leslie Ratliff, Executive Secretary *(left)*;
Dottie Bernholz, Commission member
(right).

Commission members: Judge Sanford
Steelman *(left)*, Diann Seigle, Andy Little.
Photos courtesy of Frank Laney.

NC Bar Association Dispute Resolution Section Council at the NC Bar Center, Cary, NC, 2007. *(Back row)* Joe Diab, Roy Baroff, Nancy Hemphill, Patricia Holland, Karen Britt Peeler, George Doyle, Steve Sizemore, Ann Anderson, Frank Laney, Gerald Arnold, Zeb Barnhardt, Jackie Clare, Deidre Lewis (staff); *(front row)* Andy Little, LeAnn Nease Brown, Leslie McCandless, Patti Poole, Jon Harkavy, Nahomi Harkavy.
Photo courtesy of Ann Anderson.

NC Bar Association Dispute Resolution Section 2008 Peace Award Winners were Charlotte Adams, Beth Okun, and Ruth "Tan" Schwab.
Representatives receiving the award *(left to right)*: LeAnn Nease Brown, Ann Schwab, Dan Pollitt, John Schwab. Photo courtesy of Ann Anderson.

NC Bar Association Dispute Resolution Section Annual Meeting, 2009. *(Left to right)* Andy Little (presenter of Peace Award), Justice James Exum (2009 Peace Award winner), and Ellen Gelbin (Section Chair).
Photo courtesy of Ann Anderson.

NC Dispute Resolution Section Annual Meeting, 2010, Grandover, Greensboro, NC. Robert Baker and Justice Henry Frye *(left, center)* congratulating Judge James Long *(right)* upon his receipt of the Section's Peace Award.

NC BAR ASSOCIATION DISPUTE RESOLUTION SECTION PAST CHAIRS.

(Left to right) Dottie Bernholz, Reagan Weaver, Ann Anderson, Lynn Gullick, Jackie Clare, Roy Baroff, Frank Laney, Andy Little.

(Left to right) Andy Little, Ellen Gelbin, Ann Anderson, Ken Gumbiner, Frank Laney, Roy Baroff, Lynn Gullick, Reagan Weaver, Jon Harkavy. Photos courtesy of Ann Anderson.

NC Bar Association Dispute Resolution Section Officers, 2010–2011. *(Left to right)* Patricia Holland (Secretary), Rene Ellis (Treasurer), George Doyle (Vice-Chair), and Barney Barnhardt (Chair). Photo courtesy of Ann Anderson.

Andy Little presenting the Peace Award to Judge Ralph A. Walker. Photo courtesy of NCBA.

NC Bar Association Dispute Resolution Section Council Meeting, 2005, Wake Forest University School of Law. *(Back to front)* LeAnn Nease Brown, Frank Laney, Andy Little, Sherrill Hayes, Ann Anderson, Rene Ellis, Rick Igou, Judge Pat Morgan, George Doyle, Bill Wolcott, Steve Savia, Lynn Gullick, Patti Poole, Ken Carlson, Ellen Gelbin. Photo courtesy of Ann Anderson.

NC Dispute Resolution Commission Chair Judge W. David Lee and Executive Secretary Leslie Ratliff at a Commission meeting on September 10, 2011, in Asheville, NC.

NC Dispute Resolution Commission meeting, September 9–10, 2011, Asheville, NC. *(Front row)* Lori Cole, Martha Curran. *(Second row)* Karan Whitley, Judge Jessie Conley, Lynn Gullick, Dawn Bryant, Judge David Lee, Judge Gary Tash, Judge Joe Turner, Ed Hay. *(Third row)* Andy Little, Bob Beason, Jackie Clare, Judge Ann McKown, Ann Anderson, George Doyle, Larry Hudspeth, Frank Laney. *(Back Row)* Judge Michael Morgan, Victor Farah, John Schafer, Leslie Ratliff. Photos courtesy of Judge Jessie Conley.

INDEX